IN SEARCH OF ME

A PERSONAL JOURNEY FROM LAND'S END TO JOHN O'GROATS

CAROL YOUNG

IN SEARCH OF ME

A PERSONAL JOURNEY FROM **LAND'S END** TO **JOHN O'GROATS**

MEMOIRS

Cirencester

Published by Memoirs

MEMOIRS
PUBLISHING

25 Market Place, Cirencester, Gloucestershire, GL7 2NX
info@memoirsbooks.co.uk www.memoirspublishing.com

ISBN 978-1-909544-13-0

Printed in England

Dedications

To my father, Albert Graham Edwards (Dad), a lover of the great outdoors and always at ease in the mountains.

And

To my mother-in-law Muriel Judy Young (Momma), a woman of great integrity, who completely understood my need to do this.

I owe a great debt of gratitude to them both.
They were wonderful parents and grandparents.

This book is also dedicated to those who have suffered meningitis, and their families who are still living with its consequences.

"Let the sea be the expanse of your visions.
Let the mountains be the heights you wish to climb."

C. Young 2010

Acknowledgements

Firstly to David, my husband, thank you for sharing the walks from Bristol to the Severn Bridge and Birkenhead to Chester, for supplying maps on the South West leg, for buying the 'Passion Wagon' enabling us to see Scotland together, and for your quiet support from a distance. XXX

To Katy and Ben, my most treasured fans. XX

To Paula, for suffering all those blisters, forever smiling and tolerant, and for caring and sharing the ploddy bits across the Somerset Levels.

To Bob, for being an honourable and companionable gentleman on some of the more remote parts.

To all the friends I made on the West Highland Way and Cape Wrath Trail.

To Shauna, for joining me on the West Highland Way and tolerating me. I'll always manage to fly alone now.

To Chris and Richard of C-N-Do Scotland Holidays, for being great leaders on both the Cape Wrath Trail and West Highland Way.

To Mrs T, for putting me up at such short notice.

To Gertrude my mascot, who quietly accepted being in my company for the duration and is now broadening her travels to far-off places like Thailand and Vietnam.

Not least, to all those numerous citizens I encountered en route who provided brief interludes of passing kindness, conversation and interest, and to the wonderful campsites, youth hostels and B&Bs I had the good fortune to stay at.

Finally, I would like to thank The Great British Weather for giving me a taste of absolutely everything it could offer from its most varied seasonal menu. Where would I have been without you? Your unpredictability added an unforeseen daily flavour and I am grateful for your changing moods, which in themselves presented a challenge.

I thank you all. Carol x

Brief note by the author

So that it is easier for the reader to follow my route, I have set out my account in geographical order, that is to say from Land's End to John O'Groats. This may help those of you who wish to plan your own. The route is not an official one nor indeed follows any particular course.

If you are a perfectionist, which I am not, the ferry rides I take may seem a bit of a cheat, but for obvious reasons I couldn't walk! I now apologise in advance to those readers. But I don't apologise for enjoying the rides. They were and are part of this journey.

Each chapter represents another stage of the journey and at the beginning of each chapter or day's walk I have attempted to sketch that part of the route indicating villages or towns I passed through.

Because Offa's Dyke, West Highland Way and Cumbrian Way are well published and I used these trails in their entirety, I suggest you buy the Trailblazer British Walking Guides or Cicerone Guides coupled with the Ordnance Survey maps required. On these occasions I haven't drawn any pretty pictures! Theirs are far superior and more accurate.

You will note that the dates of each chapter bounce back and forth across the country as I utilised my time well, meeting old friends, using known National Trails where possible – sometimes on my own, sometimes with a companion or with companies who specialise in long distance walks – and seeing cities I hadn't visited before. All managed within time frames that fitted my busy working life and my personal one too.

I did not plan the whole route. It planned me in many ways. This will become evident as you peruse these pages.

Introduction

Sometimes in life we meet someone, or an event inspires us to set ourselves a challenge.

A challenge can be miniscule or monumental. It may seem insurmountable to some and to others 'a walk in the park', but to that individual it is an achievement nevertheless.

In 2004 I set myself such a challenge – walking from Land's End to John O'Groats.

It was to be an amazing journey. It was not what I expected it to be, but more. It tested my physical and mental strength, durability, sustainability, determination, integrity, knowledge of maps and undoubtedly my vulnerability. I can honestly say I found it exciting, exhausting, scary, romantic, awesome, breathtaking, bewildering and highly amusing.

During my 'great expedition' (excuse me if I seem a trifle over excited at the acknowledgement of completing it) I have met some marvellous people of all age groups. Their small acts of generosity confirmed that humanity still exists. Their colourful, interesting characters showed how enriched this society is by its diversity and complexity.

Although I probably only walked 40% of this journey on my own, the remainder was shared with like-minded outdoor folk whose passion for walking and experiencing the broad range of Britain's changing landscapes, geology and fauna, coupled with snatching glimpses of its wildlife, only enhanced my own experience. Their companionship, be it in a group or singly, added that vital but special ingredient. I would liken it to spice for the curry or ketchup for the chips. I hope my companions also enjoyed the experience as much as I enjoyed their unquestionable ability to put up with me.

This challenge has examined my reasoning for being here. It gave me time to ponder my attitudes and outlook on life. It gave me the opportunity to listen to others and, perhaps selfishly you may think, determine that life is for living in the here and now and that sometimes to understand yourself you have to push back the comfort zone to find the real you. Most importantly, it gave me time to reflect, to appreciate what I have and to question what I could do better in the future, giving me a sense of peace within.

I hope that you enjoy sharing my journey. I hope you can be inspired by it. Six years ago I would not have believed it possible or achievable. I now know that if you truly want to finish something, however difficult, you will.

Dear Reader

Originally, this diary was written down in date order, covering the different legs of my walk as I tackled them. However, you'll immediately see that it wasn't completed as a single linear walk, but one that involved taking time off work when I could and planning accordingly, bearing in mind the time required and what holiday leave I could realistically request. This was problematic and equally challenging.

For everyone's benefit therefore, this account of my walk follows the geography of Great Britain, rather than my personal timeline. I hope you don't get confused by the dates of the walks but see this book as a series of short stories diarized to simplify it and make it more interesting, with a little bit of background knowledge thrown in so you understand my blonde reasoning.

To make it easier to grasp the overall route there is a concise resumé of the locations, trails and mileage covered. This is just in case for some silly reason you might find it useful for planning your own route!

So let's start at the beginning and set the scene so you realise how limited my experiences were beforehand, considering I was 46 years of age!

The seedling of my eventual challenge was the Youth Hostels Association (YHA) holiday I took in July/August 2004, walking the Coast to Coast route. This was to be:

1. The first time I had been away from my family for two weeks, and only the second time I had ever ventured out of Hampshire travelling alone.

2. The first time I had ever challenged myself to walk such a long distance.

3. The first time I was to live for two weeks with strangers whom I may or may not have got on with.

4. The first time I had complete back up for my husband – just in case! (With my husband having suffered meningitis four times, possibly five, you get a bit edgy about these things.) The arrangements included: (a) His parents and mine had my itinerary and contact phone numbers. (b) The neighbours, bless them, were put on alert to keep a watchful eye on him. (c) He had plenty of medication. (d) My GP was aware I would be away. (e) There was plenty of food in the fridge and cupboards in case he didn't feel like going out. (f) The garden was tidy with no vegetables to look after. (g) There were 'post-it' notes to remind him of the comings and goings of the children. (h) Most importantly, a letter was prepared for A&E just in case he had to be admitted to hospital and they needed to know his full medical history and allergies.

5. The first time I could hand over responsibility to our children for looking after their father – with help – in times of emergency. Even though Ben was surfing in Newquay the first week and Katy was away for the first few days on a work trip.

6. The first time I was to feel free of responsibilities (albeit briefly).

7. The first time I met myself again as Carol – not as a full-time worker, housewife, mother or carer.

8. The first time my mind was liberated of clutter and I was remembering everything just for me and not for everyone else.

9. The first time I felt the old self-assurance and confidence seep back into my bones.

10. The first time I would make some lasting friendships and meet others who inspired those around them, so I could think of doing something as mad as walking from Land's End to John O'Groats.

11. Most importantly, I found a sense of spiritual wellbeing, I found where I truly belonged, and the inner peace that I discovered whilst walking can only be described as the sanctity of prayer on the move. For I can honestly say that my brain emptied to allow me to absorb the beauty of my surroundings and finally to thank God for being alive.

This YHA holiday turned out to be pivotal. It was the seed sown for the bigger challenge I could not miss or ignore. I'm sure my husband at many times regretted saying 'yes' to me going on that trip, as the many stories to come will show how much he has had to endure as I have rediscovered the old adventurous me. However, on a positive note, he has been right there behind me and I can't fault his agreement, encouragement, patience and graciousness in allowing me to pursue a dream. Particularly as many of his own had fallen by the wayside and if anything had gone wrong he would have been solely responsible for the children, which would have taken up any energy he had remaining.

Lands End
to
John O'Groats

Cape Wrath
John O'Groats
Ullapool
Torridon
Mallaig
Fort William
Dunfermline
Edinburgh
Glasgow
strathaven
Carlisle
Ulverston
Prestatyn
Liverpool
Wrexham
Chepstow
Bristol
Bridgewater
Exmoor
Hayle
Penzance
Lands End

CHAPTER ONE:
A NERVOUS START

LAND'S END TO STRATTON.

DISTANCE: 101.5 MILES VIA ROADS

AND THE SOUTH WEST COAST PATH.

DATELINE: MAY BANK HOLIDAY WEEKEND 2005.

When the YHA assistant leader had spoken with such enthusiasm and casual fluency of her achievement in walking from Land's End to John O'Groats in three months, I knew that, given the opportunity, I too could do it. Such was my euphoria after achieving the 190-mile Coast to Coast walk (St Bees to Robin Hood's Bay) in two weeks in July/August 2004. Listening attentively to her stories at that time, I came home bolstered, confident and positive. In my mind, a challenge had been set, a seed sown to do the same, but in my own blonde way. I wasn't sure yet when it would be; I just knew it would happen.

By Christmas 2004 I couldn't contain myself any longer. With Christmas money I purchased my first Ordnance Survey (OS) Explorer Maps: 102, 104, 106, 111 and 139. (Make-up,

1

clothes and smellies out of the window then.) These maps would see me up the north coast of Cornwall. Now that I had them, there was no backing out. I booked my week's holiday with work and then proceeded to examine the route.

Looking at the maps it all seemed simple. Pretty easy, nothing to worry about; I was confident, wasn't I? Could I do the distance in that week? Would I be safe? Would I scarper at the first sign of trouble? These questions bounced around the blonde brain.

My deliberation was not unfounded. The truth is, I have always loved the outdoors. I had climbed, walked, canoed, sailed, served as an assistant Venture Scout leader, lived down the bottom of our garden in a den as a child, camped in terrains across the country in all kinds of weather BUT never on my own. In fact, up to this point in time, I had barely been out of Hampshire alone.

Scary or what? At 47, this girl had a lot of catching up to do. I knew I had weaknesses and fears to face. I had never travelled on my own, I didn't like the dark or, what was more to the point, solitary places, or large towns. I had a fear of men and a fear of making such a colossal navigational mistake that I would have to rely on someone else to bale me out. To exacerbate these fears I have a very vivid imagination. I was to be kidnapped, raped, fall off a cliff, collapse from hypothermia or heat exhaustion, and have a heart attack – and all this before breakfast. The possibilities were endless as my mind swirled in Alfred Hitchcock movies fast-forwarded. However, on top of this, as a mother, carer, sister and daughter, the responsibilities of 'what if?' weighed the heaviest. People were reliant on me returning safely. I was loved. I held down a full-time job, money was needed. I was the key worker and earner. My children were still dependent on me to a certain extent, and my husband David, who had been so ill much of his life, needed my support. So you realise now the extent of the mental challenges facing me.

Not deterred, however, my next purchases were a bivouac tent, a down sleeping bag, and a Thermarest ground mat. The tent weighed 1.5 kg, with only two carbon poles and made out of ripstop waterproof Gore-Tex. Its maximum height was only two feet, so I would have to get dressed lying down. It was six and a half feet in length and the width allowed just enough room for me to roll in and drag my rucksack beside me. The sleeping bag plus a silk liner weighed in at 0.98 kg and together they became a warm three-season sleeping bag. The Thermarest mat was the weight of tent and bag combined. I didn't mind this as if you're warm on your back, you have no chill factor and some comfort does help with morale.

One cold frosty weekend, I tested it all in the back garden. It was heaven. I do like camping; it's great. I was only sort-of warm though. I made a mental note that taking my son Ben's thermals would be wise. I soon changed those on other trips, as his had a hole where I didn't need one! Not lady-like.

Next, fitness: I highly recommend this. I had always maintained some levels of fitness through cycling, tennis and swimming. However, during the winter months I took to doing at least three cardiac exercises a week, undertaking a combination of the above with a few walks thrown in at weekends. At Easter, I spent an arduous weekend with my brother and his friends scrambling and walking in Snowdonia, which set me up nicely. Cor blimey, didn't I ache after that?

My route was now evolving and would entail our dear friends Dave and Jan in St Austell putting us both up for one night, and David for five nights. This was an excellent way of catching up with them. They were delighted to be used for a purpose, but also just to have the company. I was really looking forward to seeing them again. It had been a couple of years for me anyway.

We planned to stay Friday night, then David would drop me off at Land's End, then they would all visit the north coast at Treyarnon one evening for a meal with me. David in the meantime could spend some relaxing time with them and meet me on his motorbike, dropping off maps. I didn't realise how useful that was going to be.

My route was:
- Road to Penzance, across to Hale, then the South West Coast Path to Gwithian Campsite
- Gwithian to Perranporth Campsite
- Perranporth to Treyarnon Youth Hostel (booked)
- Treyarnon to Tintagel – via Padstow Ferry (Cheat No.1) – Youth Hostel (booked)

- Tintagel to Bude Campsite
- Bude to Bideford and then home

By the Thursday, the day before departure, I had packed and repacked my rucksack several times as we had to have things capable of fitting into three panniers, with the rucksack and its main contents strapped and covered on the back of the motorbike. Katy, my daughter, had given me Gertrude the cow as a mascot, to hang on the back of my rucksack. She has gone the entire journey with me, poor cow. She hung there miserably, wrapped in a plastic bag. I apologised for the treatment and told her things would get better.

So for anyone wanting to have a go, here was my list of essentials in the sack:

Clothes
- Thermal hat and gloves, sun cap, thermal first layer (used for pyjamas as well)
- Berghaus Paclite jacket and trousers (these have never let me down, I have always been dry)
- Boots, flip-flops, 4 pairs of walking socks (always keep feet dry, sweaty feet are as bad as wet-from-rain ones)
- 1 two-litre water bladder and 1 x 500 ml bottle for nights
- 1 pair of shorts
- 2 walking shirts base layers
- 2 short sleeved T-shirts
- 1 pair of zip-off trousers

- 1 pair of plain trousers
- 2 sports bras (they're extra – men don't carry those)
- 2 pairs of knickers and 12 panty liners (to save weight)
- Bathing costume
- 1 large fast-drying high absorbency towel and 1 small one
- 2 thermal jumpers

Hardware
- Tent, sleeping bag and mat
- Maps, compass, whistle, Swiss Army knife
- First-aid kit
- Sunglasses, Maglite torch, Headlite
- Pen, pencil and paper
- Money (paper and plastic), pictures of the children, essential telephone numbers and addresses – all wrapped in a plastic bag and stored in a body belt
- Antihistamine tablets, Paracetamol, Ibuprofen, antiseptic wipes (for all purposes), spare plastic bags, blister plasters of various sizes (I find Superdrug's own brand equally as good as Compeed), tissues, deep heat gel, sun cream, sole repair cream, double cream, no, not that, Vaseline lip balm!
- Toiletries, all in miniature – easily obtained from a good drug store
- 1 small bottle of perfume and moisturiser – my little treat and a reminder that I am a lady and must keep up some standards
- 1 fold-up hairbrush and miniature mirror
- 1 nail file and miniature foot rub emery board

Food

My rations for walking per day:

- 1 Go Bar
- 1 bar of chocolate
- 2 breakfast bars
- 1 miniature packet of raisins
- 1 packet of nuts
- 3 or 4 boiled sweets

All packed separately for five days. Some people may require more than this but I find it easier without, and drink plenty of fluids instead. In any case, if I require more I buy pies or sandwiches as and when the opportunity or need arises.

Personal safety protection

- Personal Alarm
- Condoms (a pack of three!)

You may question condoms. Well, this was David's idea and I laugh about it a lot. Ben had been given some as an introduction to college life! As a precaution, the colleges just gave the students a pack as a reminder of what to do if... They had been lying about the house for ages, so David reckoned if I took them, perhaps if I got attacked (oh, thanks then) I would have time to suggest that the assailant should put one on. Can you imagine, "Oh by the way, before you rape me could you just pop this on please, it would be terribly decent of you." I just laughed as little scenarios crept into my mind – "Which size would you like?" – and I am giggling as I type. However, in all seriousness, because it was so bizarre it could be effective as a stalling technique and then I'd kick him in the goolies.

Fortunately I had done some self-defence in Police College but, as they said there, nothing prepares you for surprise and strength. As you will note, this could only happen three times!

The personal alarm had been Katy's idea (much more sensible, or so you would think). She had been given it for her own protection whilst travelling to and from London as a student. It was a bright, chunky, lightweight, yellow object with a quick release pin and easy clip-on device which could go on any belt, strap or even the outside of a rucksack. I tested it, it worked. That was good enough for me.

All together, the rucksack weighed in at 16 kilos. Not bad but I wasn't taking cooking equipment. That would prove interesting on another leg of the journey.

I cannot express how necessary it is to have an even, well-packed rucksack and one that fits you. I can honestly say mine is just great. It fits so well that at the end of the day it is just as comfortable as at the beginning. Rucksacks incorrectly fitted can cause all sorts of back issues and feet problems. I have seen that happen. Tied to the front of my rucksack, my companion Gertrude the cow was to be my closest friend (more on this later).

Out of all my equipment, my boots were the most important. They are very comfortable, flexible and reliable friends who inspired the 'Boots' poem found at the end of the book. It is a must to have the correct boots for this type of walking.

I tend to my boots as a gardener does his flowers. I talk to them nicely, saying how far I am expecting them to take me. I wash and dry them, replenish the outers with Nikwax proofer and debug the inners. I make them as tidy as possible and, touch wood, they have never let me down. After every walk, this has been the ritual and the norm.

I will not repeat this essentials list again as it became standard throughout the walk.

We kitted out the bike Thursday evening (it took all evening). On Friday, I would come home from work, have a bite of tea and then go, go, go.

I was so excited. I pivoted between anticipation and fear and consequently I didn't sleep Thursday night. Groggily, I worked through the next day and finally we donned our leathers and set off.

Friday April 29th 2005.

The journey down was hell. Bad traffic and then at Dorchester, a fine mist and drenching drizzle started which stayed with us until Bodmin Moor, at which point it turned into foggy pea soup, taking our speed down to 30 mph all the way to St Austell. Having left the house at 4pm, we arrived at 10pm, an hour and a half over the normal time. Our friends Dave and Jan were as funny and warm as usual with, "What time do you call this? We thought you had bypassed us to get an early start, suppose you want a drink, it's do it yourself time, we are off to bed!"

With warm hugs and plenty of chat we rearranged our belongings, hung our wet gear in their kitchen and then crashed out for the night. Well, I only crashed until two-ish;

the route revolving round and round in my brain. Had I remembered everything? Had Katy got back from London okay? All the self-doubts and nerves flooded my pickled brain. Why was I doing this? Finally sleep enveloped me, but I still woke at 6am ready to go.

Saturday April 30th 2005. Land's End to Gwithian Campsite - 22 miles.

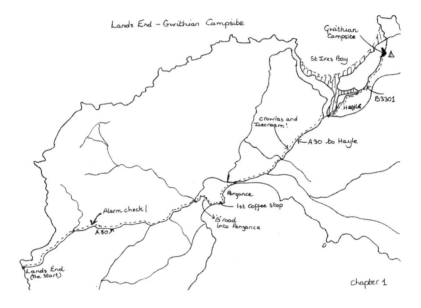

We did Dave and Jan the honourable thing of waking them up (haha!) and providing them with an early cup of tea. I could only manage a light breakfast. Blooming butterflies were flapping about like crazy.

Oh my God, this was it, but beyond that, a gritty determination had gripped me; the desire to achieve something different was immense.

There was a heavy mist when we finally set off, the air chilly and damp. It was 7.30am. I was trembling. For the time being, it took all my concentration to get my husband on the right route to the 'End'. We arrived later than expected; I hadn't realised the distance nor anticipated such foul weather.

It was 9am. The weather had cleared. We wandered around the closed gift shop and David took some photographs of the motorbike and me, still clad in my leathers. There was a group of cyclists getting ready to set off. They too were taking this journey, only in 12 days maximum. They boasted high specification racing bikes. There were three support vans, one for carrying the bikes, one for making cups of tea and one for sleeping accommodation. I felt quite small. They were laughing and joking and here I was, anxious. I was still in leathers, the rucksack ready to roll and nowhere to get undressed in privacy.

Ignoring my moralistic virtuous head screaming at me, I stripped there in front of everyone, trying not to bring attention to myself. As the sweaty leathers wouldn't come down over my knees and the knee protectors got stuck coming over my feet, I started to hop around the car park desperately trying not to lose my knickers while getting the bloody trousers off. The ground was too damp to sit on. I shouted to Day (that's David when I am in a panic) "Give us a hand!" and as he, embarrassed by my antics, held my shoulder all eyes from the vans turned towards the commotion. Not too much attention, then. Carefully keeping hold of my knickers and modesty, the leathers finally gave way, thus I stood, half dressed in the bare, damp car park. Freezing, I tried to remember which pannier I had packed my trousers in. "Oh bollocks," all privacy lost without inhibition and much to David's amusement, I pranced about the bike in my underwear, finally putting on my zip-off trousers to reinstate my equilibrium. Still, I had forgotten my nerves. Such was my initiation to what would come later.

Finally, at 9.30am, kissing David goodbye, bracing my shoulders and expanding them for courage, I set off. The early mist was lifting. Chatting to Gertrude, I told her the adventure had begun.

Oh blimey, that first mile! I was so animated, so pleased it was happening. I barely noticed my surroundings. I couldn't feel the rucksack, only an amazing beckoning in my feet. I practically skipped along. It was only when David overtook me heading back to St Austell that it struck me I was on my own. Suddenly, overwhelming and unreasonable doubt entered my head. I was now alone and vulnerable. I felt the first jangle of nerves and the bleakness of my situation. Cornwall was quiet. And nothing stirred. Well girl, here is your first test, this is what you wanted. Shake yourself and get on with it.

With renewed energy, I forgot myself and followed the A30 quite happily for another mile, crisscrossing the road for safety. I had just passed a school outside of Sennen when I had my first incident. A local bus had come haring round the bend I was on. With not much room to spare, I flung myself into the hedges which covered the stone walling behind them. Well, that was fine but then, extricating myself from the brambles, nettles and ragged robin, I inadvertently pulled my personal alarm.

Oh my God, didn't I jump! The blasted thing was so loud. I couldn't find the pin to stop it. Being attached to my waist belt, I couldn't get rid of the noise. "Stop, stop!" I shouted, but of course it wasn't going to. Then I thought, no, don't say that, people will come. Oh my God, I'm supposed to blend into the countryside, not make myself obvious. Like a demented chicken, I frantically looked for the pin. Oh shit, oh shit, where was it? Then, as if to goad me, there it was dangling from a branch protruding from the wall. Never before have I been so pleased to see a piece of yellow plastic.

Putting the pin back in and switching off the sound was such a relief, only for the silence that followed to scare me to death. Eerily, the hedgerows stared at me. The stone walls became giants. Oh no, my imagination was going into overdrive. Get a grip. Whilst the commotion was going on, my concentration had been totally focused on finding the pin. Now I was aware someone may have been watching, alerted by the noise. Knees trembling, I brushed myself down and furtively glanced about.

I stuffed the offensive safety mechanism into my pocket and pretended the fiasco hadn't happened at all. A piece of cake.

For the next mile, I can only describe myself as unhinged. No, I wasn't going to ring anyone. Forget it. Sing a song. Eventually I calmed down; the next six miles flew by. The A road became busier as I headed into Penzance. It was now noon and I walked nine miles into the outskirts of the town.

I couldn't believe it. I had promised to rendezvous with David at a café we knew along the harbour front, but it didn't happen; he hadn't expected me so soon. So I had a coffee, reflected on my journey so far, envied the relaxed passers-by and set off towards Hayle and the north coast. Feet good, energy levels good. Weather breezy, but sunny.

I met David on the side of the busy A30 dual carriageway. He pulled over near a roundabout. We only had time to exchange a few words. He rode away again and I walked on.

I was very much relieved to walk into Crowlas at 2.30pm. Thankfully, there had been a path the best part of the way to this village. The traffic had been quite noisy, this was tiring. The weather had turned warm. I had now stripped to a pair of shorts and a T-shirt, with a baseball cap to keep my long blonde hair tucked up inside and the sun out of my eyes. I treated myself to an ice cream and a rest. I hadn't eaten much. This was a welcome treat and a boost for my sugar levels.

Walking into Hayle was disappointing. The tide was out, exposing the mud flats, which probably didn't help my initial impressions of this tired, untidy Cornish town. Even the toilets were locked and had graffiti on them. Oh blast! There was nowhere to go, it would just have to wait. The whole town had such natural beauty around its harbour wall but behind the concrete there was rubbish on the streets. The houses were run down; weather-beaten, their painted brickwork faded, lacking the vibrancy of fresh colour.

However, here was my first encounter with another human being's generosity. I staggered into a greengrocers, unsure whether to buy a tomato or a banana. The greengrocer must have wondered where I had come from as I felt quite knackered by then. Kindly he said, "Here take it," putting the tomato in my hand, "you look like you need it." He didn't want any money so I gratefully accepted his kind gesture. I could have hugged him. Believe me it was wonderful not to have to hunt around for money but it was equally humbling to accept charity. I thought of all those people around the world who have to accept charity every day, about how desperate their plight is and how pathetic mine had been.

Only four miles to Gwithian. Yippee!

The B3301 leading to Gwithian was just one of those roads that slowly and interminably went up. I couldn't find a way onto the coastal path, and by now all I wanted to do was to crash into the campsite. It took an enormous effort. I recall stopping several times to find a place to have a pee. In the end, my bladder complaining bitterly, I just had to scooty by the side of the road at the gate of a farmer's field and hope no one would pass in their car. How unladylike was that? Over the course of my journey, I became more proficient at the speed I could have a wee, and be off again!

Gwithian campsite was great when I arrived at 4.30pm. What a sight met my eyes: campers eating cream teas. Ashamedly, I probably looked a mess and smelt worse. The proprietress, however, was fantastic. After explaining what I was doing, she charged me £5 for the night and gave me a free cup of tea and a scone. Wow, what a reception. Can you see me singing and dancing? Well, such was my joy. When walking you get so easily pleased. I sat at a table in pure ecstasy, watching the world go by. I can honestly say it was the most savoured and devoured cream tea I have ever had.

Clotted cream, mmm, lush. Sipping my tea, the third hot drink of the day, I felt my legs begin to seize and cramp. Rummaging in my rucksack, I found the supply of salted peanuts and ate a handful with my scone. What a mixture!

Wearily I decided to make one last effort to put up the tent and get my kit in order before treating myself to a shower. My feet were complaining. "Let us out," they cried, "we need to breathe!"

Anyone watching me talking to my legs and feet at that moment would have sectioned me. "Okay guys, this is it, last ditch effort then you are in for one hell of a treat, my friends. You can do it, don't seize up on me now."

The campsite was spotless; it was very family orientated. I chose a spot between two camper vans. They had families in so I felt less vulnerable, albeit it was quite amusing being watched by them as I put up my little tent, made my bed, sorted out my towel and toiletries for the showers and took off my boots. Phew, what a feeling. It would have been so easy to lie out on my bed and sleep for a while.

As it was, I knew I needed to get out of my sweaty clothes before I cooled down completely. So I headed for the shower blocks.

The showers were amazing. Do I sound over enthusiastic? Probably. They were in pristine condition, looked clean, smelt clean. Was my brain having illusions due to fatigue? I don't think so. A woman had designed this shower block. It was heated and comfortable. Only women would know how much space a woman needs to have a shower. I have never since come across any better on a campsite. They were A1. After all, how many showers have a bench to sit on, a row of four pegs on the door, a wide shelf for putting your toilet bag on that wasn't going to get wet because the area in front of the shower was large enough to fit two or three adults. Under the bench there was a shelf for shoes. The shower itself was a power shower. Oh joy, heaven, but even better, the piece de resistance was the shower tray: clean and sparkly. No tissues, no sand, no sanitary towels, no streak marks! It was home from home. No flip flops required. It even smelt of lavender.

I took my time meticulously inspecting my feet for warm spots and rubbing my legs to stop any cramps.

Refreshed I returned to the tent and worked out my route for the next day – Gwithian to Perranporth along the South West Coast Path. I filled up my water bottle again and packed next-day meals at the top of the rucksack. My money belt still around my waist, I gathered my mobile phone. It was 6.30pm now and the outside temperature had chilled considerably. The light would be gone in another hour and a half and my stomach was calling for nourishment.

Quickly I rang Dave and Jan and confirmed my safe arrival. They had been waiting. I apologised for leaving it so long. I then walked over to the pub. It was practically opposite the campsite. It was busy. I was a bit nervous stepping inside alone. Vulnerability flooded my brain. But boldness is the key.

Confidence is the answer and with this I shouldered my way to the busy bar and ordered a half pint of shandy, a cup of coffee and a bowl of leek and potato soup.

Waiting for my change, I was aware of a man watching me. He was giving me the eye. I shivered. I loathe that leer of a lech who has no regard or respect for the woman he is slowly undressing with his eyes. I shudder as I type. Oh yuk!

Giving him one of my best glares, I chose a spot in the pub where he wouldn't be able to see me and waited nervously for my supper. It is very peculiar going from being a people watcher to now becoming the victim. Was I paranoid?

It felt as if the whole eyes of the pub were on me, so it was some relief when my supper arrived. It smelt good and tasted even better. I gobbled delicately! Far too quickly, the soup and huge chunk of bread had disappeared, my stomach's gurgling quenched. Slurping my coffee, a wave of exhaustion crossed over me. It was time for bed. Only one more thing to do – walk out of the pub purposefully, confidently and briskly. The man was still there. I slinked out via another door, checked no one was behind me and dashed across the road like a frightened rabbit back to the campsite. That was just as planned then!

It was 8.30pm. With the sun down, the campsite had a quiet hum of babies trying to be laid in bed, children complaining of having to brush their teeth and the sea behind the dunes providing a regular rhythm. The wind had got up slightly. Inside my sleeping bag, I snuggled against my lover of a rucksack. My lips and nose pressed against its cold metal buckles. Outside, the chilly breeze rattled the tent like a plastic bag. My thoughts drifted. Would I need a pee in the night? Will I sleep with the noise of the pub later on? Will I be stiff in the morning? I wish I had a pillow. Goodnight Gertrude, thank you for a great day. Tiredness and a warm glow of contentment overwhelmed me. At last, now relaxed and very cosy, I succumbed to sleep.

I can't remember any more until approximately 11.45pm. I deduced the noise was caused by the pub emptying. I was just thinking, oh damn, I could do with a wee, when I promptly fell asleep again.

I cannot describe how I felt when I was awoken at 4am from a very deep sleep. A large hand was pressing heavily on the side of my face and head, forcing the cold damp tent to cover one eye and half my mouth. In my stupor, my first recollections were *I can't breathe* followed quickly by *I think I should scream*. It was most bizarre. Fear didn't hit me until I fully came to. Trying to scream, my attempt came out more like an owl screech. Moving slightly, I was released and all that remained was the wet tent on the front of my face. I lay there slowly fumbling for my knife and headlight. I listened intently to the outside for noise but the wind against the bivi made it sound more like I was in a washing machine, so any human noise seemed to be drowned out. Although I thought I heard a grumble, it seemed an age before I had the courage to climb over my rucksack and roll out of my tent, but it all happened in a very short space of time.

Although my heart was absolutely thumping, I still felt numbingly calm. It was bleak outside, the sky clear. The wind was bitterly cold, blowing through my thermals quite easily. I looked at the tent, a dishevelled mess. Both of the looped pole ends had collapsed inward as both guys and pegs had been pulled out. I could just make out from the angle of one pole that it had pushed itself through the fabric of the tent. This made it awkward to reposition the guy rope and poles so the tent could be erected again properly. I made it stand as best as I could. The two camper vans either side were silent, nobody stirred. To be honest I felt rather embarrassed. Shivering, nerves jangling now, I looked about but there was no one to be seen. Had I dreamt it? What if everyone had heard me scream and I had woken everyone up? Looking at the tent in the dim light, it was evident there had been some force to break the pole. All I could do was to return to my sleeping bag before I caught hypothermia.

Remarkably, logic stepped in. Someone must have tripped over the tent and fallen backwards onto my face. And, typical me in a real crisis, my back aching, my legs cramping and head pounding, I fell back to sleep and still woke at 6am.

In the morning, I felt very vulnerable now it was light and there was a good old sea mist again. The campsite was eerie. Not venturing outside the tent, I dressed and packed my rucksack, all while lying down. Gracefully, I then rolled out of the now collapsing tent once more and decided to go over to the showers.

I didn't look at the damage to the tent again. Instead, I gathered it and all my belongings and dumped them in the shelter of the linen washing area of the toilet block. I then went and had a therapeutic shower to collect my thoughts about my route and to warm up. My nerves were shattered. I kept checking to see if I was on my own. Again the vivid imagination went into overdrive as 'Fatal Attraction' came to mind.

Top tip: When unsure of oneself have something to eat. It is a great morale booster.

After munching a cereal bar, Plan B was evolving – try to get hold of Mrs T in Mithian. It was five miles off my route from Perranporth, five miles short of my planned day. It was one of two options and would change my route plans entirely. The other option was to get David to meet me at Perranporth and I would find a B&B somewhere, but as it was Bank Holiday there was no assurance of that. I really didn't want to put him out. I decided the first option if possible would be best, and anyway I would get a chance to see Mrs T again.

Returning to my beleaguered tent, I folded it down as best I could. It wouldn't go into its bag; the poles were at an awkward angle. They needed the elastic cut that ran inside them. The tent was wet through. I was so livid now. Forcing the tent into my rucksack, I ranted and raved. Then a poor, unsuspecting gentleman who had wandered innocently over to the shower block for his first morning pee asked, "What's up?" Without replying to his question I just barked at him, "Have you got a knife or something or pair of scissors, this bloody tent won't go in. I need to cut the elastic to release the pole." If I had thought clearly, I did have a Swiss Army knife – duh! I could have easily dealt with it myself. Such was my anxiety to be away from the campsite.

Bless the gentleman, after running back to his caravan he meekly held out a pair of scissors to me. He looked quite shocked. I don't recall him even getting to the toilet. I apologised for my behaviour and thanked him graciously, stuffed my tent properly in the rucksack, handed back the scissors and left.

Sunday May 1st 2005. Gwithian to Mithian, near St Agnes - 17 miles.

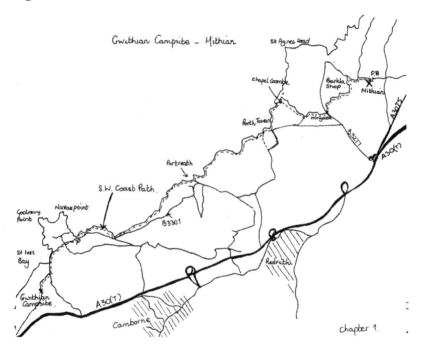

Was I going to be scuppered at the first hurdle? I thought not, but I was digging deep to control my fear, and shouldering against the damp I strode out with some reservation.

My emotions dipped and soared as the first two miles were eaten up. I kept looking behind me for the first mile, such were my concerns of being followed. I chose not to head out immediately to the coastal path and walk around Godrow Point, but instead waited until the road literally joined the path at a known beauty spot approximately two miles away.

My camping plans were now over. I was so glad I had booked two nights in YHAs, with only this night and the next to overcome. It was too early to ring David or Mrs T, so I decided to set myself the time of 9am before I could do anything and relaxed into the walking.

At 7.15am I hit the coastal path. There was a café there but I didn't stop; I was getting into my stride. The early mist was showing signs of breaking and a hint of blue promised it was going to be a good day. I was really looking forward to being on a real path. My spirits rose.

From here, with the sea to my left, the comforting weight of the rucksack on my back and the rocky path undulating, the walk finally became a source of enjoyment and elation. This was what I wanted to do.

The air was still, the mist burning off fast now. I managed to take photographs, enjoy the views and admire the fauna of red valerian, thrift, periwinkle, spring squill, wild primroses, celandines, sweet violets, vetch and ragged robin. They lined the path in a profusion of yellows, blues and pinks where the sun had woken them. An intangible peace swept over me as I bounced along, willing myself up and down the wiggly path towards Portreath. I selfishly forgot everything and everyone as I wallowed in the ambiance of the day.

At 9am the sun burst through and at 9.30-ish, I walked into Portreath. I hadn't phoned anyone yet. I had had to negotiate a group of diddy caravaners parked on the coastal path which had taken me off the track for a bit. I wasn't going to brush with them. Their dogs had warned me of them before I was anywhere near close!

Portreath is a most pretty village. Nestled in a valley between high cliffs, it urges the walker towards the sea and its secluded harbour and beaches. The views across the bay are stunning. On the north side of the cove there is a tidal swimming pool and the south side is a quiet haven overlooked by old fishermen's cottages.

For me it was the café's open sign that beckoned. "Yes Gertrude!" I cried. Slumping thankfully into a chair, I ordered a double bacon butty and a large mug of coffee. Whilst waiting I used the toilets. Bliss! Here I took the opportunity to have a quick wash and freshen up before breakfast (I do have some standards). Toilets are wonderful places where you can readjust all sorts of clothes and all manner of items; they become a refuge.

I tried to phone David. No signal. Well, there's a surprise. It would have to wait until I was up high again.

The bacon butty was scrummy and scoffed far too quickly. It was the most welcomed refreshment ever. But at 10.15am I was on my way again. It was a rude awakening for my legs as I climbed the steep road and track out onto the headland again. Just before reaching the coastal path once more, I managed to get a weak signal and phoned David in St Austell, explaining the circumstances and what I was hoping for.

He waited for my next call. I rang Mrs T; she was delighted to hear from me and was more than happy to put me up for the night. "It would be lovely to have some company," she said. The previous year Mrs T had lost her husband and life was a bit hard. "Expect to see me around four-ish. I'll ring you nearer the time so you can get the kettle on!" I couldn't thank her enough before I said, "Goodbye and see you later."

Once more onto the coastal path (stiff climb) and the views of the village below were spectacular. I was heading for Porthtowan. It was soul-stirring. I soon got into my stride. Although sunny there was a cool breeze. However, it wasn't long before I stripped off my zip-offs and sweater. As the sun became stronger so did the glare that reflected off the sea. In the shallows below the cliffs, the inlets and ravines constantly changed. The sea's movement and the colours alternating between jade and a deep blue mimicked my own depth and intensity of purpose. As I climbed various heights and dropped down to virginal bays only accessible by boat or on foot, I felt a true sense of achievement. I didn't meet anyone.

I kept up my fluid intake. Top tip: Every 10 minutes take a good swig of water, whether or not you feel thirsty. It keeps you hydrated and maintains some rhythm in your day. It is so easy not to take enough fluids on board. Believe me, you get a cracking headache at the end of the day if you don't.

As I ambled along, I let my mind wander free for a bit. I was aware that I hadn't had much time for me. The children: forever ferrying them here and there over the years, guiding them through decisions on schooling, college, and university. Coming to terms with my husband's ongoing illness and the need to work full time. I didn't begrudge their needs. I just recognised that if I didn't do something as an individual, I would become invisible. I knew my confidence had been waning. I was losing my sense of self. Who was the real me? Where had I gone? The person who wasn't the mother, carer, wife, or supervisor; the person who always used to be happy, nutty and carefree.

On that second day I found myself again. It shook me rigid. I recognised I was truly happy. I bounced along literally on the balls of my feet. Suddenly I was 17 again, cut loose, liberated of worries. I thanked God for the beautiful day and then thanked my family for letting me go. On this day there was no guilt, no anxieties, no emotions of doing the right thing to please, pacify or support.

I was ungoverned, almost autonomous with a sense of laissez-faire. A tide of abandonment washed over me and my 'self' began its long journey to growth.

I hit Porthtowan around 12.30pm. All I can say is, it's a great place for pasties. Coming off the path, the walker literally finds herself next to the baker's shop; the smells beckoning this ravenous walker to partake. It also acted as the local post office, so whilst basking in the sunlight I sat and wrote a few postcards and enjoyed every last scrap of a warm 'stringer'.

There was a family on another table deliberating over who should have which type of pasty. I smiled at the banter and then feeling bolstered with confidence I wandered over to the pub opposite and had a shandy. I didn't feel threatened in any way.

Having gulped down my drink, I took the steep road descent into Porthtowan. This was very narrow. It is treacherous for walkers who can't be seen around bends. Climbing up again was tough as I headed for Mithian.

I savoured the remaining coastal path part of the day until I reached Mulgram Hill. It felt like I had been climbing all the way from Porthtowan. It was exhausting and exhilarating. Below me, the ravine stepped away with Chapel Porth in front. Here I parted company with the South West Path as I descended into Chapel Coombe, and then up its valley towards Mingoose. From here it was road. I was quite pleased; by this time I was very tired and knew I still had a fair way to go.

On reaching Goonbell, there was a red telephone box that worked and still required money. I was so pleased because I had no signal on my mobile phone. I was just two miles from Mithian, the kettle was on. It was the longest two miles of the walk but worth it. It took me an hour. It was now between 4.30 and 5pm.

Mithian is a quiet, quaint Cornish village. It boasts a church and pub. Most of the houses are thatched and whitewashed. This was my home for the night.

In the year of my absence, little had changed at Mrs T's. Warm hugs were exchanged as we slipped into companionable chatter and giggles. She was still grieving but we talked about the children, her grandchildren, the 'good old days' when I was a child and it was just her and I when her husband was away at sea. And here we were again, just us. I was given a lovely roast and Mrs T enjoyed it as much. "Not worthwhile cooking a roast for one." I knew what she meant.

After tea we fed the cats. They took to my lap with ease as Mrs T and I had a game of cards. David arrived and took my failed tent off me and gave me another map. I kept the sleeping bag just in case I needed it for extra warmth at the youth hostel. He spent the next half an hour having a cup of tea and chatting. Then he was gone, the dashing cavalier, away on his bike once more.

I was knackered. I ran a bath and had a lovely soak. Legs very tired, feet in excellent condition (thank you boots). By 7.30pm I was ready for my bed but we carried on chatting until about nine-ish. I had to be away by 7.30am as my route had changed and I had to get to Newquay before hitting the coastal path once more to Treyarnon.

I promised to make Mrs T a cup of tea and feed the cats before I left. I was to sleep with the cat Kalamazoo. He was quite possessive about the bed as this is where Mrs T's husband had spent his last days. Kalamazoo was his cat and still pined. Creepy or what? I shivered, how spooky the room felt. My imagination began to run bananas. I undressed hesitantly, quickly glancing around for ghosts and praying he wasn't watching. I dived under the bedclothes. They smelt familiar from my youth.

I chided myself as Kalamazoo made himself comfortable against my back. We tussled for position. "No, you aren't getting right in," I said, placing him firmly behind me. As the companion of my bed, I have to say Kalamazoo purred very loudly (on a par with snorers!) It was rather comforting and I fell asleep very quickly.

I was awoken at approximately 3am with a present. *Crunch, crunch, crunch*. The beast was enjoying his midnight snack. Kalamazoo had thought it wise to share his present with me but I was so tired I just remember thinking, don't jump up here after that, and promptly went back to sleep.

Morning came. Groggily, I staggered towards the bathroom. My feet found the sticky blood and remnants of the feast; a mouse, the tail still intact. A piece of bone stuck to my big toe as I limped to the bathroom desperately trying to shake it off. It flew across the room and stuck to the radiator. I left it hanging there, a blob of congealed matter. I was desperate for a wee. I sat on the throne, deliberating arse, toe or radiator? Decision made, before wiping my arse I wiped my sticky feet and radiator then cursed the cat. Of course, he had already gone out. The culprit had left the building.

I made the tea, had some cornflakes, fed the cats and returned upstairs. Mrs T was delighted: it had been a long time since anyone had given her tea in bed. Shortly afterwards, she came downstairs while I refilled my water bladder. Thanking her once again, we exchanged great big hugs. I put on all my wet weather gear and left.

I didn't know when I would see Mrs T again but I knew I would be buying flowers on my return home. She had never let me down, and my allegiance to her goes back a long way.

The time was 7.30am. Do you sense I am a stickler for time?

Monday May 2nd 2005. Mithian to Treyarnon Youth Hostel - 22.5 miles.

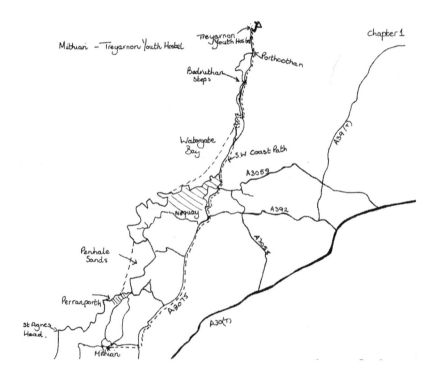

misty as I picked a minor road route out of Mithian to hit the A3075 to Newquay.

I was quite pleased with the weather conditions. Although murky, it offered me the excuse to wear a hat to hide my hair. With all-weather gear on, to all intents and purposes I could have been a man. It is not until you hit an A road that as a walker you feel so vulnerable. The users and the speeds they drive at are frightening. Stone walls offer no protection. As a walker you are only able to lean into them. There are no verges when cars and lorries are too close! Main roads also create stalkers and kerb crawlers asking if you would like a lift.

I briefly stopped at Perranzabuloe. It was nine-ish. I had a drink, snack bar and piece of chocolate. It had been slow going along the minor roads. It had taken a while to negotiate them and I am convinced they were longer than the signposts said they were. In any case, it was 10.5 miles to Newquay and seemed to take forever. I had to make up for the three miles lost the day before. By now the day was very warm again as I moseyed into Newquay.

What a difference a town makes. Although I came in on a quiet route, the front seaside road was packed with people. The noise level was perforating. Leaving Newquay to the surfing addicts with their choice of seven beaches, and the bright, tacky amusement arcades to entertain the hordes of people milling the streets, I left the B3276 and headed onto the coastal path once more at Whipsiderry Beach. It was a great feeling. There was a stiff westerly breeze, high clouds and sun. I had stripped off my outer gear some time ago and was happy to get back into shorts and walk. I had a long way to go yet.

Could I sustain this speed? Did I have the strength to do all the ups and downs of the path? Surprisingly, I was so pleased to be out there with the miles covered, this hadn't really occurred to me. Although tired, I bounced along; just exhilarated that I was achieving.

I was probably doing about three miles an hour including the ups and downs. I had surprised myself with the fitness. My legs and feet felt good.

Although Watergate Bay was stunning, it was quite tiring walking its length on the road and then back up onto the track above the sea. I was up high now as I came to Bethruthan Steps car park. And people. (Up to this point I had only met one lady out walking her two red setters.) Here, I took the track onto the road which led me into Porthcothan; another small surfing beach with fine sands. The only thing that spooked me was a gentleman peering out of his windows behind curtains. He was in the top half of a derelict looking farm, his face quite pale as he watched me. It sent shivers down my spine as 'Hannibal Lecter' crept into that vivid imagination again.

From Porthcothan I was now on the final stretch (haha). The route twisted its way across the cliffs as it zigzagged round headlands and down onto tiny beaches and up again. I finally staggered into Treyarnon Bay with the welcome sight of the youth hostel across the beach. I was very warm, my feet complaining, and hungry and knackered. It was 5pm. I had made good time. In fact I couldn't believe it.

I had come from Mrs T's and that seemed a distant memory. A stiff breeze blew across the beach. The sun was lost behind clouds. Now was a good time to go in the sea and cool down, wasn't it? I had to use my swimsuit once, didn't I? How cruel was it to have the sea beckoning all day? The beach was deserted I stood demobilised in my swimsuit for a while. Perishing, I ran down to the water's edge, my only concern being keeping my bag in sight. My feet were already singing my praises. *Thank you, thank you* and *Hallelujah*.

I didn't stay in for long. It was numbingly cold. Two minutes with shoulders underwater was enough. Running up the beach I noticed some people had wandered into the bus shelter that was on the path to the youth hostel. I had planned it to be my refuge for getting changed, as it was out of the wind. Now I couldn't use it. Shivering, teeth chattering, my fingers blue, I cursed and messed about getting myself dry and changed as a bemused mother, grandmother and two children watched this unsightly spectacle. "Oh I just had to do that," I said.

Inspecting my feet for warm spots and rubbing my legs to get the circulation going again, I was pleased although cold. The effort was worth it. Refreshed, I could look forward to a warm shower, sort out my bed, order breakfast and 'dress up' for a meal with David, Dave and Jan. I had planned to meet them at 6.30pm at the hostel, which didn't give me much time.

Just as I contemplated going into the hostel waiting area, the family in the bus shelter did a very charitable thing. They offered me a cup of coffee from their flask. How cool was that? I gratefully drank the sweetened coffee and savoured the warm cup in my hands. The children eyed this crazy woman up and down.

"Where you goin' then," they asked. "John O'Groats, but not today," I said and grinned. I think this was lost on them. I got the distinct feeling from their puzzled stares that they weren't sure where that was. I sat with the family chatting until they caught the bus. Such a short spell of time, but a very pleasant one. Then I walked into the youth hostel.

Treyarnon YHA is a great hostel. It boasts brilliant views of the sea from its glass frontage and is geared to the leisure pursuits, primarily surfing, that are offered at this location. It is roomy, very friendly and open all year round. I ordered a continental breakfast to be left out for 7am. I was going to have another long day getting to Tintagel.

I found my bed and made a quick dash to the showers. I had to be ready and 'dressed up' to go out. I wasn't of course. 'Dressing up' consisted of a clean pair of knickers and bra. Clean hair, teeth and a touch of perfume. A fresh T-shirt and dry trousers rounded off my 'going to dinner gear'.

I apologised to my hubby and friends for being late. They had booked a table for dinner at the pub in St Merryn. I was knackered and my face was glowing. I just wanted to put my head down. I can recall feeling 'spaced out', especially after the steak and chips! It was great to see everyone. We shared a few giggles. David and I exchanged maps again and agreed not to meet the next night as it was too far over on the motorbike all the time. However, he wanted to meet me before I left Padstow in the morning. He said that it gave him a purpose to get up and going.

He seemed pleased at this prospect. Later in the day Dave, Jan and he were going to go out somewhere else. I was glad because I wanted him to enjoy the break. He did look tired.

Returning to the youth hostel, I knew I would not see Dave and Jan again for some time, so after lots and lots of warm hugs I waved them goodbye. I met my fellow room-mates on my return. They were an interesting bunch, two French-Canadians and one Australian girl with whom I took up conversation. She was travelling round Britain catching buses and staying for one or two nights in places and walking from there. We discovered she was going to Tintagel tomorrow but as she put it, "I am getting there the smarter way, by bus. I'll see you there and have the kettle on." That was the last I remember as my head hit the sack.

Tuesday May 3rd 2005. Treyarnon Youth Hostel to Tintagel Youth Hostel via the Padstow Ferry - 22 miles.

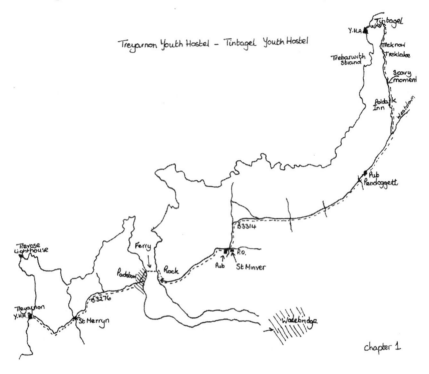

I have a built-in alarm clock and at 6.30am I quietly left my room to get my breakfast. It was very quiet at the hostel. My breakfast was in the chiller. I was not disappointed. It consisted of a croissant, butter, yoghurt, cheese and a slice of ham.

It was 7.15am when I vacated the building and set off. Again the early sea mist, the overcast sky and the dampness that hung in the air gave promise of another glorious day.

Today was where the 'alternative' part of my route came in. I was to use the Padstow Ferry. I hadn't been on it since I was eight and I was looking forward to it. First, I had five and a half miles of road walking. I was meeting David between 8.30am and 9am so I had to get my skates on.

It never ceases to amaze me how fast I walk on my own. The mist was thick and shrouded my view of the landscape, so I could only see 100 metres in front of me. A blanket of doubt came down as I realised I was not alone. I became quite spooked by this person. Just outside of St Merryn I had caught up with a hooded male who was walking 25 metres in front of me. I assumed it was a male by his gait and the way he slouched along. He appeared to be holding something and occasionally he looked behind him, furtively. I couldn't make out his features. I was extremely indecisive. There was no alternative road route. Should I stay behind him? Should I stop and let a good distance get between us? But what if he wasn't friendly, would he wait in ambush for me? I dribbled behind him, keeping a distance so as not to lose him out of my sight altogether, but far enough away to make a fast dash to safety. Heaven knows where that would have been if he had chased me. I kept looking at the map, checking my position relative to buildings available for refuge. My mind was in overdrive. The relief of reaching Padstow, where the chap was swallowed up in the town, was immense. I could have cried when I saw the familiar steps from the car park down into the little streets below. I practically flew down them. It was 8.45am. I had made good progress despite my fears. I quickly made my way to the quay and found where the little ferry left from.

No sign of David or the ferry! The sea mist was heavy. I wondered if I would be going across the river. I sat and waited. I was chilly from nerves.

Isn't it strange how we as humans make assumptions and categorise people before we do them justice? For, walking towards me was the hooded creature of the mist. A tall young man of no more than 16 years, walking with a young lady and in his arms a small Border collie puppy. How gentle the boy was treating this dependent creature, and seeing his face I smiled. (Some of which was relief, I must confess.) He could easily have been my son. An innocent keeping another warm and safe from harm and exposure. I apologised inwardly and chastised myself for being so foolish.

David arrived shortly after that. He had had an awful journey on his bike from St Austell. We exchanged one or two items. The ferry had come and was already leaving, so I ran to the quayside shouting, "Wait for me, I won't be a mo!" Grappling with my kit, I said my goodbyes to David as the ferry turned around to collect me. How sweet was the ferryman to do that? That small act of kindness saved me at least half an hour on the day.

I was the only person on the ferry. It was a treat. I savoured the moment. Surprisingly the mist seemed less thick here and the estuary was quite calm. I do so love the smell of the sea and the sense of freedom that being on a boat can give you.

The ferryman was a kindly Cornishman, chatting as he went. He had done the same trip for 10 years and still enjoyed the estuary's moods. I suppose he liked the company as the day promised to be a slow start. I reached the other side safely and waved goodbye. His weathered face creased with a smile.

As I disembarked from the tiny boat, for the first time I felt a little weary. Nerves had taken their toll. The puppy incident had wound me up slightly. I was drinking an awful lot of water and my two-litre water bladder was running low by 10.30am when I reached St Minver.

Here I found what I can only describe as the smallest possible post office that I have ever come across. Set in the front room of a tiny cottage, amazingly it was open. I say this because at first the door was shut. However, it also doubled as the local paper shop and someone opened the door. "You look 'bit lost. It 'ud be pension day down 'ere even though, come in." I couldn't believe it – I must have looked astonished for there was a queue inside this tiny dwelling, four people to be precise, plus me. They were chatting amongst themselves, so I didn't like to push forward and ask for water. Obligingly, I bought a post card. I then asked politely if I could refill my water bladder. "Oh yes o'course, but use the ou'side tap of the pub, 'e won't mind. I can't give 'e non." I said, "Are you sure he won't mind?" "No," came the reply, "we all use it at some point. Tis useful for 'osing the flowers. T'will be fine for your bottle." The postmistress smiled. Conversation finished, she pointed to the tap on the outside wall of the pub and shut the door. Job done she returned to her work.

I was left standing and a little bemused by the assumption

it was okay to use the publican's outside tap. I filled my water bladder guiltily and prayed I wasn't going to get the wrath of God come round the corner in the shape of an angry publican. The postmistress had been so matter-of-fact – blunt even – but sincere in her actions. What a character.

The mist still hadn't lifted as I headed towards Westdowns on the B3314. My boldness had escaped me and the thought of walking further out of my way towards the coast in the mist made me feel inadequate and uncomfortable. Reaching Pendoggett some eight miles further on by 12.30pm, I found myself damp, sweaty and craving for something to quell the rumblings in my stomach and in need of a quick caffeine intake. The mist had barely lifted but a welcomed pub appeared by the roadside. Despite my concerns, the desire to rest won out.

A little anxious, I stood at the bar and ordered my drink and a packet of plain crisps. There was an elderly man propped up at the bar and two lads playing pool. It was good to have something warm and the complimentary cinnamon biscuit was a treat. Supping my frothy coffee at the bar, I was interrupted by the authoritative voice of the gentleman sat next to me. "What are you doing here today young lady? Where are you going?"

My ears pricked up. Who was this calling me young, I'd take that any day. Facing the gentleman, I was able to assess his face a bit more. At a guess in his seventies or eighties, liked his beers, but also his whisky. Face bloated by drink but cheery nevertheless. Always mindful of company and surrounding ears, I explained I had walked up from Land's End and was meeting my husband in Tintagel.

"Jolly long way I say. Let me see." He eyed me up and down. "Do you work for the NHS by any chance?"

Keeping a straight face I said, "Yes I do." I didn't elaborate. Perhaps he thought I was a nurse, I don't know, but he continued in his plummy voice. "Knew you were." (Very pleased with himself.) "All NHS staff has to communicate, yes communication is the key."

Top Oh, I thought.

He left me for a while. I couldn't dislike him. He just ordered another drink and carried on chatting to the barman.

"I come in here every day," was the next thing he said to me. Yes I thought you might, I thought.

"By the way, which route did you think you would take?"

Careful guard up, aware of the lads in the background, barman listening, I shrugged. "Not sure yet, mist still a bit thick, probably the most direct route." Still evasive: giving nothing away. I listened. No choice.

"Well," he bustled, "let me give you a good tip for the most marvellous view. Take it from me, if this wretched mist lifts you will not be sorry. Make your way along this road for a bit and then take a little road leading to Trebarwith and Treknow, this takes you into Tintagel the back way so to speak. You will get a glimpse of Trebarwith beach. It's where some of Poldark was filmed."

He looked at me expecting me to be puzzled over 'Poldark'. But I had been an avid watcher of the TV series – the first in colour for me. No, I hadn't known it was filmed there, but I didn't say anything. I had already seen the road on the map and if it hadn't been so eerie in the mist I wouldn't have given it a second thought. However, I did want to be near the sea again.

I thanked the man for the information, drank the last dregs of my coffee and hauled myself off the bar stool. I had become far too comfortable and that wouldn't do. I was not in my teens now, drinking in the 'local' with the locals.

With reluctance and seizing limbs, I soldiered on and did take the road in question. My instincts were screaming at me that there may be trouble ahead. I must say I was a little nervous and anxious. I kept checking no one had followed me from the pub. Soon after passing Poldark Inn, the road climbed slightly and there in the mist was parked a white Ford Fiesta. Oh joy. I knew beyond this was an old quarry and water splash, and my brain went into overdrive. I passed the car on my left. A man was reading a paper in it. He looked up and his eyes bore into mine (well that's what it felt like). I can tell you, I really did pick up the pace, and with my heavy rucksack on I pelted down the road and didn't stop running until halfway up the other side, just before entering the tiny hamlet of Trebarwith. I didn't dare look back. My chest was heaving and heart banging. I started to break out into a cold sweat. What fun.

The hamlet was a relief. The sun was just bursting through so I sat on a convenient bench and had some chocolate in order to gather myself together. It barely touched the sides. The intense adrenaline surge made me shake. Or was it those nerves? It had been five and a half miles of walking extremely fast. My fear had been immense.

I stood up, asking my legs not to cramp up on me. My reward when the mist finally cleared was just as the man in the pub had said: "Marvellous." But it was only the briefest of glimpses of the sea. I chastised myself for being OTT – blasted imagination!

Another challenge over, I took stock of the situation and calmly packed away my hat and waterproof, savoured the now bright mid afternoon sunshine and commenced walking again. As I strolled, a new confidence arose from my previous panic, or perhaps it was a realisation that not every hedgerow or white Fiesta had beasties in them.

So then, the final push to find the youth hostel out on the coast, a further 3 miles away via Tintagel village. I think it was sheer bloody-mindedness that pushed me forward as I ate up the remaining miles. I don't know where the energy comes from. It's just there. I ask my legs for more and they oblige. I can't say I enjoyed the last bit of the walk that day because it felt like a rush and it was. I wouldn't do that mileage per hour again on reflection. I know now that even walkers can miss really important parts of the countryside if they don't stop. My only excuse was nerves. Car travellers miss masses of views, smells and peace, and I had done exactly the same. Still, it was a lesson. It was my first adventure and just walking alone had been the biggest challenge of them all. I cannot seriously explain how nervous I had been. It had been my intention to use the South West Path most of the way and I had done very little of it, my own inadequacies disallowing me that enjoyment.

I can honestly say I shuffled into Tintagel. Very tired, feet burning from walking and running too fast, sugars low and in desperate need to sit down. I probably ponged too. I can remember praying that somewhere would be open for something nourishing to eat. My rations for the day had been adequate but the thought of another peanut or chewy bar did not fill me with enthusiasm. I needed something substantial. My salvation came in the form of a café that was open (thank goodness it was closing at 7pm as it was now 5.45pm).

I cannot describe how relieved I was as I salivated over the menu and how positively delicious the fish and chips were that I ordered. The lady who served me waited patiently as I exhaustedly decided what I would have. I kept apologising for not thinking straight. It took me at least five minutes to stop shaking. I was aware people were looking at me but I was just too tired to care. A family were sat opposite and I asked them to keep an eye on my rucksack. I was desperate for a crap and wee and any hole to relieve myself was welcome.

Standing in front of the mirror was not a pretty sight. I was sweaty; my hair all over the place. I sniffed under my arms. Not a pleasant aroma. So I did a strip wash there and then and hoped no one would come in. Using the soap from the dispenser and my hands, I washed my face and armpits as best I could and dried myself off with my sleeves and toilet paper.

The blow dryer didn't work very well. If you've never tried

putting your face or your armpits underneath one, take it from me it's difficult. Contortionist comes to mind, especially when your legs are beginning to seize up.

Combing my hair with my fingers and looking in the mirror, I thought I looked better. Putting my sweaty shirt back on with its large wet patch, I can't say the aroma had disappeared!

I walked out, refreshed, relieved and revived, well almost. Slumping into my chair and thanking the family for looking after my rucksack, I eagerly awaited the arrival of my din-dins. I loosened the laces on my boots and let the air to my feet. Unfortunately, the bouquet coming out was whiffy! But this was soon forgotten. Oh boy, the mug of tea came out. Oh boy, oh my. That mug of tea was just the bees' knees. I even put some sugar in it. It barely touched the sides as I gulped it down. Then looking up, more people were staring. I just shrugged the 'it's been a long day today' shrug. And I carried on slurping.

I couldn't have given a monkey's for what people thought at that moment, and that's the truth.

I was not disappointed at the meal. It was enormous and really I was over faced, but somehow it just went down. Then I sat in the café until I felt I could muster up one more effort to find the youth hostel. After the food, my brain started to tick properly again so I became embarrassed about how I must have looked and smelt. My feet were begging me not to stand up as they were hot, very hot. I apologised but we had to move on.

Tintagel was still busy as I slowly made my way out to the coastal path to find the youth hostel. Past the chapel and over the common land dropping down towards the cliff, there, nestled in the rock, was the best positioned youth hostel I had ever been to. It was idyllic, looking out to sea facing west towards the burning sun. It was going to be a brilliant sunset.

A surprise awaited me, for there in front of me, by the gate and waving madly, was the young Australian girl I had met the previous night. "Do you want a cup of tea? What took you so long?" I just grinned and yes I did want another cup of tea. How special was that? I was so pleased to see her and even now I can't remember her name, just her kindness.

I checked myself into the self-catering hostel. The kitchen was bustling with people preparing their dinners. A couple of motorcyclists were biking John O'Groats to Land's End via the B roads. They had slowly meandered down through Britain and had taken six weeks to get this far from John O'Groats. Both were retired. I thought it was a fantastic way to operate. They were delightful and had had a great time visiting little villages across the country. There was also a gentleman walking the South West Coast Path in stages, with his long suffering wife as the support wagon. She thought perhaps he ought to join me but I wasn't getting into any domestics.

My bed was comfortable and the shower adequate. No blisters yet, just warm spots. I declined my friend's invitation to walk back into Tintagel for a drink. She had enjoyed her day, first catching the bus to Tintagel and then walking the coast and seeing the castle and other tourist magnets. She thought I was mad but I was too tired to care. I needed to be off the next morning. So we chatted a while and she went to the village and I happily turned in to write my diary.

Sat outside, in front of the youth hostel, the wind had

dropped and the orange sun was blanketing the sea before disappearing. It was a wonderful sight, a beautiful and touching end to the day. I left a note on my new friend's bed wishing her a safe journey wherever she was going next and a safe return to Australia. I was asleep before she returned and gone in the morning before she woke. I have never seen her again but I will always be grateful for that cup of tea.

Wednesday May 4th 2005. Tintagel to Stratton - 18 miles.

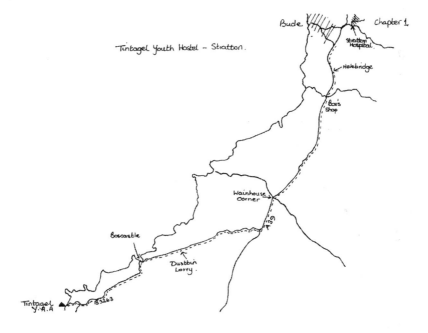

Up early: 6.30am. Had a cup of tea. Bikers up. Prepared feet, put some blister plasters over warm spots from yesterday – a preventive measure. Did some stretch exercises; legs a little sore now. Checked feet again, miraculously good, no blisters. I was very lucky. But my rucksack seemed heavier today.

I chewed on a cereal bar and had a piece of chocolate for breakfast and drank a large mug of tea.

Circumstances were forcing me home. David was very tired; I could hear it in his voice. This was to be my last day, so I wouldn't be going to Bideford this time. I was going to be picked up in Bude or Stratton, whichever was easier towards the end of the day. I remember feeling a bit downhearted but determined to enjoy the last day of freedom. The weather forecast had promised another warm day but at that time it was still very drizzly outside. Wet weather clothes were needed. I was quite pleased actually; I didn't look so ravishing in all my manly clothes.

I set off at 7am and retraced my steps into Tintagel. All was very quiet. A light rain started to fall. I passed by the early morning dustcart at 8am. I was on my way to Boscastle (what was left of it).

Earlier in the year, a terrible storm there had damaged the youth hostel, forcing it to close. Many other properties near the quay had been washed away or were structurally beyond repair. The appearance of Boscastle had changed considerably.

It was a steep climb on the B3263 out of Boscastle and this was a wake-up call to my legs. With the misty rain in my lungs, I found it quite difficult to breathe so I huffed and puffed my way to the top. I was overtaken once more by the dustcart and then by a lady in an estate car. I think it was a Volvo. She pulled up short and asked if I wanted a lift. I declined and she went on her way. I carried on for a bit only for the lady to come back again past me and then a little later she drew up by the side of me again and asked if I wanted to get in. I firmly said, "No," but she was very insistent that I should have a lift, which was a bit unnerving. It did cross my mind was she queer? But then who was the odd one here?

That was it for a bit as I gradually climbed for three miles. It was very peaceful and the farmland spread for miles. The lanes were deserted. This was fantastic stamina training, just like when I used to take horses out to exercise.

It was just at the final rise that I saw it. Through the murky drizzle the white monster of a dustcart loomed. It was parked in a lay-by. I could feel the panic setting in as my imagination played havoc. Looking at my map there were no boltholes. No houses to run to; just fields. I started to shake. What a way to go, I thought. Minced, bagged, packaged, parcelled, tied and munched into tiny squidgy pieces. Clearly I had watched too many Tom and Jerry films over the years. Oh Gertrude, we could get squashed, this could be it, just don't rape me first, oh yeah I've got my condoms.

All these thoughts hurtled into my mind as I shouldered up and sauntered along briskly past the dustcart looking like a man as best I could. My winter hat disguising my hair and my raincoat large and baggy, I hoped it would be enough.

The men were eating their breakfast. Too busy tucking into their sandwiches, a flask was balanced in front of the window and two pairs of feet were on the dashboard. They didn't even look up. I scuttled off down the hill and only stopped walking fast when a single bungalow came into view.

What a prat! Logic finally brought me to my senses. For goodness sake, I scolded myself, settle down and enjoy the day, Gertrude will be getting seasick.

I stopped for a snack at Wainhouse crossroads. It was about 10.30am. The rain had stopped. It was warming up. I was on target for an early afternoon pick up. As I devoured my snack bar I began to realise how sad I was. It was my last day. If my tent had been available I would have selfishly continued. Sensibility kicked in, it was meant to be, time to stop. It was a learning experience that had taken its toll. In truth, I was physically beginning to weaken and mentally tire. The navigating, making choices over the route, personal safety and my level of awareness had questioned my capability to do the next leg alone, or indeed any of the route alone. Was I going to be this nervous every time? And if so, was it really worth the angst?

Looking back now, I had been weary, my rationale unclear. It had been my first endurance test and an interesting insight into how the mind is affected under duress. Over the next legs, I learned to recognise this tiredness and use it as a marker to chill out and stop for longer breaks.

Nothing much happened for the rest of the day. I was on the busy A39 again and much of the time was spent just listening to traffic. Not incessant but the road was fast. At two-ish my efforts were rewarded by a highly recommended café at Helebridge, selling the most enormous baked potatoes. I couldn't believe their size. Orgasmic and organic. A walker's hallucination? I ordered a good old boring cheese one and lashings of salad and coffee, total £3.50. I was not disappointed. It was only matched by the toilets. (Here I go again.) These were plush, plush, plush. They even boasted a bath – which I could have used!! Well, highly tempted, I declined. It was explained to me that originally the café had been the family home. And, "Yes, occasionally we get people like you who need a wash."

Was that woman hinting? Surreptitiously I sniffed my arm pits; umm…not bad. They will do for another half day. At this point I rang David to come and collect me from Stratton near the hospital.

This seemed a good place to stop and by the time I had my lunch I would probably be walking into Stratton at approximately 4.30pm. I made light work of the potato then used the plush toilet again. I rinsed my face, and set off on my final sprint for Stratton!

So, this was it, only two miles to go. I dolly-stepped along, delaying the inevitable. Freedom would soon cease to exist again. The mother would return and the carer would support once more. I cannot fully express the sense of peace, pride, jubilation, guilt and loss that enveloped me on that final stage. I was excited by the prospect of finishing and bereft at the thought of possibly not having the chance to do the next stage. This may all seem odd to you, but for a very long time I had learned not to assume anything and that my life would be permanently on hold.

True to his word, David arrived with the motorbike at 4.30pm. I couldn't stop grinning. I was very pleased to see him. I was completely drenched in sweat and sort-of unscathed by my adventure. We exchanged hugs. He looked drained and I knew it had been right to stop when we did. He has never really slept well away from home. It's easier to manage pain in your own surroundings and be yourself, even though our friends perfectly understood him. It would have been too much to hunt around for a place to sleep so that I could continue to Bideford.

To David's embarrassment, I was so sweaty and beginning to get chilled, so I stripped off down to knickers and vest, to let the air dry me off properly. I only hope this loose behaviour was not noticed by too many of the residents of the quiet side street where I had chosen to do this. Hopefully they were all holiday bungalows.

We messed about for about half an hour repacking the bike and putting everything back as we had come down, except that the tent had to be strapped separately to the bike as it didn't fit anywhere now. Then we were off.

To begin with, I welcomed the breeze and its cooling effect on my body, so for the first hour on the bike my feet were profoundly thankful to be off the ground and started to cool down. However, my adventure was not over.

Stuck now in the 'cowboy' position on the back of the bike, my legs and hips began to cramp. It was excruciating and the only relief was to stand up on the rest pedals for brief seconds.

It was dark now as we trundled the five hours home. It was hell. I started to get the shakes from being absolutely frozen. My sweaty body by now had cooled a considerable amount; I was beginning to go numb.

Shooting pains coming up from the base of my feet were worse. In essence I was becoming hypothermic. I squeezed David's thighs several times and made a 'T' sign in his side mirror. Thankfully he got the message and he pulled over as soon as possible in the next Little Chef.

It could not have come soon enough. In the car park, David had to gently ease my legs over the bike to even get me off, I was shaking so much. We frantically found some more layers for me to change into in the café toilets. If anyone could have seen me walk across the car park to the building they would have laughed. Tears were quietly rolling down my face as my feet took the initial shock of the ground. Red hot pins and needles shot up through my legs. I looked like I had come out of a Spaghetti Western and had just had a shoot-out with Clint Eastwood. I swaggered in unable to bend my knees and sat with my extra clothes on my lap. I had to wait for my legs to thaw enough and de-cramp so I could even put them together, lady-like. I sat on this café chair with my legs splayed apart, rubbing them and urging them back into life.

It's when you are in these positions – not that I am all the time – that idiotic thoughts come into your head. Like, gee, that was one hell of a ride. No, it was a walk I've been on. I wonder if we switched off the gas at home. I need a lie down, here will do. How did I get here? What's David doing here? What's the time? Where's the gents, no I mean ladies.

I think I had lost the plot by now. It was touch of hypothermia in truth. My husband calmly ordered a large cup of tea and a plate of chips and pretended to ignore me whilst I slinked (well, crawled) off to the toilets to get changed. My lips were blue and I really struggled getting off the leathers and putting on thermals underneath with two extra jumpers on top. I hopped about the toilets dragging my trousers off, fingers fumbling with zips and buttons. Well, I couldn't do that in the café, could I?

Composed, I walked out of the ladies' toilets greatly improved in posture and dignity. I sat, still shaking, warming my hands on the tea mug and unable to eat anything. Slowly, warmth began to seep into my bones and my legs started to become less painful as I continued to stand up and walk about, sit down and massage and repeat all over again.

Did I enjoy this adventure? You may well ask. With two further stops to defrost, it took us an agonising five and a half hours to get home. We arrived home at about 10.30pm. I was exhausted.

Two days later, I had forgotten any pain and anxiety endured; only good memories remained. The tent was replaced by the shop I had purchased it from, and two days after that I was already planning: what's next?

For me personally, I had discovered that there was life in

the old girl yet. I had passed the first test. I knew I still had a long way to go, but I was looking forward to the journey showing me. As far as I was concerned, if allowed, Gertrude and I had more adventures to come.

CHAPTER TWO:
THE PASSION WAGON TEST

STRATTON TO BIDEFORD. DISTANCE: 23 MILES BY ROAD.

DATELINE: AUGUST 21ST & 22ND 2009.

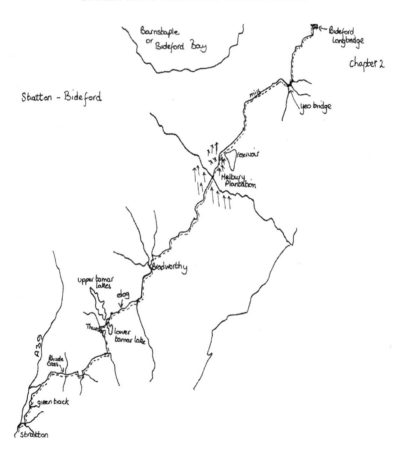

During the year (2009) there had been much discussion on how I was to complete the final stages of my journey in Scotland, when trying to use public transport was going to be expensive and less flexible. So David in his wisdom – with very little input from me – found himself looking on eBay for a suitable mode of transport. I have to be honest here. I was not amused and perhaps selfishly felt cheated that I wouldn't be sorting myself out for the remaining part of the walk. But to be fair, David had been left behind so many times whilst I had been travelling that it was only right for him to join me on my final stages.

My first thoughts concerned the cost of a vehicle. Was it really worth it? But I was persuaded that we would be able to use it in the future after my adventure! Watch this space!

I came home from work one day to find on our driveway a white Renault Romance Traffic van – converted into a camper wagon back in the year dot. David proudly presented our new possession: an eBay special bargain! On initial inspection the bodywork was rusty but satisfactory. It had four wheels, which sort of helps, and the interior – although worn, shabby, dirty, greasy and tired – was solid and had potential! "What do you think?" David looked at me all eager. Well, what does one say? "Marvellous dear, how much?" was my first reaction. My second was inside my head: *What a bloody heap*. I stood there thinking that this has got to work.

That weekend was hard work cleaning the inside of the van while David looked at the engine. I washed the carpets, the grit coming out in blackened lumps, and the wardrobe was cleansed of grease. The wagon had been used by a family who engaged in the sport of Motocross. Personally, I think this is what sold it to David as he too had an interest in the sport and it turned out our son had raced at the same tracks with the van's owner. SOLD, the van was going to be ours anyway, if you get my drift. This didn't help clean the van. Still, weekend over, the van was polished inside and out. Underneath all the grime, once finally expunged, were decent cupboards well built – in fact 'built to last'. A bit like a septic tank in the garden really. The paintwork on the outside looked... better! And the engine? Well, a little less promising, but 'it works'. The upholstery was and still is tired and so were the curtains. The seats, when put together to make beds, didn't and still don't quite line up because the stuffing has flattened, which gives you lumps and bumps where you don't want them!

The van boasted an upstairs, which was a bit of a hoot as a piece was missing, so you had to be either a very tiny adult or a child to fit on it and then there was the little matter of climbing up to it. The Wessex Climbing Club would be well impressed with the skills I have acquired since 'the purchase'. All I can say is one has to stretch all muscles as if on a medieval torture rack to get up there.

David was all agog and eager. He now had two weeks to get it sort of roadworthy. I was assured it was going to be fine as black smoke billowed out of the exhaust each time it started up. "Diesels do that you know," I was told. And when it rattled along at 40 miles an hour not picking up speed, it did cross my mind how long it might take to get to Stratton, if we got there at all.

Not deterred, David worked on the engine and altered a few odds and sods and left it at that. He did the usual checks. Oil, water, tyre pressures and windscreen washer bottle. I packed the van with, dare I say it, a flutter of excitement. This was to be another adventure and I was doing an odd bit in order to complete the length between Land's End and North Wales. In all this excitement we renamed our Renault Romance Traffic 'The Pash Wagon'. After all, one, we could always hope for 'pash' (romance), two, it certainly wasn't posh and three, there was always the prospect of pushing it! And of course my 'pashion' for walking was going to continue.

Friday August 21st 2009. Going west.

Worked all day. I was looking forward to both the trial of the wagon and the walk. We were unsure where we were going to sleep overnight but it needed to be near Stratton. David picked me up, true to his word, at 6pm. Proudly, we left the car park.

The journey was long and arduous. The A303 was filled with holidaymakers and weekenders heading for the West Country. We finally arrived in Stratton at 10.30pm and managed to find a small but adequate lay-by half a mile outside the town, which was fantastic from my point of view. We had a light tea and a well deserved mug of tea. I rearranged my day-sack, maps, boots, food and water bladder, made the beds, tied Gertrude to the rucksack (by now even she was used to the regime) and finally we turned in for the night at approximately 11.30pm. We were both a little wary of parking there. After all, neither of us had slept in a lay-by for a very long time. Not that we made a habit of it before but on odd occasions it had happened.

We had just settled down and all was dark and quiet when a car pulled up behind us with its headlights blazing and the radio boom, boom, booming, causing the van to shake. (It was that close.) David and I froze and hoped that it wasn't a gang of youths who had been drinking and were going to make trouble. Peering out of the curtain, I could just make out one person in the car and he had his head to a mobile. Clearly he had screeched into the lay-by to take a call. Relieved, the old mother instinct returned. What a good lad pulling off the road. Anyway, five minutes later he had revved up and was gone, the noise finally disappearing down the road at top speed. All was quiet and we both slept until 6am.

Saturday August 22nd 2009.
Stratton to Bideford - 23 miles.
We got up, got dressed, washed, had breakfast, packed away the bedding and then headed back to the hospital in Stratton. David dropped me off at the same spot he had picked me up back in May 2005. It was 7.30am; all was quiet in the village. My plan was to meet David in Bradworthy, the largest village on the walk, for a coffee break or dinner.

Out of Stratton, alone once more, I found a great path leading behind the original village and church; a tiny green track, firstly tarmac then a muddy path. What struck me most was my confidence. How different from those few nervous miles in Cornwall four years before. How quiet the track was and how much I was enjoying its peace and tranquillity.

The day was dull, that drizzly fine sea mist was about but it was refreshing, not eerie any more. The track finally led me to Colbrook House. Here it became difficult to find the road as the new owners had clearly rearranged their boundary and pathway compared to the map. The house had been recently renovated and a new drive had been put in, taking the walker behind the house instead of in front, which led to a stream I couldn't get over. It was covered in a thicket of brambles and gorse. I could see the road but not get to it. Back-tracking, eventually I just threw in the towel, opened their back gate and walked down their drive to the road. It was no great distance, just a bit inconvenient.

The road leading to Rhude Cross was a long steep climb but from here I had my first glimpse of the North Devon coast, possibly the Hartland Point area. Following this delightful lane, I munched handfuls of already ripened blackberries. Yum, deliciously sweet and juicy. I didn't notice the miles, just the signposts pointing the correct way. I headed towards the Tamar Lakes via Thurdon, but I was to be disappointed. The lakes were away from the road and I didn't really want to divert off my course just for that. At Alfardisworthy, there was a mill but it had now been turned into a museum for vintage cars!

It was at this point I was joined on my walk by a spaniel. He didn't seem to want to leave me. I hate it when this happens. Looking at the map, the dog came either from the mill or from one of the houses, but he didn't have a tag. All I could hope was that he would get tired of following me or that he did this often and the owners knew about it. I hung about for a while and went into the grounds of the museum, only to be greeted by a young lad smiling that he had found his friend again. "We are staying in a caravan behind the mill, sorry." The dog was clearly pleased to see the boy. I was pleased for both of them.

I walked on for another half a mile when I had 'movements'. Putting it as eloquently as possible here: I was in desperate need of relieving myself of a stool at this stage. It's always a problem and you just can't concentrate until your stomach feels better. I was brewing a good one and likely to explode. I won't pinpoint the exact location of my defecation (all done in the best possible taste). I dug my hole with the heel of my boot to about nine inches deep, hidden from the road, in a small wooded area. The relief was immense. The fern and odd bramble tickling my ass could not take away how good it felt. Everything however must be done at great speed, if you're not wishing to be noticed. Tidying yourself up, placing your dirty tissues in a separate bag and covering the offending stool correctly so animals are not harmed by it before anyone spots you can sometimes take seconds, but this still has to be properly executed. A small tip for you: Always keep your dirty tissues in the same pocket. It's no use complaining about the smell of your brown nose when you've blown it! Personally, I keep my dirty tissues in a separate bag in my right pocket, clean tissues and antiseptic wipes in my left because I am left handed and naturally I always use my left hand to grab things. This is an essential ritual when packing. Of course, you can put your tissues in the ground with your crap, but I find it easier waiting for a public loo to dispose of the paper waste.

Moving on then: I really enjoyed the day. I walked into Bradworthy about 10.30am. I was early again. I sat on a small memorial bench outside the cemetery and had a drink and some nuts before entering the village. It was still quiet.

Bradworthy is well worth a visit. Dating back to Saxon times, probably about 700 AD, it is a good example of a typical village of this time with its square in the centre and the local facilities surrounding it. It boasts the largest village square in the West Country. In mid-July a carnival is still held there and in late August the revival of the centuries old sheep fair now takes place. The church dates from Norman times but little of that remains as it was extensively damaged by fire in 1395, then rebuilt and rededicated around the 1400s.

The lower part of Bradworthy has a green called Broadhill. This green space was originally used for villagers to stack their faggots for burning and also for drying clothing. The name Broadhill is probably derived from the Saxon term 'broad estate', meaning open green.

Arriving in the square it was busy. Villagers were putting up bunting; clearly a carnival or festival was going to happen, and as a visitor I felt a little like an intruder. I had left messages for David on his mobile. Pointless: no signal. But he wasn't there and just as I was about to head off, the Pash Wagon arrived.

Parking in the square, David brewed a cup of coffee. I was able to relax and take stock of the surroundings. The village reminded me a little of Downton or Stockbridge in Hampshire. I must say that having a cup of morning coffee in a luxury seat instead of on my bottom on a mat was refreshing.

We then planned to meet in the forestry commission car park at North Melbury Wood for lunch. David had not expected me to be this far already. His comment was, "I haven't even had time to shave or wash."

Setting off again refreshed, the weather was ideal for walking: slightly breezy but sunny. The B road was quite dangerous, as it was clearly a useful way of getting to Bideford without going on the tourist route. I met two farmers laying out signs to the entrances of their fields. This was warning drivers of muddy roads and delays from combine harvesters and tractors. Whichever way you looked there were views of fields and on the high spots a glimpse of the sea.

The plantation at Melbury had for the most part been deforested. It was a working plantation that obviously didn't match my map. However, North Melbury Wood did exist, but what had once been a car park was really just a small lay-by. By the time I reached David he had shaved and washed. I stopped for half an hour.

My feet were very warm from walking on too much tarmac.

I had to put some plasters on the warm spots and change socks. If I hadn't done I am sure I would have had blisters later.

It was 12.45pm when I set of again. Passing Melbury Reservoir with fishermen dotted along its shores, I ploughed on. With Bideford only approximately eight miles away, I had made extremely good time. The road shortly thereafter became a bit creepy as I walked towards Dundridge. Here the road went past water treatment works and rose above the River Yeo. Walking under a canopy of trees for approximately one and a half miles, it was quite dark and dank as water dripped from one side of the valley, becoming tiny rivulets crossing the road to plunge down the other side. The sudden cold sent a bit of shudder through me. I could see on the map when it would open into daylight again and couldn't wait.

My reward came later. Walking towards Yeo Bridge I suddenly came eye to eye with a buzzard. She was perched on a sawn-off tree in the beautifully landscaped garden of an old mill. I was being nosey and as I peered over the fence, her head turned and stared at me. I couldn't have been any more than 20 feet away. Both of us were surprised but with gentle grace she looked for a maximum of five seconds and then flew effortlessly away. It was a magical sight. I watched her disappear beyond the mill and across the valley to the conifer woods. I remember standing there awestruck. Yes, if only for this moment, this walk had been worth it.

The road out of Yeo Bridge was steep and offensive on the now tired feet. At Littleham Cross, I had a brief view of

Bideford and the sea, then lost them again on the decent. The road had now become just a track with greenery in the middle. I didn't think the local council worried too much about this road. But it was a great route to come into Bideford on. There was no traffic until I actually came into the town on the B road at Handy Cross.

I met David in the main car park in Bideford at 3.30pm. Funnily enough he had made his way to the ice cream van and so had I. I tapped him on the shoulder. "Would you like me to buy you one?" I said. "Blimey, that was quick, I was going to look round." Thwarted again, he accepted the ice cream and we sat on the nearest bench enjoying a Devonshire Cornet. Then we walked about the town before heading back to a very treasured haunt at Croyde Bay for the remainder of the weekend.

The van had been a success. The walk had been completed. We met up with our daughter and surfed the next day before travelling home on the Monday. Fantastic. The weather stayed breezy but sunny.

David and I had shared some quality time. And best of all I would be concentrating on 'Up North' next. I was glad that this half of the country was completed. It felt good.

CHAPTER THREE:
A TRIP DOWN MEMORY LANE

**BIDEFORD TO BARNSTAPLE RAILWAY STATION. DISTANCE: 9 MILES
VIA ROAD AND TRAIL. DATELINE: SUMMER**

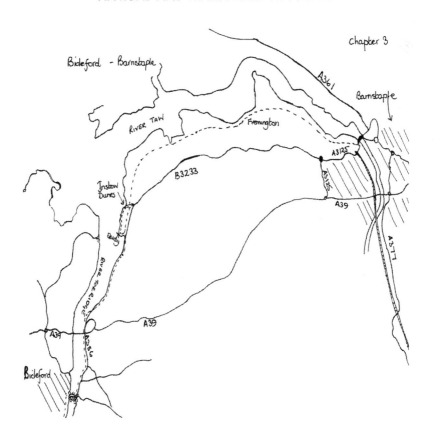

This part of the walk was one we had done years earlier. And we actually walked from Barnstaple to Bideford. It wasn't part of a bigger plan at the time. We didn't think of it as a possible route for a much longer walk. No, it had just been a walk and cycle ride, enjoyed during a family holiday when our children were young.

I've included it because it is special. Our children are special and their love of the outdoors has come from walking and cycling from an early age. As a parent seeing them still enjoying the countryside, I am rewarded with pride for this part of my journey.

I haven't wanted to repeat this leg of the walk because (a) I've already done it and (b) I couldn't have enjoyed the walk any more than I did at that time. This may sound mushy and wrong in principle or 'breaking the rules'. To this I would say my rule at that time was to open my children to the possibilities around them, encourage them to breathe fresh air and sense the freedom of space in a fun way. Memories are there to be reflected on, and reminiscing reminds me of a different era and my responsibilities as a mother and as a wife.

Our holidays spent in our trailer tent at Croyde Bay were fun. We had taken a few holidays on the Gower with the trailer tent and thought we would explore Devon for a change.

Saving for a holiday each year was difficult. A month or two before each holiday, I would gradually buy the non-perishable food items, toiletries and 'treats'. This helped with the final expenses. All year I would put money by for petrol, campsite fees, children's ice cream and spending money. This was eked out of the Family Allowance and housekeeping money. The week before leaving I would bake quiches, flapjacks and shortbread, and make fairy cakes with different toppings and homemade pasties, to give us a good few meals and lunch snacks. Even then the excitement of a pending journey rippled around the family. The grandparents helped out. We were supplied with what my husband and I called our 'Red Cross parcels'. These as often as not were in the form of money either for us or for the children, or perhaps a family pack of biscuits, ham, a special marmalade, even postage stamps for the children to send cards.

We were extremely grateful to the grandparents. Our joint income was limited then and didn't stretch too far. I didn't have a full-time job. Instead I child minded after school, became a classroom assistant and dinner lady, then some evenings I worked in the local store and pub. The holiday was such an enormous treat that it was never taken for granted by any of us in the family. For my husband particularly it was a welcomed break from the same four walls, but always a rather daunting if not tiring prospect. His energy levels were always fluctuating and he was never out of pain.

The children were eight and six years old. My husband and I walked and they cycled. We had a green Austin Montego estate then and their bikes used to live on the rack attached to the back of the boot. For our son, even though he was the youngest, it meant he could burn up all his energy. He never sat still and was always looking for the next adventure. It was a cycle ride to him, nothing more, and there was plenty of space to lark about on the bike. For our daughter, being sensitive to her surroundings, it was about enjoying the views and the interesting parts of the old railway line.

Looking back now, it seems amazing that given their ages, we had expected our children to cycle the nine miles, because of course they had to cycle back! But they had been cycling to school since they were three, firstly to playschool with the help of stabilisers and then to primary school every day, two miles away. We did however break the Devon trip down to two days. Reflecting now, I hadn't even considered that it might have been painful for my husband to walk that distance, but he never complained. He just slept it off the next day.

I have no photographic evidence of this part of the walk. In those days, I didn't take the camera everywhere with us and anyway film processing was another expense. Digital cameras weren't even talked about in our family, but they had just begun to infiltrate the high street and would eventually become accessible and affordable to all, including us.

So enough of this preamble: now to the walk itself, using the Tarka Trail.

The first part of the walk took us between Barnstaple and Instow. I would recommend spending time in both of these places, as they have significant historical backgrounds and are interesting in their own right.

Barnstaple is a vibrant, bustling market town nestling in

the valley of the River Taw. It has become a major part of the tourist industry in North Devon. Not only is it pivotal to the range of leisure activities that can be found in this area, such as walking, cycling, canoeing, surfing and fishing, but its road links allow reasonable access to Taunton, Exeter, Bideford, Lynton, Tiverton, Exmoor National Park and the beaches of the North Devon coast.

Originally a Saxon stronghold for the defence of North Devon, it was walled to withstand any Danish attacks. Its old name was Beardstaple (market of staple) which meant it was a centre of commerce and recognised as such by the kings of that time. Firstly, they established the town as a burgh or borough and then created a mint and in turn, granted a Charter that gave the townsfolk rights to hold a market and fair.

Over the ensuing centuries, Barnstaple's importance as a west coast port was strengthened by its use by the Naval Council. Ships that sailed from the town fought in many sea battles, including Drake's victory over the Spanish Armada. (Commemorated by a tablet in Queen Anne's Walk.) However, the port was not just used by the Navy. It had far more strategic importance to the woollen industry. Trade flourished as the known world expanded, and this was a time of great prosperity. Although trade was interrupted during the English Civil War, with the town being held by the Roundheads for a time, it later settled back to being an industrial centre and market town.

It is well worth a visit to the pannier market and Butchers Row. This beautiful Victorian building reminds one of Waterloo

Station in London. The current market dates from the mid-19th century when an Act of Parliament was passed to regulate markets and fairs. Previous to this, markets were shambolic. Free trading of livestock often involved harsh treatment during sales and butchery, and the so called 'stalls' and their produce were often poor in quality.

The pannier market was originally known as the vegetable market, changing its name to reflect farmers' wives and daughters bringing their vegetables and dairy products to market in large baskets. At the same time, Butchers Row was built on the north side of the market, allowing the butchers to keep meat cooler. This still exists today, however the shops are not all butchers. But the market runs on Saturdays and traders still use the vast hall, not necessarily for produce but for crafts and other interesting stalls.

Barnstaple has many little lanes, nooks and crannies to explore. It retains its charm whilst providing modern shopping facilities. The children, I remember, enjoyed walking through little alleyways where the sense of the town's history could still be felt. Since this walk we have returned many times.

This part of the Tarka Trail was not formally opened until 1991. We would have been using the trail in its infancy. Most of the trail is formed by the former Bideford Extension passenger railway line opened in 1855, which was closed in 1965 and finally removed in 1985.

We set off along the trail rather swiftly. The bonus of being an old railway line it that it has small gradients for the cyclist to deal with. The children kept backtracking because we couldn't walk as fast as them. Ben had a blue BMX bike and Katy an orange one.

From the trail there were wonderful views of the Taw estuary and its marshes. At one point the railway line feels like it is amongst the marshes and at the Fremington crossing we stopped for a rest. The children spent time looking down into the river before we trundled on again. I just remember us bumbling along and taking note of old pieces of sidings and railway sleepers occasionally still lying in the grass. Looking back now, I hadn't realised how soon after it had been opened that we had first used it. I just remember the smell of the sea, the open views and the exercise.

It was about one o'clock when we arrived in Instow. It had not taken long. I remember us eating a sandwich before going onto the beach and the dunes!

Instow is only a small hamlet. It lies at the meeting of two rivers, the Torridge and the Taw. From its shores, Appledore on the other bank can easily be reached by ferry. Its beach, Instow Sands, is used widely in the summer months as this is a suitable spot for families with very few strong waves. It is popular with canoeists, kayakers and those with small dinghies. The waters here are quite shallow and it's a wonder how the larger boats negotiate the River Torridge to Bideford. It is a very picturesque area.

The old railway station at Instow has now been turned into a museum. For the walker or cyclist it would be easy to miss the beach, as the path does not automatically take you there. I remember thinking at the time it was lucky we followed rustic signs 'to the beach'. However, it may not be like that now.

We spent an hour messing about on the beach, getting an ice cream, having a drink and walking down to the quay and the public slipway. It was then time to trundle back. Ben was tired, hooray! He had cycled miles back and forth. Katy was tired but she was never going to show it. So it was a gentle coaxing back and lots of stops and snack breaks until we returned to the car. They probably rode about 15 miles that day. We had walked 12 miles so they must easily have done more.

The next day, the Instow to Bideford leg was far easier on us, although I have to say it was noisy. From Instow, the track was very pretty to begin with, then as we followed the River Torridge it became dusty and uneven. There were open fields to our left, and the river with the tide out didn't look quite so picturesque with its muddy banks. For a pedestrian this stretch was much busier, and the sound of traffic could be heard from the main road (A39) before you could see it. However, we were soon underneath it before walking alongside the A386. This was quite busy and as a parent I was glad I was walking to make sure the children slowed down and stayed on the path as we went across Bideford Long Bridge.

This is one of the finest and longest spanning arch bridges in the country. Built in 1535 to a hung design, it has 24 arch stone spans. Originally the bridge was made from oak dating from medieval times as part of an ancient causeway.

Surrounding the timber frames, loose stones forming a scour protection known as 'stirling' can still be seen. Over the centuries, it has been widened to allow a footpath and was strengthened with girders. During WW1 a temporary train track was laid to help the war effort. In 1968, the western arch of the bridge collapsed through flooding and the Department of Transport carried out extensive repairs on the arches, strengthening the pillars below the sea bed. Later, a more modern bridge was built to re-route the strain of traffic further along, and a 3-ton limit was placed on the old bridge.

Travelling across this ancient bridge and looking westwards towards the quay and the boats was really exciting. Bideford is the home port of the MS Oldenburg, which sails back and forth the 12 miles to the island of Lundy off the north coastline. Originally built in 1958, MS Oldenburg started her new life as the Bideford-Lundy Ferry in 1986 after refurbishment. She was in dock and as we walked along the roadside by the banks the children were able to peer over.

The river was becoming higher now and some canoeists were grouping to paddle downstream. The bustle on the river with tiny rowing boats and little skits with outboards made it pleasant to watch. We wandered along the broad walk there until it was time to turn around and go back.

Bideford also has a pannier market although we didn't see it. It is held on Tuesdays and Saturdays. I also understand that Bideford is renowned for antique shops, which are to be found in the tiny alleyways called 'drangs'. This appears to be a West Country term for small alley.

Our return was uneventful. The children had enjoyed the less strenuous ride and Bideford, primarily because the ice cream van was there plus the river with all its boats by the quayside, was colourful and entertaining. The trail going back was busy with people by this time and it was quite dusty. I think I took a picture of the bridge but it's somewhere in one of our albums in the loft. Duh – must hook it out sometime.

As a walker, if I was doing this route again I would certainly use the trail. It's so easy to walk along and for a long distance walker it's perhaps a natural break from having to think about where to go next. There is no need for maps or much in the way of provisions, as there are adequate shops in Bideford and Barnstaple for grabbing something nutritious. I would certainly take my time if and when I do this trail again, and perhaps during the summer take a trip to Lundy Island for the day to give my feet a break. However, I can not get away from the fact that it's so much more enjoyable walking with the children you love.

CHAPTER FOUR:
A LESSON IN LEADERSHIP

I started to prepare for this particular trip in the January of 2008. I had the maps required – OS Explorer Map OL9 Exmoor and OS Explorer Map 140 Quantock Hills & Bridgwater.

I was really looking forward to this part of the walk. My sister-in-law had offered to accompany me across Exmoor and she and I would be backpacking again. I probably didn't appreciate how very little backpacking she had done, especially with the weight we would be carrying, so I can only apologise for my first mistake of assuming we could go long distances in a day. This proved to be pivotal in the distance we covered, as originally the plan was to walk from Barnstaple to Bristol in a week – approximately 90 miles.

Poring over the maps, I plotted a course looking for possible sites to put up our tent, and boltholes where we might have shelter from poor weather. So in January I started contacting farms that I saw on the maps, checking on the internet that they still existed before phoning. It's on these quests that you realise how kind and accommodating people are. When I explained what I was doing, invariably their first question was, "Are you doing this for a charity?" And secondly, "How many people?" I am not sure what my reaction would be if a stranger asked to borrow my garden or field for a night, but I would like to think that as a like-minded person I would be equally generous – once I understood what was happening and what was required of me. I even rang B&Bs and just asked the question, "Can we use your garden with our tent?" One lady said, "Of course, not a problem, we have a lot of people coming through here using our facilities. I can even cook you a breakfast and we have a downstairs shower you can borrow." She was going to charge us £5 each. What more could you ask. Even more amazing, I could give no indication of when the walk would actually happen, only that it would possibly be in March or April as holidays hadn't been finalised at that stage. That did not deter people. It was all, "Call us when you roughly know."

I don't know if it's down to how you approach people, but by the end of the weekend I had enough farms, campsites and B&Bs lined up to cover the distance we would walk. I can only thank them for their generosity.

Booking my holiday gave me a sense of purpose, and in February (thank goodness for forward planning) I secured my holiday dates for March. One weekend saw me booking one night in a B&B in Barnstaple and the train tickets from Salisbury to Barnstaple for March 14th. I was so excited. To the reader, this may seem so insignificant but I had only ever booked train tickets online once before and just for me. I'd never accomplished booking for two or negotiating a B&B that was clearly very popular. We only just got in for the night.

That same weekend, out came the rucksack and the other precious commodities. Gertrude, I am sure, was pleased to be out from under the bed and as I tied her on to the sack I told her all about the route and that we were having company this time. I rang Wintershead Farm, Simonsbath to check it was still okay to camp there for our first night. On reflection they must have thought I was mad, and probably didn't think too much about the dates, but at least I had warned them when we were coming through and I was very grateful the offer was still open. As far as I was concerned, I was on my way again.

My brother kindly allowed us to borrow his two-man Hilleberg tent – very lightweight, durable, waterproof and ideal for backpacking. It has two storage spaces and openings, with enough room for rucksacks to stay dry if necessary and enough area to cook in. We split the weight. Paula had the tent and I had the poles and pegs. I think I came off better here.

I packed my rucksack as before, except I put in extra thermal wear. I was so glad I did. For main meals this time, I packed five Wayfarer meals. I was not relying on pubs this time around. It is surprising how those extra items brought the weight up to 18 kilos. Wayfarer meals are substantial and weigh heavy. But I think they are well worth it, they do fill you up.

Friday March 14th 2008. Travel day.

Sunny weather. I arrived at my brother Steve's all excited, David describing me as "living with a tornado" and thank God it was leaving his camp for a week. He stayed at my brother's for a while, let the 'whoosh 'of the whirlwind out of the car to release her energies and then he left. A becalmed (for now) tornado repacked her rucksack to accommodate the tent poles, then she had another cup of tea and was then let loose with her calm sister-in-law, who drove them both to Salisbury.

Paula had used the long stay car park in Salisbury before. In my ignorance I didn't know it existed. Apparently, you book your space by phone and you can extend the time by calling. I thought this was brilliant and welcomed myself to the 21st century. Paula was so confident of what she was doing, and I followed her through the streets to the railway station like some lost child eager with anticipation of our journey.

It all went without a hitch. Proudly I produced the tickets; my little contribution! We had no problems. Changing twice, we finally caught the train from Exeter to Barnstaple. This two carriage bus-style train was delightful, with its front facing seats all in a line and covered in the brushed cotton style of another era. It stopped at all the tiny stations and the conductor pressed the button if anyone was going to get off. It was literally like being on a bus. I found it charming if not tiring.

We arrived in Barnstaple at 16.38. It had taken three and a half hours. Not too bad, about the same as in a car.

We found our B&B The Old Vicarage easily. Beautiful accommodation and friendly people. We had a tastefully decorated family room which gave us the option of one of us having a double bed and the other a single. It was a relief to dump the rucksacks, have a brush up and go back into the town for some grub. We also wanted to work out the direction of our route for the next day. It was all quite simple and by the time we found a decent place to eat, we were hungry. We had a great meal at 'Woodys' chip shop/café. Paula had cod and chips and I had fish cakes and chips. All washed down with a mug of tea. Yum. I felt stuffed.

Back at the B&B, we tried to watch a DVD but it wasn't really worth it so we just chatted and turned in. It had been prearranged in our booking that we could have an early breakfast, but on our arrival 'early' seemed to be 9am! However, after we explained, the owners kindly accepted that we needed an earlier breakfast and were prepared to do it at 7.30am. This was really good of them.

I had the double bed and had a fairly good night's sleep, but I was too excited again really. I was woken at three-ish by mice scrabbling around somewhere above me in the loft or rafters, then at about five the water heating kicked in. So it was a bit noisy.

Breakfast was duly served at the appointed hour and was very good, but I never do justice to them. Our table was situated by the window overlooking their garden. Very pretty and carefully managed; I would recommend coming here but booking is advisable.

Saturday March 15th 2008. Barnstaple to Wintershead Farm - 16 miles.

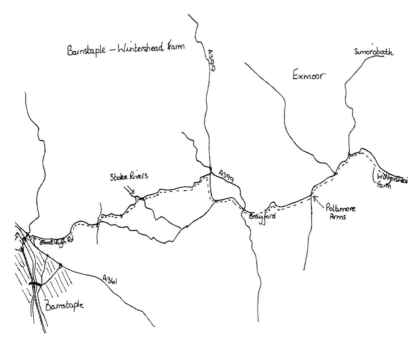

We set off after our early breakfast and hit the trail at 8.10am. Weather: overcast and chilly. I was wearing a hat so it must have been cold. Paula had a warm headband. I must invest in one of those as they keep your ears and head warm, but also allow a bit of chill on top. Sometimes hats are too warm. It had rained in the night and for now it was staying away, but the forecast was not good.

Adrenaline once again fuelled the anticipation of a good day's walking, and this kept me bouncing along. We made the steady climb out of Barnstaple along Goodleigh Road, and at Goodleigh we finally got onto our first track. I always find it a buzz once I'm off road. It's so much more interesting and quiet.

The track became our first challenge with heavy rucksacks. It lulled us into a false sense of easy walking but eventually as we came past Dean Wood, a slow careful descent was needed as the water was running under our feet and clearly the 4x4s that used the track had created deep ruts. The stones were slippery and loose.

What goes down must go up; it was a sharp but steady climb for a mile up the coombe to a dear little village called Stoke Rivers. This was just a couple of farms and a church. From here it was road again all the way to Brayford, but it seemed to be going perpetually uphill, at least to Mockham Down. By now the weather was looking doubtful. A chilly wind had sprung up but still no rain.

Reaching Brayford, we had made good time especially with so much up. It was 12.00 and we had done nine miles. It was at this point that my uncomplaining stoical companion announced "blisters" ... aargh! We sat in a welcomed bus shelter where on inspection her feet did not look good. Munching our snacks, Paula began to smile again, but morale was a bit low. Then to add insult to injury it began to rain. At this moment I now regret not saying, "Let's find somewhere to stop for the night." In my own mind I was set on getting to

Wintershead Farm. After all, we were over halfway. My first mistake in leadership: 10 miles would have been enough for Paula on the first day. I should have found the nearest bolthole and let her feet rest.

We left the bus shelter fortified, bolstering Paula along. On the map I could see a pub at Sherracombe Cross called the Poltimore Arms. The prospect of having a hot drink with perhaps some soup pushed us forward. It did cross my mind we might be able to set up camp there for the night.

The rain became a steady inconvenience. I was still feeling upbeat and sang as we trudged along. We had another climb up Beara Hill to Sherracombe Cross. By this time we were drenched. It was now 3pm and we had slowed down considerably. There were cars parked on the pub's small forecourt but it looked just like a house. There was no sign to say it was a pub but it did have the opening times on the door. By rights the door should have been open, but it wasn't.

I knocked on the door and asked if they were open. "We were," came the reply of a disinterested but bemused bloke. "No chance of a drink?" I asked as I looked inside (he wasn't going to let me over the threshold). I could feel the heat from a welcoming log fire on my face. The bar pumps still uncovered, the warmth was very inviting. "Looks like you are still open." "We aren't," came the short reply from a man of few words. Then he made an observational point. "You're a bit wet." Yes of course I bloody am, I thought, it's raining outside!

"W'ere you goin'?" he asked. "Heading towards Wintershead Farm for tonight," I said, and then hopefully, "There isn't anywhere to stay close to here is there?"

He didn't want to hear. He just said, "Long way that, y're goin' to get wetter."

Knowing Paula was just behind me and that we weren't going to be allowed in, I simply asked one small favour: could we fill up our water bottles. Begrudgingly, he took the bottles. Again we were not going to get even a foot in the door. He filled them up and I thanked him profusely for his generosity as he shut the door. No welcome there then.

All Paula and I could do was laugh, it was so funny. We stood there dripping wet, and I was so pleased to be with her to share such a bizarre moment. The conversation was so comical and dry. It was a great morale booster. The only thing we could think of that might have made them shut up shop early was that there was an England rugby match that day.

We could delay no more. We walked on silently in the rain. It was a slow process and we stopped more and more. Paula was clearly in agony, her hips and shoulders now beginning to suffer along with her feet. However, I could only admire her for putting up with my cheerfulness whilst she hurt. Even I was beginning to get uncomfortable as we walked the last watery mile into Wintershead Farm.

It was 5pm and getting dark as we knocked on the door of the farmstead. A dog barked, a light was on. The farmer was in. Opening the door, it was with a stunned silence that he absorbed the apparition in front of him. Two drenched ladies, water dripping off the end of their noses, cold, wet, hungry and desperate? Housewives? No, I digress.

"Can I 'elp?" he asked, after a while. I explained who I was but he couldn't believe it. I think from his expression he thought we were a bit mad. Wonder where he got that from! However, the reception we received was the warm hearted benevolence of friendship, as he offered us the boiler house to dry off in, cook our tea and use the toilet facilities. He also showed us where we could pitch our tent in the small orchard next to the farmhouse, promising he would keep the outside light on by the boiler house and extend the heating for a while.

The boiler house was full of pipes and had a chimney flue, a water tank and an oil tank. All were warm to the touch. The hot pipes were HOT! The tiny toilet and basin were all that we could have wished for. I could not thank him enough. He left saying, "Any other problems knock the door."

We couldn't have been more appreciative of our surroundings. It's surprising what little is required.

Our first priority was pitching the tent before it got completely dark. It was our last effort and must have been awful for Paula, whose feet were bitterly complaining. We found a relatively flat area with fewer stones. The tent went up easily. The weather had briefly eased to a fine rain. We gathered our sleeping bags and thermarests, made the beds and closed the tent down. Our minds turned to FOOD and getting ourselves dry.

It was quite cramped once we had disrobed ourselves of our wet clothes. Paula was soaked through to the skin and quickly stripped and changed into something warm. Our clothes were draped across every conceivable hot spot and our waterproofs were hung on hangers that we could only suppose were for the farmer's use. Our boots were placed on the water tank and the liners wrapped around the back pipes. I was quite lucky my wet weather gear had kept me dry, so I only had to strip to vest and thermal trousers. It was great to get the air around the body again, even if it was chilly. This allowed the body to breathe again and disperse some of the sweaty odours.

The loo is where we set up kitchen. It was the safest place we could use the gas burners. So there I sat on the throne, tending to the boiling water with our Wayfarer meals heating up and making a hot cup of tea and cocoa for us both. Whilst waiting I checked my feet. They were good. Not a blister in sight. Paula's were a bit different. They needed some doctoring but as she waited for dinner she just let her feet breathe for a bit.

Our tea was nourishing. Paula had curry and noodles with soup and I had chicken casserole. We then shared a chocolate sponge. It was delicious and most welcome. We ate some of our other snacks too. We sat on papers on the concrete floor and I looked at the maps for the next day. The boiler house was now quite warmish (compared to outside). It had started to rain again. This didn't bode well for the next day.

After tea, the loo and basin became a washing room. Morale takes a final leap when the face, hands and armpits are washed with the smallest possible amount of hot water, i.e. using a warm flannel. Other parts get an antiseptic wipe. It's the best one can do in the circumstances.

I sorted out my rucksack for the next day, leaving out the breakfast things. I then went to the farmhouse door to ask about rubbish and what they would accept for payment. There was no reply. I could hear the dog barking and I could hear water running. I left it for the moment and returned to boiler house. The wind had got up and the rain had stopped once more. It was going to be a changeable night.

I felt terribly buoyant. It takes a lot for me to get down about things, but I did make another mistake of not giving Paula enough advice or plasters for her blisters. When I look back on it now, I should have told her what I would have done and that was to pop them to ease the pressure, leave them free of plasters overnight and then plaster them in the morning to protect them for the day. I was a very poor leader at that point. My euphoria was overtaking the needs of others.

Paula was cheerful though, and we joked about the situation we were in. We did both look a mess. I was so pleased to have her company. It was now about 7pm and we were knackered.

I still wanted to speak to the farmer again so we returned to the door. Finally, Jane came to the door. I felt terribly guilty as she was in a wheelchair. She apologised for not coming the first time as she always took a bath at that time. She didn't need to explain that it took her longer than other people. She was so chatty and friendly. We stood in the doorway and met 'Tilly', the owner of the bark, a friendly Jack Russell who enjoyed the attention.

Jane wasn't going to accept anything for their kindness towards us. I said we would be off early in the morning so we probably wouldn't see her again. We said our goodbyes and then headed out into the weather and darkness. It was cold. Hats and gloves and our thermals and other layers were required for sleeping. But it helped turning into our tent whilst we were warm and we soon got cosy.

Then it poured with rain and it rained all night. Well actually, I slept through it until Paula and I were both disturbed at approximately 2.30am by a rumble that got louder and louder. It felt like whatever it was, was going to plough through our tent. There was no light to be seen. It was just the most horrific sound, as if a sheet of corrugated roofing was going to flatten us. It was still raining and blowing a gale. The tent was fine but this noise was above all of those weather sounds. Still it kept coming and then at its most clangorous, it died away. At the last roar a light flashed by. It had been a 4x4 rushing down the tiny track behind the wall where we were pitched. It thundered by. It was one of those vehicles that had a Nissan hut-like back cover and we thought its dynamics had caused the noise. It was all over in seconds but it was like standing on a precipice waiting to be pushed. Miraculously, we both managed to get some more shut eye after that.

Sunday March 16th 2008. Wintershead Farm to Pooltown - 15 miles (but we walked 19).

Wintershead Farm - Pooltown

Woke at 6am, a little sore. Hips would need some deep heat gel. Not raining but plenty of drips coming off the trees. The tent would be wet. Yuk. We lay there for a bit and contemplated the day. I was concerned about Paula's blisters.

How far would we be able to manage? Take the day as it comes. Luxborough or Treborough were our planned stops but it might have to be sooner.

These were my thoughts as we headed over to the boiler house for breakfast. Paula was terrific. Groaning a little, she hobbled over and said she felt rested and better. Hips and back a little sore. It was still semi-light: 7.15am. Inside, our equipment was dry. Well, Gertrude was still looking sorry for herself. She was still damp, so I apologised for neglecting her and promised she would dry out once we got walking again. I was like a Jack-in-a-box ready to roll again.

Breakfast consisted of porridge, some raisins and a large mug of tea. Using a micro towel, we dried off the tent as best as possible. I should have carried it. Another mistake. It would have helped Paula just a little not to have that weight and she should have had the poles instead. Again, you live and learn. Later you will read how much I came to realise the ordeal that Paula had gone through to achieve this walk with me.

We took away our rubbish and left a £5 note in appreciation of the farmer's generosity, heading off on the Two Moors Way to Withypool. I have to confess I made a huge navigational error. Why I didn't check my compass I have no idea. I didn't read the map correctly, so we ended up going south instead of east. This took us on a detour, landing us with an extra four miles to get to Withypool; a colossal mistake given the extent of Paula's blisters. I am so glad that at the time she didn't know how far she had walked that day. I kept saying *bollocks* to myself, over and over again. My concentration had slipped so badly. My confidence took a huge knock and I felt sadly deflated. Pride had taken a knock too. The good thing was it had finally stopped raining. The only consolation at this point was the weather would have been misty across the moor and we may have missed our turnings anyway, but this was no excuse.

Moving on then, we walked into Withypool. The tiny café was open… hooray. We were the only ones in there. The post office opposite was owned by the same person. Paula bought some electrical tape to bind up her feet. Stretching out on the benches in the café, we had a cup of coffee and a piece of cake. Paula did her doctoring. Outside it was cold but brighter. It was good to get the leggings off and pack away the waterproofs. We then walked on to Winsford along part of the Samaritans Way.

My spirits soon rose again. We were on the move, albeit more slowly but we were going. I can't help being cheerful. It was just a matter of getting on with it. Stopping at Winsford for lunch, we found it a very pretty place with tiny footbridges for getting across the fords and a pub in the centre with a green. We had done really well up to this point, all things considered.

Staying on the Samaritans Way, the path and track undulated all afternoon. Even I was beginning to tire. Walking through running water from Battleton Brake to Kennisham Hill wireless station, it had been a three mile, slow, steep climb. We started to look for somewhere to park ourselves for the night. I had hoped we could have camped somewhere in the plantation. However, it was privately owned and we did need some more water, so we continued on the Samaritans Way towards Luxborough.

The views were spectacular from here. It was a delightful path but we were too pooped to enjoy it to be truthful. We came off the Samaritans Way to see if Newcombe Farm would be suitable to camp at, but on arrival it was so creepy and unwelcoming that we carried on to Chargot House. Again, nowhere to camp. Then we walked into Pooltown; it was 5.30pm by now.

This was it. A tiny village, pristine in fact, with a big notice on its only piece of flat green grass saying: 'Keep Off, No Camping'. Bugger. So I went to the nearest house. It had a thatch and the lady there was cooking Spaghetti Bolognese or chilli. Anyway it smelt delicious. I asked if she could suggest anywhere we could camp. She said, "Well, you could camp on that rough ground opposite, people walk their dogs up the track behind it." I then asked would she mind if we had some water. She kindly filled our bladders. She didn't offer us any of her sweet smelling food but the water was fine, and gratefully we headed to 'the patch', no bigger than 20 metres square of rough (!) ground that was to be our pitch for the night. Well, the ground moved. It had tufts of rush, sedge, reed and moss, suggesting water, amid long rye grass all trampled down into a semi-firm consistency.

The good news was we couldn't see any dog mess anywhere. We pitched the tent as best we could, but we didn't think it would be comfortable. By the time we had dinner prepared it was dark again. Our headlights danced about. It had turned a little milder thankfully and we munched our dinner. I had stew and dumplings, while Paula had pasta and tomato sauce. More good news: no rain. We turned in for sleep at 8pm. I put deep heat gel on my legs and hips. Feet good, no blisters.

As we turned over to sleep, the ground wobbled with moisture; waterbeds came to mind before I crashed to sleep.

Monday March 17th 2008.
Pooltown to Crowcombe - 11.5 miles.

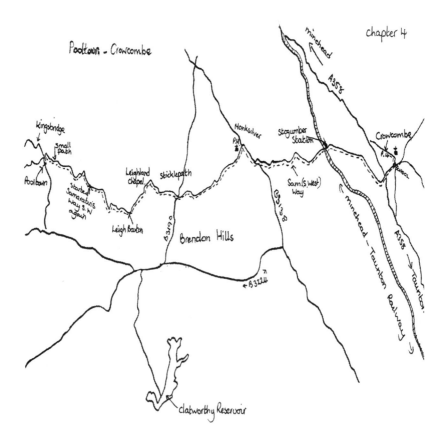

It had been a colder night. The only noises were cars, pheasants and owls. Morning came with lots of condensation inside the tent, but outside it was drier. The lady from the thatched cottage spoke to us before she drove to work, offering us the use of her outside tap again. She also commented on the spectacular light display we had put on the night before. Oh blimey I thought, she knew when we went up the track for a pee!

We set off again at 8.15am. A rude awakening was the steep climb behind the houses in Pooltown, but that brought us onto a lovely path across fields where we picked up the Samaritans Way again towards Treborough. Here there was a lovely farm. We stopped and sat on an old hay trailer. Paula doctored her feet again. The cows were very well kept. Beautiful creatures all busy munching on silage.

It was pleasant walking and being mainly off roads. Between Treborough and Leigh Barton, it was particularly nice with views of the valley of West Combe woods. At the tiny hamlet of Leighland Chapel, a path took us behind the church and slowly dropped down to Pitt Mill Farm. The path kept us above the property, which had clearly been renovated and now commanded a beautiful setting.

We really enjoyed this part of the walk as the path was interesting. At Chudleigh Farm near Stickle Path, we met a lady with a Jack Russell called Molly. The path then got even prettier as we followed the 'Way' to Monksilver. For Paula and her feet, having soft ground to walk on was better. The woodland here was very pretty and in another two to three weeks the colours would change. It was typical coppiced English woodland, a mixture of birches, beech, oaks, hazel and willow with that promise of a spring covering of primroses, bluebells, celandines and violets. I found it calming and a joy to be there. This path was what a walker walks for.

Coming off the height down into Monksilver, the route became one of those typical sunken stony tracks all the way into the village. It was 12.30pm when we walked or staggered into Monksilver. The prospect of having a pint or coffee with a soup in the pub was fuelling our desire to get there. Alas: pub closed. It was Monday. There wasn't a soul about. But our water bottles needed filling again.

I got rid of our rubbish in the big bins at the back of the pub. I met the landlord coming out and asked if it would be possible to have some water. "We are closed." That was it. I tried to explain what Paula and I were doing. "We are closed," came the response again.

"Blinking heck," I said to Paula, "what is it with people around here?" As we muttered, a lady came out and without a word placed a large jug of water on a table. As she turned, while we were still thanking her, she said something like, "Leave the jug on the table," and then she was gone, slamming the door behind her. Paula and I just giggled. It must have been something about pubs that week. We sat and ate our lunch snacks and enjoyed the bit of sunshine there before setting off again.

Paula braced herself to stand up. The next four and a half miles to Crowcombe were slow but painfully sure.

We followed the Samaritans Way into Crowcombe. This village, basically consisting of one street, dates as far back as 854 AD. It boasts a 13th century church, pub, village hall, school and workhouse and is situated in the Quantocks. We had moved across the valley from Exmoor into another area of outstanding beauty.

It was 4.30pm when we arrived here and the post office was open. We bought some treats and asked if there was anywhere to camp in the village. They were so friendly and helpful.

"When the girl comes back to the pub after picking her kids up from school, ask there. She will be in about five-ish. Just tell her the people from the post office sent you. She might let you camp in her back yard."

By 5pm Paula and I were being watched by bemused locals beginning to gather at the front door of the pub called The Carew Arms. Clearly, it was a popular venue as Range Rovers and other farmers' wagons were arriving. Paula and I were a bit concerned if the landlady said no, because it was getting late to find anywhere else. We could see, as the doors opened, that there was a pecking order with the locals. So we waited our turn in the queue.

People were booking tables for dinner. Listening to the conversation, this was definitely the place to come. There was a brief silence as we asked at the bar if we could stay the night in her back garden. A little suspicious to start with, she kindly let us camp. I explained what we were doing. She just eyed us up and down and you could see the cogs whirring, labelling us 'mad'. I asked how much we should pay her. She said, "Well, no doubt you will come in and buy drinks and have something to eat, that will be enough. If you wait a mo 'til I have served this lot, I'll show you where to camp between the garden furniture outside and there's an outside toilet you can borrow all night."

I could have kissed her. We ordered a beer and waited patiently as many locals were served, until we thought we had been forgotten. But then she showed us where to go.

It was getting dark again. We only just got our tent up and dinner cooked before the daylight went. It was a treat to sit at a table and cook our meals at waist height, even though it was chilly outside. Paula had spiced Mexican super noodles and I had chicken casserole. The landlady's children had been watching us from their bedroom windows as we pitched the tent, brewed our drinks and ate our dinner. I had never classed myself as a novelty before.

Washing had been difficult the night before, so it was good that in the outside toilet we had two loos to choose from and two basins with hot water. We both had strip washes, hoping that no one would come in.

It was a very cold evening. What a welcome the pub was. We sat in there by the fire with our boots off, giving our feet a good airing. This allowed our socks to dry against the warm flagstones. We both felt a wash of contentment after such an arduous day. I am sure many people will understand what a wonderful glowing, tired feeling it is that walkers feel, as the mixture of chatter and crisps re-cleanses the spirit. It was very cosy.

I got chatting to some local rugby players who bought Paula and I half a pint each of Otter Bright Bitter. Yum! (The beer, not the men.) The locals were very friendly and it was good listening to the banter.

We left some money for the landlady. Reluctantly, we had to leave the pub and head back to our dark, cold tent. A prospect not wholly welcomed. However, we turned in and soon drifted off to sleep.

The temperature during the night dropped to -6C. I awoke several times from cold. Looking at Paula who couldn't be recognised with her hat on, I tossed about trying to find a warm position. I too had on hat and gloves, thermals and over trousers. Fortunately, the necessity of getting up for a pee did not occur. I drifted most of the night.

Tuesday March 18th 2008.
Crowcombe to Bridgwater - 13 miles.

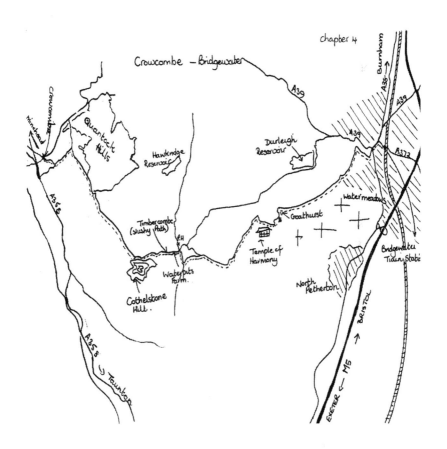

At first light, there was stillness with just the gentle sound of munching coming from the other side of the fence where sheep were grazing. At 6.30am, I got up and staggered to the toilets. It was chilly to say the least. The tent was covered in a sharp frost and all the fields were white. I grabbed our cooking bits and popped the kettle on.

The toilet was again a great place to heat up the water. The little room started to feel warmer with the cooker on, or was I just imagining it.

Paula soon came round. She had been off her feet a little longer this time but they were still very sore and painful; this became apparent once the rucksack was on her back, owing to the weight.

There was also a problem with the rucksack itself. It was clearly not designed for a woman's back or hips. The length and rigidity of the frame did not match Paula's hips or spine, consequently she had aching shoulders and back, and sore areas where the waist band rubbed against her hips.

It was clear now that we were not going to make Bristol on this occasion, so we looked at the possibility of getting to Bridgwater by evening. I was selfishly saddened and pissed off by this, but poor Paula was so stoical it really would have been very unfair of me to push any further, and from a strategic point of view Bridgwater was an obvious place to stop to catch the train back to Salisbury.

To have any chance of achieving this, it was going to have to be a very, very steady walk with plenty of stops and lots of encouragement. In truth, I had pushed too hard at the beginning of the walk and my leadership skills had been crap.

We set off at 8.30am, the weather dry, crisp and sunny. Still following the Samaritans Way path, we climbed out of Crowcombe over 'Great Hill' and followed a fantastic avenue of beech trees for approximately three quarters of a mile. I have never seen such magnificent beeches and against this backdrop the views were stunning of Bridgwater Bay, the Bristol Channel, Wales, Exmoor and Minehead.

Looking across the valley from where we had come was tremendous, as we congratulated ourselves on just how far we had walked. This was by far the best part of our walk. The track was easy to follow and gentle on the feet, and the views stayed with us all the way to the car park near Lydeard Hill. Here the track turned into a small road.

We stopped for a while to have a snack and Paula doctored her feet again. Then we continued following the Samaritans Way. At Park End, the track became a lovely path – although muddy – through some woods to Timberscombe. Then it became really wet. I have never seen mud like it. We waded through a quarter of a mile of it, desperate to keep our balance in the churned-up mess.

On a small track we came to Manor Farm, where we stopped and chatted to the farmer who had turned it more or less into rented accommodation. He had a lovely old Border collie called Jacko. He explained that the new construction had churned up the track and the people who owned the land had blocked natural waterways, causing the flooding. He also warned us that the pub at the top of the road didn't welcome walkers very much. That was disappointing we thought, and we found it to be true. So Paula and I sat on one of the benches outside, ate our lunch snacks and then moved on.

Still following the 'Way', we walked over Broomfield Hill. By this time I was carrying Paula's rucksack to give her a break. And in the short space of time I wore it – approximately five miles – I knew exactly what she meant by uncomfortable. It was so heavy on the neck and shoulders, and the hip band was so big it did nothing to support the weight from underneath as it slid over our hips.

The views again were excellent, the weather now very warm and enjoyable. Paula cursed me occasionally for being so cheerful. She was amazing. Her saving grace had been her walking poles and lots and lots of stops.

We could see Bridgwater, our destination. The tracks were great for any normal walk. Without our heavy rucksacks it would have been a pleasant bimble. We followed a path passing the most enormous free range ducks, hens and geese farm. It was great to see so many varieties all running about. Through this tiny valley towards Goathurst the path stretched approximately a mile and a half, and the views of the small villages in the distance were very pleasing.

We passed the Temple of Harmony. I am not sure Paula's feet would have called it that! At Goathurst, we stopped for a welcomed break. Sitting on the only bench on the only green, we brewed up a cup of coffee and ate our remaining snacks. A warm drink is always so welcome when life feels tough.

Neither of us wanted to move really. But having come this far, Bridgwater beckoned three miles away. It was now 3.30pm. If we could reach Bridgwater railway station and get a train to Bristol, we could catch one back to Salisbury and be home.

Reluctantly we dragged ourselves up again. Paula had doctored her feet. I was feeling terribly sad at this point. It was a slow, frustrating walk into Bridgwater as the paths became obstructed by water levels and poor signposting. We had to negotiate walking or sliding across an enormous log with our backpacks on. This was clearly the route the locals used to get over the fields of drainage systems. I have a great picture of Paula dragging herself across the log, having had to throw the rucksack as best she could onto high ground. It really was the final straw for her. I actually found it quite comical. I know I shouldn't have laughed but I did.

I don't wish to be harsh but Bridgwater did not appeal to me. It seemed run down in places and had no heart. There was an emptiness, a greyness about it that it had lost its way somehow. Most of its buildings seemed tired and a lot of the shops and small businesses were closed and boarded up – a sad testament to changes in its economy and prosperity. At one time, it was a place to lay claim to; now it's small town floundering beneath the big city of Bristol.

Both of us knackered, we staggered into Bridgwater

Station. The time 6pm. How fortunate: a train to take us back to Salisbury would be leaving at 6.30pm. It was a relief to get any train at all. It was cold on the platform and we were tired and sticky. The stationmaster, a burly gentleman, sort of took pity on us. The toilet door being locked, we asked for the key but he said it was a bit grimy. "Get rats in there," he said. "Do you want to use my toilet? It's much warmer and there's a sink in there with hot water, you can have a wash." I looked at him a bit suspiciously. His overwhelming kindness seemed just a bit too friendly. Paula thanked him and went to his boudoir! I just looked at her and made damn sure I kept talking to the bloke all the time she was in his 'little room'. After all, she was changing into new clothes and I was doing my motherly bit. I know she's only 10 years younger than me and probably 20 years older in her experience of the big wide world, but I wasn't taking any chances.

Feeling mildly more refreshed, we sat waiting for the train to arrive which it duly did, but it didn't move for quite some time. 'Incident on the line'. Our concern was we wouldn't catch the connecting train at Bristol. But we did and arrived at Salisbury by 8.50pm.

Our legs were completely seized. It was a very painful journey home. Cramp is awful and so are blisters. The worst was I hadn't finished and it was only Tuesday. Selfishly I kept thinking, what am I to do with the rest of the week? I must do something. Poor Paula was feeling terrible that she had let me down but now in hindsight it was me who let us down. My eagerness, ambition, poor leadership skills and poor decisions were to blame. I certainly would come to know what it feels like to be on the receiving end of such a tough journey, and how terrible you feel about letting yourself down and the person you are with, and how hard it is to say I can't go any further today.

This chapter was a great lesson for me. I learned a lot about myself, some of which I didn't like much. But the walk itself was a great route. I thoroughly enjoyed it. The paths were interesting and some of the route could easily be redirected onto the higher moor for future walkers.

The following day, Paula came over and apologised again for finishing early, but she was really in no fit state to drive or to go to a pending job interview. By the time she arrived, I had vented my anger and frustration on the washing pile, cried several times like a spoilt brat and thundered around the house stamping and shouting. BUT I was already planning not to waste my week's holiday. I couldn't walk Bridgwater to Bristol, so I would get the map required to do the Severn Way and walk from Bristol railway station to the Severn Bridge in a day (see chapter six). It was a little bit that just needed doing. And this time David was to join me. That was a bonus.

CHAPTER FIVE:
THE GOING A BIT EASIER?

BRIDGWATER TO BRISTOL. DISTANCE: 37.5 MILES VIA TRACKS AND ROADS. DATELINE: MAY 17TH & 18TH 2008.

For this part of the trail I used OS Explorer maps 141 and 154. I actually walked it in reverse from Bristol to Bridgwater.

I was so pleased when Paula said she still wanted to finish the bit she had said she would do. I was bolstered by this. The fact she was still prepared to put up with me and that I would have company on this leg meant everything to me. We were to backpack again, but this time Paula had invested in a new rucksack and boots that were suitable for her.

Given that we were doing this over a weekend, it was going to be long days again walking, but we weren't carrying as many food provisions or extra clothes. The days were still chilly in the morning but the weather was stable.

Saturday May 17th 2008. Bristol – Cheddar 20.5 miles

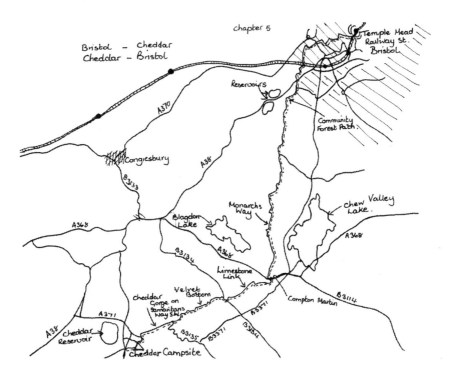

Weather conditions: excellent. Overcast but warm air temperature. We arrived at Bristol railway station at 8.30 am, and set off at 8.45am having organised maps and clothing.

Getting out of Bristol was surprisingly easy: road walking for one hour. We encountered a black man in brush cotton pyjamas like you do, carrying a coffee he had just purchased from an early morning café. "Morning ladies," he said and grinned. We scuttled by and then had a bit of a laugh about it. Luckily there was no exposure of parts on his account. We found it so comical.

We followed the A370 towards Southville then through to Ashtonville, past Bristol Rovers football stadium and out through an industrial estate into meadows, leaving the metropolis of Bristol behind. We didn't meet anyone. The streets were very quiet, clearly all were getting over the night before!

From here we had no roads for several miles, hooray. We picked up the Forest Community Path. It was impossible to tell we were only two and a half miles from Bristol. It was so quiet, except for planes flying in every 20 minutes. The path took us past Hanging Hill Wood quarry (I nearly went wrong there) and then it was a slow ascent up to Barrow Common and on to Dundry Down via Monarch's Way. From here the views of Bristol were extensive, the reservoirs clearly visible. This vast expanse of water supplied the city.

From here, still following Monarch's Way, we had our first encounter of the day with many tiresome, if not beautiful, long grassed meadows as the path meandered across pastureland towards the tiny hamlet of Hounsley Batch. This is where we hit our first road.

Having negotiated some awful stiles and gates that were not designed for backpackers, or oldies for that matter, with clear views of Winford and Chew Valley Lake and the sun getting warmer, it was 2.30pm when we stopped for lunch at Lower Strode. This tiny hamlet consisted of two cottages and a farm. We sat in the corner of a field lush with grass and cowpats, and enjoyed the warmth and a well deserved rest, with 'Walnut Tree Knoll' behind us. What a wonderful name for a small hillock.

The walking hadn't seemed too difficult, as it had been interesting negotiating our route. You forget about your aches and pains in these circumstances. Anyway, it was a useful loo break behind the bushes with long grass up your arse for company.

Fortified by lunch and with the weather getting warmer, we climbed up a very tedious hill of long grass onto a small road, then across to more grass, nettles and hogweeds all the way to Breach Hill Farm. From here, there were extensive views of Chew Valley Lake. I noted that it would be good to walk around here another time.

To our right we got a little glimpse of Blagdon Lake and its village. This is very pretty and quintessential English countryside. A patchwork of fields with all manner of greens; very pleasing on the eye. The route was poorly marked at this stage as the paths were not used that often, and there was a distinct attitude of 'we don't want walkers on our land'.

It was a shorter descent across crops and field systems for approximately a mile before we finally came upon the beautiful track called Villece Lane. This was a sunken drovers' route rutted with 4x4 marks but nevertheless a track with beautiful trees and hedgerows. Stone lined, it was much easier underfoot and a welcomed change from fields!

The track led us to the little village of Compton Martin. If you are to follow this route, I suggest using Monarch's Way, which is probably easier for rucksack carriers. We chose the more difficult route of straight up out of the village. The path was overgrown and very slippery where wild garlic proliferated, making it difficult. It was extremely steep and we were very relieved to join the Limestone Link route up the remainder of the hill as we parted with Monarch's Way.

We were now well and truly on the Mendip Hills. It was very breezy. We were on the plateau with a view behind us of Blagdon Lake and Chew Valley Lake. The walk now became an avenue of orchards either side but it was a hard road. Hazel Corner marked the end of the Link – a chocolate box cottage surrounded by hazel trees with two noisy dogs in the garden. It is here we joined the Samaritans West Way path and at the road we saw the first signs of life since leaving the Bristol suburbs. Cars on the B3134.

From here we crossed the road onto a grassy track. What bliss! We passed Nordrach House, dedicated to Outward Bound activities. There were some youngsters in the grounds. The track was what walking was for: soft and easy. We briefly stopped and had a snack sitting on some pallets, while an old terrier barked at us most of the time.

Time was pressing; it was approximately 4.30pm. However, we were in for a treat. The walk got even better as the track ran down into the most quaint valley. A hidden treasure called Shake Hole. This was originally the site of lead mining, but where disused mineshafts and waste tips had greened over to become an interesting cycling and walking area. It was a bit like being on a green lunar landscape. The path then proceeded to follow the old mining rail lines into a valley called Velvet Bottom. I've seen some bottoms in my time but this takes the prize! A wonderful description for what it was. The grass here was so soft and velvety it was like walking on a carpet. At this point, I thought it would have been great to stop and camp here but there was no water. We were on limestone.

Passing the Mendip Adventure Base, the path weaved its way along for a good two miles, with deep embankments either side slowly changing from grassy to shrubby and finally to rock as we walked into the deep sided quarry at Blackrock. This marked the end of Velvet Bottom but we continued onto the road at Blackrock Gate. Here, we were offered a lift by a man in a white camper van. Although tempting at this stage, we declined.

Cheddar beckoned but the road was too dangerous, so we crossed it and continued on the other side of the gorge, climbing up to its top. We had wonderful views of Cheddar and Cheddar Reservoir. Both of us were extremely tired. I was exhausted and wheezing, my chest really hurting from the ascent. I only had one gear and that was 'slow'. At these moments, my blonde brain kicks in and thinks all manner of crap such as what the hell am I doing this for? Which way up is the map? And I get angry with stones that are in the way, with my laces loosening, and with stops, starts and water breaks. All I want to do is get to the finish line. I think it's called desperation!! I must be awful to be with. However, walking with Paula, who was feeling exactly the same but was quieter about it, was the positive aspect of those final steps (almost an hour), as we followed the gorge all the way into Cheddar.

It was a relief after a stony descent into Lippiatt Lane, one of Cheddar's backstreets, where we emerged onto the main road and walked to the campsite. It was now 8pm and I was unsure if the campsite would even be letting people in this late, but my fears were unfounded.

Gratefully, we pitched tent quickly and after a blissful hot shower and a cup of tea (the latter given to us by a sympathetic caravan owner, we must have looked knackered) we began to prepare our food. By now it was just getting dark and a few spots of rain decided to bother us. However, on the perimeter of the camping area was a small octagonal pergola sitting area, where we were able to sit and cook our meals in reasonable comfort and out of the chilly wind and rain.

We turned in at 9.30pm. A long day. It was not necessarily the difficulty of the walk, more the time taken in route finding. The evening was very chilly but dry again. My feet were good, still just slightly warm across the instep. Hips sore, I rubbed Ibuprofen gel on them, then read for a bit and was asleep by 10pm.

Sunday May 18th 2008. Cheddar – Bridgewater 17miles

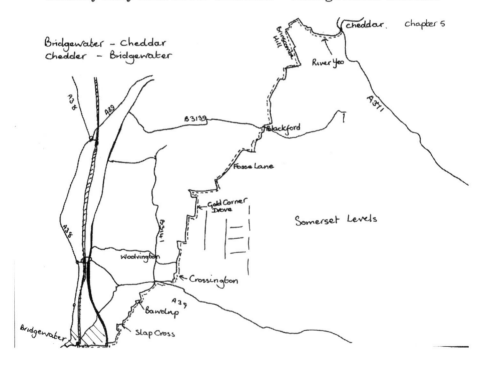

I slept well until 6am. We had porridge for breakfast, then left the campsite by 7.45am. The day was slightly chilly, with the sun beginning to burn off early mist. It was going to be a hot day.

After negotiating a new industrial site, we followed the Cheddar Yeo river. This was unforgiving arable farming land and seemed to go on interminably. It was very flat and crisscrossed with a series of drainage ditches that were deep and wide, forcing the walker to use the one path available. This was the first inkling of what the Somerset Levels where going to be like to walk amongst at a later stage of the day.

We negotiated a series of gates and again they were locked and difficult to climb with our sacks. Eventually after three and a half miles of this uninteresting and frustrating landscape, we arrived at Brinscombe Farm. From here, in theory the route would become more interesting and easier. This optimistic nature of mine gets flattened every time. The route on the map looked simple – a climb onto Brinscombe Hill shortly after the farm. Wrong! The 'simple climb' turned into a path that clearly the farmers didn't want used, as it stopped abruptly at a thicket. We could see the old signpost through the tangle of bramble, willow and hazel and so our route was correct, but the farmer clearly had other ideas and had let it overgrow. On top of which a secondary fence of barbed wire marked the boundary.

We tried walking along the edge of the boundary, but the thicket was so overgrown it was impossible to go further with our rucksacks. We returned to the original supposed exit point and, mustering all our strength, we tossed our sacks across both fence lines. Then, like First World War soldiers, we crawled under one fence and climbed the other whilst negotiating brambles in our faces and sharp sticks.

It was all a trifle annoying and had wasted precious time. On terra firma once again, we thought it would get easier but the path across the ridge was dominated by gates that were locked, poorly maintained (rusty to climb or leaning inwards and outwards), or tied up with knotted polypropylene rope – on top of which the field systems had been changed. Paths became difficult to decipher, so we basically followed a south-easterly direction until we practically stumbled into Washbrook, and from there we picked up the first easy path. Actually, we were pleased with ourselves not to have taken more time than we did. The good news was that the view from Brinscombe Hill to Cheddar was stunning and just on the horizon was Bridgwater. (There is always a plus.)

Washbrook to Middle Stoughton was easy and from here we picked up a fantastic track all the way to Blackford. Not a gate in sight! It always amazes me how quickly I forget the difficult bits. It's like having a baby – bloody painful at the time but soon forgotten ready for the next one. And you wouldn't miss it for the world. So the struggle during that part of the day was soon behind us, as the warmth and tranquillity of this sunken lane began to relax us once again.

The pub at Blackford beckoned. It was 11.50am when we reached it but was it open? Oh dear, no! The Sexey's Arms is a genuine old fashioned pub dating back to the 16th century. It clearly is popular, providing local ales. A garden for the children to play in was on the opposite side of the road. I popped my head in the door and asked if they were open. "No," came the reply, "but we will serve you. What would you like?" What a nice person I thought. "Two halves of lager and lime please," I requested. Paula and I savoured the sit-down outside, with a bag of crisps, our own snacks and a drink in our hands, soaking up the sun. Ah yes, this was more like it. The day had become very warm. We were down to singlets and shorts.

The desire to stop there forever was very strong. Begrudgingly, aware of the time and the amount still to do, we forced ourselves onward and in doing so made a big boob. We chose a route taking half an hour more than we needed to. Still, we got over that blip, only to be confronted with the monotonous roads of the Somerset Levels. Long, straight and hot. Not pleasant.

This part of walk seemed endless and Bridgwater felt further away rather than nearer. Fields and fields of meadows interspersed with wide canals of water with very few bridges now offered a choice to the walker: you either walked in a westerly/easterly direction or northerly/southerly. There seemed to be no other route to ease the monotony.

For three hours we chugged along, meeting no one on these hot roads, just occasionally a car. Paula's feet started to play up. She had changed into her approach shoes at The Sexey's Arms. I had her boots in my rucksack.

The highlights of the afternoon were a roadblock with a solitary police car and a bull in a field. Fortunately, we didn't need to go onto the closed road but we did need to use the path where the bull was. This created a diversion again and the climbing of two farm gates. Very tiring and hot. It was 4.30pm when we arrived at Cossington and we had to be in Bridgwater by 6.30pm.

At Cossington, we negotiated an even bigger gate completely blocking the disused railway path – a cycle route! It was at least 12 feet tall and tiredly we climbed it. After this, my feet started to suffer. I had jumped down onto the balls of my feet, which had aggravated a warm spot. Bollocks.

At Bawdrip we rang Steve to get him to check the railway times for the next train. It was due in at 6.30pm. We had three miles to go and it was now 5.05pm. My feet were killing me but we notched up another gear. Following little paths between the villages, we edged closer to Bridgwater. It still felt miles away, however the electricity pylons and the noise of the M5 were a giveaway that we were close. Even the last field we crossed had been ploughed to its very edges. The ruts were destroying our feet even more.

At 5.30pm, my feet finally burst into blisters. Absolute agony until I pricked them to relieve the pressure. Dressing them quickly with Paula commenting "join the club," we practically ran into Bridgwater Station with 20 minutes spare before the 6.30pm train arrived.

We were both utterly exhausted, me particularly. Paula had been there before and she was coping better than me. It was good to sit down and munch my last fudge. Burning legs seizing up and feet swelling from the heat all conspired to make me feel very uncomfortable.

The need to drink as much as possible was essential. Paula had suggested we had a quick drink in the pub before hitting the station, but I just couldn't think straight. I was so sure we wouldn't have time. So the journey home was tough. My legs could not stay still. There was no comfortable position to put them in because the coaches were full. We were crammed in unable to stretch.

Still, this leg of the journey was done. On the way home, I was elated and reflective. I was thinking north next, Wrexham here I come. Despite two days of intensive walking, we had discovered parts of England I would never have entertained visiting. It had been great for Paula to finish this leg with me, but the next part was to be on my own. Only Gertrude would accompany me on that walk.

CHAPTER SIX:
AN ENJOYABLE TIDY UP

BRISTOL TO SEVERN BEACH RAILWAY STATION.

DISTANCE: 11 MILES. DATELINE: MARCH 21ST 2008.

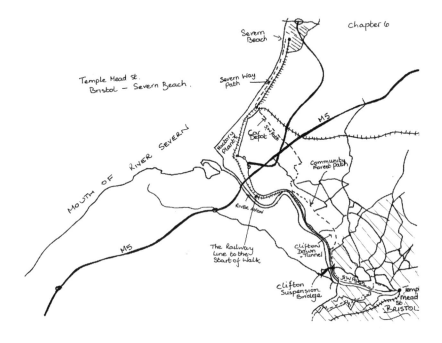

Having finished a walk earlier than expected (see chapter four), I could not waste the remaining holiday that I had booked. I needed to complete a part of the journey that just

118

had to be done. It was decided that David and I could manage this together. Well put it this way, I decided David could manage. Do I sound pushy? Yes, that is the case, but it was only 11 miles. Taken slowly, he could do this leg and it would be an interesting day out. I was positive it would 'do him good'.

On the Friday we left home early and drove to Bristol Temple Meads Station. Doing the walk in reverse, we needed to catch the 9.16am to the Severn Beach Railway (Line End). Then walk the 11 miles back along the Severn Way to Bristol. It was hoped at the end of the walk we would still have time to enjoy a little of Bristol.

The day was warm but overcast, ideal really. I was just excited to be doing a bit that needed finishing off and would have to be done at some stage. David was quite enthusiastic once we had parked the car. It had been easy to find Temple Meads Station from the M4.

The rail journey was also interesting. The single carriage stopped several times. Its route took it underneath Clifton Park at a steady incline. It stopped almost at the top for a brief while, allowing the other carriages on the other track to go by. Then it was a steady descent onto the levels of the Severn Estuary. We could see our walk.

All went to plan. We arrived at the beach at approximately 10am. At this time of the year, although the weather was reasonable, there appeared to be a brisk wind coming off the estuary. In Severn Beach village itself there was very little to admire, but we did stop and have a coffee in the local baker's shop/café before starting our walk. This was quite busy. Local traders from Avonmouth's industrial works and power plants kept the little baker's busy with requests for filled rolls and sandwiches.

We soon left the village (if that's what you can call it) and headed towards Bristol along the Severn Way, which ran parallel to the shoreline and the railway. It was a bit scruffy here.

There were bushes and reeds and the path was quite wet with overgrown brambles and hogweed. It soon gave way to a small path that was quite intimidating and I couldn't put my finger on why that was. I suppose it all looked very tired and rather bleak. I was glad David was with me as we passed the first of many derelict power station buildings. I can't say it was particularly pleasant. There was plenty of litter about. We then headed into an industrial estate on what seemed a long minor road, which had a sign saying 'café open' along its route but we never did find that café. Amazingly, the estate seemed to be dedicated to masses of parked new cars; rows and rows of them.

At this point it had turned quite warm, so we stripped off our outer gear. The road was very busy. It was a minor road but had all the qualities of an A road designed to take heavy goods vehicles and that was what it did. Once past this, it became much more acceptable as the path followed an old road behind the sewage works that was non-accessible to traffic, leading us under the M49 and over the M5 into the suburbs of Bristol.

In front of us beckoned our first and last climb of the day – Kings Weston Hill. Once through Lawrence Weston the walk became interesting as we had our only piece of forest walk (all of one mile).

The remainder of the walk was spent following the road through the suburbs of Sea Mills (we bought a pie for lunch here), Sneyd Park and onto Clifton Down. This park was full of people as we crossed it. The path led us towards Clifton Suspension Bridge and its observatory.

For those of you who have not seen the bridge, it is well worth a visit. I hadn't come since a schoolchild of 11 and at that age one doesn't appreciate the colossal engineering quality and beauty of such a fine structure. (I seem to remember being more interested in the zoo.) Designed by Isambard Kingdom Brunel and completed in 1864, it is a fitting memorial to a man who never saw its final construction. Its use, although initially for horse drawn vehicles, still meets the demands of modern commuters in their thousands every day. For a walker, it's a surprise to realise the height at which Bristol sits. This part of the city perches proudly on the rock above Avon Gorge. The views are spectacular.

We didn't cross the bridge to its visitor centre in Leigh Woods. Instead we climbed down the numerous steps onto the bottom road and walked along the riverbank for a brief while, before following the road in towards the docks and the floating harbour. We ambled at this point, enjoying the scenic route into the city alongside the river. It was busy but the pedestrian walkways were very accessible.

Across the river, the SS Great Britain dominates the dry

dock. This ship was an engineering masterpiece in its day. Launched in 1843, it was designed by Brunel in collaboration with Thomas Guppy. It boasted a host of technical advancements. It has an iron hull with a screw propeller and a one thousand horsepower steam engine which, on its maiden voyage across the Atlantic, broke the speed record. It was capable of 12 knots and continued sailing until 1886.

Used as a floating warehouse for over 40 years, she was left abandoned in the Falkland Islands in 1937. In 1970 she was salvaged and brought back to Bristol where she had been originally built. The ship is now a working museum and open daily to the public.

The remainder of the day was a slow bimble back to the railway station. We enjoyed our brief visit and managed to find our way out of Bristol easily, stopping at a well-known beefburger bar at Ower for our dinner.

We got back home again by 7.30pm. It had been a lovely day, albeit tiring for David. The weather had been kind, extending the daylight somewhat, allowing us to enjoy our time together.

CHAPTER SEVEN:
THE TWO BRIDGES

SEVERN BRIDGE TO SEVERN BEACH RAILWAY STATION AND BACK,

THEN SEVERN BRIDGE TO CHEPSTOW.

DISTANCE: 13.5 MILES. DATELINE: EASTER WEEKEND 2007.

Disappointment had spurred me to do this part of my adventure. I had booked a fortnight's holiday with C-N-Do Scotland to do 'A Cape Wrath Trail' in June 2007. Alas it had to be cancelled (not enough interest). I lost my money on a cheap return flight to Glasgow plus one night stays at Glasgow and Stirling Youth Hostels respectively. That will serve me right for booking early. Still, I was promised that the following year I would automatically be put on the holiday list if required for 2008 but I had other plans for then (probably having a bolshy moment), so I deferred it to 2009.

The trail had been my only plan for 2007. I felt lost after the news but this did not deter me. Instead I created two little journeys: equally special.

Friday April 6th 2007. Severn Bridge (Aust Service Station) to Severn Beach Railway Station and back - 8 miles.

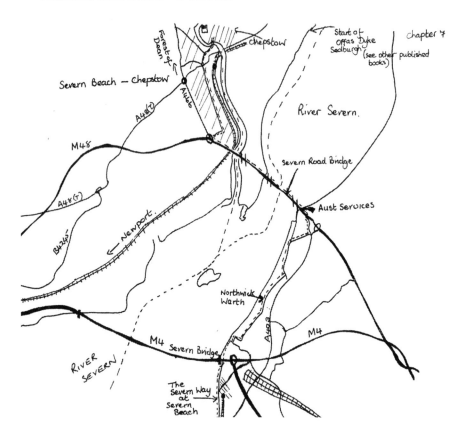

That Good Friday, David and I travelled up to the 'bridge' in my little Mazda MX5. It was a sunny morning, but chilly. Nevertheless we had the roof down, which makes for a far more exciting journey. We arrived at our destination about 11am and parked the car at the hotel service area. We asked permission to leave the car there, explaining our reasons. They happily obliged after we had provided them with our registration number.

We soon found our route over the motorway. This was rather exhilarating. We stood above the traffic waiting to go onto the Severn Bridge as vehicles queued to pay the toll. Looking along the length of the bridge from above is quite something. From this angle, the arched curve of the bridge is accentuated far more than from a driver's perspective. It is possible to see what a beautiful piece of engineering the bridge truly is. Its ghostly white steel towers dominate the skyline, rising to 136 metres above mean high water of the River Severn.

As a walker, you are dwarfed by the size of this bridge. When first opened in 1966, it became the sixth longest suspension road bridge in the world. Interestingly the bridge, although seen as one edifice, actually consists of four component structures: Aust Viaduct, Severn Bridge, Beachley Viaduct and Wye Bridge. In all, it has a total length of two miles, spanning from Aust to the outskirts of Chepstow across the Severn Estuary and the River Wye.

We walked over the bridge and joined the Severn Way, which took us onto a path running parallel with the shore of the Severn, an embankment above the mud flats commonly known as Northwick Warth. In years gone by this grassy level and embankment was used for horse racing, competing for the 'Waterloo Cup'. There was a stiff breeze coming off the estuary. Although it was a relatively warm day, this kept us chilled. The tide was out.

Here we met a chap and in a very local, dulcet toned voice, slow and deliberate, he said, "No bodies today." Not a 'hello' or 'morning'. It was comical and I couldn't help myself from smiling, but I was soon put in my place as he swiftly but morosely continued with his morbid stories of floating bodies or the body parts of those who had jumped, with a glance at the bridges. Now having attracted our attention, he proceeded to say, "Good day," and left us. We stood there absorbing the new information and gazed at the bridges with a humble respect. I recall feeling very alarmed at the prospect of finding a body, and I remember looking at a lady further along the beach with her dog, wondering if she had found any bodies in her time. It sort of put a new slant and meaning on the walk, if you get my drift (excuse the pun).

As we came closer to the Second Severn Bridge Crossing, we became aware of the rumble of traffic that could not be seen. For me the bridge dominated the landscape as we walked closer; being so tiny against something so grandiose was intimidating. We stopped often to admire this monster of a structure. For your interest: work began on building the bridge in 1992 and it was finally opened in June 1996. Its total length is 3.2 miles. A cable stayed bridge in design, the central part is called Shoots Bridge, as this spans the deepest section along the width of the Severn at that point known as 'The Shoots' channel, allowing the passage of shipping underneath this section. The bridge approaches from the English side at Severn Beach, Gloucestershire and crosses in a gentle S shape, finishing near Sudbrook, Monmouthshire on the Welsh side. Standing underneath one of the bridge pier foundations on Severn Beach is to be recommended. The enormity of the 37-tonne concrete slabs, combined with the noise coming from above, is overpowering to the senses. As a mere mortal, the walker is lessened by the beauty. Personally, I am not generally enamoured with concrete, but standing on the shores looking along the undercarriage of this structure I can honestly say the walk was worth it, just to see the bridge from such a different perspective. As a driver having crossed it many times since, I now eye it with respect.

We walked along the remainder of the embankment into Severn Beach and found the station. We didn't stop but on our return we met some interesting characters in the form of two dogs – a Jack Russell, blind, ear torn and hobbling excitedly after a Doberman type breed that was equally boisterous. Clearly the larger of the two was guiding the blind dog. They were very friendly and excitable. They were so pleased to see us. Me being me, I was concerned for their safety. Looking about, the owner, if there was one, could not be seen. They didn't look starving and the large dog had a tag on him with a telephone number. I wasn't going to leave them there, although the dogs seemed happy to stay with us. I rang the number and a gentleman answered. Grateful, he said he would come and collect them. Apparently the Jack Russell wanders off and gets himself lost and the Doberman goes and looks for him to bring him home.

Finally, after explaining our location, in the distance across the fields towards Northwick we could see a man waving. The dogs were clearly so pleased to see him. They danced about all excited. We chatted for a while and then walked back towards Aust once more.

We had lunch/tea in Aust Services and drove home. It had been a great day. David was knackered and would need to rest before the next bit.

I had planned to return on Easter Monday, this time by motorbike if the weather held. There is nothing like using as many modes of transport as possible. This made the walk far more interesting and adventurous. The plan was for me to be dropped off at the services area again and then walk over the old Severn Bridge into Chepstow, where I could join up with the Offa's Dyke Trail that I completed the following year (see next chapter). David would collect me from there.

Monday April 9th 2007. Severn Bridge (Aust) to Chepstow (Bridge Street) - 5.5 miles.

We left home on the motorbike at 10am, arriving at Aust Services once more. This was becoming a habit. I quickly changed out of my leathers and into walking gear. This time there was no need to gain permission to park; David wouldn't be staying there that long. However, he was keen to walk some of the way over the bridge, just to experience the height.

Following the cycle path, we walked onto the bridge a little cautiously. I was surprised how many people were using it.

Primarily runners and cyclists, and on that day we were the only walkers. The first thing that struck me was the wind and the movement of the bridge. Although a gentle breeze, on the bridge it felt quite strong.

Our senses create extraordinary tricks on the mind and on our balance. It was strange peering over the edge looking at the brown, swirling mass of the estuary. The tide was ebbing. I had not registered how fast the movement of water is there. For me personally, I felt quite giddy as I pondered about those who 'jump'. The sheer height was enough to keep me looking at the route ahead. I could not peer for long however, as the movement of bridge and water made me feel queasy. Looking up at the tall towers was even worse. It was like being in St. Paul's Cathedral again, but that's another story.

David returned to the bike as I happily marched across the bridge, occasionally glancing at Sedbury Cliffs, the water below and towards my destination of Chepstow. It truly is worth walking the bridge; the views are fantastic.

The road was not so busy now. I had this feeling of being in no man's land, humbled by walking over something so delicate but strong. It was the first time I had acknowledged how reliant I was on a man-made structure. Yet driving over it I had never felt that. Some would say: 'You should get out more'.

The remainder of my walk quickly took me into Chepstow. I completed it by 2pm, finishing in Bridge Street on the north side of the old bridge over the River Wye (now replaced by the new bridge of the A48). I stopped where the Offa's Dyke Path leads in a south-easterly direction to Sedbury.

I phoned for my lift which duly arrived. After I had changed clothes (once more hopping around in a car park), we spent a little time wandering around. We met up with old friends of ours, a pair of keen motorcyclists who were enjoying a day out riding. It was great to see them and warm hugs were exchanged. Apparently the Forest of Dean is a great place for bends in the road. Motorcyclists like those.

Chepstow is worth stopping in for a while. It is a bustling market town. Many of its tiny streets are a reminder of its history, with its growth dating from Norman times. In medieval days, Chepstow was the largest port in Wales, with a vast tonnage of shipping using the Wye for the import and export of goods. It has a choice of pubs, restaurants, shops and other facilities for the community including a hospital. Its castle is worth visiting, noted for being the oldest surviving stone castle in Britain. It was commissioned in 1067 by William the Conqueror himself, as a means of guarding England from the attacking Welsh. The castle was built at an ideal location, at an important river crossing between England and Wales. Set high above the Wye, it utilises the gorge as part of its structure. It was used as a defensive stronghold, military barracks and prison until it was finally abandoned in the late 17th century.

Chepstow is also renowned for its racecourse, built in the grounds of the now ruined Piercefield House. The grounds are still open to the public and part of the Wye Valley Walk runs through Piercefield Park.

We travelled home on the bike and arrived about 6pm. Another special day and another part of this journey finished. It had been satisfying to do something positive with the Easter break. David had equally enjoyed the motorbike trip. He does go rather fast on the bike and travelling along the motorway at high speed is a little bit daunting. I must be getting old; still it was a new experience for Gertrude.

CHAPTER EIGHT:
UNDERSTANDING LOSS

OFFA'S DYKE PATH - PRESTATYN TO SEDBURY CLIFFS, CHEPSTOW.
DISTANCE: [182MILES. DATELINE: JUNE 24TH-JULY 8TH 2006.

A little history lesson first. The Offa's Dyke Path follows the border between England and Wales. It roughly parallels the ancient earthwork boundary that gives the path its name. Much of the earthwork is still visible, constructed of ditch and rampart with the ditch on the Welsh facing side. It is estimated that the earthwork was 27 metres wide and eight metres from bottom of ditch to top of bank. It is thought the construction dates from 785 AD and it is not entirely known whether Offa (King of Mercia) had it built as an agreed boundary or as a defensive system against the Princes of Powys at a time when there was trouble in the border regions.

The path rarely follows the earthwork for any length of time, instead it crisscrosses the border nine times. The route is diverse. The walker is treated to a variety of changing landscapes. Traversing the Clwydian Hills, vales, towpaths, drovers' routes, river walks, the high ridges of Hatterall and Hay Bluff, passing through historical towns and castles en route... all provide a true sense of walking through history. The path is challenging in the height covered and the many stiles (approximately 677 according to books) that have to be negotiated. For this 12-day walk, on average it was going to be 56 stiles per day! Tiresome to a walker with a heavy backpack on a hot day. However a little consolation; during this walk just 627 stiles were accounted for, as there had been gates to go through as well. Weren't we lucky.

Pre-ramble.

In the year of 2005, having finished the first stretch between Land's End and Stratton, I had been determined to do more of my walk but it wasn't to be. Instead there was the loss of two great parents and the year of my husband's 50th birthday. I arranged a celebration for David's milestone in the August. We had a great gathering of both families and my husband's old and new friends. A sunny afternoon was spent in the garden with a barbecue and birthday cake. It was to be the last family get-together for my father and my mother-in-law. To this day, I am so pleased that they were both there to enjoy this special occasion together. It was a miracle that David had reached the ripe old age of 50 but you never know what is round the corner.

David's mother had been suffering terribly with rheumatoid arthritis. She had been wheelchair bound but a new drug had given her a new lease of life, allowing her to manage without the wheelchair for a little while, so she was able to walk into the party. Although still in pain, she looked happy and truly pleased to catch up with people. She never complained, just thought it was 'a bit of a bugger'. My father was pleased to see her. He didn't know it yet but he was harbouring a virulent stomach cancer.

My brother remarried in early September and that was a grand occasion too and a happy one.

Christmas came, and neither my dad nor mother-in-law ('Momma' as she was affectionately known) were alive. Momma had passed away in the November with respiratory failure and Dad had wasted away before our eyes and passed away with cancer a month later, in the middle of December.

It was a double tragedy for us. As a family we were gutted. I poured myself into my work but that really wasn't the answer. In hindsight, I should have taken plenty of time off. As 2005 closed, I vowed I must keep going with the walking challenge, because they would have wanted me to.

The need to do something – to do something to cheer myself up – was relentless. So in the middle part of January 2006, I booked my place with a reputable walking holiday company to do this walk.

When the itinerary came through, I did question whether or not I would be fit enough to do it. The walk was described as 'quite strenuous' and some days involved considerable ascent. In total, we were to climb more than 28,000 feet over the 12 days of walking.

There had been little time for preparation as my work had

been demanding. The remaining parents suffering loss and my own family's many needs had taken my energy. As a quick fitness burst I took once more to swimming, cycling and walking the Purbecks. I was really looking forward to the break. I did not foresee any trouble with meeting new people. The Coast to Coast in 2004 had been a challenge but I do generally get along well with everyone.

I didn't receive the full itinerary of when and where we were going to be staying until two weeks before the start date of the holiday. At this point, I bought my train ticket in advance – a single from Southampton to Llandudno Junction booked online. Even this was a concern. I can remember becoming quite anxious about giving out my bank details. Again I was nervous at catching the train alone. Crazy really, but this was all part of the growth, I was just a green shoot. Also my concerns turned to the wonderful bed and breakfast accommodation that I would be staying in. In my naivety, I didn't guess the type of person who would book on a walking holiday with such extravagant tastes. I just thought, blimey this is a bit posh and left it at that.

The week before saw me packing my day-sack, boots, Gertrude and a holdall with plenty of changes of clothes. This was a treat. Just as a last-minute thought I packed a skirt. That was to prove a saving grace. The weather boded well. I was really excited now.

Saturday June 24th 2006. Travel day.

David dropped me at Southampton Station at 7.15am. The

journey, despite my fears, went without incident. I enjoyed the ride. I changed trains twice. The last journey transported me back to the 1950s as families clambered aboard the coach-like train, all going on holiday to Prestatyn and other towns dotted along the Liverpool estuary coastline.

The chatter was really noisy. The parents were all shouting at each other excitedly. The grandmas were keeping the children in check. It was rather endearing to watch.

As I came closer to my destination, the noise subsided as the crowds got off the train with their possessions of suitcases, buckets and spades. I arrived in Llandudno Junction at 2.30pm. Here I met another lady, Karen, who was also going to Bryn Corach Country Hotel. She had used the walking holiday company before. She wasn't walking Offa's Dyke, but I felt a touch relieved that she was going my way. I hadn't been looking forward to the taxi ride on my own.

It was not difficult to find the taxi rank. It cost £3.57 to travel the mile up to the hotel, and Karen and I shared the taxi.

Bryn Corach Country Hotel is rather splendid. Its location commands a wonderful view looking down towards Conwy Castle and beyond into Conwy Bay, with Snowdonia National Park as its backdrop. Bryn Corach means 'dwarf hill'. The house, as it was then, was the first to be commissioned in 1913 for Holiday Fellowship Holidays. It is a beautiful Victorian building copying the castle architecture, providing a sense of majesty and wealth. The turrets and buttresses on the house, walled gardens with topiary, and a miniature bowling lawn and archery lawn on separate levels were all in keeping with the façade of the era. Pergolas led down to a small wood, which allowed any would-be explorer onto a lane down to the town.

I found it instantly charming. The gentleman who had it built was known as 'Dai Sixpence' because that was what the labourers earned a week. They were also allowed to bring their families to live in the gardens in chalets. Not too dissimilar to families who live and work on the motorways today.

We had a very warm welcome and were shown to our rooms. I had a twin room to myself. This was a surprise. It was very tastefully decorated in a soft, Georgian colour. The beds were comfy, that was what mattered. There was ample room with an en suite shower and bathroom; pure luxury as far as I was concerned. The views from my window, although in the back, were equally stunning – the mountains rising behind Conwy and the woodland valley sweeping down to the town. I couldn't believe I was staying there.

I had a quick freshen up and went downstairs. As promised an array of coffee and tea with a delicious choice of homemade cakes awaited me. That went down very well as I sank into a luxurious settee in a colonial conservatory overlooking Conwy Castle and Conwy Bridge. The lounge area was massive, with beautiful wood flooring covered in thick colourful Persian carpets. There were plenty of bamboo settees and chairs, a long coffee table and papers to read.

I did feel a bit lost, so I wandered out into the garden. I could see in the distance that the tide was out, exposing Conwy Sands.

By this time it was still only 4pm, so Karen and I went into town. She left me there as I had not explored it before and she went off to do some shopping. I walked onto the town's walls.

I cannot give you all the facts about Conwy as it has so many attractions and I would certainly like to go back to explore further, but here are three highlights: Conwy Castle and Town Walls, Conwy Suspension Bridge and Conwy Railway Bridge.

Conwy Castle and Town Walls were constructed in King Edward I's reign between 1283 and 1289. The combination of castle and walls represents one of Europe's finest surviving medieval towns. The walls are complete and intact. They are three quarters of a mile in length and have 21 towers. It is possible for a visitor to walk along the top of the North wall and also around the walls at their base. The castle had an outer and inner ward, with each ward protected by four towers.

One of the first road suspension bridges in the world, Conwy Suspension Bridge was built by Thomas Telford and completed in 1826. It spans the River Conwy and replaced the ferry. It is now only passable on foot. A new bridge is now used for local traffic and the main A55 goes under the river via a tunnel.

For its part, Conwy Railway Bridge was designed and built by Robert Stephenson. Completed in 1848, it opened the next year after tests proved it could carry heavy locomotives. The bridge is the only remaining example of a wrought iron tubular bridge of this time. It is still in use, with very little added reinforcement.

It was sunny that afternoon but a bit breezy. I made my way down to the quayside and from there walked along the river estuary towards the bay. It was good to stretch the legs after so much sitting. Returning, I came across 'The Smallest House in Great Britain' with dimensions of 3.05 metres x 1.8 metres. Painted red, it couldn't really be missed and is worth looking at. Apparently a six foot tall fisherman was the last person to live there! It is still owned by descendants of that resident.

I slowly made my way back to the hotel and I didn't see Karen again. By now other residents had arrived. A tall American and four other people who knew him plus a singing group were all having tea in the lounge. I made a mental note that this would be a good place for Mum and I to go for a singing weekend; my parents were not very far away in my thoughts.

Our walk leader arrived at 6pm. By now the whole walking group had gathered. There were nine of us including the leader. At this stage we weren't formally introduced but we had practically overcome that already. Our leader thought it would be good to go and walk the town walls and then be back for supper at 7.30pm. I was happy to troop back down to the town and connect with the companions with whom I would be travelling for the next two weeks. Everyone seemed amiable enough. The tall American I recall had a booming voice.

On returning to the hotel, I went to my room and saw my reflection in the mirror. I looked haggard. The nervous energy had taken its toll, and the previous months had been exceptionally difficult. After a lovely shower and change of clothes, I braced myself for supper and the holiday ahead. I felt very tired.

Supper was a gourmet delight. The food was delicious. What a feast of meat and fish. Copious amounts of different curries and cold meats, salads or roasts. I couldn't believe it.

The dining room was huge and filled with plenty of tables, all circular with eight settings on each. People intermingled and sat where they liked. I found it a bit disconcerting that everyone was dressed up for the occasion and I was still in my walking trousers. This was the first sign of why the holiday had cost a little more than I would usually pay for a holiday. I felt uncomfortable at this.

I was on a table of singers, walkers, painters and local interest parties. It was a great way to meet everyone in the hotel. I did notice that the group of five people who seemed to know one another stayed on the same table. Even at this stage it was a bit of a worry. The leader was on my table and was very interesting to talk to. He seemed okay but a bit aloof. However, to his credit, he put everyone at their ease on our table so I really enjoyed the supper.

After the meal, the walking party was finally properly introduced. Our leader took us to one of the many conference rooms and talked about the itinerary, answered any questions and laid out his plans for the following morning. He wanted us all to be ready by 9am to travel to Prestatyn by mini-bus. Then the group adjourned to the bar.

I decided that I didn't really want a heavy head in the morning and anyway, to me walking means appreciating the Countryside and freedom, not carrying a hangover or wasting money. So after one drink I joined in with a singing lesson until 10pm. It was great. I explained I was an alto and part of me wished I was staying there for the weekend. Everyone was so welcoming and warm.

I turned in at 10.50pm, looking briefly out the window, small lights peppering the hillside. It was very peaceful. I slept until morning, something I hadn't done in months.

Sunday June 25th 2006. Prestatyn to Bodfari – 12.5 miles (2,790 feet of ascent).

Morning broke on a dampish day. I was refreshed and ready for the challenge, packed and prepared for the day ahead before breakfast.

Breakfast was another gourmet feast of unimaginable choices. Personally, I couldn't walk on a heavy stomach so I chose a light breakfast of orange juice and cereals. The main topic of conversation was whether we were going to be back to watch England v Ecuador in the World Cup on the television that night. I was quite bemused by this, for as much as I love football the walk appeared to be unimportant.

Everyone seemed very sluggish putting their belongings in the mini-bus. It was frustratingly slow. I met one of the party coming down the stairs complaining about her room-mate and the fact that she had specifically asked for a room on her own. Oh dear, I thought. This proved to be the first rumblings of complaints. Sadly uncalled for, this continued throughout the holiday.

I would describe this particular walking companion as

friendly but direct, forthright, strong-headed, strong-willed and abrasive at times, and often lacking diplomacy. Her anger at not having a single room was vented at every possible moment on her night companion, who was an eccentric, friendly, true blue stocking, highly intelligent, lonely, institutionalised character who bordered on having Asperger's, making her highly vulnerable to verbal abuse and being ignored.

From the first day I could already see the differences between them and I remained friendly with both sides. I could see how one's intolerance and the other's monotonous indifference to situations and her egoistic manner were never going to work. I just didn't want to be a part of it, but by the end of the holiday everyone was involved. I shudder as I type.

We arrived in Prestatyn ready to begin walking at 9.45am. On the beach we took photos and started walking back through the town southwards. It was an abrupt climb up limestone cliffs into open countryside and onto the Prestatyn Hillside Nature Reserve. I was glad our leader took the lead and made it a steady climb. I had been worried about asthma as there was damp in the air. I needn't have worried; I was fitter than I had thought.

I finally began to enjoy myself. By now it was really warm. I stripped down to vest and shorts at the earliest break. Our first view was beautiful. In one direction was the Liverpool estuary, the other way looked towards the Snowdonia mountains, and below us was rural life, expressed in patchwork colours in the valley.

It was constantly pleasing to the eye as we walked along

the Clwydian Range. We spent the next hour or so going through undulating open meadows, passing Henfryn Hall. A coffee break was spent at Marian Ffrith, the site of a quarry. We ate our packed lunch at Moel Maenfa. A feast of nuts, fruit, salmon and mayonnaise sandwiches, homemade blackcurrant flapjack and chocolate, you name it, we had it. It was a bit chilly up there but the views stayed with us. For me, I had just relaxed into it all and was happy to spend time on my own with my thoughts.

Overall, for me the day was very interesting. A great path, it was changeable from open heathland to road and tracks to farm meadows, with stiles becoming ever noticeable.

We were picked up by mini-bus at 4.30pm. I had found the leader a little up himself but we stayed at a reasonable pace. He seemed quietly arrogant and although cordial, he didn't put himself out on that first day to blend the group together or get to know anybody.

We arrived back at the hotel by 5.30pm, in time to see the second half of the football match. We won, Beckham looked knackered. I found the contrast between a day of walking and watching something so loud and intrusive tiring. Clearly the group had not left television behind yet. I was glad to have a room of my own.

Evening supper was a repeat of the previous night. Prawn cocktail starter, then roast beef followed by homemade cheesecake. Delicious. Our leader left the table and did not socialise after dinner. I was more than happy to go to my room and sort my out day-sack.

I was fully relaxed, and I was not prepared to listen to the feuding walkers. I made a mental note to mention to both that if either wanted a room on her own, I was more than happy to share. I had left work with all its staff problems behind and I really didn't want this hassle on this holiday.

I rang David; all was okay at home. Then I wrote my diary. My last thought for the day was I hope this group becomes less service orientated and expectant.

Monday June 26th 2006. Bodfari to the A494 (Clwyd Gate) - 12 miles (3,290 feet of ascent).

I slept six hours, good for me. Breakfast: superb again. All our kit had to be ready, including the holdall, because we were moving to new accommodation. All in the mini-bus by 9am. The driver was a very sing-song Welshman who gave us plenty of gossip about the locals, not that I can remember what he said. I was too busy trying to overcome motion sickness.

We commenced walking at 10am, in perfect walking weather – warm but a gentle breeze. No wheezing today. I was fit and found the climbs great. The group was polite but there wasn't much interaction, most people just concentrating on the difficulty of the ascent. Some were a little unfit.

A steady climb brought us back onto the Clwydian Hills again. Some of the hills form a line of Iron Age hill forts. We spent all morning going over some fantastic open heathland and skirted the shoulder of Moel y Parc. We went over the mound of Penycloddiau, the site of one of hill forts, and finally after a switchback of hills and valleys we climbed to the summit of Moel Famau – a height of 1,818 feet with its Jubilee tower built in 1810 to mark the jubilee of George III but never completed.

This has to have been the best day. Lunch was spent looking out from the tower towards Liverpool and the Snowdonian hills, but there was a misty haze and a chilly wind. We only stopped for 20 minutes. The food was fabulous again – sandwiches yum. I thought I was eating too much. There were plenty of people visiting the summit, a great place for walking with paths going off everywhere. It would be nice to go back.

My legs were feeling good; no blisters. It was so good to be in the fresh air. Slowly the path descended across open heathland and the afternoon continued along the remaining switchback of hills overlooking Ruthin in the valley below. Eventually we came onto the A494, 300 metres below our highest point of the day at Moel Famau.

This marked the end of our day. We had been walking for seven hours and the group was tired. I was exhilarated. The friendly mini-bus driver picked us all up and transported us to our new accommodation – Eyarth Station, Llanfair DC, Ruthin. This was a converted railway station run as a guest house.

I would recommend this place. The host family were very welcoming and geared up for walkers. Again I was the single occupant of a splendid double room. The bed was deliciously comfortable. There were also plenty of teas and coffees. I always have the same routine if on my own. Put the kettle on, and whilst waiting for it to boil sort out the food bag, tip away the remaining water from the bladder bag, and lay out my wash kit and clothes.

I savoured my shower and reflected on the day. It had been the best Monday in ages. Supper was at 7am, so I had time to ring David. He was okay and he could sense I was really enjoying myself despite the issues with the group. I still hadn't had a chance to speak to our leader about sharing a room with the so-called 'offensive woman'. He had seemed more relaxed today although not talkative.

Supper was delicious. Grapefruit, followed by chicken and mushroom in herb sauce with roast potatoes and broccoli. Followed by citric torte. Yum. They ordered wine. I just raised my eyebrows. I really did not want to be putting money into a kitty for wine. I had given myself a budget to spend and this early on I didn't want to break into money just yet. I wouldn't have minded taking turns buying one bottle and sharing, but six of them were getting through expensive house wines and I really couldn't justify it. I declined the kind offer of a glass and ignored the indifference they showed towards my lonely companion, who tried to make conversation without success.

Again our leader left us shortly after dinner, stating what time he wanted us to be ready the next day. After that I made my escape to write my diary and read up on the next bit of route.

Tuesday June 27th 2006. A494 (Clwyd Gate) to Castell Dinas Bran - 13.5 miles (2,440 feet of ascent).

Restless night. The bed was comfy but I couldn't get warm, perhaps I was sickening or overtired. Bowels painful… trapped air and constipation… must drink more and eat less today I thought. Breakfast looked equally as good as the day before, but I declined a cooked meal and just ate cereal. I drank masses of tea and orange juice. That will do the trick, I thought. I did some exercises in the bedroom. (Bowels finally relieved.)

Our lunches were packed with stodge. I took as much fruit as possible. The walking that day can only be described as brilliant. Our day had started with wet weather gear as it was drizzling. We began earlier than usual at 9.30am, to cover the southern end of the Clwydian Hills. Again it was changeable from hills to valleys.

Our first climb of the day up the side of Moel Gyw was a bit tough on the legs. We then passed up and over our last summit, the hill Moel y Plas at 1,460 feet. We went through Llandegla, the highest village on the walk. Here we stopped for a very welcome ice cream. The weather was very warm. Some of us sat on a small seat outside the church. It was very quiet.

From here it was a steady climb up and into Llandegla forest. This is managed by the Shotton Paper Company, much of it pine. The path slowly ascended to a height of 480 metres until it finally emerged onto open heathland. We had a short break here (phew), before following the path out to a small road between Minera and World's End. *Map ref OS 256 235495.*

(See chapter nine) Because that is where I cut away from the offas dyke to start my walk towards Wrexham.

The next part of the walk was stunning. At World's End, we had wonderful views of the vale of Llangollen. We did however have the company of midges in amongst the trees, so we didn't stop long but progressed along the best path of the entire walk. We traversed this narrow path in the shadow of Eglwyseg Rocks, at a height that allowed us to view the valley forwards and backwards for its entire length. The valley was bathed in sunlight, the rich green pastures dotted with just a few farmsteads creating a memorable picture. If you don't do any other part of this walk, I would suggest this bit. I can honestly say I found a great inner peace on this section.

I was totally relaxed and blind to others and their problems. For me it was a great healing day mentally. We were nearing the end of our day's walk when we met a dishevelled group of walkers. They had huge backpacks and looked a little disorganised but happy enough.

We stopped finally and I enjoyed the remainder of my stodgy food, looking towards Castell Dinas Bran, a castle dating from the 13th century, whilst waiting for our chirpy Welsh driver to pick us up. It was still warm. We were then accorded a wonderful bus journey back to Eyarth Station via the Horseshoe Pass. It was a bit of a switchback ride and by the time we arrived back, I was feeling positively sick. I was glad of my own room.

The food was great again, although I probably didn't do it justice. I stopped longer that evening and chatted to everyone, but they were still not giving our eccentric walking companion any let up. They were so mean to her. I found this behaviour childish and selfish, so I retired early again. I really did not want to get involved. If anything, it should have been the leader sorting it out.

Wednesday June 28th 2006. Castell Dinas Bran to Trefonen - 16 miles (2,275 feet of ascent).

I had a better night's sleep although I was awake at 4.30am (curtains too thin). I felt replenished. Feet good. Felt fit, just a sore thigh. Breakfast was another feast but I only managed grapefruit and yoghurt. I still felt full from night before. The weather was fine again; a T-shirt day.

Today was to be our first time actually walking on Offa's Dyke itself, albeit briefly. We had to collect all our belongings as we were moving on to Welshpool.

Dropped off at 9.30am, we continued below the crags with marvellous views of the vale of Llangollen until we dropped down into Llangollen itself and onto the Pontcysyllte Aqueduct, which carries the Llangollen branch of the Shropshire Union Canal over the River Dee.

The aqueduct was built by Telford between 1795 and 1805. A masterpiece of the Industrial Revolution, it involved a 1,000 foot long cast iron trough supported on stone arches 120 feet high. We stopped before walking over the aqueduct. I bought an ice cream and went over to the turning basin to look at the canoes and the boats.

Some of the others were sitting and savouring ice creams

too. Our leader checked that everyone was happy about walking over the aqueduct before we set off. No one was squeamish as we walked single file along the path by the water trough. We enjoyed the scenery although we didn't stop for long!

The day passed easily. We climbed away from Froncysyllte and briefly touched Offa's Dyke, although it was overgrown. We walked alongside it for half a kilometre. The ladies stopped briefly for a pee. In a line, we squatted. I don't think anyone had a camera.

I managed to talk to people today. The walking was easy, however the group tended to get lethargic after lunch and required motivation. The packed lunch was stodgy again; I wasn't looking forward to that. The scenery changed many times from uplands to rolling farmland and slowly rose to Chirk Castle. Now managed by the National Trust, this was built in about 1300 by Roger Mortimer and has been lived in by the Myddleton family since 1595. We walked down its avenue of trees towards the path, which is only permitted in summer and has a different route in winter. We were fortunate to lunch in the grounds. I remember a cockerel that was persistent in scrounging food.

After lunch we followed some superb stretches of Offa's Dyke and then walked the route of Oswestry Old Racecourse and its grandstand (only the foundations still existed). The path then entered woodland that gently descended. A great path for the remainder of the day.

My only concern at that point was that I was waiting for

my period to come, and it was causing enormous pain in my bowels as I became more constipated. I hope you don't me mentioning that. It's just that I am a woman and no fictional novels or even factional ones I've read ever speak openly of what a bloody nuisance it is (excuse the pun). Walking helps relieve the pain, so it could have been worse.

Staying at the Royal Oak in Welshpool was great. I was ecstatic; the room was finally basic. And it was just the bare essentials – a single bed, a dilapidated though serviceable bath, a large dresser, a wardrobe and a single mat on wooden floors. Finally I felt at home. This wasn't luxury any more. It was my little heaven.

Originally the pub had been a coaching inn and once the manor house to Powis Castle. In my room it didn't take any stretch of imagination to appreciate its former uses. I used the bath to wash my clothes. It was very useful. I had approached the leader about sharing my room with my new found walking companion, but he didn't take it up at that point. I had also offered my room to the other character, but by then she had accepted the situation to some extent and just gave her room buddy a hard time.

Unbeknown to me, they had both been giving our leader an earful each day about one complaint or another, and as I would be told later, all of the group had complained about something each day. He should have done something about it. Coming down the stairs, I could hear complaints again. I wandered onto the streets and found the cash machine. My month's pay had been paid in. Perhaps tomorrow I would withdraw some money and have a drink. I had seen the pub's pumps and there was draught Guinness, so that would be a treat.

Wandering back in, I had tea. I was too tired to make that much conversation. It was at this point that my holiday came to an end as far as I was concerned, when one of the walkers announced her purse had gone missing. From then on we never heard the last of it. I have always been one of those people who feel guilty when they haven't done anything wrong, who always feel somehow responsible for someone else's problems, and this was no exception. With five people in the group knowing each other so well, immediately there was this awful suspicion placed upon the rest of us.

I tried to speak to the walker concerned about Llangollen and the conversation I had overheard in the tiny shop there, about a purse that had been found and the shopkeeper had held on to it. Everyone in the queue – including other members of our walk (the Americans) – would have heard that conversation. But the purse owner wasn't listening. So I just told her to ring the shop and left it at that. She was so unapproachable. Perhaps I would have been like this in her situation, having to cancel cards and with no money for the holiday. One of the ladies who knew her apparently gave her some to tide her over. I was just glad to retire. It was a tense end to what had been a good day.

Thursday June 29th 2006. Trefonen to Welshpool – 16 miles (1,050 feet of ascent).

It was a noisy night and in the early morning I was woken by dustbins being collected and loud conversation. I couldn't get my brain to stop thinking about 'the purse'. Maybe I should have spoken to the leader but in truth I didn't mention it. I was too fed up with the group to be bothered.

Now I wish I had. Even as I type it still leaves a sour twist in my stomach. The holiday turned into a psychological disaster for me and all the grief of the previous months just poured out of me. I had cried buckets that night. A total outpouring of everything bottled up. I felt so sick.

At 6am I got dressed and organised my case and looked out of the window onto the street. I could just see the newsagent was open. It had a cash machine next to it. I needed to relax so I would definitely draw out money and get a drink tonight. I also needed some more batteries for my camera and the newsagent might have them. Plus I needed to buy rations that I could eat at lunchtime without having stomach aches.

It was rather pleasant stepping out at that time and wandering along the empty street. I enjoyed choosing some crisps, nuts and small bars of chocolate. I then collected some money from the cash machine. I wasn't going to be buying wine, just a beer at the end of the day. Feeling slightly better after my shopping, I wandered back and had a wash. It was going to be another hot day.

Breakfast was a quiet affair; not everyone was there. The

atmosphere was stilted. I gathered my bag and waited downstairs. Some other bags were there. I said to our leader that I would be back marker today. He was happy with that. I stood there with the bags and waited what seemed like ages. I wasn't comfortable. I felt nervous and kept thinking about the family. I kept telling myself to calm down.

We were given our packed lunches. They were enormous. The orange I was given equally so. This was great considering the weather we had during the day. We finally set off at 9am as we needed to get an early start.

The day was spent thinking. I was back marker, which meant I could burp and fart as much as I liked but also I could think. In doing so, the walk paled. I don't remember much of it, just that it was extremely hot and a bit of a trudge at the end of the day.

The morning was spent climbing to the summit of Moelydd, which wasn't far. The views were marvellously clear and on the horizon was a heat haze. The views stretched from the Berwyns in the west to Long Mynd and the Church Stretton hills to the south.

During the morning I could feel myself close to tears again. I hadn't cried very much when my father died. I found myself talking to him and Momma, saying at least they know I am not guilty. I beat myself up all day. As the day wore on, the heat was intense. Everyone was suffering. The group became very slow. I found being back marker frustrating as the loiterers and retrogrades slowed up the walk terribly. Even my feet were beginning to burn.

We spent the afternoon walking alongside a river exposed to the sun and then rejoined the Shropshire Union Canal and then again onto the open flood embankments to Buttington Bridge, finally walking into Welshpool. I vowed to take a wet hankie tomorrow and put it round my neck. I was grateful not to experience another mini-bus ride today.

Dinner was another big meal. On arrival I bought myself a Guinness and our leader a drink too. On reflection this was probably misjudged, as again the evening was spent going on about the purse and even our eccentric companion was a bit of a pain. The best bit was that David had sent a postcard to the hotel. He must have had second sense. I guess I had rung him more times than usual. I was delighted to get it. Up to then I had felt so isolated and I was tickled he was thinking about me. It was a moment of hope and warmth amongst what was slowly becoming paranoia. I was glad to retreat to my room.

I repacked my case as we would be moving on again. It was very warm and sticky. Then I wrote my diary and turned in.

Friday June 30th 2006. Welshpool to Kerry Ridgeway - 17 miles (15.5 miles from Buttington Bridge) (2,200 feet of ascent).

I did not sleep well. Why am I a thinker? I kept going over the Llangollen shop incident. What if I had seen something? Why had I not remembered to ask the group when I got outside, instead of looking at the canoes? Did the American people think I took it? They had been in the queue, had they taken it?

It struck me that I'd had a conversation with the leader in the Royal Oak when buying him a drink, saying, "I've got some money now." Did he think I had taken it? I tried desperately to calm myself, knowing I was innocent. But like a washing machine it just kept going round in my head. Not helped by the same old conversation at the dinner table about 'the purse'.

I could feel the accusations in the atmosphere again at breakfast. It was palpable.

I was first to be ready again. Taxis had been ordered to take us back to Buttington Bridge and still people weren't ready. Again I was left with the baggage downstairs to look after. This made me feel very uncomfortable. It seemed aeons before another of the party appeared.

We finally got going at 8.30am. Negotiating many stiles, it was a long slow climb up to the summit of Beacon Ring Iron Age hill fort. Whilst doing this, we hadn't been walking for long when someone announced that their camera was missing. My heart sank. Oh God, not again. The conversation then just revolved around missing items. The leader just heaved a sigh; he looked pissed off, as someone rang the hotel. The reply came back: "No we haven't found any camera but there are a load of clothes left in a wardrobe. We will forward them on." The lady they belonged to hadn't even noticed they were missing, but the camera still was. Fortunately, she just shrugged it off and left it at that but for me who had been left with the baggage, I suddenly realised I had placed myself in a vulnerable position once again.

I started to shake as the conversation turned to someone stealing things in the vicinity. On top of this, the continuing saga of the two people sharing a room together and how they weren't getting on was just intolerable. The constant back-biting and hurtful comments got me down. In the end, all I could do was try and close my ears to it, but I felt like I was back at school, that's how childish it all was.

By now it was 9.30am and the sun was very warm. I had put two litres of water in my rucksack and a wetted scarf for later in the day. Shortly after climbing the hill, a farm mongrel terrier decided to join the group up to the top. We had a welcomed break there but the views were distorted by a fir plantation and the actual summit had two unsightly masts. A plantation of pines and beech commemorated the coronation year of 1953. Sadly, this masked the enormity of this Iron Age hill fort and its ancient history. The Beacon once housed a small village that survived by hunting and farming, however the site has a much older long barrow or burial mound suggesting that it could once have been a sacrificial site.

The dog stayed with us for the duration of the snack break and only turned away once our picked-on companion had ordered it home. Again she was criticised for her manner, but to be fair her authority was exactly what that dog listened to. It seemed the group wished to destroy any harmony they had. All views and breaks were not relished; the chance to moan seemed to be far more important. I felt terribly isolated. I sat away from them trying to enjoy the view of Welshpool settled in the very green Severn Valley, and Powis Castle standing magnificently against the hillside, its brick-red construction in stark contrast to the greenery below.

From here we rambled across moorland until reaching the grounds of Leighton Estate with its hall. The estate was self-sufficient, having its own village that was occupied by its workers. There was a village school and church. Originally it was developed by a wealthy Liverpool banker in the mid-19th century. They pioneered farming improvements, gas lighting and water power.

As walkers we could not see the hall. We just had the experience of walking through its magnificent exotic gardens. A wonderful woodland of mixed conifers, Chile pines, monkey puzzle trees and other species met our eyes. The coolness and quiet solitude of the wood finally silenced the group. I thoroughly enjoyed this serenity. We passed a couple of holding reservoirs that had been used for water power, including one named Offa's Pool. The reservoirs were surrounded by huge brick walls, and what were once water pools now had enormous monkey puzzle trees growing out of them.

We rejoined Offa's Dyke itself after a tedious road walk. The oaks that lined this part of the dyke were magnificent. They were enormous and I could not guess how old they were. The trees were evenly spaced with huge boughs, and no sign of decay or disease. The best I have ever seen. We stopped there to admire the Camlad and Caebitra valleys and had our lunch.

I managed to ring home; everything was okay. My stomach

was bitterly complaining. I was still 'on' and getting heavier instead of lighter. I had been pleased for the small break, but from those who needed a longer rest there were more grumbles and groans, and the unfit among us became frustratingly slow.

The remainder of the day was relatively flat. We went through fields and fields of barley and corn, finally passing Montgomery and its castle to our right. It had become hot and dusty. Time to put my wet scarf around my neck. The others were all getting hot and bothered and feeling physically battered. Some had developed blisters. We stopped whilst first aid was administered. I still had plenty of energy.

Much to everyone's consternation the last stretch was a 500 foot ascent. Our leader didn't say anything. No words of encouragement. I overtook the group and ploughed on up to the top. It was just a small step onto the road; we had finally finished for the day. Amazingly 10 seconds after reaching the road, from around the corner came our lift. Fantastic timing.

Our destination for the night was Milebrook House Hotel. A beautiful three star country house hotel, family run. It was once owned by the famous explorer and writer Sir Wilfred Thesiger. If you get a chance to stay here it is well worth it. Tastefully decorated, it retains its colonial furnishings and delicate colours.

I was allocated my room. Well, I can only describe it as opulent. Although the bath was quite old and basic with poor running water, the room was very pretty. A mighty Queen

Anne bed with brass bedstead and a mattress to die for. Soft peach furnishings in a Laura Ashley style, with the tiniest attic window allowing light into the room. Ivy grew around the window, hiding it from observers below on the veranda. They could not possibly see me. But I could see and hear them.

I was attracted by the view of the gardens below the veranda. Lawns and formal gardens, colourful shrubs and climbers stepped down to the kitchen gardens, which provided many of the vegetables for the restaurant, with little passing and sitting places. Polytunnels were further along the garden, enabling a gardener to bring on younger plants with protection. I was fascinated. The evening was still, blackbirds and chaffinches chattering in the coolness with just the interruption of occasional traffic.

I opened my case and had a semi-cool bath. It took forever to fill. I was very glad I had packed a skirt as an afterthought. I had one clean white T-shirt. I couldn't decide whether to tie my hair back or leave it loose. I certainly didn't have any make-up or fancy jewellery. Oh sod it. This was a walking holiday, not a fashion parade.

The Americans then came to have a look at my room. I was a bit annoyed and wary of them. They thought it was 'quaint and gorgeous, how lovely to have such a beautiful bedroom'. If only they had known. This was so removed from what I was used to on walking holidays.

I wandered down to the bar and bought a lager. I handed my key in at the desk, and I turned to find the leader watching me. I felt guilty and for what? I didn't want to keep my key and lose it. Ben had lost his on a beach and had come back to the hotel only to find all his belongings stolen. Since then I have been very careful to hand in my key.

Supper was at 7.30pm. The sun was still warm as I met my travel companions on the veranda. Looking at their clothes I felt underdressed. Feeling distinctly out of place, I left to walk in the garden and explore. The paths crisscrossed. One garden led into another past a statue and a seat. A path led me down to the river. It was so peaceful, tranquil and quintessentially English. The river was shallow but running fast. I took the opportunity to dabble my feet. My thoughts moved to my family at home.

Picking up pebbles, I had five minutes of childish pleasure skimming them across the water until I had this eerie feeling of being watched. It was most peculiar and this area was secluded. I felt a shiver run down my spine, gathered myself and headed back to the house.

Dinner surpassed itself. I had Welsh lamb and goats cheese. The service was slow but refined, deliberately careful in its execution. David and I had never stayed anywhere remotely like this. The waiters all wore white gloves. I struggled not to grab anything or spill or gobble, a bit difficult for me. I couldn't believe it when people started moaning about something again. I then switched off. I didn't drink wine, it was so unnecessary. I noticed our leader took another bottle away with him. I was beginning to question his leadership. Was he a quiet alcoholic?

I retired early, and returning to my room I sat on the bed

and cried. I was so tired mentally of having to be diplomatic with the group, having to be friendly yet inside seething with their total lack of comradeship. The guilt of sleeping in such luxurious surroundings, something that David and I had never been able to do, was unbearable. I spent the night sleeping on the floor wrapped in the eiderdown. My last thoughts before going into this restless sleep was at least my body felt fit and my legs and feet were still very good.

Saturday July 1st 2006. Rest day.

I woke at 5.30am, with noisy birds outside my room. I ran a bath and put all my dirty washing in it.

The eccentric but practical walker and I had already spoken to the owners and they had agreed to allow us access to their washing lines. I was so pleased to get things washed properly. The 'wash and go' tube was useful. I hung the clothes out early. It was going to be a glorious day. I took the opportunity to walk down to the river. It was babbling and so peaceful.

Back in my room, I was very tired and lay on the bed chiding myself for being over dramatic and vowing to sleep in it the next night.

Breakfast was at 8am. It was a slow affair, no rush. I had a kipper and cereals. One of the group had booked two taxis for us all to go into Knighton at 9am. I spoke again to the owner about what I had done with the washing, and she even offered the iron for later. I was delighted as it meant my skirt could be a bit more respectable.

The morning was spent in Knighton. I grabbed a newspaper and my lunch – a peach, a pizza and a custard tart – and found a spot by the river to relax in the shade. By now the temperature was 23 degrees and rising. Knighton itself is very quaint and many of its building date from the 16th and 17th centuries. Knighton means 'the town on the dyke', which is literally true as it straddles Offa's Dyke and is the only town to do so. It also marked the halfway point of the walk.

The Offa's Dyke information centre and headquarters in Knighton is clearly designed to impart information to children on field trips and educational outings. It is well laid out and worth a visit. Outside its doors the Offa's Dyke Park and stone mark the official site of the opening of the path in 1971.

I was quite jumpy that morning and didn't really relax. I wandered about the town, bought a few toiletries and peered into the many antique shops and art galleries. The taxis then brought us back to the hotel.

No sign of our browbeaten friend today, although I noted her washing was on the line. I spent the next three hours writing and sitting on the veranda. Its vines of wisteria provided a welcome shade with the sun on my back. It was Saturday July 1st lunchtime and the hotel was full of day visitors. It was all very exclusive and the service excellent. I hadn't eaten my peach, so I sat looking out on the garden and eavesdropping on a family standing on the veranda waiting for lunch. It was all rather lah-dee-dah and amusing. The conversation ranged from the housing market and prices to children's education and catheters!

I had almost finished my diary when the leader joined me and spoke of my challenge. He seemed sort of interested and asked for my address so he could send me some details of different routes to consider. I never did receive those, so I suspect he was trying to check if my contact details were the same as my booking information. Such was my feeling of being watched.

After he left, I cannot describe the peace as I sat finishing my writing, compared to the inner turmoil and upheaval of the past year. My thoughts turned to Dad and Momma. Dad would have loved this walk and Momma would have appreciated this garden.

I then checked the washing and it was dry. I borrowed the iron and packed everything again properly. It was a relaxing day on the whole and I began to warm to this hotel. David and I will definitely have to visit it.

Sunday July 2nd 2006. Kerry Ridgeway to Knighton - 12.5 miles (3,250 feet of ascent).

I slept in the bed overnight, after a warm drink and a read. I managed a good rest. The day dawned bright again and it was going to be a hot one.

Breakfast was good but the service terribly slow. I only ate half my porridge, my stomach gurgling. I felt sick with 'the curse' still going strong. Our leader could not hide his annoyance; he looked like he had a hangover.

I went outside and took some early photographs of the front garden and the already sparkling river.

The mini-bus driver warned us the walk would be a switchback today, indicating it would be the longest day. By the time we started walking it was late and already 23 degrees. Today my problem was flooding. Any opportunity to stop and relieve it I did. Crudely speaking, the body gets so sticky and uncomfortable, even though I had all the wipes possible. Again I make no apology for sharing this with you. It's just life and something us women have to put up with.

After a slow start and a climb, we went through Nut Wood and a plantation. We followed the dyke up and across the undulating country of the Shropshire Hills, an area of outstanding beauty. The scenery was very pretty and forever changing.

We left the Montgomery plains behind and moved into small villages and farms. Our first break was at Churchtown with its delightful chapel. Looking around the building was an emotional break from the bickering of the two sleeping buddies. They were driving me mad. The remainder of the day I spent on my own and just savoured the walk. It was great. I was fit enough to enjoy the views. The air was hot but clear.

We crossed the Clun valley at Bryndrinog, a splendid half-timbered farm near Newcastle. Three miles away was the village of Clun, immortalised by the poet A. E. Houseman who is probably best known for 'A Shropshire Lad'. Clun became the ideal setting for his poems of loss and lost innocence. How appropriate was that?

From here we passed the quaint village of Lower Spoad.

There was another medieval farmhouse here, so pretty and isolated, but we weren't able to stop. Instead, it was a long dusty climb out of the valley towards Llanfair Hill. At Springdalehill Farm the valley stretched below us. It was a brilliant view. I noted they had a small campsite for backpackers. I wished I was doing just that. It was fabulous walking after this, as we accompanied the massive banks of the dyke. Llanfair Hill marks the earthworks' highest point at 1,408 feet. It was great now striding out with no stiles!!

I felt very comfortable. However, one of the walkers had again been bending the leader's ear. It was almost a child's petulance but I could only feel sorry for her. We stopped for lunch near Selley Cross, the views stunning. At Selly Hall I filled up my water bladder again, from an outside tap meant purely for walkers. I had already gone through a litre and a half, so I was glad I would have enough water to last the final five or six miles.

We passed through the most enormous field of free range hens. It was a pleasure to watch their enjoyment basking in the dirt bowls and sunbathing and strutting their stuff across such a fertile grassy meadow. They looked so happy.

I took the opportunity to ring home. David was surprised to hear from me and immediately realised I wasn't enjoying myself. I would never normally ring in the daytime. I couldn't divulge much but he sensed it. I then lay back and savoured the sun, but my brain would not stop thinking. I had hoped our leader would take me up on my offer of sharing a room with one or other of the bickering walking companions. I wish I had had a tape recording of how sad and thoughtless it all was. Actually I preferred the 'blue stocking' one the most. She didn't faze me at all. She really was a lonely troubled soul in need of some serious TLC. The plus side was that she was so practical.

These thoughts dispersed on our final break in the afternoon when we were met by a pair of seasoned leaders from the walking holiday company. As we walked, they spoke to the lady who was missing her purse and chatted to some other members of the group. I was just walking and thinking, oh God, here we go again. The guilt I carry and for what. I wished this holiday would stop. I shook for the remainder of the walk, my nerves in tatters. On reaching the hotel I retired to my room to sort myself out. Bleeding was dreadful now. Looking back now, I am sure my period was worse because the whole holiday was so awful.

Unfortunately, once I was in my room the remaining group were stood under my window on the veranda and I heard every word. I heard quite clearly someone discussing the fact I had gone to a cash machine in Welshpool. And the fact I spent time going off on my own at breaks. (My period duh.) Clearly I was a marked woman. I felt physically ill. I had a wash and with no confidence I went downstairs, bought a drink and went to speak to them generally on the veranda. Nothing was mentioned. So that was it. The other leaders had gone, having not spoken to me at all. Such was my paranoia, I felt the group had made their decision. This was shit. I walked down to the river feeling desperate. Not even the solitude could quell the inner turmoil. At this point all I wanted to do was run. But what would that have proved? I look back now on this walk, trying to come to some logical explanation for it all. Perhaps it was all coincidental and hearsay and I took it all to heart. But it still resonates and I feel scarred by it.

I was so tired and my period didn't help. Reluctantly I sat through dinner, another opulent meal. Our leader's attitude was awful, slinking off again after dinner. No conversation, taking his freebie bottle of wine with him. Not once on this walk had he stayed with us. It seemed terribly selfish considering the group was so divided. As a leader, he should have been joining in the discussions. If I had been leader I would have shared the bottle of wine. I decided maybe he had 'ghosts' of his own. He certainly gave that impression.

After dinner I retreated to the garden, my solace. It was still warm. I was rewarded by meeting two kittens and their mum curled up in a basket left for them in the sun. I didn't touch them but they each meowed, acknowledging me. The evening was beautiful and the fragrances wafting through the air and insects flitting about in the late evening sun were a poet's dream; the tranquillity and colours awakening the senses. I looked back towards my bedroom window. I could just make it out amongst the leaves. I could paint this scene; so much growth and vitality in the colour.

I peered into one of the domed polytunnels and it had rows of lettuces, tomatoes and cucumbers all at varying stages.

There was a herb garden and nasturtiums grew everywhere. Everything was used in the kitchen.

I returned to my room and repacked my holdall. Everything was clean. Fantastic. Tomorrow might be better; ever the optimist. It had been decided between the leader and the offended walker that I would be sharing a room with our misinterpreted companion. Hooray you hear me cry. She didn't know it yet though. This bothered me.

Monday July 3rd 2006. Knighton to Kington – 13 miles (2,250 feet of ascent).

We got going late again, at 10.30am. This was another beautiful easy day of walking. Still no blisters or aches and pains. I just bumbled along on my own and wondered how I was going to speak to this person about sharing a room with me. However, that was abruptly rectified when at some point in the day, the new arrangement was loudly announced by a now joyful walker who was getting her own room. How tactful was that?

The packed lunches were good again. The liquid intake of 2.5 litres was only just enough. It was that hot. After a steep climb out of Knighton we followed the dyke and its massive earthworks over hilltops. The walking was grand. We descended to Dolley Green and could see the Malvern Hills and Brecon Beacons.

The weather was so kind to us. Enjoying it, I forgot the angst in the group. I felt so fit I could really take in this stunning scenery. I disregarded the group and enjoyed my own thoughts. Dad would have loved this. We crossed the English/Welsh border four times during the course of the day. I truly felt I was walking somewhere historically special. Considering the start time, we made good progress into Kington and arrived about 5pm.

Kington is a small border market town. It's very pretty, with many of the houses built of flint and painted white or pink. Very picturesque. Our accommodation, The Burton Hotel, was great. For one thing, it had a sauna and swimming pool. Yes! I was delighted, my excitement transparent. My swimming costume came straight out once we were allocated our rooms.

"Are you going now?" my new room-mate asked. "Damn sure I am, are you coming?" I responded. She started to dither. "Oh come on, let your hair down!" I said. "If you have your cozzy go for it." My enthusiasm persuaded her to join me. I then ran a bath and said, "I'm washing my sticky clothes in the bath and I'm going to leave them to soak whilst I have a swim. Do you want to put yours in as well?" I left her to think on this as I got clean clothes out of my holdall and slipped them on, knowing I would be clean after my swim. I gathered all my toiletries and watched her do exactly the same.

Immediately she and I hit it off. I could see her relax. She found her swimming costume, stayed in her old clothes and we went to find the pool. It was brilliant. We had the exclusive use of it. They provided towels which was fantastic. I cannot describe the joy as I slipped into the pool and did my first length underwater, allowing the submersion to wash all my cares away. I came up replenished. It felt so good. It was utter bliss – refreshing, invigorating and calming. My companion enjoyed it too and then another walker came and joined us briefly. Finally, I was left alone and stayed in for three quarters of an hour. Oh yum, my body felt good.

I enjoyed the shower and hair wash. Going back to our room I found my new friend using the bath and washing her socks out. "You don't mind, do you?" she asked. "Of course not," I replied. "No need to stand on ceremony with me. Do you want a cup of tea? I'm gasping." She asked, "Are you making one then?" "Course I am, I wouldn't ask if I wasn't," I grinned at her. "Yes please then," she said, in her jolly hockey sticks voice.

Whilst the kettle boiled I hung my costume out of the tiny window to dry and proceeded to wash my day clothes. It was mainly my top and as it was quick drying I knew it would be ready by morning.

Evening dinner was chicken casserole or salmon all beautifully cooked. The person in the group who had lost her camera the week before finally mentioned she had found it the same day in her main suitcase. Her little clique already knew this but the other three of us didn't. So we were surprised and expressed our relief.

I had another swim; it was going to a warm night. I don't know what the others did. Then I went to our room and started to read, but my companion wanted to talk about how life was with her and about the holiday. I wasn't going to comment on the holiday but listened to what I can only describe as an interesting but closeted life. I enjoyed her company. She had been to so many places and had achieved so much, but her understanding of people was non-existent. Anyway, she enjoyed being waited on. I seem to remember making most of the cups of tea until I ordered her to do the next one. I assured her I wouldn't complain how it turned out!

Tuesday July 4th 2006. Kington to Hay-On-Wye – 14.5 miles (2,115 feet of ascent).

Out at 8.30am, hooray. We ascended Hergest Ridge, a grassy moorland hill, passing the old Kington racecourse and the Whetstone, a large glacier boulder. At Newchurch we stopped at the tiny chapel and admired 'The Great House', a cruck-framed hall dating from approximately 1450. We then started to walk along drovers' roads that historically were used by farmers taking their stock to Hereford market.

This is Kilvert country: Frances Kilvert (1840–1879) was a local curate who kept diaries describing this part of the world with honesty and a keen eye for detail. The day was very pleasant and easygoing on foot until the tedious trudge at the end. This was probably because of the heat. The best part was walking through Bettws Dingle, a dark and shaded glen where the path took in a plantation of conifers with a river running through it. We stopped here for a while. It was a welcomed break from the sun, which had brought the temperature to 30 degrees.

The banks of the River Wye eventually saw us into Hay-On-Wye, renowned for second-hand bookshops and its place on the world stage of literature, hosting the annual Hay Festival of Literature where the great and good amongst bibliophiles promote or speak about their latest edition.

There were canoeists in the water and children swimming. Oh to have joined them. It was 2.30pm and our coach wasn't picking us up until 4.30pm. There was now time for us to enjoy the town and its books. I was delighted to be able to peruse the numerous second-hand bookshops and look for an early edition of the Scarlet Pimpernel by Baroness Orczy. I was not disappointed and managed to pick one up, a second edition, for a price! Katy would be tickled I had thought of her.

Apart from books, the town itself is very pretty. There are numerous cobbled streets and fine Elizabethan style houses that have picture galleries and curio gift shops as their frontages.

I ended up having a coffee with two of the group near the coach park. It was here that I recall was the last time I saw my Offa's Dyke walking guidebook. I didn't know it was missing until the following day. This was a bitter blow.

The coach duly collected us at 4.30pm. It was still very hot and the coach ride made me feel sick. Back at the hotel I had another swim and had time to write my diary. My companion opened up a bit more tonight. What a sad existence she had. I was mentally exhausted with her demons; I had enough of my own. We were moving to Monmouth tomorrow so everything had to be packed.

Wednesday July 5th 2006. Hay-On-Wye to Pandy - 18 miles (2,480 feet of ascent).

I can honestly say I was looking forward to this stretch. I had walked some of it before but my parents had talked about it warmly whenever they went to Pandy to stay. However, the loss of my guidebook just before setting off unnerved me once more. I approached our indifferent leader to say it was missing but his comment was, "Around the country there are people's belongings." Logically I worked out I had probably left it either in the coach park toilets or on the coach itself. I was devastated, as I had enjoyed following the maps and being able to write up my diary accurately at night. I had lost my friend as far as I was concerned.

I became quite short with my companion, only because she needed constant reassurance and I was feeling crap. I knew I had been her saviour but this day I just couldn't be bothered. I had come with such high hopes and spirit to this holiday, and I couldn't believe I had spent much of it being a sounding board and a diplomat, careful and adaptable in volatile situations. It was worse than work!

Still, the Black Mountains beckoned. Walking out from Hay-On-Wye we made the steady climb to the slopes of Hay Bluff and then ascended it gently until on top. Once on top of the Hatterall Ridge it was easygoing for nine miles. We had early sun but dark clouds were forming and our leader pushed on.

My legs were great. I really enjoyed the path and the views, which were magnificent to begin with. The ridge marks the line of the English/Welsh border and the eastern boundary of the Brecon Beacons National Park. It became quite cold but the weather held good. We didn't hang about though and the leader didn't stop for long. He didn't want us to be in the middle of a thunderstorm without shelter.

Unfortunately the views were not much towards the end of the walk. But I thoroughly enjoyed the open space and the freedom to go at my own pace. No stiles, hooray. I became very excited when I realised we were coming down from the Cat's Back towards Pandy and the Lancaster Arms. I could see Tim Todd's Caravan Park where Mum and Dad had stayed for some of their best holidays. When we finally came down to the car park, I sat on the wall and rang Mum. She guessed immediately where I was and could picture the pub. I felt very emotional. Dad had been with me that day. I had become spiritually uplifted as the day went on.

I knew tonight I would be sharing my room with the lady who had lost her purse. I had already decided this was my opportunity to speak to this person concerning that purse. I wish she had checked out the shops at Llangollen, but for all I knew she had. I wanted the air clear. She was so edgy. I can't say I was looking forward to my next two nights. I would have been happy to stay with my eccentric friend but they seemed to think I wouldn't be. Oh well.

On arrival at the Riverside Hotel it was chaotic and checking in was poor. By the time we had all checked in, our volatile walking companion had flipped about something wrong in her room. She exploded. We were all tired. My new sleeping companion and I found our room, small but adequate. I had a shower then went into town for more provisions.

Later, I cried when I spoke to the woman about her purse. I think she was surprised that I hadn't mentioned it before. I explained that the attitudes of the group had got me down. I think she took the hint that that meant her as well. I also explained that I had lost two parents the previous year and had inherited money. If she thought I would steal money, I wanted her to know there was definitely no need to. I was just not used to overspending or drinking and all I had wanted from this walk was for it to be peaceful. She didn't comment on this. I think the penny dropped as she realised I had suffered a lot over the holiday listening to her and the others.

Dinner was great despite the complaints about the rooms directed at our leader. This could not deflate me any more than I already was, so I found amusement in our waitress who was a Somerset delight. "Ther' you 'r' m'dear," she said as she served us, a great smile on her face. Nothing was too much trouble. I wish the group could have appreciated her.

I spoke to the leader later, but he acted surprised and actually said I had been the least of his problems this holiday. It was then that he explained that one of the walkers had lost his camera on the first day and that had been reported to the police. I was shocked he had not mentioned it before, but clearly those who were with the camera owner when he lost it had known. No wonder everyone had been on edge.

The leader was surprised I didn't know. He asked if I had any reason to suspect anyone else regarding the purse. I explained about the shop and who was in the queue at the same time as me. I also spoke about the dynamics of the group. He agreed but then he hadn't done anything about it. All he said to me was, "At least you know what you don't want to do again," and this was true. People had acted so spoilt on this trip.

I found out there and then how vulnerable the leader was and that something was terribly wrong. He spoke of having had a loss. I could sympathise with him there. I talked about leading groups. He agreed I would be fine at it, but remember I could get groups like this. Feeling a bit more cheered, we went into the bar. The Americans were there with a wodge of money on the bar counter. I moved away. I didn't want to see them. I bought a Guinness, I think the leader had a lager and we had a pleasant conversation with some gentlemen who were judging a national terrier competition in the area. I finally relaxed; these chaps were so comical. They had terrier attributes themselves – wiry hair, quick beady eyes and nervous twitches. I just smiled.

I finally slept, and I don't know where my sleeping companion had got to.

Thursday July 6th 2006. Pandy to Monmouth - 17 miles (1,360 feet of ascent).

After another feast of a breakfast we were back at Pandy by 9am. Another long hot day and lots of stiles. Feet just a little warm today, their first signs of complaint. The solitary lady was quiet today as she had not enjoyed sleeping alone. I must say I was looking forward to sleeping by myself on the last night, but I wouldn't have minded if it was with my belittled friend.

Not much happened this day and the walk was easy again. We went through many fields and pleasant farmland following the Trothy Valley and the River Trothy, a tributary of the Wye. The most impressive part of the walk was the 12th century White Castle. This is one of the three castles used by the Lords of the Marches to defend Monmouth. Sadly, we were unable to look around it. The other lasting impression of the day were the apple orchards. Guarded by high security fences, the trees were dedicated to the production of a well-known commercial cider. The path passed through one of the fields and made for difficult navigation. This was the only time I saw our leader dither.

The remaining part of the walk was lovely and there were no incidents or conversations that caused any harm. We walked straight into Monmouth and to our hotel.

Monmouth was the largest town we had stopped at since Prestatyn. It is dominated by its south entrance where the Monnow Bridge crosses the River Wye. This impressive bridge with its rich, red brick fortified gatehouses draws the visitor into town. Monmouth was the birthplace of both Henry V and Charles Rolls, aviator and co-founder of the Rolls-Royce Company.

Back at the hotel: feet a bit sore, blisters healed, body fit, mind crap. More complaints about the hotel. Nothing bloody right. Still, they may as well continue to the end. Oh get real, people.

Friday July 7th 2006. Monmouth to Sedbury Cliffs (Buttington Tump) - 19 miles (2,870 feet of ascent).

How do I describe this last day. A vague sense of achievement, as a part of my plan had been ticked off. It was to be the last day of hassle. I had never in my life wanted a walk to finish, but this was the exception.

Breakfast good, we slowly dawdled out of Monmouth and set off towards the Forest of Dean. We had a steep climb out of Monmouth to the Kymin, site of a pair of buildings built by the 'Gentlemen of Kymin Club'. The roundhouse was built in 1794 and contained a kitchen and banquet room in which weekly meetings were held.

At Redbrook we joined the Wye again and then climbed above the valley at Highbury Farm where we met Offa's Dyke once more. From here the path passed through lovely woodland. It was warmish again and so welcomed, although you had to keep an eye on your feet with roots along the path ready to trip you up. We descended to the river once more at Bigsweir. This is the highest tidal point of the Wye.

From here we strolled along the river to Brockweir, and then climbed again to stay high above the river overlooking Tintern village and the ruins of Tintern Abbey, built in 1131. It was quite difficult to see the ruins with all the foliage on the trees. There was only one real vantage point from Devil's Pulpit, named following a local legend of the Devil's attempt to corrupt the monks down below. We continued on this delightful path until finally we came out along the top of limestone cliffs at Wintour's Leap, with the river 200 feet below. From here, Chepstow is easily seen. Then we walked past the old cast iron bridge over the A48 and on towards Sedbury Cliffs.

We made our way past some houses and the last remaining fields, which took us to Sedbury Cliffs. I felt relieved as we arrived at our final destination. I had no feelings of exhilaration or real sense of achievement. On the last stretch my minimalist friend had turned to me and said, "Thank you for being the only genuine person on the trip to make it bearable." I just said, "It's me being me. It's okay." I suggested she got the dog she had discussed. "Do you think so?" she asked earnestly. I said, "Perhaps it will be company for you and it will certainly enjoy the walks you give it." She grabbed my arm and thanked me for being human, then wandered off.

I watched her go, this lonely figure, and then continued to the end with the others. She took herself down to the beach, but I declined her pleading eyes to join her. I had had enough. I took photos of the group and shared in their achievement but it wasn't mine. The jibes at our unhappy walker going off to the beach soured the occasion. It just summed up the holiday. If perchance you're reading this my friend, I can only say to you that you were the strongest walker of us all and I hope you are still travelling and that life has been kinder to you.

We got into taxis at Buttington Tump. My friend would only go in the same taxi as me. We arrived at Castle View Hotel in Bridge Street before the others. She was agitated as she was given her room key. Our leader followed shortly. One of the others went upstairs and came swiftly down saying the lady was crying, ranting and raving. She had already been abrupt to the receptionist and had mentioned that she wasn't going to stay. I asked the leader if I should go and speak to her but he said he would sort it. He came down in a while and explained that she was leaving right away.

By this time the others had arrived and we were all congregated in the reception area. A lonely figure came down the stairs, looking washed out. As she made her way to the door I said, "Come on, I don't mind sharing a room with you." "No Carol, thank you for your offer but I cannot stay another night with such a hypocritical group of people. They have enjoyed their holiday at my expense and it would be hypocritical of them and me to share their success." With that, she stormed out. She was right of course. The reaction of the others was one of selfish arrogance. It didn't seem to occur to them they had caused her such misery.

The walker who had had to endure sharing a room with this sorry woman said her pathetic last words on the subject. "That is fine, now I have a bedroom to myself." Yep, that truly summed up the holiday.

The group exchanged email addresses. I gave mine out but I certainly wasn't going to be emailing anyone. However, the evening was quite enjoyable. A Guinness was bought for me. I had arranged a collection and we gave our leader another bottle of wine. He didn't really need any more wine but what do you give someone you don't know?

Later I rang David. In the quiet of my bedroom I was able to relay the disastrous holiday. That night I slept well.

Saturday July 8th 2006. Travel home day.

After breakfast I left the hotel at 8.30am and the train departed Chepstow at 9.10am. All went without incident; a very cheap ride home. One of the gentlemen and a lady from the group took the rail journey with me, as they were going on further travels. I arrived in Southampton at 2.30pm. I cried and cried and held on to David in the station. I was so glad to be home.

Although this holiday was a disaster, the walk itself was excellent. I will do it again one day by myself and relish every moment. Even the stiles. I have just put this stage down to 'life and death' and the way I reacted to it at the time.

CHAPTER NINE:
THE WHITE WATER WALK

BETWEEN MOLD AND LLANGOLLEN (MAP REFERENCE OS 256GRID
REF 235495) TO BIRKENHEAD FERRY PIER VIA WREXHAM AND
CHESTER. DISTANCE: 39.7MILES. DATELINE: MAY 8TH-10TH 2009.

Four reasons made this part of my walk special.

1. For my 50th birthday the children had given me a voucher to go white water rafting at the National White Water Centre, Canolfan Tryweryn near Bala. I was going to fit this in as part of the walk. I couldn't wait.

2. David was coming with me and it was hoped he would walk from Birkenhead to Chester with me. If he felt well enough.

3. I was to meet with Janine, a friend since my Police College days in Wrexham. I hadn't seen her for 15 years although we had been in correspondence frequently. To see her again was going to be such a treat.

4. It was just 37-ish miles of walking and would allow the crossing of the Mersey to be my stepping-stone northwards through Liverpool. Another cheat perhaps but I had always

fancied taking the 'ferry across the Mersey'. This is the romantic in me and shows my age.

We used the little Mazda for this trip. What an effort jamming, cramming and juggling everything that needed to go. Packing is an art form in a sports car. We had to take enough clothes for two days, my wetsuit, socks and gloves, wet weather gear for David and me, three days of snacking items, and my walking rucksack with spare water bottles for David.

I was so excited about this leg of my journey. I am not sure which bit was making me most excited. I just knew it would be great if all our plans came together.

Friday May 8th 2009. Between Mold and Llangollen (grid ref 235495) to Eccleston via Wrexham – 18.5 miles.

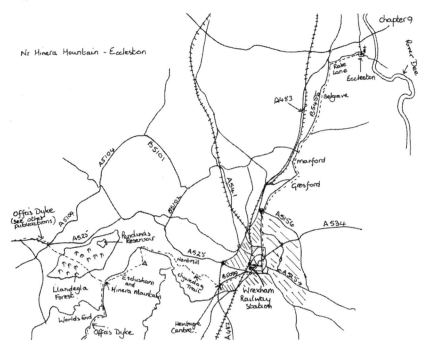

We set off at 5am to ensure I was at the start of my walk for approximately 10am. The weather was overcast but a good temperature for walking, although rain threatened. Leaving David behind at the start point, the plan was for me to be in Wrexham by lunchtime to meet up with Janine for a couple of hours and then walk on to Chester.

Amazingly I started walking at 10.10am. We stopped the car exactly where two years previously I had walked with the Offa's Dyke group. A stone marked at the verge confirmed I was starting at the correct place. I waved goodbye to David, looked at Gertrude and said, "It's just thee and me," and headed off along the road in a north-easterly direction. I then took the path over Minera Mountain before dropping down into New Brighton.

Oh it was so good to be on a path again. The damp sweet smell of heather mixed with moorland grasses was welcoming me home again. But it was cold. I had hat and gloves on and walked briskly. The views of Wrexham and the Minera Valley were clear. There was a lot of debris on the mountain, the remnants of intensive lead mining in the area. I couldn't hear a thing. It was so peaceful.

At New Brighton I picked a lovely path called Clywedog Trail. It followed the River Nant for two miles. This was great – I hadn't expected to find such a pleasant path. Nant Mill Wood and valley is so pretty. The river tumbles over limestone rocks under dark fauna, creating little grottos. It felt like something out of Robin Hood television programmes.

Clinging to the sides of these rocks were enormous oaks and beeches. It really was very secluded. As I progressed, I was treated to a marvellous display of bluebells and wild garlic carpeting the ground. I sat on one of the rocks and savoured the moment.

The wood continued with huge cedar pines towering above me. It was a cocktail of sensual delight. I would recommend this little walk to anyone. Children especially would love it.

The path ended at Caeua Bridge by the beautiful church of Bersham in all its redstone glory. As I passed under the A483, I saw the old ironworks had been turned into a heritage site. Unwittingly I had chosen the best possible route into Wrexham for a walker. Well done this blonde.

The B road was quiet and I was only two miles from Wrexham railway station. I rang my friend. Her reaction: "Bloody hell woman, that was quick! I'm not dressed yet." There were a lot of other words but I can't repeat them!

The fields soon passed and I walked into civilisation. It was easy to find the station. David was already there and I couldn't stop grinning. I had a drink, ate some sarnies, tidied up a bit and waited for Janine.

We heard her before we saw her. As her car swept into the car park with horn blowing, she was shouting like a washerwoman, laughing her head off, pointing a finger at me and calling out, "Look at you!" She parked slap bang next to us. We could barely get out of the cars in excitement. We just hugged each other for ages and then started crying. It was so good to see her again. Nothing had changed: a wonderful warm, hard-headed woman. Janine grabbed David and practically crushed him. She was all dressed up and I probably smelt high. It didn't seem to matter.

She was meeting a friend later so we literally only had about two hours to catch up. We went into a local supermarket café and had a very long chat. David was surplus to requirements at this stage; you know what we women are like when we get chatting.

When we said our goodbyes it was rather sad. I promised to make a longer trip up next time but neither of us committed ourselves, as we both realised our lives are very busy. Janine and I will always be there for each other, and for friends that is all that matters.

Shrugging off that 'moment', I set about the task of walking out of Wrexham. It was now 2.30pm and I had nine miles to go to get to Eccleston. Getting out of Wrexham was problematic though. It took me some time to get onto the right road out of town. Asking was no help. I never quite believe how locals aren't able to give clear instructions.

The remainder of the afternoon was a matter of slogging it along various roads. Up there, the roads are not as busy as here in the south. My feet were warm. I had given myself three hours to do this part and I needed it. I was knackered when I finally crawled into Eccleston. Originally my plan had been to walk to Chester, but the next three miles would have to wait.

Eccleston is one of those villages I wouldn't have known

about and made me glad I encountered it on my walk. If you are ever up in the Chester area do go there. The village and the land surrounding it are owned by the Duke of Westminster. The church was built by the then 1st Duke in 1899. It's an impressive red sandstone ashlar building designed by Bodley and has features similar to Liverpool Cathedral. It cost £40,000 to build, equating to £3.34 million at today's prices! There's a fine pair of 18th century gates that lead into the churchyard through an avenue of lime trees. It is stunning and pristine.

The school and schoolmaster's house was also designed by Douglas for the Duke and built in 1878. It has a Gothic appearance with its octagonal turret, belfry and steeple, and is constructed of red sandstone with a red tiled roof. It is so pretty and is still used as a primary school today. All the houses and cottages in the village can only be described as quaint. Most of them have wonderful twisted Victorian chimneys and delightful red tiled roofs, with tiny lead latticed windows.

In the centre of the village is a pump. The roof of the old village shop slopes completely to the ground and there's a veranda with grass sweeping down to the roadside wall. I noticed a plaque stating that Eccleston had won 'village of the year' awards. Many of the properties are Grade 2 listed buildings.

David picked me up and we made our way to our B&B for the next two nights at Rhydydefaid Farm in Frongoch, about a mile from the White Water Centre. We had used this accommodation before; the owners had been very welcoming that time when we took Katy there to experience the water.

They are geared up to organising breakfast at the right time.

We arrived there about 7pm. It had been a long day. We were welcomed again with a cup of tea and cake. The lady was very pleased to see us again. She showed us to our room, and we were in the back this time. It was very comfortable. We had a shower and then went back into Bala for ham, egg and chips. It was good to back in Wales. So far the plan had come to fruition.

Saturday May 9th 2009. White Water Day plus Chester to Eccleston – 3.2 miles.

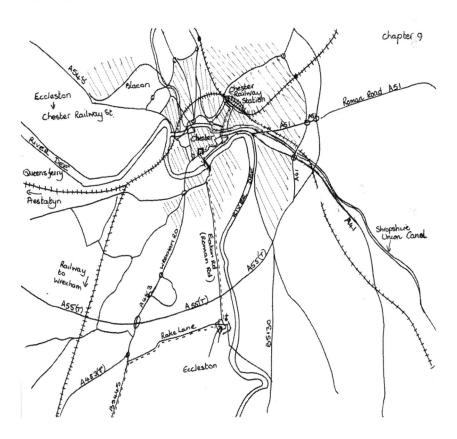

David was unwell in the night, with a bad headache: too much travelling. Breakfast was very leisurely at 9am. Very civilised. Everything was beautifully cooked and I managed the full works. I was nervously excited about the next adventure. I didn't want to damage myself for the Cape Wrath Trail later in the year, but I knew I was going to love this.

There were some bikers at the breakfast table so of course we got chatting about their BMWs. Beautiful bikes – ideal for touring the Welsh roads.

The weather was dry, but windy and chilly. Did we expect anything else? Not really.

All I can say about the next two hours is thank you children for giving me one of the most exhilarating adventures I have ever had. It was the best. It was great to be on the water. All my fears just disappear as soon as I am in the challenge, so to speak. I threw myself into the fun and excitement, making sure I got one of the best positions on the raft to get the biggest dunking and thrills. We lost two people after the second run. One had gone overboard which put another off, so it wasn't easy. Our instructor was terrific, making sure we had a chance to ride the waves and waterfalls, paddling like fury. The stoppers on the water are the worst because the raft hangs there for a brief second and then does what it likes. By the time we had finished I was freezing. The centre had provided wetsuits and lifejackets but I was so drenched all the time I couldn't feel my hands. I would just love to go and repeat this exercise again. Brill. The memory makes me grin every time.

After this adventure we had a spot of lunch and made our

way to Chester railway station. I planned to walk from here back to Eccleston, as the next day would mean catching a train to Birkenhead Ferry and then walking back to Chester. It meant today we could get train times and work out where we could park the car for the day.

We arrived in Chester at 3pm. Parked at the station, fantastic. We looked at the timetable for the morning and had another drink. Then I set off for Eccleston on foot at 4pm. It was now sunny and it was easy walking out of Chester. I went down to the River Dee, past the park where families were playing football, having picnics and enjoying clarinettists in the bandstand. I walked over a beautiful iron bridge and took pictures of the weir there, then came onto the old Roman road (now called Eaton Road) leading out of Chester directly to Eccleston.

Looking behind me, I could see the Roman entrance to Chester, now a tower of sandstone. I felt almost reverent of the route I had chosen, which was by chance. Within five minutes I was in open countryside. The silence enveloped me as I meandered along happily with the Dee to my left a few fields away. I arrived in Eccleston bright and perky.

This time we had a good look round the village and took photographs. A lady was mowing her grass. She had lived in the village all her life. Driving back to Bala, we put the roof down. It was lovely. The route was less winding than the day before and the last sun on the mountains and the Clwydian Hills was breathtaking. We then had an enormous tea at our favourite café.

I was sick in the evening. My fault: I had over eaten. It had been a great day, and our room was a delight to collapse into. David had done so well to keep up and pick me up at the various places. He had enjoyed watching the rafting, and in another era he would have joined me.

We had achieved everything and our plan was still on schedule. But for David to manage the walk on Sunday, it all depended on his ability to sleep that night. We booked a 7.45pm breakfast, which bless her our host duly supplied. It is supposed to be later on Sundays.

Sunday May 10th 2009. Birkenhead Ferry to Chester Railway Station - 18 miles.

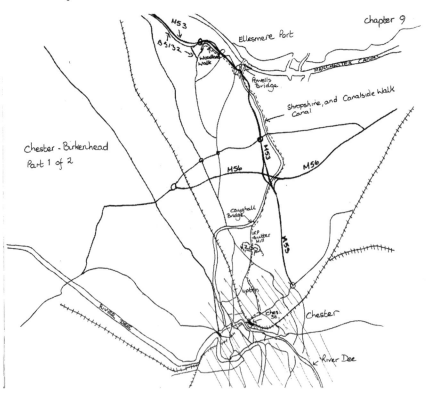

Breakfast was right on time. The bikers were up and we chatted to them. It was a lads' weekend away. They had been in the Orca rides yesterday on the water, spending most of the time in the water! They were off to do the 'high ropes' at the centre. We spoke about bikes again and then we were off.

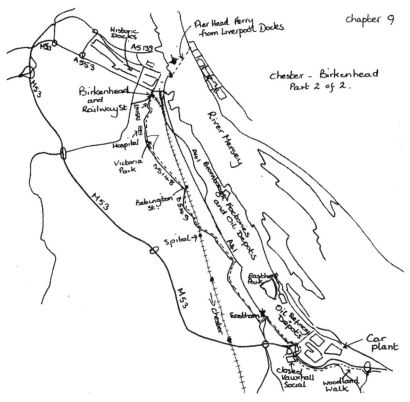

We made good time to Chester, arriving at 9.50am which meant we managed to catch the 10am train to Birkenhead. We left the train at 10.30am and began the slow walk back to Chester. We didn't stop to look at the Mersey too much because of the time it would take to get back.

I was very aware that the walking pace had to drop to two and a half miles an hour for David to manage this walk or he would not make it. I was so pleased to have his company and for the day it was easy to forget he was ill.

Birkenhead I would describe as a 'once was place'. Many back-to-back streets, old yards and tattered signs showed it had once been a prosperous area of industry. Much of the town was a mixture of 1950s council housing and Victorian homes. Grant Hospital was a good indication of the modern versus the old. In amongst the dilapidation there were pockets of pleasantness, Tranmere School Park and Victoria Park being havens amongst streets upon streets of derelict shops, graffitied walls and people doing nothing. The only shops faring well seemed to be off licences, tattoo parlours, betting shops and small newsagents. We saw no large supermarkets or greengrocers. Maybe we just weren't in the right area.

It all seemed very poor with a mixed race culture. It wasn't until we reached Bebington that we had a glimpse of what once had been, when we finally came onto a quiet minor road and followed a copse that hid a housing estate behind. The walk then became more wholesome (I do sound rather snobbish, I apologise). An avenue of trees lining the route and playing fields on both sides of the road led us through Eastham.

We took the minor road here. The original village was very pretty. It had retained the country tranquillity and as we headed along Rivacre Road we could sense how the Wirral had once been a very rural area until Ellesmere Port and Birkenhead had industrialised it. At one point we were walking parallel to the M53, which hides the extensive motor vehicle factories and Vauxhall works, sadly much of it redundant now. Interestingly, we passed by the Vauxhall Social Club House, Hotel and Conference Centre with its golf course, all up for sale!

Rivacre Wood was a brief interlude. A pretty wood with bluebells and garlic and bees. A lady was sitting on one of the many benches admiring the bluebells. She was quite a large lady, and as we passed her we asked which path to take for the minor road that we wanted. She explained that she and her husband used to come here and sit. He had died of diabetes complications and he would have understood why she walked the woods daily. We thanked her for her local knowledge, which actually saved us from coming up against the barriers of the motorway. My map had not been updated with this latest change to the woodland route.

We finally joined the Shropshire Union Canal at its basin, where it joins the Manchester Ship Canal. There is a museum there, a desperate attempt to invite visitors into a failing area, but it would be worth a visit. There were canal boats moored. What struck us were the rows and rows of empty warehouses.

From here it was good to put the map away and just wander along. We still had a long way to go and it was 2pm. We were halfway but David was slowing down. So we had a break and ate our sandwiches. I hoped it would give David the energy burst he needed for the next stage. The canal was dirty with plenty of flotsam – polystyrene blocks, bikes, even a burnt surfboard at this end – but as we moved away from the port it became far more rural and very pretty. Fishermen lined the banks. The day was very warm, and I am glad I had brought the two litre water bladder and two 500 ml bottles.

We bumbled along taking it steady and enjoying each other's company. We even held hands. For a moment it was all very romantic. By now it was 3.30pm. As we went under one of the numerous bridges, a signpost indicated it was 7.5 miles to go to Chester along the canal. I got the map out. My concern for David was paramount in my mind, as he had now developed a blister. After administering first aid, I chose a route which took us off the canal. This would cut two miles off our journey.

At 5pm we left the canal at Caughall Bridge onto a cycle path that led into the suburbs of Chester via Chester Zoo. We ended up walking on a track that had the zoo on both sides. We went past the back of the elephant house and on the other side we could just make out lynx. And all for free. It was a great track. The blonde had done well. It spurred David on as we came into Chester through lovely tree-lined areas. We crawled into Chester railway station at 6.30pm. What a journey. It was still so warm this evening.

We were going to stay at a Chester backpacking hostel but that turned out to be a disaster. I had already paid for it, so we just used the room to freshen up, got some supplies and then left to drive south through the evening, finally getting home at 1am on Monday morning.

The weekend had been a great success. I can only thank my husband's stoical effort. I was very proud of him. I was also very grateful for his time and graciousness. Only those who really know him would truly understand how difficult that walk had been and how many painkillers he had taken to achieve it!

For me, the white water rafting was the icing on the cake. Janine was the jam tart!

CHAPTER TEN:
A SLIGHT DETOUR IN MY PLANS

**VARIOUS REMAINING TRACTS IN SCOTLAND & ENGLAND.
DISTANCE: 0 MILES! DATELINE: LATE AUGUST 2010.**

Sunday August 22nd 2010. Preparation.

We were nearly packed ready for the last remaining miles to be traversed in this long journey of mine. My feelings were varied. The journey from Land's End to John O'Groats was almost at an end. I couldn't or didn't wish to contemplate what was next after this challenge.

If I thought for too long, it filled me with melancholy and irritation that the achievement would be consumed and forgotten, that I wouldn't recall or retrieve the experience again or do anything quite so grandiose to put claim to. On the other hand, my excitement could not be suppressed or contained. Yesterday in a flurry of activity the camper was loaded. My faithful boots winked on the doorstep, begging me to pop them in the van. Romantic or pathetic, you decide. I chose the two blue pairs and placed them together. I wondered which pair would take the final honour of walking the final steps with me. Daft aren't I, the old sentimental fool.

The rucksacks were given the same gentle treatment. Placing them in the van, I noted that they too had travelled all those places across the country and had never let me down.

Today I was restless with anticipation. I baked cakes to take with us, and phoned friends whom we would meet. I had prepared myself physically and would walk on Monday across the forest to give my muscles a final stretch.

Even then, I had reservations about 'what if?' We were dependent on our vehicle – the Pash Wagon. Since our previous trip to Scotland (see final chapter twenty) the story and notoriety of the 'wagon' had become a standing joke; something out of which black comedies are made. On reflection, the seriousness of our demise if it had let us down in April cannot be emphasised enough. The beast had caused us problems since on four or more occasions, having been towed twice off the motorway and escorted by police. (That is another story.) All you need to know is that she had had her head skimmed, as well as a new head gasket, new steering rack, new thermostat, new radiator, reconditioned injectors and some welding underneath – not forgetting some attention to the rust on her bodywork. Plus for comfort we had new channel runners for the windows, to ensure we were draught free and water wouldn't seep in.

I knew if she failed this time I would be gutted. But optimism prevailed and David gave me his assurance all would be okay. What's that? Oh no, we now needed a new clutch cable. David went on eBay as I wrote these notes. The only remaining items required were the fridge contents, along with our passports!

So here was the plan. Leave Wednesday, travel to Glasgow or further then go on to Torridon and walk back to Strathcarron and the small piece near Ratagan. Travel back to Fort William. Walk from Fort William to Mallaig. Travel back to Glasgow and walk to Milngavie with Mandy. Return to Liverpool and finally finish by crossing the Mersey to Birkenhead and back. Then walk through Liverpool to Knotty Ash. 80 miles in total. Bring it on.

Wednesday August 25th 2010. Let's go...

The day arrived, my pillows were packed. Work would be a doddle this morning. I had my bag full of clothes to change into.

Thursday August 26th 2010. Well... !

Guess what? Back at work today, it was not meant to be. I can laugh now, that bloody van. I could have happily taken it the nearest cliff and pushed it over. We had reached the A34 Winnall Roundabout this time before we broke down. It was pouring with rain. We managed to limp home via Winchester and Romsey. Well, perhaps I deserved it. After all, you do something for your own pleasure and eventually you pay. Perhaps I was not meant to finish this walk. Anyway, at least I hadn't lost too much holiday. Work very kindly took me back. What a waif and stray I am.

Not to be too downhearted, a plan was already forming... Cinderella, you *shall* go to the ball. I *shall* book a B&B for at least the Liverpool bit and worry about the other bits later. Such was my determination to finish the whole walk in 2010.

CHAPTER ELEVEN:
A ROMANTIC WEEKEND FOR TWO

CHILDWALL (LIVERPOOL LOOP LINE) TO LIVERPOOL (MERSEY FERRY).
DISTANCE: 9 MILES. DATELINE: SEPTEMBER 3RD-5TH 2010.

I could not book any accommodation over the August Bank Holiday weekend 2010. Instead, I managed to secure two nights at the Somersby Guest House in Childwall the following week.

It was excellently placed for the one and a half miles back to the Liverpool Loop Line then a return trip of seven and a half miles back into Liverpool city centre. It is strange looking back now how nervous I had been booking anything over the internet, because by now it had become second nature to do all my holiday booking online. My confidence in just getting on with it had grown.

Friday September 3rd 2010. Off to Liverpool.

I worked all day. Bit of a back problem, my kidney region hurting. David picked me up from work at 5.30pm. We travelled well until eight miles from Oxford. Because of heavy traffic, we did not pass Oxford until 8.30pm! "Travel teaches toleration," so said Benjamin Disraeli. Then we had a brilliant run.

We arrived at the guest house at 10.10pm. No breaks, very tired. A very warm reception, a chap called Dave putting us at ease. The house was in the leafy suburbs of Liverpool. It was very comfortable. We had a shared bathroom and toilet which wasn't a problem. Our room was adequate and more importantly had a comfy bed. Downstairs there was a guest kitchen and lounge, which enabled people to cook their own meals. We crashed out at 11.30pm.

Saturday September 4th 2010.

The day had dawned bright and fresh. There was a clear autumnal bite in the air, a promise of winter. The sun was glorious. It was 7am and I was excited to be up and on our way. I had a lovely bath to freshen up. It had been a long day yesterday and my back was still sore. David had fallen back to sleep again. No surprise, it had been a long drive. His usual headache woke him early and the need to sleep again after his drug fix was essential to ensure his wellbeing for the day.

Breakfast was ample and at the reasonable hour of 9am. David was feeling better, but packed plenty of painkillers for the day.

We set off at 9.45am, having spoken to a carpet fitter next door to get bearings on which little road I was on according to my map. We were soon into our stride. We passed Liverpool Hope University. It was a simple walk back to the Liverpool

Loop Line. Standing on the old railway line once again was a wonderful reminder of the previous walk (see next chapter).

We stopped briefly then made our return back towards Liverpool, joining up with the cycle route of the Trans Pennine Trail, which makes its way into Liverpool docks (Pier Head). It was at Childwall Church that we saw the prettiest vicar ever. People were gathering for a wedding. The groom was there with his best man, guests and photographers, all standing outside the church and in amongst them was the vicar. Well, she was gorgeous. She had a stunning black dress on and legs up to her thighs. Long hair, high heeled shoes. Beautiful figure and wearing her dog collar just accentuated her neck and fine boned face. I had to look twice to make sure I was looking at a vicar. Yes she *was* one, she was carrying the Bible in her hand and greeting everyone and making everyone welcome to her church.

We skirted Calderstones Park with its botanical gardens, and then went through Sefton Park. The weather was very warm as we enjoyed an ice cream in the park. It was all very leisurely. There were so many people out by this time. Many families were enjoying the river and lakes. Sadly, once out of the park and walking through the streets of Toxteth, we saw how run down the area was. Many small shops and businesses had closed. It was very scruffy and intimidating. However, my wee break for the morning was at Elim Pentecostal Church. There were volunteer gardeners and cleaners tending the church and they let me borrow their toilet. Oh bliss!

It took us until 12.50am to reach Pier Head. The ferry

across the Mersey would be going again at 2pm, just enough time to have lunch and buy tickets. The lady at the ticket office explained what we could do. Having told her my story, she gave us concessionary tickets costing £5 between us for a round trip of an hour, or a later return. This was a very grand gesture. It meant we could get off at Birkenhead if we wanted, or come back straightaway.

The ferry ride was very breezy. We finally found a place to sit at the bow of 'The Royal Daffodil' and near one of its address systems. If you haven't had the pleasure of this trip I urge you to go. As passengers, we were given a brief 800-year account of the Mersey's history and the ferries that have operated during that time between the Liverpool and Wirral Docklands. Although the narration was a bit contrived and romanticised and the tune 'Ferry Across The Mersey' overcooked, for me it nevertheless added another interesting experience. Furthermore, the diversity of the passengers in culture, creed, social class and size was illuminating. I found it highly entertaining and a pleasing demonstration of British citizenship.

As we boarded the ferry, I had been struck by the Liverpool people themselves. There was a large family tucking into beefburgers and chips, all chatting away as large as life itself. I could only admire the women, their vibrancy. Clearly a day out on the ferry is something to dress up for.

The women had on bright red lipstick, their eyes glossy with mascara and shadow, and wore tight fitting clothes exposing all the bulges! Nails were in all colours, faces rouged, their hair bleach blonde, gothic black or copper bordering on ginger. Some were in matching outfits, some not! Shoes were of the type requiring ladies to get help keeping their balance going down the slipway. So much effort had been put into their femininity, but it didn't quite match their language. In between mouthfuls of beefburgers, they were laughing and joking and generally taking the piss out of everyone, including themselves. Their husbands or partners were equally loud but they had respect for their women. What's more, they couldn't have cared a hoot about anyone else. They appeared unburdened. It was rather refreshing, this 'take me as I am' attitude of pride that came from them. There was a passion about their city and life in general, with a true sense of belonging. I think this sums up Liverpool.

I sat watching an elderly couple who were 'out for the day'. Sheltered from the wind, they were immaculate. She was dressed in well-pressed cream trousers and matching lightweight jacket and cardigan. He looked cared for, his trousers ironed with military precision. Shiny brown leather shoes, his warm sweater, shirt and tie covered by a loose, clean matching jacket. They barely spoke but sat in companionable silence sharing a flask of hot drink. They were a tiny couple with hard, determined, weathered faces, watching the world go by with knowing eyes.

Families of cyclists, university students, people going to work and many foreign people of all nationalities were aboard. There was a lot of excited chatter as the ferry got closer to Woodside, Birkenhead. People were deciding where they were going, how long they would be, which ferry they would get back on. We stood on the edge of the dock where I had been on the earlier part of the walk. It was great to join it all up. This was what I had set out to do. Another cheat I know, but this is my personal route from Land's End to John O'Groats. Alternatively, for those who wish, there is a route from Wrexham following the Cheshire Ring Canal path into Runcorn, then onto the Trans Pennine cycle/footpath into Liverpool, adding another 20-30 miles to your journey.

The ferry rides all too quickly came to an end. Returning to land once more, it was now 4pm as we made our way to the bus station. Fantastic service, all automated timetables with the screens telling passengers what bus would be arriving next and at which bay number. The 86C at a cost of £3.60 for both of us took us back to Liverpool Hope University, five minutes from our accommodation. David was very pleased, he was so tired. We had a lovely cup of tea and relaxed, had showers and then returned to The Brickwall Inn we had visited in 2009 (see next chapter). Sadly, it was now boarded up with weeds growing in the car park. So instead we went to the Falstaff pub in Childwall. Lovely grub – £11.85 for both of us, including half a pint of beer. Not bad.

Sunday September 5th 2010.

I slept like a log. David was very tired; we would have to take it steady today. We had a leisurely breakfast. I would certainly come here again. Dave, our host, was very easy to get on with.

The plan was to do more sightseeing in Liverpool all day and then return home in the evening. So we parked near the docks and put four hours on the meter. We could always return. We decided to take a bus tour of Liverpool. This would give us a brief overview as we hadn't much time. The bus stopped at the main attractions – Albert Docks, Pier Head, The Liver Building, Liverpool shopping centre, Cavern quarters, museums and galleries, two cathedrals, the Chinese Arch, Cains Brewery, Rodney Street and Hope Street. It was a whistle-stop tour but we must to go back sometime and enjoy the culture properly.

It was such lovely weather and we spent a great deal of time wandering the streets around the docks and visiting the Albert Dock Museum. Well worth a visit. Exhibitions ranged from Customs and Excise dating from 1500 to the present, the Titanic, Lusitania and Forgotten Empress exhibition (Titanic was registered in Liverpool but never touched its shores), Shackleton's Antarctic Adventures and a feature on International Slavery from early 1500 to Apartheid to present-day slavery. All very informative and tastefully laid out. It was child-friendly. Sadly we didn't get to the Beatles exhibition next door; that's for another time.

We left Liverpool at 2.30pm. David had had enough but we had managed it together. It had been lovely to share his companionship in a remarkable city. We arrived home at 7pm.

Waking up on Monday September 6th, our next plan was to get up to Scotland. First, the van needed to be fixed. David was under it as I wrote these words in my diary.

CHAPTER TWELVE:
NORTHWARDS HERE I COME

LIVERPOOL TO ULVERSTON. DISTANCE: 111.5 MILES. DATELINE: SEPTEMBER 26TH-OCTOBER 1ST 2009.

From this segment of the walk onwards, I can state most emphatically that all the walks gave me immense pleasure. This particular leg offered me the chance to walk on my own again (David would share the experience albeit on back up duty) and I'd be exploring a region of the country I would definitely not have gone to normally. This was an opportunity to find the confident old me again. I loved the peace of my own company, the camper van working, and David supporting me.

Friday September 25th 2009. Heading off.

We left my workplace at 5.30pm in beautiful sunshine and by 6pm we were heading towards Newbury. We had a really good run and came to the outskirts of Liverpool by 10.30pm. Leaving the M62, we headed for a small village called Tarbock Green. Of course it was dark and finding somewhere to stop and pull over for the night was difficult. However, in the village the landlord of a pub called The Brickwall Inn allowed us to park for free in his spacious car park. We patronised his pub by getting in a half of bitter and sat by the log fire and enjoyed the rest. Outside, the glow from Liverpool's streetlights could easily be seen. Back in the wagon, we slept soundly until 7am.

Saturday September 26th 2009. Liverpool (Childwall) to Ainsdale-on-Sea beach - 23.5 miles.

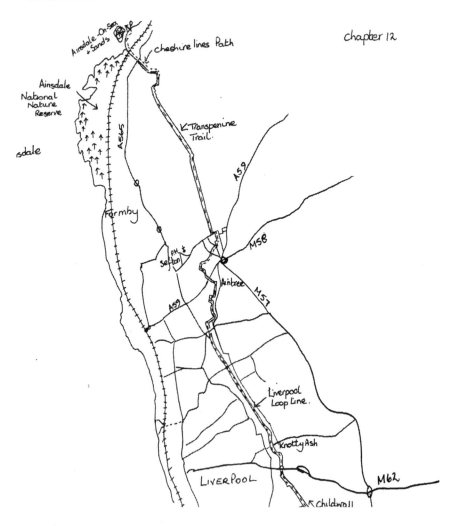

The landlord's wife offered us some breakfast. We declined, but it was a very friendly gesture. We tried to give them some money for staying in their car park for the night but they declined. An extremely pleasant couple, so it was sad to see the pub boarded up when we came back the following year (see chapter eleven).

It had not been planned but to my amazement, the little village was only five to six miles away from the start of my walk at Childwall, where I would commence my walk along the Liverpool Loop Line (part of the disused railway line that once served the city). This meant we followed very quiet lanes into the back of Liverpool and didn't meet any people or traffic.

At 8.39am exactly, I started walking along the wide but darkish railway line. Although it was a great path, the tree lined embankment made me feel a bit enclosed and vulnerable. It was extremely quiet and only occasionally did a cyclist come by or the odd keen jogger. I met one shopper and four dog walkers. Clearly, after a Friday night Liverpool wakes up slowly.

Shrugging off any anxiousness, I started to admire this trail. Here I was walking through Liverpool with the streets above me. The only noise I heard from the conurbation above was the occasional siren and youngsters enjoying football training sessions. I saw signs for Knotty Ash and started singing: *We are the diddy men, diddy, diddy, diddy men.* I would recommend it to anyone; it's a happy marching tune.

I passed cycle route signs to Tuebrook, West Derby, Norris Green, Clubmoor, Walton, Bootle and finally Aintree. The worst part of the railway line was walking through a long tunnel that had a curve in it, meaning it was black for a few moments. At this point, I did scuttle through pretty damn quick and just before coming out of the darkness I saw a man walking in. I think he was a bit bemused by this woman with her rucksack bumping up and down and boobs flopping about, but I wasn't stopping.

I soon settled down again. Compared to my first walks, I was far less nervous and enjoyed reaching the small milestone of Aintree Racecourse. I stood for some time savouring this moment. The walk had brought me unwittingly to somewhere I would never have gone. To stand outside the home of the Grand National was thought provoking, with its brick frontage built in the shape of a superior stable block embellished with horses and their riders. It brought back memories of my grandfather studying the form of the horses, and watching the races on the television on a Saturday afternoon to see if his predictions were correct. I have never enjoyed horse racing but the Grand National had been the only race the people at work used to have a flutter on, or indeed my grandfather ever placed a bet on.

From Aintree I then picked up the Cheshire Lines Path, which eventually became the Trans Pennine Trail again. This was an enjoyable mile of walking the banks of the Leeds and Liverpool Canal. At first it felt eerie but I soon enjoyed the company of moorhens, Canadian geese, ducks and a single heron stood on the bank watching the river carefully. At Netherton, I left my original planned trail briefly for a well deserved lunch break with David at The Punchbowl, a delightful pub in a village called Sefton. This tiny hamlet dates back to the Middle Ages. The village is built on the flood plain of the River Alt, and to get to it my detour took me across a few meadows with ditches similar to Somerset but not on such a grand scale.

After sustenance, wonderful toilets, a leisurely coffee and a brief look in the delightful 12th century church, I was ready to walk again. The time was 12.15pm and I was probably just under halfway in my day's walk. I left David to find a campsite for the night and we arranged to meet near Ainsdale.

Alone again, I picked up the Cheshire Lines Path near Maghull. Basically, I turned left in a westerly direction along the five-mile disused railway line now converted into a multi-use route for cyclists, walkers and horse riders, and part of the much larger route of the Trans Pennine Trail.

The railway line originally belonged to the Cheshire Lines Railway Company that operated its services across the Lancashire mosslands between Liverpool and Southport, and which closed in 1952. Here I was treated to a wonderful cooling breeze coming from the coast. The air temperature was ideal for walking. My path stretched before me, rising above the open plains. I could see for miles but my objective was such a small dot on the horizon. I settled into an easy pace with only the occasional cyclist passing.

I had time to think here. I had no reason to watch my feet constantly and again that enjoyment coming from solitude was cleansing. I felt fit and happy. Fields and small farms stretched either side of the railway line. The flood plains, a patchwork of ditches and dykes, were very arable and fertile.

I congratulated myself on finding a pleasing pathway through Liverpool and its outskirts. As a walker though, you can have enough of a straight line, so it was with pleasure that I finally came to the end of the railway line, with a signpost saying 'Liverpool 20' and 'Southport 7'. Gosh, had I walked 20 miles already? It certainly felt like it. My feet were beginning to get warm.

The best path of the day came at this point – Sixpenny Lane, a narrow lane between farmers' fields and a small copse. It was soft underfoot, a welcomed break for my hips. I savoured the last peace and quiet before passing a golf course and riding stables and into civilisation again. In all, on this stretch I only met six people. The noise of the traffic as I walked on the road towards Ainsdale-on-Sea was a shock. However, the enormity of the beaches and the dune systems here (Ainsdale Hills) had me awestruck. I can only thank this walk for bringing me somewhere I had not expected to find so interesting.

I chastised myself at this point for not knowing enough about my country. I had just walked into one of the largest sand dune systems in Britain, making up part of the Sefton coastline which is approximately 12 miles in length. The National Nature Reserve at Ainsdale is a 508 hectare site comprising one of the most extensive and developed dune systems and woodland habitats in the UK. Large sections of this area have become designated sites of special interest and have been declared an EU Special Protection Area of Conservation. The reserve has a vast diversity of rare and special species like the Natterjack toad, great crested newt and red squirrels. Its wildflowers include the dune helleborine, seaside centaury and yellow bartsia.

It was now 3pm. I had done well but my legs were tired. As I walked along the road (part of the Sefton Coastal Footpath) with the dunes to my left, I couldn't see the sea at this point. It wasn't until I actually got to Ainsdale-on-Sea – with its railway cottages (now a hotel/pub), Butlin's Holiday Camp, boating lake and parking area – that I fully appreciated the enormity of the beach. The sand looking seawards went on forever. The sea was so far away on the horizon that I was unsure where sea and sand met. The tide was so low that the oil fields were in touching distance. Of course they weren't, but such was the perspective that gave the illusion.

I found David and we parked the Pash Wagon on the beach. This natural car park was incredible. We drove along the sands to it. I had never done anything like it before. Our view was second to none. But we were in for an even bigger treat. There also happened to be an air show on and so we stood on the beach as Spitfires, bi-planes with wing walkers strapped on, The Red Arrows and a Hurricane flew above, giving us a free display. What a fitting end to the day. Wow!

As we savoured a cup of tea and biscuits, we watched sand carts and kite fliers and all manner of other people using the beach. It wasn't particularly warm but we stayed until the sea seemed to be a little closer. Even then, when we tried to walk out to its edge, I was too tired to reach it.

David thoroughly enjoyed this part of the day. We had two hours of quiet contemplation and relaxation, and he took numerous pictures before we headed off to the campsite a couple of miles away. Called Willowbank Holiday Park, this was a 3 star AA campsite with showers. Marvellous. I made tea, then prepared my rucksack for the next day. I noted that my legs were slightly sore.

Sunday September 27th 2009. Ainsdale-on-Sea to Cocker Bar - 21 miles.

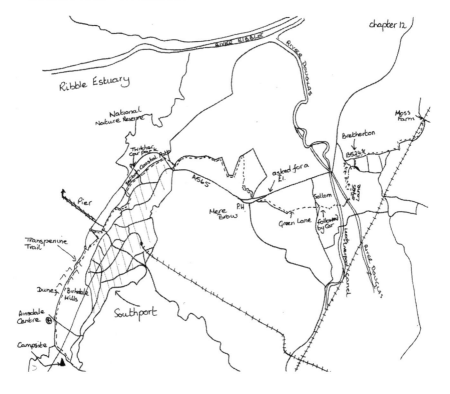

We were up at 7am and David dropped me off at the start point at 8.10am. It was going to be another fine day for walking, with the weather still steady. It was expected to be warmer at midday, so it was good to get a refreshing start. My legs were still sore from too much road walking at speed, but my feet had no blisters. I soon got into a rhythm though.

I chatted to Gertrude, as the two and a half miles into Southport was tedious. There were dunes on both sides of the road. It felt quite claustrophobic with the Birkdale Hills to my right and the Ainsdale dune system to the left. However, I had learned to relax by now and enjoy what I see. I would like to return to much of this journey, as I felt quite nomadic when I was there and humble and apologetic about not being able to patronise the area.

Southport was unexpectedly very pretty and clean. The council have really got it sorted with beautiful parks, a yacht club and a lovely marina. The promenade is dominated by the impressive Royal Clifton Hotel. This enormous hotel with its grand Victorian facade must have the most panoramic views of the north-west coast. Opposite the building was an equally impressive structure: the longest pier I have ever seen (3,650 feet or almost three quarters of a mile). In fact, Southport Pier boasts of being the first leisure pier built (1860) and the second longest in the country. It has had its history of disasters and was almost demolished in 1990 by Sefton Council because of rising debts. It was reprieved by the setting up of a Pier Fund and also received monies from the Heritage Fund, finally being restored to a fully functional pier in 2002. A battery-run tram service operates along its length daily except for Christmas Day. I would recommend anyone to go there. It truly is a beautiful structure. A marvellous piece of Victorian architecture, and a reminder of passengers who once disembarked there from ocean steamers.

I left Southport reluctantly, but time was creeping on. My route was going to follow the Sefton Coastal Footpath for a while longer but the air show had diversions in place, so I followed the roads around the perimeters of the Southport Municipal and Hesketh golf clubs and back onto Marsh Road to pick up the path there. Here, I was now exposed to the elements. I recall it was slightly overcast and blowy but a great temperature for walking. I was glad to be meeting David for a coffee and anyway I needed a crap.

The car park where we met belonged to the RSPB. It was very quiet at first. As I sat on the throne, a horde of twitchers arrived and much to my embarrassment I had to pull the curtains pretty quickly!

I changed into shorts at this point. I was so glad I did. I can honestly say I was really enjoying the walk. I also enjoyed the cup of coffee with David, and soon set off on my way again with a great sense of achievement.

I was eating up the miles. We had not planned where we would meet next. He had a copy of my route but his task was to locate and phone our next campsite for the night. He had an idea of roughly where I would be stopping for the day and that was enough. If all failed we would return to Willowbank.

I followed the Sefton Coastal Footpath for another mile or more. This time it was a pleasant path passing along an old disused embankment or dyke. Looking across the marshes there were Canadian geese flocking in. This area again reminded me of the Somerset Levels, with very few paths to choose from and the roads very straight. It became hot and tedious. I passed rows of greenhouses and fields and fields of corn and beet. My feet were beginning to complain, the tarmac surface not good for them.

Finally, I found a welcome soft track which took me onto a lovely path across country towards a place called Mere Brow. This was a change from my drawn route for the day, but it was actually quite a shortcut and a godsend for the feet. By now the sun was very warm. Mere Brow boasted a pub, so I texted David and soon after we sat and had a very welcome drink of local beer and toasted sarnies. He had found a place for us to stay – a small Camping and Caravanning Club site at Moss Farm in Little Hoole, near Much Hoole (what wonderful names). This was a fantastic location and only some three miles off my route.

David then suggested we meet again at Bretherton to see how far I was going to take it for the day, and this would be my tea break. I was getting used to this wonderful back-up person. I was determined to stop somewhere within spitting distance of Leyland. I was not looking forward to crossing this town, so walking through it early morning was going to be my best option. Ideally I wanted to be further than Bretherton before I was picked up, but my legs were a bit sore. Not deterred, I left David with this overall picture in mind.

Taking the B5246 towards Holmes, I encountered my first

spooky hitch of the day. If it had been the first chapter, I probably would have been completely unhinged, but I was definitely used to my own company by now and confident. As I took a very green track (on the map it's depicted as a road) a gentleman ran across to me and said very abruptly, "Have you got a phone, I need a phone now!" "Yes," I said carefully, "what for?" "I'll give you a pound if I can borrow it." He was very earnest, very flustered, with short cropped hair and right in my space. I repeated the fact I did have a phone but needed a reason. Apologetically but very hurriedly he explained he was further up the track, his car had bottomed out, he was stuck. Looking at the path I was intending to go down, I did wonder how a car had got down there. He insisted it was true and his sons were in the car. "How old?" I asked. "Fourteen and eleven and they didn't want to help push it," he replied, continuing, "Look, can I borrow your phone? I need to ring my sister to get my brother-in-law to help me out. I am going to get so told off for this, she is going to hit the roof." I handed him the phone very undecidedly but he was immediately on to his folks, explaining where he was. I relaxed a bit then, especially as a boy came running down the track shouting, "Dad, Dad, have you got hold of Mum?!" The boy then got told off for leaving his brother behind in the car, and he buzzed off back up the track.

As soon as the man managed to get hold of who he wanted he handed back the phone, thanking me over and over again. He produced a pound from his pocket. He probably didn't realise how unnerved he had made me for a while. I was just thankful to be on my way. I passed the car further on down the track, the two boys messing about, and hurriedly left the scene. I didn't wish to speak to the dad again.

I soon settled into a steady pace again. My legs were tired now. The lane was long and straight and very bleak. I did feel rather isolated. With rows of drained fields, it did cross my mind that if it had been raining it would have been even more bleak. I finally came to farms near Sollom and found a great path that would take me northwards to Bretherton. I had passed a red Vauxhall Nova at that stage. A young lad was driving it. I walked on by, not giving it a thought and turned onto a track that said: 'TO FARMS ONLY footpath access only'. At this point the red car overtook me and continued down the track. I just thought it was going to the farm but as I went over the River Douglas, it was parked on no-access land. I then started to have a glimmer of nerves. I had another mile or so of this track and then it would go into a wood. It was very quiet with absolutely no boltholes or another path. I continued as the car went past me again. On the map, the track was depicted as a road, generally four metres wide or less, so I tried to reason that perhaps they were entitled to be there and it was only locals who had put up the signs. After all, there had been fishermen at the bridge.

I next encountered the red car parked approximately three quarters of a mile further along. I could see it clearly. At this point I rang David, gave him my location and explained that after I passed the car I would be going into woods that should come out at the rear of Bretherton. David was already parked near this village.

His reply to my frantic phone call was, "What do you want me to do about it?" I just said, "If I don't walk into Bretherton in the next half hour, start looking for me in the woods."

I sped past the car at breakneck speed. Looking into the window of the car the lad, with his dark shades on, just followed me with his eyes, although I couldn't see them. Boldly I squared my shoulders and walked into the wood. I kept looking behind me but the car didn't come. Thankfully, an elderly couple came out of the woods. I stopped and spoke to them for some time, giving me space to think and breathe better.

I didn't see the red car again. The track turned into a delightful leafy lane and then I saw many Sunday walkers as I came into the affluent village of Bretherton. Some of the houses were exquisite. I found David parked in a side road with the kettle on. It was now 3pm. I was mentally exhausted and my legs were very tired, but I wanted to do at least another two and a half miles towards Leyland.

Setting off again along the B5248, I finally arrived at Cocker Bar at 5pm. It was with relief that I got into the van and we trundled back to Moss Farm at Little Hoole. The site was adequate; it had a toilet and a basin in one of the barns. That was all we needed. We turned in at 9pm, the weather still kind if not overcast. Rain was expected tomorrow.

Land's End

In the generator dry room at Wintershead Farm

Heading towards Yeoland, Dundridge, Bideford

Crowcombe in hard frost

Looking towards the new Severn Bridge

Before setting off to Chepstow

World's End, Llangollen

About to get a full dunking - wild water rafting, North Wales

Transpennine Trail, Liverpool Loop Line

Views of the Leven Estuary, Morcombe Bay, Cumbrian Coastal Way

Bigland Tarn, Cumbrian Coastal Way

With full backpack at the start of Carlisle to Glasgow

Camping at Glenvalatine, Lowther Hills below Wanlockhead

Pricking blisters and dressing feet on the veranda of the Tree House

The Start of the West Highland Way, Milngavie

Walking down to Kinlochleven (West Highland Way)

Mallaig (eastern shores) B & B

Beautiful Knoydart: lunch stop at Dubh-Lochain

From Ratagan Youth Hostel, looking across Loch Duich

Swardalan Bothy, near Glen More

Views from the forest near Carn Allt na Bradh

New walking companions on my way to Torridon

Sheildag

ET Rock below Beinn Eighe

Near the Heights of Kinlochewe

Swimming ledge on the River Oykel at Oykel Bridge

Ullapool in the evening sun

Achmelvich Beach

Kylesku Bridge

Durness campsite

Highland cattle near Laird

First snow - layby near Hope

Ben Loyal, walking towards the Kyle of Tongue

Osprey seen near Kyle of Tongue

Walking in sleet towards Gills Bay nearing the end

John O' Groats

All my 'reliable friends' (a good advert for Scarpa!)
and Gertrude in the foreground

Sundew

Wild primrose

Mutated form of sea buckthorn near Ainsdale on Sea

Thrift

Spring squill

Monday September 28th 2009.
Cocker Bar to Bilsborrow - 15 miles.

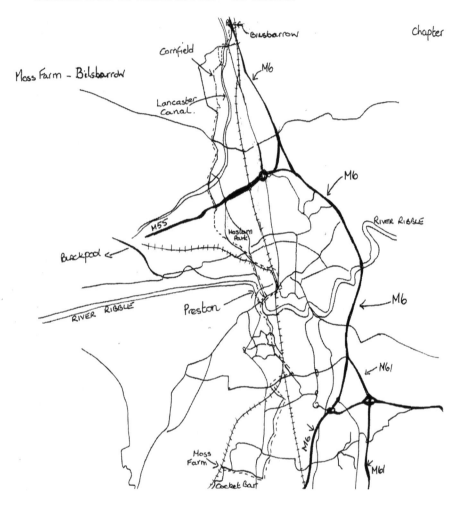

We were slow starting today. David had a reasonable night, but I felt a bit fluey and had a sore throat. My legs were a wee bit sore but my feet were in excellent condition. Thank you boots once again.

Today was about walking through Leyland and Preston. This is what had been so fascinating about the journey. I would never have dreamt of going to these places. Who in their right mind would entertain visiting such built-up areas of industry and commerce? Certainly not me, so this was to be a challenging day. I am quite fearful of walking alone in large cities. I am definitely a country bumpkin.

The weather was damp and drizzly, the air temperature good but clammy. At least I knew I would be needing my waterproofs today. I started walking at 9am. The B5248 was quite busy but pretty all the same. The affluent side of Leyland I suspect. At least there was a path to follow and I found it all rather easy walking through the outskirts of this town. It was quieter than I had expected.

I managed to get off the B road and follow a much smaller road into Farington. It was near here where I managed to find a fantastic bakery and bought a very warm sausage roll. Devouring it far too fast, I marched onwards to the outskirts of Preston. Actually, I was so busy watching my route that any concerns I may have had about walking in this district didn't surface. I started to rather enjoy the various village areas – Penwortham, Middleforth Green and Lower Penwortham.

At Broadgate I picked up the Ribble Way, albeit briefly. This path looked down to the River Ribble. It followed a crescent of Georgian houses, not unlike Bath. The street was lined with beeches and huge horse chestnut trees. I savoured this moment before changing course and walking towards the centre of

Preston itself. It became a little tiring and noisy from here for a bit, as I negotiated the A5071 past the university complex.

Only here did I catch a glimpse of how tired the area was. At Maudlands I followed the railway line for a bit on the B6241, and this was grim. By now the drizzle had stopped and it had become warm once more. Haslam Park was to my right but there was no footpath I could get onto, and it was with heart in mouth that I walked along the grass verge of this busy road until I reached the point where the Lancashire Canal went underneath the road. Thankfully, I then picked up a lovely path that led me through a sports park and a new estate out towards Cottam.

Suddenly I was in the country again. Cottam marked the start of passing very small rural villages. I had agreed to meet David at Lower Bartle, where a tiny lane crosses the busy M55. It was great to see the van. David had done well to find me. Having already had a sausage roll and nibbled my own supplies, I was just thankful to be out of the chilly wind and to sit and slurp a coffee.

We decided looking at the map that there was a pub at Woodplumpton and perhaps we could have a drink and snack there. Sadly, being Monday, as with so many rural pubs it was closed, so we used their car park to have a brew up in the van and for me to use the toilet. Relief. Walking through the town had slowed me down. Negotiating traffic and crossing roads for safer walking and better noise levels does take its toll.

I think it was about 1pm. The path got better in the

afternoon. The weather, quite changeable, had become sunny and warm. My route to Bilsborrow was through lovely lanes. Past Moons Bridge, the path went over the Lancashire Canal once more. It was a popular watering hole for canal users and there was a marina.

A welcomed break for my feet came at Carnforth – a field track that was a shortcut away from roads. I met a woman walking towards me and she was amazed at what I was doing and verified that I could use the track across the farmer's field, then get out onto the Lancashire Canal towpath. I skirted the farmer's field and took the track. In front of me was the most enormous field of sweetcorn. To begin with I could see the diagonal line. It should have been simple but then the rows changed and I hit problems.

I hope never to repeat the experience that ensued. I have never been so claustrophobic in all my life. I couldn't see above the corn. It was wet and like a jungle. The leaves were constantly slapping my face, so I dropped to the ground and headed in an easterly direction to the edge of the field. This went on for at least half an hour. I actually was so frightened I began to hyperventilate. My problems were not over at the field boundary, but I could see where I needed to be. Beyond the next field system lay the towpath. But there was nowhere to get through. I walked the edge of the boundary thinking I was going to end up back at the farm at this rate.

Finally I found the corner I needed but the gate, or what was left of it, was completely overgrown with brambles and a barbed wire fence had been put up. All I had to do was get through it into the next field and onto the towpath. I was sweating buckets. I was desperate to get away from the cornfields. I felt they were closing in on me. I rang David to calm myself down and explained I was in a bit of a pickle and if he didn't hear from me in a short while it could be because I was injured. I explained to Gertrude we had a bit of climbing to do. I put on my gloves – thank God I had put them in my rucksack – and started to beat down the nettles and brambles as best I could. I prised back the barbed wire off the corroded gate, threw my rucksack as far as possible, apologising to Gertrude, and climbed the unstable gate as best I could. At one point the brambles just tore through my fleece and scratched my arms something awful. The gate as I tried to climb it hung perilously inwards and wobbled into the vegetation.

Adrenaline makes you achieve remarkable things, for on the other side of the hedge the path dropped away. I could see the original path to the gate but the farmer had ploughed right up to the hedge line and my rucksack was in yet another field of corn. All I had to do now was jump. Easy. I lowered myself down the now swinging gate (only brambles keeping it together) and I leapt into the hedge line with its stinging nettles. Great! Elation is how I can only describe it. Scratched, bruised and stung, but no twisted ankle – all bodily parts intact – that was good enough for me.

Brushing myself down and collecting my nerve, I walked

around the next cornfield, found the gap onto the towpath and pretended nothing had happened! I rang David to confirm I was still alive and enjoyed walking the towpath. It was sheer bliss I can tell you. I now look at ants in a new perspective and in admiration!

It had been a long day; it was now 4.30pm. David had sorted out our next night of accommodation. Another Camping Club site and only a couple of miles away, I was delighted to hear. He picked me up at Bilsborrow and we then enjoyed an evening at a very plush site, with showers. I cooked dinner, did all the usual preparations for the next day and attended to the many scratches that had become swollen and sore. I took a antihistamine tablets and put some cream on the cuts.

It was a bright, cold evening and I was able to dry out my damper clothes from the morning. We turned in at 9pm. My feet were still remarkably good.

Tuesday September 29th 2009.
Bilsborrow to Lancaster - 16 miles.

We were up at 7am and I was walking by 8.30. It was only four miles to Garstang where David and I had agreed to meet for coffee. David was tired, and it showed. He was going to have to pace himself. I was looking forward to this day, because much of my walking was to be on a trail called the Wyre Way, which I was to pick up at Garstang.

The weather was great again. Cloudy with a slight breeze, although rain had been forecast for the afternoon. It was ideal walking temperature.

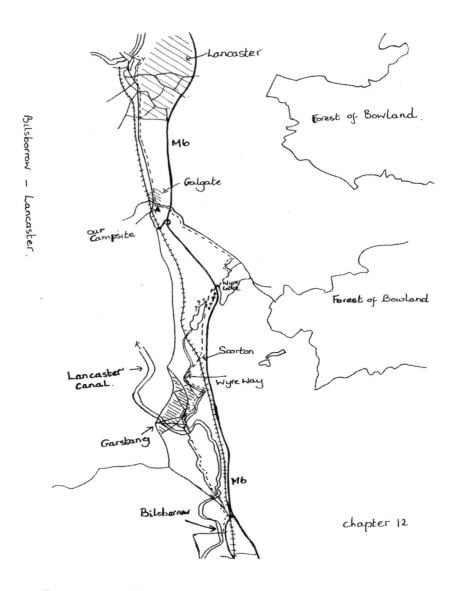

Just outside Bilsborrow I found a very interesting sight (well it was to me). A very old farmhouse and its surrounding fields had been isolated over the years by the industrial revolution, with all its changing methods of transportation up to the present day. At the bottom of the farmhouse fields were the Lancaster Canal, the Northern Railway Line and the M6 motorway, and to the front was the original road – the A6 heading north. I found it remarkable to see all those transport eras represented within such a short distance of each other, yet reflecting almost 300 years of history.

I arrived in Garstang at 9.45am, the few miles not taking me long. My legs had overcome their soreness and were enjoying the stretch. David and I had a lovely cup of coffee in a tiny family run café. Everyone was so friendly that we actually had two cups and a bun.

David needed to rest as much as possible. His next challenge was to find another place to camp for the night. We perused the camping club directory for something outside Lancaster. There were a couple of options and I left him with that task. We had an amble round Garstang for a bit and then I left him and headed off on the Wyre Way path.

What a treat for the feet and for the eyes. The peace was wonderful once more as I bumbled along the river, meeting the occasional fisherman. This was a lovely walk. I followed the Way through Woodacre, which has a railway works, then on to Scorton. This is a very pretty village and clearly embraces walkers as it has a public convenience for their use. You pay 20p but the loos are fit for a queen, which of course I am.

Scorton is a pristine village, well worth a visit. Only eight miles south of Lancaster, it's on the edge of the Bowland Forest. For such a small village it's a busy one. Developed as a result of the cotton mill industry, it is much older than that and probably originated back in the 17th century. It boasts a Bikes and Barrows Festival where people dress up a bike or barrow in a given theme. It is also the host for The Society of

Archers and *The Antient Silver Arrow*, a competition dating back to 1673 designed to maintain the target archery skills of longbow men. It is reputedly the world's oldest and longest established sporting event. The winner is the first archer to hit the black three-inch centre spot from 100 yards.

From Scorton I followed the river once more through woods and out towards Nan's Nook, a farm close to the motorway. It was very quiet as I skirted a place called Sunnyside. It had a campsite and chalet area purpose built for fishermen to enjoy all the lakes of the Wyre in this locality.

From there I hit road again but it was extremely quiet as I walked into Galgate. Here I met up with David at the campsite he had found. It was great to walk into where we were actually staying and it was only 1.30pm (this was meant to be a half-day walk). The weather had become quite chilly and rain was looking more of a possibility. We brewed up and then took ourselves into Lancaster in the van. This was somewhere I was looking forward to seeing. I also could see the potential of walking back from Lancaster to Galgate after wandering round the town for a bit. It also meant I had a couple of hours with David.

We parked near the fort and castle walls, then we walked along the River Lune for a bit before heading into the town itself with its cobbled streets and wonderful museums and buildings. I would like to spend more time in Lancaster. It clearly has a lot for the visitor to enjoy. The castle alone is well worth a visit, steeped in over a thousand years of history. It is owned by Her Majesty the Queen, who is also the Duke of Lancaster. It is reputed to be one of the oldest imprisonment castles in Europe and was allegedly where the Witches of Pendle were tried, convicted and sentenced to death. Sadly, we didn't have enough time to visit the castle this day. We must return.

There are wonderful views of the town from the Ashton Memorial in Williamson Park. We enjoyed window shopping and a drink, then made our way back to the car park. Dark clouds were forming. I said to David I would walk back to the campsite; I didn't think it would take me too long. Haha! At a quick march I could be back in an hour. I finally crawled in at 6.30pm, having left the centre of Lancaster at 5pm. Negotiating myself out of the town was dreadful. Anybody you ask in a town doesn't seem to know where they are! It was three and a half to four miles to Galgate, and as David left me in Lancaster the skies opened up and did not stop pouring with rain until later in the evening. I came in like a drowned rat.

I couldn't be bothered to make tea so instead we went to one of the local pubs in Galgate and had the most enormous meal and a pint of Guzzler beer. It was brilliant. David and I both felt replenished after that. It had been a cracking day, albeit a wet end.

Wednesday September 30th 2009. Lancaster to Sampool (Foulshaw Lane) - 18 miles.

A bright start. David dropped me in Lancaster town centre at 8am and I set off at a brisk pace, following the Lune Valley path/cycle route. This was extremely quiet but an easy way out of the town. Soon I was crossing the River Lune via the Lune Aqueduct that was completed in 1797. The aqueduct rises some 61 feet above the river. It has a span of 664 feet and consists of five semicircular arches each spanning 70 feet. The trough of the canal is 20 feet wide. It was an amazing start to my day. I stopped and savoured the views along the river. Lancaster seemed a distance away.

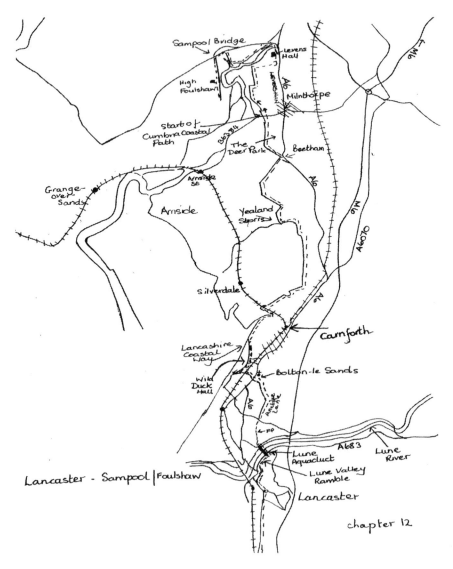

From here I took a delightful path on farm tracks northwards towards Bolton–le-Sands. Eventually this path turned into a quiet road serving just the local farms. It was very rural. I headed towards the coastal path known as the Lancashire Coastal Way. I managed to get hold of David; he was going to meet me at a place called Wild Duck Hall. I was really enjoying the navigation and walking on my own.

Arriving at Bolton-le-Sands, at last I could now see across Morecambe Sands to my destination across the water: Ulverston. But I was still a long way away from there. It was quite chilly but I had my windproof jacket on. The cup of coffee and biscuit was a welcomed break. So was the toilet. The van had been so useful for that.

By now it was 10am. I enjoyed having a rest and spoke to a lady with a pushchair and baby who were talking to some ponies in a field. Then I set off again, leaving David to again track down a campsite that we had previously seen on the map at Meathop Fell caravan site. I wasn't sure if I would make it that far on this day, but I was going to try and get as close as I physically could. In my mind I was hoping to finish the route the following day. This would give us a free day to travel slowly home.

I continued on the Lancashire Coastal Way, skirting the edge of the estuary of the River Keer all the way to Carnforth. The tide was out and I had some difficulty following the markers on the green marshy path I trekked along. Crossing the railway line, I headed towards Warton. Then I arrived at some hills and the road started to undulate in height. As it did so I passed through the villages of Yealand. It was an extremely picturesque area.

My next surprise was the deer park I had to walk through to reach Milnthorpe. The tiny road that leads through the park had deer to my left. I stopped and had something to eat while I watched them for a while. There have been deer in the park since the 17th century, part of the Dallam Tower Estate with the River Bela running through it.

Milnthorpe is a delightful market town dating from the 1300s. It owes its name partly to the fact that it was once a port built on the Bela. Watermills used the river, hence the name. My feet were a little sore by now; I didn't have any blisters but they had become warm. As I walked through Milnthorpe onto the Cumbria Coastal Way, I arranged to meet David at Sampool. At this point the road became a long flat slog just like the Somerset Levels. The roads seem to go on forever. I could see my destination but the Milnthorpe Sands and the River Kent estuary had to be circumnavigated, which meant going back onto the A6 past Levens Hall and back out again.

Not all parts of the route were tedious. The walk through the grounds of Levens Hall was a brief interlude from the road. I passed High Sampool and its caravans then returned back to the main road to wait for David.

Unfortunately, we had a bit of a disagreement here. The road was extremely dangerous and for David coming from Ulverston it was easy to miss the Foulshaw turning. So I carried on walking towards Foulshaw Cottages, but then retraced my steps to the main road again. My legs were by now very sore and had started to cramp. I was very pleased to see the Pash Wagon finally coming towards me. It was 5pm and it had been a hard day.

Meathop Fell caravanning site was brilliant. The showers were hot and we were able to relax for a while. I felt a flutter of excitement as I could now see the end in sight. If I was fortunate enough to feel good tomorrow, it would be achievable to finish the walk. I explained to David that he needed to go off and enjoy the day without worrying about me, as the route would be taking me into the fells. My plan was to continue out of Meathop towards Ulverston and if I felt well enough, David would drop me back to Foulshaw Cottages and then I would walk back to the Meathop site again. It was so central to the walk.

We had tea and then turned in. I slept like a log. My last thoughts were excited ones but I was too knackered to acknowledge them.

Thursday October 1st 2009. Foulshaw to Ulverston - 18 miles.

This was to be the best day of the walk. I started from the caravan site, slipping away quietly at 7.45am. I left David in bed as there was no need to disturb him. The sun was already starting to show but the air had an autumnal chill to it. It was going to be another cracking day.

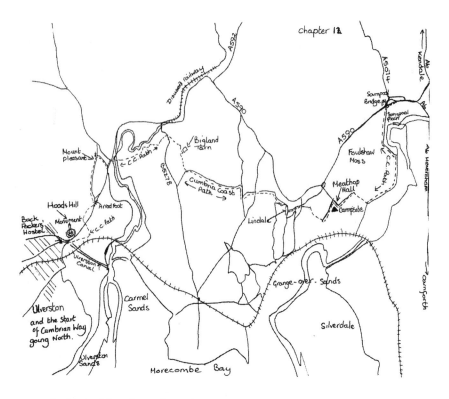

At Low Meathop I took a ram track across to Lindale. The animals didn't notice me passing through there. I followed a delightful lane to Field Broughton past a large outdoor activity place. All the time, the roads went up and down with sometimes extensive views of the southern Lakeland Fells in front. At Grassgarth I picked up the Cumbria Coastal Way again. I had been a little hesitant at this point, because this was to be my only bit of open moorland. But I needn't have worried. Oh it was so good to feel the bounce of moss and grass beneath my feet. The route up through High Stribers Wood was great; it opened out onto Bigland Heights. Here I finally rested and sat on some craggy crops to admire the views.

The sun was shining. I was so elated to be there. It was truly a magical, wonderful feeling. Before me Morecambe Sands stretched into infinity and Ulverston beckoned. I allowed myself a well earned break. I stayed long enough to devour a sandwich and chocolate bar, just wishing this moment didn't have to end. I was very isolated but at total ease with myself.

How far had I come since 2005? How much stronger was I? Reluctantly I shifted again and enjoyed walking over to Bigland Tarn, a well stocked fishing lake, down through another wood with open views of Rusland Valley and Haverthwaite. This was brilliant.

I followed the Cumbria Coastal Way all the way to Greenodd, where a large girder bridge spanned across the River Leven. Now that I had reached the A590 I was dreading this part of the walk, but at the bridge I met an elderly couple walking their dog. They were locals and advised me to cross the road and walk into Mount Pleasant and Penny Bridge. It was far safer to take this route to Arrad Foot than walk along the busy road with no path. They even offered me a cup of tea along with David when I had finished the walk. They were delightful and so enthusiastic about me doing this journey. I shall not forget their kind hearts.

I followed their instructions and I could see the road on the map to which they were referring. Further along I popped into a church I encountered. The volunteers were preparing for Harvest Festival and the church looked very pretty.

From Arrad Foot my path into Ulverston was a bit fraught. I tried to use a footpath that led uphill across quarries, but it was covered by fallen trees, bracken and brambles. In the end, I rejoined the A590 rather scratched up again, and walked on its grassy edge. It was very dangerous. So I was relieved when finally a footpath appeared as I walked past The Walkers Hostel below Hoad Hill in Ulverston (which brought back warm memories of earlier in the year – see next chapter) and on to Booths, the shop, to meet David for a coffee.

It was 1.30pm and I had travelled an enormous distance from early morning. We ate a Danish pastry each and chatted about me returning to Foulshaw Cottages, the last stretch still to be done. My legs were like jelly, they were so tired. I had pushed them hard. My feet were warm but not complaining. I was so grateful to them.

We didn't stay too long at the café as my legs were beginning to cramp. I had two packets of crisps to counteract this. David then dropped me back to Foulshaw Cottages and as I waved him goodbye I felt a sudden loneliness and loss. I don't know why it just came to me that I had almost finished my long journey, and what would I do after this. Shrugging off this dampening spirit, I rose to the challenge ahead – almost five miles of hard track, oh yuk. But I was in for a surprise, for the coastal path followed a grassy dyke along the banks of Milnthorpe Sands and the Leven Estuary. I followed a shepherd and his dog. There were many sheep grazing on the dyke and I could see Arnside on the opposite side, with the Kent Viaduct in the distance taking the railway line across the sands.

Once the heat of the sun had gone the day became rather chilly. Winter was looming and darkness would fall even quicker. I was aware of the time and moved swiftly past a lovely cottage and some horses at Crag Wood. From here it was a matter of picking up the road that led into the caravan site. I had made it. It was 5.20pm precisely.

I saw the van parked in its usual spot and waving my arms, I ran the last bit, punching the air and shouting, "I've done it, yes!"

I was so delighted with this part of the walk. I had spent all 111.5 miles of the route alone. David had not troubled me particularly. He had done a marvellous job in catching up with me at coffee times and finding our campsites, and he had stayed reasonably well. I had had no navigational hiccups either. I may have changed some of the route but not a lot, and I finished earlier than expected. Although to you it may have seemed rushed, for me who loves to walk at a reasonable pace it didn't feel like it. Yes, there were places I would like to revisit now, but that's for the future when I am older. This was all about the challenge and *finding me*.

This section of the walk certainly did that, in bucket loads. I had enjoyed just Gertrude for company. The fear of being alone had gone since those early days and I knew that finishing Scotland on my own was going to be something to really look forward to – provided the van kept going!!

CHAPTER THIRTEEN:
LETTING MY HAIR DOWN

**THE CUMBRIAN WAY – ULVERSTON TO CARLISLE.
DISTANCE: 70 MILES. DATELINE: MARCH 29TH-APRIL 4TH 2009.**

When a walking companion offered to do this part of the walk with me I was pleased yet reticent. Pleased because the route would take me through some remote parts, but reserved about walking alone for a week with a friend who was male. Rising above self-inflicted constraints and inhibitions, I was inwardly excited at the prospect of walking an interesting route. However this new liberation played on my mind.

I was twenty one years of age when David contracted meningitis for the first time. As a newly-married couple our friends were supportive, but they had lives of their own. David's subsequent long stays in hospital having operations and various tests and more attacks often left me isolated. The need to work was paramount, particularly when the children were young. In many ways I had had to be so independent and practical as I balanced working life, caring for the children and caring for David, while going out, letting my hair down, enjoying other people's company and affording it were put on the back boiler. I have now been married to David for 33 years, and for all his medical problems he has remained consistent in his determination to stay upbeat and has had the graciousness to allow me to retrieve some lost time, even if this time it involved walking with another man.

As I voiced my concerns about leaving him to go off on this next stage, David just laughed. 'You silly bugger, you book it, you know you will enjoy it, be grateful someone is going to put up with you' he said. In his defence he hadn't fully understood how much I had held back as a person to socialise and be me. Over the years he had not understood the inner struggle with the guilt I placed on myself even for going out for a night with the girls or for walking with my brother and his group for the odd weekend, or just taking myself off to the beach for a swim or leaving the children in some other person's care whilst I went to night school.

Unknown to David, this chatty, confident, happy and friendly person had often found herself bawling her eyes out at the bottom of the garden, taking her frustration and anger out on the weeds that dared to grow in the borders. How unjust life was! How come I was healthy and couldn't make him better? Why us?

It was David's mum who once said, 'You were too young to have the responsibilities of looking after an ill husband. You have never had time to be yourself or find yourself'. I shall never forget those understanding, sanguine words after David contracted meningitis for the fourth time. That left him unable to work, and it was twenty-four years ago.

So with David's understanding, permission and support I meticulously began planning the route and accommodation. The route is very popular, so finding accommodation was a bit difficult, but again I was amazed at how helpful people were in offering names and addresses of other people who 'may be able to help'. I will also be eternally grateful for our first hostel, as they were prepared to keep Bob's car there for free until our return, and Millbeck Farm Bed and Breakfast, where the proprietor certainly understood my need for a separate room and didn't charge us extra (what a gem she was). There was only one night Bob and I had to share a twin room - gulp! I fretted about this a bit as I would have with anyone, even a female, because although I knew him, I had never had to share a bathroom with another man before and the thought struck me "I hope he doesn't snore". It's all about your own personal space.

So here I was on the eve of the big day, tossing and turning most of the night, anxious about walking with a male friend alone, yet so bubbly at the prospect of what looked to be a great walk. To me it was a step forward in completing my adventure. Everything would be fine, wouldn't it? Would I keep up the pace? Would my navigating let us down? As companions, would we fall out over something trivial?

Sunday March 29th 2009. Heading up north.

David and I met up with Bob at Salisbury College car park at 10am. After exchanging last-minute arrangements, David's eyes comforting my anxious fears, and loading my belongings into Bob's car, we set off. The day was sunny and warm. Although tired from no sleep, I was so excited and I definitely wasn't going to nod off.

I still wasn't sure about my companion. But I don't know why I worried. Congenial conversation made for a pleasant journey up north, although I did get a bit nervous when Bob suggested lunch at The New Hollies. As we left the comfort of the M6 and headed off onto the A5 (an unknown area for me) I did get slightly edgy. Where on earth was he taking me?

Lunch at The New Hollies, the greasy spoon truckers' cafe of the north, was a great eye opener for me. If you haven't been there, do go. I ordered a vegetable soup and mug of coffee, whilst Bob tucked into a full breakfast! It was quiet by usual standards I am told. There were people even having their Sunday lunch in there. Still, the food was served with gusto and hearty chat. Mugs of tea and coffee on tap. Fantastic. I felt myself warming to this place.

Going to the toilets upstairs in this place is an experience in itself for a woman. You never know whom you might meet. I was greeted by a burly bloke stepping out of the men's block. "Ladies loos are locked luv, use the men's, no one in there at the moment." Gingerly I crept in. He was right. The smell however was not overly pleasant! I made for a hasty pee, only to bump into another bloke coming in as I made my escape. Flustered, I muttered, "Doors locked," and gave a cheesy grin. As we passed on the landing I had a quick glimpse of the makeshift bedrooms. Clean and basic, fine for truckers getting their head down. Raising my eyebrows, all I can say is I am not a snob but coming down the stairs the handrail felt sticky and tacky, if you get my drift.

We arrived in Ulverston at 4pm. This market town still retains some of its cobbled streets and old buildings. It is the birthplace of Stan Laurel of Laurel and Hardy fame and has what is reputed to be the shortest, deepest and widest canal in the UK, which actually made Ulverston officially a port in 1796.

The Walkers Hostel was very welcoming and only cost £16.50 a night. We had a cup of tea, found our beds and then went into the town to locate the start of our walk for the following day. It was good to stretch the legs. The evening was glorious. First we climbed the 430 feet up Hoad Hill on which stands the Sir John Barrow Monument, built in 1850 by public subscription. This 100-foot high limestone monument, modelled on the Eddystone Lighthouse, honours Ulverston's most famous son Sir John Barrow. Born in 1794, he became 1st Baronet, was a naval administrator, an explorer, a founder of the Geographical Society, a writer (including biographies, Mutiny on the Bounty and reviews in Encyclopaedia Britannica), a foreign diplomat, and a mathematician. He died in 1848 having outlived most of his friends and associates in Ulverston. He was interred in London's St. Martins-in-the-Fields, but his parents are buried in Ulverston.

The monument was closed. Renovation work had begun in the year 2000 and was near completion. But the views were stunning of Morecambe Bay, the Leven Estuary and the Lakeland Fells we would be heading for, all bathed in lowering sunlight. Leaving the monument, we walked into Ulverston to find the start of the walk for the next day. This we finally located after a much inebriated woman pointed us in the right direction. It was only 6pm and she was plastered!

Having affirmed the start we wandered back to hostel to cook jacket potatoes and beans. Followed by fruit salad.

The evening was spent in The Swan drinking Coniston Bluebird Bitter. Ummmmm... I downed one and a half pints and Bob had three. I wasn't sure I could keep up this rate and I remember raising my eyebrows as he commented on the fact I was a 'lightweight'. I grinned at his cordialness but aware I better not drink any more. I needed to be alert in the morning – and now!

I thoroughly enjoyed the pub. It was good to be doing something different than working. Turned in at 11pm. Bed comfortable.

Monday March 30th 2009.
Ulverston to Coniston - 15 miles.

I slept very well until 6am. The excitement was overwhelming. I crept downstairs and had an early cup of tea. The day outside looked grey, with a fine drizzle in the air. I thought here we go, wet weather here we come. How wrong I was to be.

I supped my tea, contemplated the route and mulled over my company. It was going to be alright. I just hoped I would be fit enough to keep up with Bob and that the route was not too difficult to navigate.

We left the hostel at 9.10am after a light breakfast. The weather did look a bit ominous. We had our wet weather gear ready! Making our way to the start took 20 minutes, so we actually commenced at 9.30am and eventually arrived at Holly How Hostel, Coniston at 4.10pm. Not bad for 15 miles with heavy backpacks.

It was a cracking day. After following the beck out of Ulverston and through various undulating farmland we reached Gawthwaite, a significant point of the walk as we passed through the informal southern boundary of the Lakeland National Park. It had started to drizzle, so we had been togged up to this point. But from then on for the remainder of the walk, we didn't need to put on our wet weather gear again! The sun came out. There was high cloud with a cooling breeze. We could not believe our luck. It was an ideal walking day.

We passed a tiny church at Netherhouses. There were wonderful views southwards looking back towards Morecambe, Heysham Power Station and still, just visible, Hoad Monument. Northwards the fells beckoned, and it was so enticing. The countryside here in many ways is similar to the Yorkshire Dales.

At Tottle Bank just before our first real climb over Blawith Fells, it became quite warm. Our lunch break was at a brilliant location near Wool Knott Fell overlooking Beacon Tarn. We were out of the wind. After a 20-minute rest we cracked on towards Coniston.

Interestingly, on the other side of Blawith Fells there is another Tottle Bank on the map. Here the views of Coniston Lake are great. From there we dropped down very quickly to the lakeside. It was then that the walk became a little tiring, as the route turned into a purpose-built hard pathway of undulating tree roots and gravel. However, the lake looked stunning. It was calm, the reflections were amazing. I loved every moment of it even though my hips and feet were complaining!

The YHA couldn't have come soon enough. Although we couldn't get into our rooms yet, we were allowed to make ourselves a cup of tea. Well, actually several. We were eventually allocated our rooms. Showers okay, it was a relief to get out of sticky clothes.

They have a licence here for drink, which meant we didn't have to bother walking into Coniston again. I have to say I was glad about that.

Dinner was a gourmet delight. They certainly know how to cater for hungry walkers. Bob and I both had tomato and basil soup, then I had pork loin and vegetables whilst Bob had bangers and mash. We bought beers then went into the lounge to rest. It was very comfortable, with only us in there for the moment. Bob drifted off to sleep as I wrote up my diary. It was still sunny outside.

Later we found the TV room in the basement of the building. There was a Chinese guy already there. We watched television until the 10pm news. When the Chinese man left, it was only then that nerves crept back in. But I was fine.

I then met a lovely girl, just like my daughter Kate. She was a medical student walking with her boyfriend, going over places she had visited with her parents as a child. I do so love these small friendly chats with strangers. They are in my life for such a brief moment of time.

Tuesday March 31st 2009. Coniston to Dungeon Ghyll (Millbeck Farm) - 11 miles.

I slept great. I usually do when I am away. I get more sleep doing something like this than at home, where I average 4-6 hours a night.

We left the hostel at 9.30am after a large breakfast! The weather was dull again, the sky promising rain. But it stayed away and it was another brilliant day. This was to be our easiest day – a bimble of a day.

We walked past Tarn Hows. This brought back old memories of when my brother and mum had swum across to the small peninsula that juts out into the tarn. I was 12 and still unable to swim well. Now I had my swimsuit with me as I had promised myself a dip if the sun came out. It didn't happen as the wind was chilly, but it was delightful to return to this gem of a place in such different circumstances. I was getting sentimental again.

The mountains and fells were all around us and getting bigger. I can't describe my joy of walking through this part of the country. I think Bob was enjoying it too. We stopped for a quick snack at Colwith Force Waterfall. Because the rivers were so high it really was a tremendous force and very loud. Munching my snack bars, I was so grateful of Bob's company. He was so congenial and easygoing. He didn't complain about me taking photos along the way, although I did try to do that whilst I was walking.

The path stayed interesting all the way to Elterwater and from there we followed Great Langdale Beck up through the valley into Great Langdale itself and its undulating, rocky path all the way to New Dungeon Ghyll Hotel and Millbeck Farm. It had blossomed into a very warm day. Blue skies all the way.

A warm welcome awaited us at Millbeck Farm B&B on our arrival at 3pm. Our host Sue was delightful. As promised, we had separate rooms. I was so grateful. She was a forthright woman and soon told us not to give the dogs any attention. "They are working ones, don't have pampering." It was not said unkindly, just firmly. She had a bit of a crisis going on at the farm. A calf had to be brought back in her car, so she left us alone with homemade cherry cake and plenty of tea and said to make ourselves comfortable.

The bathroom boasted a bath. After several cups of tea and a wonderful shower and bath I left Bob to take his turn. He had another kip (I think it must be his age) whilst I went to take more pictures, sit in the sun and write.

I couldn't have been more delighted. Bob had a twin room close to the bathroom and shower, and I had been placed right down the other end of the building next door to the sheep barn! Clearly, Sue saw I would be safer with the ewes. From my bedroom window there were extensive views of the valley and its mountains.

The sun was really warm and I enjoyed watching all manner of finches, sparrows and a nuthatch enjoying the bird seed, and then a lesser spotted woodpecker came by. What a treat.

A woman dropped by to pick up 'half a frozen sheep' like you do. I apologised to her that we couldn't help but would pass on the message that she had called. As I relaxed in the sun, I couldn't have felt any more content. I wrote my diary and leant back on the stone-walling, with a dog at my feet (whom I was trying to ignore) and soaking up the sun.
This little poem just breezed in as I sat.

Cleansed, tranquillity bathed,
The sun beats warmth on tired brow,
Crags disappear in this hedonistic glow.
Rise swift the thrush and sparrow,
Beat your glass from melted snows.
To delay and dally on this fertile day,
Would spoil this lifted soul.
Oh flushed this animated heart,
Peace descends, haply now.

I took photographs and wandered back indoors, the bright sunlight chasing me in eventually. I lay on my bed and drifted. I was so relaxed. I hadn't been like this for a very long time. I found myself nodding off (I must be getting old). I was physically spent. Marvellous.

Approximately 6.30pm, after Bob had had his bath, we took the brief walk out of the farm and down to New Dungeon Ghyll Hotel for our first beer of the evening. I was beginning to get used to this! We had Thirsk Extra. I had two halves here and then we moved on to the Sticklebarn pub where we ordered our supper whilst consuming Lancaster No. 1 beer. This was very smooth and slightly sweet. I had another two halves. Oh boy, I was slightly tipsy.

Supper was huge. It consisted of an enormous plate of chips and homemade steak and Guinness pie. It was so rich and filling. I was stuffed. Though it did soak up the next half pint of beer!

Bob was finding it all a bit amusing as I staggered up the short mountain path back to Millbeck Farm. It was dark. There was the tiniest of bridges to cross, which I recall finding difficult. We then sat and watched TV in the sitting room whilst I sobered up on Horlicks and tea. I cannot describe to you what we were watching on television. All I will say is it brought up some interesting conversations.

Sue came in to check I/we were okay and stopped to chat for a while. I was pleased she did. She had a very understanding way about her and we had a good old banter at Bob's expense. (Sorry Bob.)

Sleeping was slightly difficult. I had had too much to drink, the sheep in the barn next to me kept banging their heads against the wall (apparently they clean their heads against the stone) and the couple in the next room were banging all night!! When I finally did go to sleep I awoke with a very sore throat. I clearly had been snoring. That's what drink does to you.

I rang David to check if he was okay. More hassle: Ben's car needed fixing so that would fix him. Selfishly, because I was having such a wonderful walk I tried to blank it out of my head.

Wednesday April 1st 2009. Millbeck Farm to Keswick YHA - 16 miles.

This was to be our toughest day for ascent and the weather promised glorious sunshine. We started off at 9am prompt in short sleeves, after a very large English breakfast, all home produce. Very good poached eggs.

The walk led straight out of the farm and onto the track. It was great. The walk into the Langdale Pikes and up Great Tongue was long. Following the route above Mickleden Beck, the path slowly ascended then abruptly went up over Stake Pass. This was a bit of a wake-up call but we made good time and without problems. We stopped and spoke to a group of path-laying volunteers. The leader was an Australian conservationist. It was his full-time job making the paths in the Lakes more protected against corrosion. He explained that sometimes they started work at 5.30 in the morning because it took them two hours to reach where they were working. In the summer months they often didn't finish until nine at night.

On the tops the walking was tremendous. It felt like we were the only ones on the earth. Brilliant. Slowly we descended into Stonethwaite, Rosthwaite and Borrowdale. It was here I recognised where I had walked through on the Coast to Coast. I got all excited. At Rosthwaite we sat on the bridge over the River Derwent and had lunch. It was great to dangle the legs for a while. There were quite a few walkers out here. Mostly I noted older, retired, fit people who had plenty of time on their hands. Borrowdale is a particularly pretty part of the Lakes with good walking in all directions.

Another six miles to go to Keswick, this time round the edges of Derwent Water, a bit of a repeat of Coniston Water. Nevertheless, reaching Keswick YHA was easy enough.

That mug of tea we had every day after walking was always the best. We sat in this huge lounge drinking several cups. Again we had arrived at a reasonable time (5.30pm) which allowed us to relax.

Showered and changed, we went to a pub called The Bank. Here I was able to test which beer I would like. I was definitely getting hooked on this life. To me it was pure escapism and I don't apologise for it. Again, the food was fabulous. Bob ordered lamb and I had braised beef. By far too much to eat but Bob seemed to have an enormous appetite and polished everything off!

We came back and watched television for a bit. I then headed off to bed early. This time, my dormitory was full of Japanese girls. I became a bit of a mother hen. They decided to hit the town at 11pm when I was turning in and I couldn't relax until they came in safe. That was 3am. They were very noisy but finally I could drop off.

Thursday April 2nd 2009. Keswick to Caldbeck – 17 miles.

Up at 7am, all the culprits were still asleep. I groggily got out of bed and showered and changed. I was pleased to be getting out. It had been a hot sticky night.

Breakfast was served at 7.30am. There was no sign of Bob, but it didn't really matter. He needed time away from me anyway. He might even have gone out last night, for all I know.

The weather dawned beautifully. I took some pictures of the river and towards the direction we would be going. I had breakfast with a professional photographer. He had his maps out and was looking for the ideal early morning shot. He was only a young guy. Then I was joined by some chaps planning the route for the Lakeland Dash competition. Their job was the fell running bit and they were going to be laying out the course for the competitors. It was like an enormous Triathlon Race but in teams.

Waiting for Bob, I sat out in the morning sun by the river. It was pleasant. He was ready by 9am, which was fine by me. I was just enjoying being away and getting fresh air.

From Keswick, we headed north towards the car park that leads up to Skiddaw. The path towards Skiddaw House was wonderful. The sun was out, there was a gentle breeze. I couldn't be happier. Bob and I walked along in companionable silence. To me this was just the ticket. I could have my own thoughts and appreciate the surroundings in full. It was very uplifting as all that could be heard was the constant babble of the Glenderaterra Beck, and occasionally, skylarks, buzzards and sheep. It really is a great path as it stays high but not on the tops, giving the walker a different perspective of the Lakes.

At Skiddaw the path divided. Walkers can choose a path that is easier but longer as it circumnavigates the fells, or take the north-easterly route going over the Caldbeck Fells, with the highest point on the entire walk called High Stile. I was so pleased it was beautiful weather and I had Bob with me, because we chose the latter. No argument; it was too good a path to miss. We were not disappointed and the day got better. It was so warm.

This day was so special. We ambled along on our obvious path. We only met three people, a lady with an Airedale dog, a man on a bicycle, and a lady emerging from the Beck below us. We slowly descended to a point where the path meets the road at 'Paddy Gill', before turning up the long slow path towards Hare Stone. It was a gentle ascent for most of the way until the final climb up the sides of Grainsgill Beck. Here the path turned to nothing and was very similar to walking in Scotland. I could see how easy it would have been in poor conditions to miss the path turning off towards Hare Stone.

We stopped for lunch by one of the numerous waterfalls and their deep pools of water. I stripped off my shorts and waded in. It was delicious. I think Bob probably thought I was a bit mad because it was freezing. However it did the trick. My feet and legs were cooled and I am sure I enjoyed my lunch far more than usual.

We finally reached High Stile. The views were panoramic

although slightly hazy. We could see across to the first hills of Scotland and the Solway Firth and ultimately our goal of Carlisle. A bit of sadness crept in here as this was where we would be leaving the fells behind.

Caldbeck was beckoning and it should have been easy from this point to reach it. "Just head north," we both said. Nether Row was elusive below us as we negotiated the quarries and slate mines that pockmarked the remaining fell we had to walk over. By the time we reached Caldbeck at 5.30pm, Bob and I were both frustrated with this part of the route, but the B&B was easy to find.

The accommodation was adequate with a comfortable twin room. The bathroom was next door. I was pleased about this. Then I became a little nervous. I had never shared a room on my own with another man other than David. Yes, I had dossed down in bunk houses with groups of men friends of my brothers but this closeness was a major test for me. Bob seemed totally oblivious to my nervousness or so I thought. I have to say he just humoured me along and was the perfect gentleman. I had relaxed in his company over the past few days so I felt confident I would be okay.

From our bedroom window I could see whence we had come. It was a glorious sunny evening. I took the opportunity to wash some smalls and hang them out our window, whilst Bob had his kip. On the outside of the house, glancing up it must have looked like Widow Twankey's place. That made Bob smile.

After the usual showers we went in search of food. We sat outside The Oddfellows after we had ordered our food and waited in the dying sunshine. Bob had steak and I salmon. It was very good value with beautiful fresh vegetables. Again the beer was good. We congratulated ourselves on having found such decent pubs to eat and drink in.

I was tired, and after a whistle stop tour of the village where we found a clog shop (!) and then sorting out our route for the next day, I was happy to lie on my bed and write.

In my diary I wrote: *'Today was a memorable day, one that will stay in my mind. I feel blissfully free of cares or responsibilities. Is that wrong of me? I have had a good companion to walk with. It is good to walk with someone who walks at the same speed and in quiet thoughtfulness. I have enjoyed every minute and am very grateful. I hope Bob has enjoyed it too and I hope he would be honest enough if he hadn't. Tomorrow is Carlisle, I only ask my feet for one more day and then it is home. Something I do not want to think about yet, although I miss David. It is him who should be here.'*

Friday April 3rd 2009. Caldbeck to Carlisle - 11 miles.

I woke at 6.30am. Bob was still sleeping. Our walk, according to the book, was not going to be the best bit. As it turned out, we thought it was okay and a stark difference to the fells. It just became a bit of a trudge the last two miles into Carlisle, but often that happens as you near towns. Particularly as it was warm and humid.

We set off at 9.30am after a decent breakfast and Bob diving into the sweet shop for more supplies. The day was warm but we could feel that the temperature was changing. It was going to be one of those days where outer clothes kept going on and off.

It was a gentle, muddy walk through Parson's Park. Here they boast red squirrels but we didn't see any. We followed the meandering Cald Beck for much of the morning, passing through Sebergham, a tiny pretty village very similar to those of Wiltshire and Dorset. Pristine farms and large halls were in evidence – what I would call ideal horsey country. The daffodils were stunning along the roads. We then followed the River Caldew. It was very pleasant and easy on foot. At Rose Bridge a sea mist came in and the air temperature dropped dramatically. Behind us stood the impressive Rose Castle but it wasn't that clear.

This castle was built for the Bishops of Carlisle and dates from around 1340, Strickland Tower being the oldest part. Many of the original buildings were destroyed during the English Civil War and then restored by the bishops in 1760, and then more recently by Bishop Percy in 1852 under the guidance of the well-known architect Anthony Salvin. It is not open to the public.

Moving on, we passed other large houses – Lime House School and Hawksdale Hall. At 12 noon we were at Bridgend. This was halfway, such was the flatness of the walk. The next stage was a little hard on the feet as we followed a hard track beside the river all the way to Dalston. Sadly, although pretty, it was our first encounter with noisy industry since leaving Ulverston and was a bit of a culture shock.

Dalston marked the beginning of the end of our walk. Six miles of cycle track; the only saving grace was that there weren't many people on it. We had plenty of time to reach Carlisle, so for lunch we found the only piece of woodland next to the river, with the cycle track behind us. It was a good opportunity to check the feet as they had become very hot on this last stage. I was not going to spoil the remaining bit by hobbling. We both thought that if we could get into Carlisle early we could rearrange the train we already had tickets for. It was a possibility and a motivator.

We finally got to Carlisle Station at 3.45pm. We were very tired and frustratingly the station had been difficult to find. Anyway, we rearranged our tickets and with five minutes to spare and the good grace of the train driver allowing us on early we caught the 4.05pm back to Lancaster, then the 4.53pm to Ulverston.

It was a lovely finish to the walk. The train ride was brilliant as we passed around Morecambe Bay and across the sands. We could see Hoad Hill once more.

We arrived back at The Walkers Hostel at 6pm. Very relieved, as we weren't due in until 9pm. This meant we could relax with more tea! And more tea!! We then had showers, and went out for an Italian dinner to celebrate. Brilliant.

We arrived back at the hostel only to find that some festival performers had made late bookings. Bob and I had been put into this tiny bunk room together – gulp! The proprietor apologised but he warned us we would be better in the same room. He needed the business but they could be noisy! It was a once a year event. We understood his reasoning and we were just grateful he had looked after the car. For me, having settled down in Bob's company, I felt okay but oh dear, Bob was the least of my worries as it turned out, and actually I was glad he was there.

Disturbed at midnight by loud knocking on our doors and walls, a party of well-oiled performers were enjoying 'relaxing' at our expense. The language and what they would do with the women they were with, coupled with cigarette smoke drifting in through the window from outside, was not good. It was abusive and obscene. They were all drunk and loud, it was awful. I checked the door and asked Bob if he was awake. "I am now," he said. I felt really bad. Actually, I was concerned about his car. A large van was parked awkwardly across it. I just hoped it was alright and there was no damage.

The behaviour carried on as these people played cards until 3pm. When they came upstairs it felt like they were going to walk in on us. Finally, with loud grunts and burping and farts, they crashed out. I didn't dare go to the toilet and I was dying for a pee.

Saturday April 4th 2009. Home again.

I finally slept and when I awoke, I made sure I made a lot of noise past the men's dormitory. I thumped the door and banged the walls at 6.30am. My little protest. Then I went and made a cup of tea.

The night did nothing to quell the achievement of the

week. It had been a wonderful walk. I sat in the window of the hostel thinking how good I felt.

We drove home and made good time. The weather was kind to us. It had been a fantastic walk, comparable to the Coast to Coast with its changing scenery and different challenges. I would recommend this walk to anyone, it is so doable. Most of all, I had walked with a person who had accepted me as I am. He had been a guardian and companion, a male I could finally trust besides David.

I know David was grateful that the walk had been a success. I can only thank my companion for making it one of the most memorable parts of my journey, for all the right reasons.

CHAPTER FOURTEEN:

COPING WITH MY FIRST AND LAST BLISTERS

CARLISLE TO GLASGOW. DISTANCE: 112.6 MILES. DATELINE: APRIL 30TH–MAY 9TH 2010.

The Pash Wagon had not been that reliable during the winter months of 2009/10. David was having some problems with it. We had travelled down to Katy in Devon and had been escorted off the motorway by police! It was frustrating. I wasn't going to rely on it. I also felt I had to finish the whole journey in 2010. Something about round numbers. It then would have taken me five years – and six years didn't sound so good!

Christmas came and went. After much deliberation about this leg of my journey, I decided I would use a tent. First I needed to buy one that I could use for this trip but it also had to be useful for subsequent trips I did on my own. In the end I plumped for a Nordic Wild Country two-man tent – a high-spec lightweight (2.4kg) variant designed for backpacking.

Next it was booking holiday time and then persuading Bob he did want to accompany me again. Much of it was to be on

263

roads, but there would be two and a half days in the Lothian Hills, which were quite remote. To be fair he was reluctant and in hindsight rightly so. Roads were to play a significant part in this story.

In physical preparation for this trip, Bob and I walked the Clarendon Way one weekend to see if carrying the weight would be alright. Although we had the tent, David came and picked us up and Bob stayed over at ours. The weight was fine. I had 15 kilos with some food and water to go in. The final weight was 20 kilos.

I had no reservations about walking with Bob again (see previous chapter). He is a gentleman, and so reliable. David was fine about me going. I can only thank him for allowing me to go. Not every bloke would allow their wife to sleep in a tent with another man! Even so I was a bit nervous at how this was going to pan out. I could see no problem except having my own privacy, or he having his, if you get my drift.

Friday April 30th 2010. Off to Carlisle.

Picked up at 8am, we arrived in Carlisle at 3.30pm. We sorted out our accommodation at The Steadings B&B just outside the town. I would recommend this place. One of the units was called The Dovecote. It slept five and we had it to ourselves, so we each had our own choice of room. Phew! We would also be using the cottage on our return. The people here were very friendly. The farm and its outbuildings had been converted into either spacious cottages or small businesses. There were plenty of tea bags and milk available. It had been a good choice. Again, these kind people were going to allow Bob to keep his car there for the duration of our walk.

Once we had drunk masses of tea, we sauntered out to find the start of our walk, which would take us across meadows firstly and then onto the road required. This didn't take long.

The evening was spent in the Near Boot Inn. The dinner was delicious, gammon and chips for Bob and steak pie and vegetables for me, all downed by two and a half pints of Pedigree Marstons. The two-mile walk back to the B&B sobered me up.

We found the cistern in the toilet was blocked on our return; it didn't flush properly. We watched television for a bit and read the paper, then went to sleep.

Saturday May 1st 2010.

Carlisle to Kirkpatrick-Fleming - 13.5 miles.

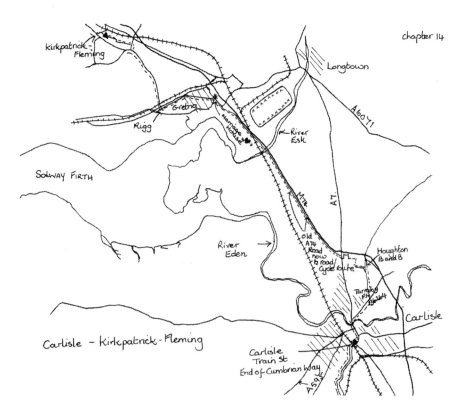

Breakfast was enormous and we got going at 10.10am. The weather was chilly but bright. It was a noisy hard slog beside the M6. We followed the old A road that ran parallel to the motorway nearly all day. At one point there was only a fence between us. Not a pleasant start.

My feet got very hot from walking fast on tarmac. I would not sustain this speed. I had brought different boots, my newer lighter weight ones. Bad mistake. They had never given me trouble before but as my feet swelled, this left less room in the boots and they started to rub. Oh dear.

Reaching the campsite at Kirkpatrick-Fleming could not have come soon enough. The campsite was great, all facilities good. We had made it in quick time. It was 3.30pm. The air temperature was quite cold and windy.

The tent went up very easily. Fortunately, we didn't have to cook. We just had a large mug of tea and then our showers. On inspection, although my feet were hot they were fine. I was concerned about the next day though. We still had lots of road to do and the distance would be a mile longer than today.

We went to a local pub for another enormous meal and sat with a Yugoslavian couple. Our conversation was a bit stilted with the language barrier.

Sunday May 2nd 2010. Kirkpatrick-Fleming to Lochmaben - 14.5 miles.

I slept well and felt deliciously comfortable in the sleeping bag, nice and toasty. The weather outside was good. My feet felt fine again.

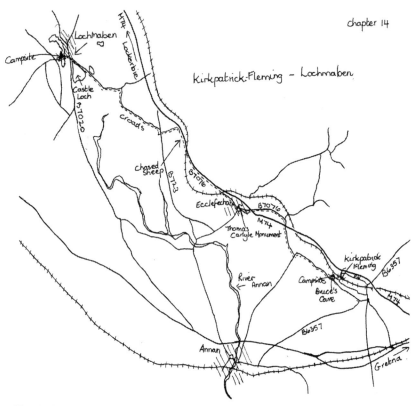

We left the campsite at 9am. Weather still fine but a chilly wind was blowing. We were lucky really that it wasn't raining.

The walk to Ecclefechan was good. We had lunch there. My feet were just beginning to get very hot again. We had not been so close to the M6 until this point, which had made it less noisy. We sat on a bench and ate sausage rolls. It was good to get the weight off my feet. They were becoming very warm and in danger of breaking into blisters, which they duly did about two miles out of Ecclefechan.

I had already put on blister plasters as a preventative but with three eruptions on one foot and two corkers on the other, life suddenly became painful.

The only event before we reached the campsite was finding a sheep walking along the road all by itself. We had a bit of fun trying to get it back in its field. Bob shouting instructions and trying to herd this sheep was quite hilarious. After this I used my poles to ease the pressure on my feet. It certainly helped, but my feet continued to get worse. I could feel more blisters erupting. I cannot describe the pain. It was excruciating and only worsened by the constant pounding on the tarmac surface. I slowed Bob down, which was annoying for him and for me, but we still maintained a pace of two miles an hour.

Actually, we probably went faster, as it only took us seven and a half hours to do the 14.5 miles and that included all the stops. I didn't think that was too bad, considering the 20 kilos I was carrying.

We arrived at Lochmaben campsite at approximately 4.30pm. It couldn't have come soon enough. I was hurting. I thought of Paula coping with her blisters. But I was still upbeat.

We had to wait for the proprietor to come before pitching. It was a beautiful tranquil evening, although my feet didn't think so. The campsite was by the loch (I was glad it wasn't midge season) and the sun was just setting on it. It was very pretty; there were swans at its edge. The caravans had the best spots overlooking the loch and our pitch was above them on the grassy, flat edges of the local playing field and dog walking facility! This Bob discovered to his cost as we were putting up the tent! After much cursing and swearing, and seeing a side to the man I hadn't yet witnessed, I (please note this) cleared it up! Apparently as a woman 'I am used to nappies'. I just found it all rather amusing. On the plus side we did have a wooden fence to hang our washing on.

The tent went up quickly and the shower block was ideal again. There was a beer festival going on behind us and a rock band was playing in one of the pubs. It didn't last all evening, thank goodness! We walked into the village and located the route for going onwards the next day, and then found a great pub for another delicious meal. The Railway Inn provided us with steak pie and chips, all for a tenner. I had one pint of Guinness and Bob had three pints of Pedigree. I was never going to catch up!

The pub was very busy as a group of rugby supporters were in, celebrating something and slowly getting pissed. It was only 7.30pm. There was a great family atmosphere in there. It was enjoyable to people watch.

Much fatigued (well I was), we turned in for the night just before dark. 9pm!! We were going to have hot chocolate but it had turned bitterly cold once the sun had gone and a breeze had sprung up. It was lovely to be horizontal and I was just savouring my sleeping bag.

Bob was still getting changed when we had a visitor. It was priceless. This West Highland terrier came into the tent and started sniffing about as Bob was just getting his trousers off. Well, the explosion of abuse. I turned over to find Bob face-to-face with this terrier who was now being backed out of the tent rather quickly, as a stream of F***s and B***s and what owners should do with their dogs were loudly vocalised. It was so funny. I couldn't stop giggling, which probably made it worse. All that came to my mind was, 'There's nothing like being caught with your trousers down!' Of course, it wasn't his fault that he had left the tent door open!

Still smiling, I nodded off and slept like a top.

Monday May 3rd 2010. Lochmaben to Gubhill Farm (Dumfries) - 11.2 miles.

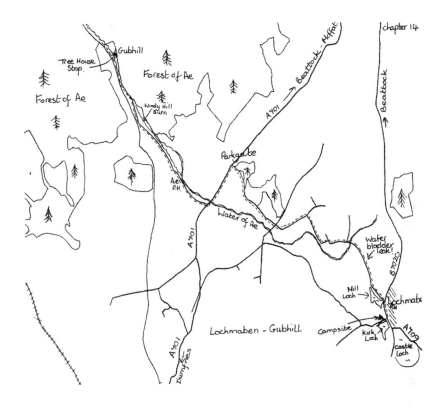

Waking at 6am, I was dying for a pee; all that beer. It was chilly. Outside there was a frost but a clear sky, the weather sunny with a cold wind. I didn't really want to get up; I was all toasty again. My feet needed dressing. I had left them to breathe overnight with no plasters on, so I could clearly see the extent of the damage. Five medium blisters on the left foot and still two corkers on the right, possibly another coming up. Oh bugger. Another painful day ahead.

Before breakfast I took some painkillers and redressed my feet. I was so glad that this time I had over-estimated how many blister plasters I would need. I knew I was going to have to pace myself or the whole trip was going to be agony. I also knew once I got over the blistering stage I would be fine. My provisions were going down, so was the weight of my sack. What kept me going was experience really. I had wanted to do this stage backpacking, so bugger it – I would achieve it and sod the pain. I just felt terrible about letting Bob down, as he would have liked to walk faster.

I have never given in and I wasn't about to do that now. I just kept thinking of Paula and how she had coped.

We let the tent defrost and dry for a bit, setting off at 10am. We stopped at a shop to get Bob's dinner. But his rucksack sprung a leak! His water bladder had dislodged inside, allowing the water to flow out of the connections. Oh dear!

After this was sorted we continued. Finally we would soon be getting off tarmac and heading towards the hills. Our reward today was following a red squirrel along the road for a while, until it decided it was better off in the trees.

We pressed on quite quickly, my feet complaining bitterly. I started to use poles. It was agony as I could feel more eruptions. This tarmac was not conducive to long distance walking. It was so bad when we reached Ae that I was not prepared to walk a hundred extra yards downhill to get a cup of coffee. My sense of adventure just deserted me! I had drink with me, but a coffee would have been fantastic. However, the sheer effort was enormous. I took my rucksack off and said to

Bob to go down and have a cup. I could see he was annoyed and frustrated. He didn't go. I think he thought it really wasn't worth going on.

I just needed to slow down. Watching Bob later, walking on in front, tears of pain rolled down my face. I wasn't sure if it was the pain of the blisters or the fact I was letting Bob down. I was annoyed at myself for having boots that just weren't right for the job. To be fair, I didn't know that at the start. They had never let me down before.

I had already circled an area two miles north of Ae at the top of the valley, before the trees at Gubhill. On the map it looked like there were a few buildings and a river. Perhaps we could wild camp there. If I had felt better, we would have travelled further on but as it was, on reaching Gubhill, there was a farm offering cottage accommodation (now that would have been nice). The lure of resting up in a cottage for two or three days was rather appealing, but that couldn't happen. I had to be back for work.

The owner of the cottages was in the fields. He was hand spraying some crops and grass to prevent disease. On asking him if we could put up the tent, he looked around and said, "How many of you?" I just replied, "Us." "Oh well," he said. He was reticent and rightly concerned. After all, it is not every day that an odd couple arrive out of the blue. "I've just sprayed these fields, I can't put you on them. I suppose you will want water?" "Yes, that's it," I said. I explained what I was doing and how bad my blisters were and bless his heart Mr Stewart kindly took pity.

"Right, okay, I do have somewhere you could go if you don't mind walking across the rough ground over there." He pointed quite some distance from the farm buildings. Further away from the house was a patch of rough ground with trees, ferns and brambles and a stream running through it. And in the middle of it was the most amazing hut/tree house/den built to very high specification, with polystyrene insulation and huge front windows.

We discovered it housed a lovely double futon mattress. There was just enough room for a little table. The den boasted a veranda made of decking and a large log had had suitable footholds cut out of it, allowing people to climb up. It truly was manna from heaven.

Not having to put the tent up was fantastic. Bob kindly went and brought back water. He had a great water container that weighed next to nothing and collapsed into next of nothing.

To me this place was like a dream come true. The views from the tree house were a naturalist's delight. The farmhouse could barely be seen, and the valleys in front dipped and stretch upwards. Green fields surrounded by stone walling had sheep and cattle in them. Conifers rose behind and in front, the trees providing shelter for birds and mammals. The 'house' was only six feet off the ground, but built on a large raised mound. We were able to put our rucksacks under it in the dry. Everything had been thought of. Away from the tree house in a sheltered hollow was a table and chairs. By this I mean two large cords of sliced tree trunks provided seats and then a thinly sliced piece (two inches thick) of tree trunk was the table and cooking stand. It was brilliant. We were out of the wind in the hollow and the last rays of sun were just hitting where we sat. It was still too cold to leave our jumpers off and we did keep our windcheaters on too.

Tea was a three-course menu! For starters we had soup, followed by a main meal of stew and dumplings courtesy of Wayfarers Meals, finished off with cheese and biscuits. It was very satisfying. Most of all, a bit more weight had gone out of the bag. I felt bolstered again.

I sorted out my feet and had a bowl wash. Managing to burst the blisters, I saw they now comprised eight large ones on one foot and four on the other. With the fluid out and the pressure off them, at last I left them to air for a bit. Bliss. I was a happy bunny. Finishing the walk early and having air to my feet was going to give them the best chance of recovering and drying out. Fortunately I had brought socks to change into each day and my boots dried out very quickly.

Mr Stewart had given us a spade for our ablutions. He told us exactly where we could do this, which was a good few hundred yards distant over very rough ground, away from the tree house and out of sight of the farmstead.

Digging a sod out when you are dying for a crap is difficult. I was very grateful for the privacy though. Visiting the latrine a second time round was difficult in flip flops. All I can say is don't try this. Having reached the spot, my feet damp and slippery in the flip flops, as I lifted the sod out again my left foot slid ungracefully into the hole. It's at these times one is glad to have antiseptic wet wipes on one's person!

By 8.30pm we were in our sleeping bags. It was still light.

The last sun was hitting the window, making the hut feel warm even though it was cooling down rapidly. Bob was reading as I wrote my diary, face and feet glowing. I had the bottom zip on the bag open to allow the air to keep drying my feet. They certainly were saying 'thank you for stopping'.

As darkness fell, we saw the last buzzards going to roost and a barn owl swooping through the valley. I just couldn't believe where we were, and I was so pleased we had stopped and asked. The futon was very comfortable for me, but I think Bob found it a bit spongy with the head rest in the wrong place. I dropped off to sleep with Bob still reading, thinking there'd be no great rush in the morning, no tent to get down.

I was awakened by Bob at 11pm, wondering what beasties might be eating our rucksacks below, as we could hear noises. We both had pees and looked about. Then we went back to sleep.

Tuesday May 4th 2010.
Gubhill Farm to Glen Valentine - 18 miles.

Waking at 5.30am, I laid there watching the view out of the window. It was so peaceful. I cried quietly. I was thinking I would have never seen this place but for the walk, I'd never had this chance to see or do something so special. It was like a childhood wish come true.

Amazingly, the sun was just starting to shine across the surface of the valley. There had been a frost. Everywhere had that luminescent sparkle to it. Then I looked at Bob, who was snoring. I just smiled to myself. Let sleeping gorillas lie.

I stayed still until 6.30am. Don't you wish sometimes you

didn't have a bladder? Sod it, I was going to have to get out of my cosy bag. Afterwards, I crawled back in trying not to disturb Bob, still sleeping or pretending to. I wrote more in my diary. It was very cosy.

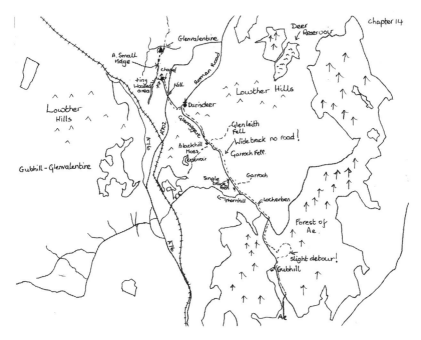

Today we were finally heading into the hills properly. I had been looking forward to this part. Especially as it would be better on the feet!

I made tea at 7.30am, having to break up the ice in the water bag. It was easy to pack up. We took it slowly. My blisters were infinitely better; three had started to harden. Thank God. It took time getting plasters on and I knew if I could get over today, all the blisters would soon harden and my feet would be great again.

I was just so pleased with the weather. It was extremely cold but we hadn't needed our coats for rain, just wind-proofing. The sun had come out for us and that had been a bonus.

We set off at 10am, leaving the spade in the barn as directed and our rubbish in one of Mr Stewart's bins. In so doing, we made a bit of a navigational error and turned right up the track instead of left. Whoops! After climbing out of the Forest of Ae and making a detour of about a mile, we finally saw the Lothian Hills in front of us. En route we were followed by two hares, and saw a heron, a redshank, a lapwing and another squirrel, all within the space of three miles.

This was to be our best day. At Garroch we finally walked on a grassy track. Here we met a lovely farmer driving a four-wheeled buggy with his sheepdog in the back. He explained what a devastating effect the winter had had on the sheep stocks right across the southern borderlands of Scotland, particularly towards Edinburgh where the snows had come in so suddenly.

Leaving the farmer behind, we set off on the best path of the walk. Grassy and spongy underfoot, we moved along very quickly. It was great. My feet could bear the weight on such easygoing ground. The path wound its way through the valleys of some lovely hills and mountains for six miles towards Durisdeer.

We stopped twice for breaks. The wind chill didn't allow for long. At Blackhill Moss I lost my navigational head, Bob seeing me straight. Too many boundaries and changes to fences confused me for a bit, yet my logic was telling me which way I should go. The compass came in useful at that point, clarifying everything.

Moving on we came into Durisdeer. It was early afternoon. Here we finally stopped for a rest. My feet were beginning to protest badly. Again I had trailed behind Bob, quietly crying with pain. I was so bloody mad at myself for having the blisters. I didn't expect any sympathy and I didn't get any. I have always maintained these things are character building. I think Bob was just ready for me to give up. I am not like that though. I go kicking and screaming. But things were improving; I hadn't needed my poles this day. I had taken painkillers a couple of times, which helped.

We stopped at Durisdeer on a welcoming bench. What a relief. I sat and ached, willing my feet and body to keep going. I was in agony again.

Durisdeer is well worth a visit if you are passing. It is a quiet little hamlet, its fame coming from when it was used as one of the locations for the 1978 film version of The Thirty Nine Steps. It was once a pivotal meeting place during Roman times and the original Roman road with its well preserved fort can be found along a path to the north of the village.

The parish church serves Drumlanrig Castle, home to the Duke of Queensberry. For all its plainness, behind the church stands the Queensberry Aisle, burial place for all the dukes. This marvellous room houses some of the most impressive marble carvings by Jan Van Nost. We would have not known of this beautiful structure had not a kind person showed us around the back of the church. It's truly a hidden gem.

From Durisdeer, we were looking for somewhere to camp for the night. Thanks to Bob's determination to keep me going for another three and a half miles, we finally plumped for the best location possible. Having staggered along a lovely green ridge for one and a half miles, the views marvellous, the path finally dropped down into the valley at Glen Valentine. Here two rivers met with a wonderful soft mossy green ledge set just back from them. It was an ideal spot for the tent.

Our route, visible in front of us, would take us over Wanlockhead to Leadhills. The sun, although weak, just hit the spot where the tent went up, and we managed to have our dinner before the wind became too chilly and the sun finally dropped out of sight. Today's menu was soup followed by pasta chicken and cheese and biscuits, all washed down with three mugs of tea.

The running water was so inviting. I staggered over with my wash kit. With my companion out of sight, I was able to have a strip wash. Actually I was so knackered and hot, flippantly I couldn't have cared if he was watching. The water was freezing but delicious on my feet and now somewhat sticky body. It's all very basic but it is a woman thing to try to keep clean in the most primitive of situations. The best bit is cleaning the teeth. I always feel better after that.

I dug a hole for the toilet away from the bend of the river behind the tent. This was a bit tricky, the ground very stony. I always feel guilty about this bit. I try to find somewhere where animals will hopefully not be affected, leave no sign of mess and take dirty tissues away with me in a separate bag.

The temperature soon dropped, and we were in our sleeping bags by 7.50pm. I was toasty as the first spots of rain hit the tent. We had been so lucky up to now, but at least the low cloud meant it would be less cold during the night. We were very dry in the tent. I wrote my diary while Bob read, both of us pooped.

Wednesday May 5th 2010.
Glen Valentine to Glentaggart Quarry - 16.8 miles.

I slept until 5.30am after a brilliant night again. Outside there was very misty drizzle. Yuk, today we would have our toughest climb and the tent would be heavy. Great! But my feet were hardening, fantastic. The thought of climbing up that height made me snuggle back into my sleeping bag. Still, the bladder complaining as usual, I got up at 6am in the drizzle. I made porridge and a cup of tea. Poor Bob: that woman bothering him again to get going.

We left at 7.35am. We then started the slow but sure ascent up the valley following the Enterkin Burn, until leaving it to walk around the edges of East Mount Lowther to Whiteside – a height of 572 metres – before dropping down to Wanlockhead.

At Whiteside we met a man who was walking the Southern Upland Way. He had stayed in Wanlockhead for the night and was relatively dry, while we were soaked. The cloud and mist was still heavy at this point. Going uphill had been laborious and difficult with the heavy backpacks. I had slipped a few times on the long tufts and hidden rocks. My chest was heaving and I had had to get the Ventolin out. I could feel an asthma attack coming on as the damp air filled my lungs. They felt like bursting. Again, I was willed on by the fact I was enjoying this trek! And the fact that Bob was disappearing into the mist ahead.

Wanlockhead saw our first rest and a decent toilet. Here Bob was very patient with me. The visitors centre was not open; it was only 10.15am. So I was looking to be going on to Leadhills to catch the shop. But Bob was wanting breakfast and was waiting for the centre to open at 11am. We didn't quite communicate enough, well perhaps I didn't. I was still getting over the trauma of the climb. So we ended up going to Leadhills. The tiny shop was open, thank goodness. They provided coffee and plenty of choice of hot pies and sausage rolls for Bob's breakfast. I bought a tomato and chocolate. It was a welcomed break.

By now the sun had come out. It was 11.30am. We relaxed in the sunshine for a bit. We still had our woolly hats on though! But food becomes a real pleasure at these times and makes the effort worthwhile. Effort with a capital E, this walk was. I was to dig deep every day.

We sat outside between the shop and the pub, which are owned by the same person. When the shop closes at noon the pub opens. The shop isn't open every day so we had been lucky. She breathed a sigh of relief!

It was a steep but short climb out of Leadhills onto a track which led us over Hunt Law to Snarhead, Priest's Pool, and finally out of the hills where the track meets Duneaton Water at Eastertown. This was a great track that had wonderful views of the Lothian Hills. It was a brilliant day and the weather stayed kind. Sun out, but chilly wind; ideal really. Again my feet were tired but the blisters weren't quite as bad, although we did have to take it slowly. I even changed my socks halfway again. I really enjoyed this stretch, in a sadistic sort of way, I thought. I was terribly sorry for Bob who had never really seen me struggle before, and I had bent his arm so much to come with me on this trip. I can only apologise for that. I felt terrible at letting someone down. I was aware he was quietly cross.

By afternoon it was warm. We pushed on now looking for a place to camp for the night. The countryside had changed into rolling pasture land and small forestry woodland. It was pretty and the views extensive. Again we were so lucky –

another great wild camp just on the edge of a forest. We walked away from the road following the river upstream for a while and found a suitable spot to pitch. Time: 4.30pm.

It was a bit spongy but at least we had water and there was a private area to go to the toilet and have a wash. The only sound we could hear was the occasional lapwing and there were swifts nesting in the banks of the river. The evening was much stiller and we were quite sheltered. Again the clouds looked ominous but we were able to have our three-course meal sitting outside again. Today: vegetable soup, Lancashire Hot Pot, cheese and biscuits and Caramac chocolate washed down by two mugs of tea. That pack must be getting lighter, I thought. Bob's trousers had ripped during the day, and they were now done up with safety pins.

I needed deep heat gel on my legs, knees and thighs that night. The tent smelled like a pharmacy. At 8.30pm I turned in, knackered. Bob read for a time.

Thursday May 6th 2010 - Election Day.
Glentaggart to Strathaven - 15.2 miles.

Overnight it became very sultry and humid. Woken at 1.30am, I found it very hot and it was raining. In my sleeping bag, I took off my thermals without making too much noise and tried not to thump Bob in the ear. Down to my bra and pants, I was irritated constantly by a prickly heat and started to scratch. I was trying to sleep but then I got another itch until finally I thought I have got to get out and have a pee and cool down. I was just trying to be polite and stay still.

Then a voice said, "I need to have a pee and check the river." It turned out Bob had been awake thinking the rain might make the river rise enough to flood our tent, so he wanted to get out and check. He was being polite too. We took turns in going outside.

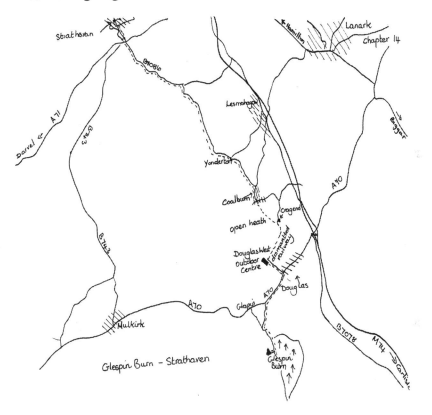

Oh dear! All dignity gone in the wind and rain! There I was in the quietest of places (except for the river) having the noisiest pee, half naked outside my tent with water squelching underfoot. I could feel the mud oozing between my toes. I started to giggle. I just couldn't help it. I stood there laughing in the rain, daft muppet. All I had to do now was clamber back into my sleeping bag – wet, muddy, but cool! Bob was very good; he turned over as I clambered unladylike into my bag. I shivered a bit so I put on my thermals again and guess what? In the damp I fell asleep until 5.30am.

When I woke the rain had stopped. I had breakfast and woke up Bob with tea. We left at 8am, having dried off the tent as best we could. Today I was wearing no plasters!! Hooray. My feet had finally hardened despite the mud last night.

On outskirts of Douglas, a lady in a bungalow accepted our rubbish. She did peer a bit suspiciously at me and looked around for other people. I must have an honest face, for she pointed to her bins around the back of the bungalow and then closed the door. It was really very kind of her.

A plan was unfolding. If we could get to Strathaven we could probably find a B&B to give us a break from the tent. It also meant we could dry out the tent and sort out our belongings. This seemed to be taken as a good idea.

From Douglas we made our way to Douglas West, a small hamlet which now mainly comprised of an outdoor centre. The hamlet had once been the train station for Douglas. We followed the old railway embankment from here and then onto what should have been a shortcut across the moor towards Coalburn. After much deliberation and taking a compass bearing, we set off on a difficult course. In hindsight it would have been easier by road but we came out at the back of Coalburn. A small shop that allowed me to use their toilet gave

Bob the chance to get some breakfast. They also did hot drinks, which were very welcome.

A taxi driver asked where we were going and he kindly explained a lovely road to take us into Strathaven. As it happened, that was exactly where we were going. The weather was kind to us and the views at South Brackenridge across the valleys were excellent. We didn't meet anyone on our way.

My feet again became unbearable as a new blister burst forth at Sandford, a mile out of Strathaven. Bollocks!

Strathaven was a wake-up call regarding noise. This was the largest town we had come across since leaving Carlisle, and the busy evening traffic with its one-way system was a little confusing. I had already enquired about B&Bs and had seen 'Rissons at Springvale' advertised. This turned out to be a great choice. I would recommend it to anyone. Mr Baxter could not have been more obliging or helpful. We had lovely twin accommodation with an en suite shower. Heaven!

Looking at my reflection in the mirror, it only reiterated the pain I had endured. I looked completely haggard, with red face, bruised eyes and grooves where I had never had them before. "God," I said to Bob, "have I looked like that for very long?" I was mortified as he nodded, affirming the worst. Oh joy! Not even a shower was going to give me a quick fix. I needed some serious plaster filling. Rather shocked at the apparition in front of me, I felt quite embarrassed to be going out later.

We could have had dinner out but instead, to relieve the load in our rucksacks, we ate two Wayfarer meals each and also had soup followed by cheese and biscuits. We then left the tent to dry in our room and went to the pub for a well deserved beer.

The Weavers was a very pleasant pub. We sat in a deep lounge settee, supping beer opposite a couple of elderly ladies there for a night out. It was a busy place with 1960s retro decor and modern flooring. A drop-dead gorgeous bloke served us a couple of beers. Hell; how is it us women look our worst at the least inopportune moments?

We returned to the B&B suitably tired and watched television. The election results had just starting to come in. Not looking good for Labour. I couldn't stay awake and with Bob still watching the TV, I dropped off to sleep as the smell of clean linen on my deliciously comfortable bed wafted in my nostrils.

Friday May 7th 2010. Strathaven to Dechmont Farm - 10.4 miles.

Morning came much too fast. It was with reluctance that I had another shower, put on a clean walking shirt with the same old smelly trousers and savoured a cup of tea in a cup!

We took our time over breakfast. I particularly enjoyed the smoked haddock, and eating off a plate instead of a tin can! We were in no great hurry to move fast, as this was an easier day. All road again but not the distance. And at least our loads were lighter.

We headed north out of Strathaven on the A726 to East Kilbride. It was uneventful, except Bob's safety pins came

undone on his trouser leg. It was sunny en route but with a
chilly wind. No rain again; we were so lucky.

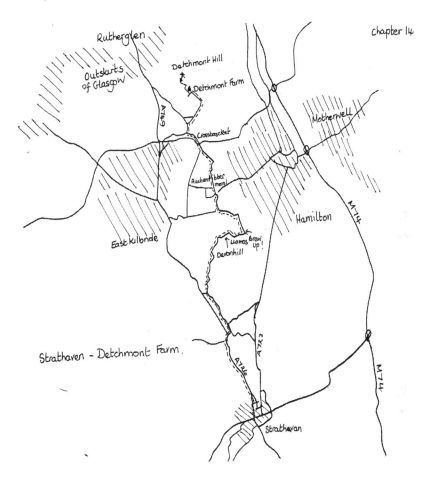

Strathaven - Detchmont Farm.

At Chapelton we took a minor road that was to take us to
Dechmont Farm, practically on the outskirts of Glasgow. It
was a treat for us to stop for the first time and have a brew up
by the road. However, it was chilly so we didn't stop for long.
A small forest offered a well needed toilet break.

The most interesting thing we passed at this stage was a llama farm at Devonhill. They came and spoke to us briefly. The views of Glasgow were panoramic from this hill. We could just pick out the Clyde and the urban towers of Maryhill..

The road continued, now slowly descending all the way to Crossbasket, where we had to negotiate the numerous roads and roundabouts of Hamilton. Just prior to this we passed a substantial memorial to those fallen in the First World War who lived in Auchentiber and the surrounding areas. It seemed a most unusual setting and as a walker you come across it at the roadside most unexpectedly. However, Auchentiber has now shrunk to a handful of houses, whereas once it was part of the Hamilton Estate. The memorial's pillars were from Hamilton Palace and marked the start of where garden walkways would once have been.

Hamilton Palace was demolished in 1921, having been one of the most substantial palaces in Scotland. Originally it was built in 1695 for the 3rd Duke of Hamilton on the site of a 13th century tower house. The palace then had major extensions added, following the plans laid out by the 5th Duke in the 1730s. The Palace was finally completed by the 10th Duke in 1842. It stood in enormous parklands, which were then landscaped. Within these gardens and parks were a three mile tree-lined avenue and the High and Low Parks, adding interest and height. A hunting lodge was also built.

The staterooms housed one of the finest private collections of art, including the works of Rubens, Titian and Anthony van

Dyck, and the palace had the finest furnishings. In its latter years it was used as a hospital for the Royal Navy during the First World War, after which time it was in such decline from neglect and required such vast amounts of money to preserve it that all its furnishings and fittings were sold off, before its final demise.

We arrived at Dechmont Farm at 2.30pm. Very early! William, the son of the farmer, was surprised to see us but after some explanation about when I had rung, he proceeded to find us a spot where there were no cattle. This was in a field that lay behind the milking shed towards the back of the farm. The track leading on towards our destination behind the farm was next to the field. We quickly erected the tent and then proceeded to walk up Dechmont Hill, 186 metres to the trig point, to find our route for the next day.

Dechmont Hill was the site of an Iron Age hill fort but in more recent times it was generally known as Dechmont Rifle Ranges. These date back to the early 1900s where there had been huts built for the purpose. The RAF used it for a practice live firing range during training. In 1941 it was recorded that there were 17 huts here. The views from the top were fabulous. Although chilly, the sun was out and we could see clearly for miles towards Glasgow and the hills beyond. Ben Lomond was there in the distance.

It took us rather a long time to find our route off Dechmont Hill. The map did not indicate how overgrown with gorse it was at its base, nor how deeply rutted its slopes were, gouged by cattle and used extensively for army cadet training. Below us we came unstuck trying to navigate a path through gorse and barbed wired fences. There also was a military firing range wall and marshland scrub. On its western flanks were a golf course and a small pine forest leading down to the back of another farm. In the end, this was the route that seemed the least inhospitable.

We met William again, who had come to feed the cattle grazing on the top. By this time my feet were really screaming to be let out. A chilly wind had blown up. It was now 6pm and we hadn't had anything to eat. I was very much relieved to be going back to the tent.

We had our last meal of the trip. By now it was cold. Bob collected our water from the dairy shed. Ann, William's mum, came and chatted for a while. They were so pleasant. The farm had been their lives for so long. I could have quite happily stayed there for longer. I find fascinating this affinity I have for the land and the countryside and how it evolves as a working landscape. I am always drawn to its simplicity and rawness; the people so rounded in their attitudes to life.

It was our final night in the tent; tomorrow Glasgow and then the train back to Carlisle. It had been a tough walk. I was exhausted, including my feet. The night was extremely cold. I think when we were having dinner my body temperature was not warm. I needed thermals, jumper and a hat on that night. Bob was reading whilst I wrote my diary at around 8.30pm. Shame there was no pub close at hand.

Saturday May 8th 2010.

Dechmont Farm to Glasgow - 13 miles.

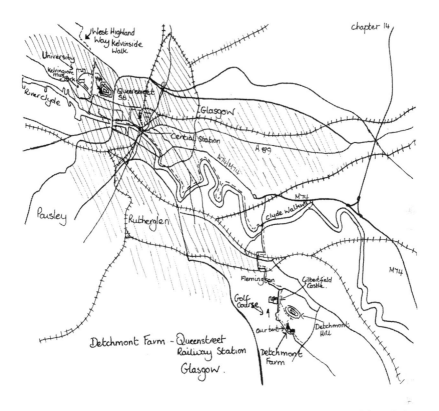

We woke to a very hard frost, after an uncomfortable night. Bob got the tea, and had to break the ice in our water container. Our fuel was low, the colder temperatures having taken their toll. We had half a canister of fuel left.

The tent was rigid. It was completely frozen outside but the skies were so clear where we were. The views from the tent were stunning. Below us, the cloud hung in the valley with rays of sun shining through it.

My adventure was almost over again. It had been extremely tough physically and mentally, yet was the journey worth it? If repeating this part, I would recommend another route from Carlisle, perhaps walking some of Hadrian's Wall and then going north. Another leg almost over though, I couldn't help feeling the flutter of achievement amongst the exhaustion. Bob was tired too. Road walking is not good.

We set off at 8am. Most of our walk was along the banks of the River Clyde. I was very surprised how pretty it was and how quiet, since we were only a stone's throw away from the heart of the industrial city. We had one last brew up along the banks of the Clyde before reaching our destination.

The weather was very warm. There was a regatta and rowing competition going on as we came closer to Glasgow city centre. We walked across the parks and into the station at 1.40pm. We managed to catch a fast train with its first stop at Carlisle. Fantastic. We only had to wait for a while, just enough time to nab an egg and tomato baguette.

We were in Carlisle by 2.45pm and back at The Steadings by 4.50pm, having grabbed a bag of chips to eat en route. Arriving earlier than expected but having rung ahead to say we would be back a day early, our hostesses put us up again in the same cottage. They were so accommodating and friendly, especially as they had been so busy the night before. Again we drank copious amounts of tea and coffee, then put our smelly gear in the car, had showers and went back to the Near Boot Inn for dinner.

Both of us were ready to tuck into something nutritious and we were not disappointed. It was with relief and not celebration that we had finished the walk. However, that did not dampen the fact my final destination was now very close and we drank a beer to that. It was not because of the alcohol that I staggered back to the B&B that evening, just that my bloody feet were still hurting.

The next morning, John gave us a wonderful breakfast again. We learned about his keenness to fish and how expensive licences were for some of the rivers in Scotland. We then left at 9.45am, the cistern still not working! Even worse, with large dumps in it! The day was bright but rain was forecast.

Our journey home uneventful, Bob kindly dropped me back about 5pm. It had been a mentally and physically exhausting adventure. I can only say I found out that I have no tolerance for blisters. Consequently I shall not walk with those boots when I have a full backpack again. This painful journey had tested my vulnerability and sustainability and I am proud I didn't give in. I can only thank my companion for accompanying me on one of the most gruelling parts of my journey.

It took two weeks for the blisters to heal!

CHAPTER FIFTEEN:

CATCHING UP WITH A FELLOW COAST TO COASTER

GLASGOW TO MILNGAVIE. DISTANCE: 10 MILES. DATELINE: SEPTEMBER 11TH–13TH 2010.

In hindsight, I can only say thank you to the Pash Wagon for breaking down! The van was still in bits and at this stage I could not see me finishing Land's End to John O'Groats this year. There were still two walks left to do in Scotland. Dampening my disappointment, my spirits were lifted by a piece of kindness. A friend was going up to Scotland with someone else and offered me a lift. If I could get myself into the city, they would drop me off at Glasgow Airport.

I was so excited by this opportunity that I rang my friend in Edinburgh to see if she would like to join me on this minute leg. Doing this little bit, if the van did get going later, it would mean I would not have to stop in Glasgow but instead get up to Strathcarron and then drop back to Fort William for the final piece. Just a glimmer of hope was enough for me. Having arranged a National Coach journey for my return (another new experience) and booking two nights at Glasgow Youth Hostel on the internet (I was getting good at bookings now), I accepted the lift.

The thought of being left at an airport would have worried me sick five years ago, but I had already used Glasgow Airport twice before, so catching a bus back into Glasgow was no concern. I had also previously found the youth hostel easy to locate and very comfortable. One could say I was becoming a seasoned traveller. I cannot express how much confidence I have gained from this walk. After all, I had not ventured out of Hampshire alone before 2004.

However, the most exciting part of this walk was to meet up with my friend from Edinburgh, a fellow Coast to Coaster (Wainwright's Trail). We had stayed in touch since 2004 and now the prospect of catching up once more would be great. Unfortunately she would not be able to join me on this walk but would be meeting me afterwards. That was fine by me.

Saturday September 11th 2010. To Scotland again.

How appropriate. I became a Great Aunt when baby Arran was born today, named after the Isle of Arran. My father would have been very proud. Ross and Catherine will make wonderful parents. I couldn't believe it – my brother a granddad!

I was picked up at Cadnam Roundabout outside Southampton at 5.30am. The weather was dry and bright, and we didn't come across rain until Manchester. We made good progress until the outskirts of Glasgow, and I was dropped off at the airport at 12.50pm. Taking the 500 bus to Buchannan Street bus station was a useful exercise, as this was where I had to catch the coach homewards on Monday morning.

I easily located the YHA, booked breakfast and a taxi for Monday morning (it was very early and I didn't want to be walking through the streets at that time) and found my room. It was 2.30pm. After freshening up, I bimbled into Kelvingrove Park – literally a stone's throw from the hostel – to find the start of the Kelvin Walkway, which leads out of town and towards Milngavie.

It is well worth a visit to Kelvingrove Park itself and allowing enough time to visit the world famous Kelvingrove Art Gallery and Museum built in its grounds, all of which are free! In fact, I would allow a spare day to wander Glasgow, as there is so much to see. I have seen so very little of this city and would enjoy a return visit.

For your interest, Kelvingrove Park was created as West End Park in 1852 by Sir Joseph Paxton, a noted English gardener of his time. The park is 85 acres in size and located in the West End of Glasgow. The land was bought by the town council, who recognised the need for a park as a place of sanctuary and recreation for the now expanding population of the industrial city and a contrast to the slums of the impoverished city centre. The park straddles the River Kelvin and has become an urban haven for wildlife. Herons, cormorants, kingfishers, mallards, foxes and otters frequent the area.

The park itself contains a bandstand, skate park, bowling and croquet greens, statues and monuments. Some of the monuments are very impressive. The largest one is the Stewart Memorial Fountain, built to commemorate Lord Provost Robert Stewart, who designed and became the major influential person in safe sanitation, building the water systems from Loch Katrin to Glasgow and thus providing the city with clean water. There are also monuments to Lord Kelvin (physicist), Field Marshall Lord Roberts, Joseph Lister and Thomas Carlyle, along with memorials to local regiments.

The park sits below the contours of a hill that had very desirable mid-19th century townhouses built on it. The houses are built in rows forming crescents similar to the Circus in Bath. The views are spectacular from these elegant buildings, Park Circus as it is known, overlooking Glasgow and the Clyde. When built, the new middle class of the time could easily escape the smells, noise and chaos of the city, whilst overseeing their manufacturing empires from a distance. Elaborate gates and steps led down to the park.

Some of these houses that had fallen into decline have now been restored, but converted into apartments or exclusive residential sites, or are home to solicitors and small businesses. The YHA occupies one of these spots and has marvellous views from its windows. Below stairs these days is the café, and not domestic servants.

Kelvingrove Art Gallery and Museum is a striking building completed in 1901, built in the Spanish Baroque style. It follows many other Glaswegian buildings in being built of Dumfriesshire red sandstone. The two main towers are inspired by the church of Santiago de Compostela. The interior is built in blond sandstone from Giffnock and on its pilasters are carved the 14 names of the Guilds of Glasgow Trades House. Relief panels on the upper levels are carved with the names of 36 'composures' and in the south end of the great hall is carved the arms of Scotland.

The building houses one of Europe's finest civic art collections. These include the Old Masters, Dutch Renaissance, Scottish Colourists and French Impressionists. Perhaps the most prestigious work – and indeed the most controversial when bought – is the painting by Salvador Dali of Christ of Saint John of the Cross.

The museum is the third most visited in the United Kingdom outside London. On entering the newly refurbished building, the visitor is struck with awe at the beauty and enormity of the flooring, with its three storeys of surrounding galleries. It is stunning. There is plenty of space and as a visitor one doesn't feel enclosed despite the museum's popularity. Many of the 8,000 exhibits appear random, including a Spitfire aeroplane hung in the lofty hallway. And a large Asian elephant called Sir Roger who lived and worked around the Glasgow area in the late 1800s. When he died, taxidermists preserved this well-loved animal. He was given a set of wooden tusks, as he never had any in life.

The diversity of exhibits is wonderful. In 2006 it had only just been re-opened after refurbishment and Shauna and I had the delight to visit all too briefly. It is one of those places that have ever-changing exhibits from local artists and renowned artists. Sadly, we didn't get to view Salvador Dali's painting as the museum is so vast. It is a must to return and savour this place.

I spent the early evening in an Italian coffee house which does fantastic coffees and wonderful pasta meals. I then turned in at 9pm. My room had three other ladies in it, two girls from America and a woman from Canada, all very easy to talk to. They were using the tourist buses to go on excursions from the youth hostel. This seemed very reasonable and ticks the 'must do later' boxes.

Sunday September 12th 2010.
Glasgow to Milngavie - 10 miles.

The day was bright. I had had a brilliant sleep from 9pm to 6.30am. How good was that! I already had everything packed for the day and crept out of the room. An adequate continental breakfast was ready for me by 7.15am and I was on the walk from 7.50am.

Kelvingrove Park was quiet. I easily picked up the route and headed out of town on the pretty Kelvin Walkway along the river. Surprisingly it was really enjoyable and I easily ate up the first three miles. I was not aware I was walking through a suburban area, as there was thick tree cover along the banks and the cycle path passed above the river. I came across a lovely weir and a place where a flint mill once stood. On the opposite side of the river there were botanical gardens.

Everywhere was so peaceful. I met two walkers and a cyclist along the route. Finally, I passed the last high rise flats of Maryhill and came out on the A81, crossed over and began the countryside section of this walk. Looking behind me as I crossed the parkland and past the riding stables of Caldercuilt, the views of East Dunbartonshire and the suburbs of Glasgow were extensive.

I was so pleased I had chosen this route because it certainly finished off the West Highland Way for me. If I was suggesting to anyone to do the West Highland Way, I would certainly recommend this as a warm-up exercise. It was a pleasant pathway that followed the Kelvin to Balmuildy Bridge. It skirted the edges of a wood and followed, for a little while, the remains of the old railway line, before the path abruptly ended at the edge of the A879. I had in mind to cross over and follow the path at this point, but the grass was long and I couldn't see a reasonable path clearly, so I followed the road to where the route meets the River Allander near the Tickled Trout pub. From here I followed the Allander along its canal-like banks almost into Milngavie.

I crossed a large steel footbridge called The Prescott Bridge constructed in 1990 and dedicated to SSGT Jim Prescott (bomb disposal unit) who gave his life during the Falkland War. A solemn reminder of our freedom.

Soon I was in Milngavie, reaching the granite stone marking the start of the West Highland Way that I had so thoroughly enjoyed in August 2006 (see next chapter). It was 10.20am. I stopped in the high street and had a café latte to celebrate. I couldn't stop grinning. The walk had been no effort.

Sat in the coffee shop my phone rang; friend Mandy was going to meet me at the youth hostel in two hours. A lady with a buggy pointed me in the right direction for the train. I walked right onto the platform, onto the train and headed back to Glasgow. I was so excited. I would have just enough time to walk back from station, have a shower and be ready to meet her. Sitting on the train savouring the walk, I can only say the achievement was bubbling up inside. The possibilities, a glimmering thought of still finishing the walk completely in 2010. If only... the van...?

When I came down the stairs of the hostel after having a shower and tidy up, Mandy was waiting for me. It was great to see her. After warm hugs and photos taken on the steps of the YHA, Mandy took me on a brief tour of Glasgow, including the area in which she had been brought up and amongst the cloisters of Glasgow University. What a beautiful peaceful place of learning. The entrance gates boast the initials of some famous people, including James Watt. Founded in 1451, it is the second oldest university in Scotland and the fourth oldest in the English–speaking world. As I walked around its quadrangle and touched its stone walls I could sense the history. All those students and academia absorbed and preserved through the passage of time.

We had lunch in a tiny Italian café just a small distance from the University. Sat outside on the sunny walkway, we reminisced over the Coast to Coast walk and caught up with news of our respected families. We then walked back to the hostel and Mandy took me in her car out of town to Bardowie

Loch, a small loch where she had learned to sail. This was so unexpected. It was delightful to be shown a place I would have never gone to. The day just got better and better. I was so glad we had stayed in touch and I could share with her a fragment of time on my walk.

The gates to the sailing club were open. We had a small wander around the yard. It was an ideal spot as Mandy was transported to her youth and explained about the days gone past.

She left me back at my accommodation at about 6pm, then I had a small snack in the café below the hostel before having a shower and getting my belongings ready to go home on the coach the next day. I had arranged for a taxi to pick me up at 7.30am, to catch the coach leaving at 8.10am from Buchanan Street.

Monday September 13th 2010.

Everything went to plan, but it was a very long journey home. We stopped several times to drop people off and pick up other passengers. At Birmingham the coach was full. It was then a long, tight journey to Oxford before the crowd thinned out again. I disembarked at 8.20pm at Southampton coach station, very tired but replenished, excited and jubilant about another triumph. It had been the very first time I had been on a National Coach; I was impressed. And another little step of my journey had been completed.

Now all I needed was a van…

CHAPTER SIXTEEN:

HEADING FOR THE HILLS OF BONNIE SCOTLAND

**MILNGAVIE TO FORT WILLIAM (THE WEST HIGHLAND WAY).
DISTANCE: 95 MILES. DATELINE: AUGUST 11TH–20TH 2006.**

After my 'group' experience on Offa's Dyke three months previously (see chapter eight), I was a little nervous at joining another group but excited to be doing another bit of my journey in special Scotland, of which I have marvellous childhood memories with my parents and with school. And I was sharing it this time with a friend who fancied doing the walk. I couldn't imagine ever going to Scotland and not enjoying myself.

The last time I had visited Scotland had been when I was 15 years of age and had climbed Ben Lomond and Goat Fell. This had been on a school trip. We had had wonderful weather, and the geographical importance of the trip was lost on me as the fresh air and the climbing took my attention. I also had my first taste of leadership here, with my skills put to the test looking after the 'First Years' at my secondary school.

This time I was determined not only to enjoy the walk but also to understand a little bit about the geology and geography. The company we were going with had a good reputation for this.

I will always be grateful to my friend Shauna, who was extremely good at booking everything. At this point, I was still very inexperienced in using the internet and buying online. I didn't even use internet banking then; I was still back in the Dark Ages. Worst still, the prospect of flying without the family on a small plane was not going to be the best part of the journey.

I had been to Cuba once with the family and the Channel Islands twice. That was the extent of my travelling on airplanes. Then I had acted calm for the children's sake. However, it was David who had coerced me through these events, as my nervousness about noisy waiting lounges and confinement made me sweat.

I have to thank Shauna for showing me the ropes in how to be relaxed, casual and chilled about these things. I don't know if she knew how nervous I was, but I can remember being a hyperactive blonde with excitement and anxiousness all rolled into one. What a naive person I was at that time; how quietly understanding Shauna had been.

Friday August 11th 2006. Travel day.

There had been some degree of uncertainty about how we would reach Scotland today. We had no idea if the flight would even go. During that week, the police and MI5 had averted what may have been another 9/11 type of attack on an airline flight from Britain to America. Since then flights had been experiencing cancellations and delays due to the tightening of security. Passports were definitely required even for internal flights, there was a clampdown on bottles carrying any form of liquid and sharp objects were being confiscated. (Lady razors being one.)

Fortunately our flight scheduled for 8.30am was only delayed by half an hour. Even so, on scrutiny our hand luggage had to go in the cargo hold and our bottles of water left at the desk.

We even had our walking boots taken from us and the soles inspected. I found this very nerve racking. As I have said before, I am one of those people who feels guilty even seeing a policeman. Still, Gertrude got through. It was to be my mascot's first flight and I hoped they would treat her gently as she dangled from the rucksack, looking a bit woeful as she went onto the conveyer belt and through the aggressive plastic doors. We had never been parted at this point. It was probably best that Shauna was not aware of my quirky thoughts at this time. She is by far the more sensible of us two.

Our flight was fantastic. We had marvellous views of the English countryside as the weather stayed bright and we were below the cloud line.

We landed in Glasgow at 10.20am and after collecting our luggage, we were out of the airport by 10.50am, heading for the interlinking bus. We were aware of more security presence at the airport, with armed policemen outside the front entrance. After two minutes' wait on the bus, a 15-minute ride brought us to Glasgow's Queen Street Station. By 12.30pm we were at Stirling Youth Hostel and booking in. Now we had all afternoon to relax. Fantastic.

Stirling Youth Hostel is situated in the old part of the town, a five-minute walk from the castle and set behind the facade of an historic church and next door to the Old Jail House. Now open to the public, this relives the story of Victorian jails at that time – with all the gory details! How appropriate I am typing this on Halloween night!

The hostel has a four star rating. We had a comfortable en suite twin room. It could not have been better. After leaving our luggage, we visited the castle and very impressive it was. Well worth a visit. There was so much to take in and really we needed longer to appreciate it. I was particularly fascinated by the weavers creating the Stirling Tapestries, a project which it is hoped will be finished by 2013.

Having a cup of tea in the castle café was very pleasant. Then we wandered into the town to find somewhere for an evening meal. A pleasant pub suited us, with its homely atmosphere. We went back to the hostel and to bed quite early and read.

Saturday August 12th 2006.
Milngavie to Drymen - 12 miles.

As usual I slept fitfully in anticipation of the walk. The weather was fine on awakening, and our meeting point for the group was at Stirling railway station for 8.30am. We had a leisurely breakfast and sauntered down to the station to greet everyone.

Well, just one member of the group named Michael. The C-N-Do van soon arrived and we met with others who were already aboard, having been collected from C-N-Do's headquarters.

We just had one more member to pick up who hadn't arrived yet. He was waiting back at their headquarters and when we arrived there, some of us took advantage by making one more trip to the loo.

Altogether there were seven in our party, plus the van driver Chris who doubled as the chef de cuisine for the week, and our mighty leader (tall) Richard. Almost immediately I felt at home with everyone.

From the start it was clear that C-N-Do went out of their way to put everyone at ease. It was evident they wanted us all to have a good time and to achieve the walk. The mickey-taking started over the luggage and the amounts people took.

Our leaders were clearly good pals. They were like chalk and cheese in many ways, especially the colour of their hair and their accents! They were a bit like a comedy act. They took the piss out of each other constantly, but equally they respected each other and any decisions were carefully planned for and executed. They took their job in leadership very seriously.

Our journey to the start of the walk was fun and we soon introduced ourselves to each other. Two people were French, one person came from Luxembourg, one was from London, one from Ireland and then Shauna and I. What a mixture but what lovely company. From the very start our redheads hit it off. Our Irish friend Nicola was so bubbly, infectious and wildly outspoken that our redheaded leader had great fun winding her up. The banter started from a mile up the road. I can remember soaking up the atmosphere on the bus and smiling to myself, but also feeling rather sick as we journeyed along the roads.

We arrived in Milngavie at 10.45am and had numerous pictures taken at the granite obelisk in the town that marked the start of the walk. Everyone was so upbeat, so gregarious and warm that instantly I knew I was really going to enjoy this walk. No one was too reserved. I was so eager to get going, and probably very loud and nervous in anticipation of the walk, questioning whether or not it would be too hard.

At 11.30am we set off at a brisk ambling pace. The way was flat as we walked along gentle paths through Allander Park and Mugdock Wood. Our first taste of climbing was past Craigallian Loch and on towards Carbeth Loch. It was quite windy but dry.

As a group, we settled into chatting and getting to know each other. For me it was lovely to be out again. I could feel the year's tension dropping away. I enjoyed my own space for a while and much of the time I was preoccupied with my own thoughts of Dad and his love of Scotland.

Near Blanefield we caught our first glimpse of Ben Lomond and the hills of Dumgoyach. Here I felt the sense of promise of the later hills. We continued walking across our first stretch of open moorland with its dramatic views and open spaces, with Dumgoyach Cone to our right. This cone is just one of the volcanic remnants in this area (The Campsies) where lava has been pushed upwards to the surface in successive layers and is almost certainly pure basalt.

I was beginning to feel at home. It is the smell that gets me every time. I do wonder sometimes if in my former life I was a cow or horse. I just love that wet earthy boggy smell that oozes from the rough pastureland and open moors of the valley.

We stopped for lunch near Dumgoyach Farm. Later, as we walked along a long flat path running parallel with the A81 past Glengoyne Distillery – this was the disused Blane Valley Railway Line opened in 1867 and finally closed completely in 1959 – we were relieved to stop for a welcomed break at the Beech Tree Inn. I was delighted to use its facilities!

It was warm as we all sat outside, and I had an orange juice. I surveyed our group. Yes, everyone was likeable, there was definitely going to be a sense of camaraderie just like the Coast to Coast.

From here, we ambled along the track until we reached the A81, where we crossed the road and fields and headed along a minor road into Gartness. At this small hamlet we crossed Endrick Water. Further along this river, in medieval times, once stood Gartness Castle, at one point home of the Napier family.

We followed the road with wonderful panoramic views of the fertile farming area of Strathendrick. Passing Drumquhassle Farm, we slowly ascended to the brow of a hill. The day had turned warm and I was glad I was in my shorts.

The views were extensive of the Campsie Fells, the Kirkpatrick Fells and northwards to Conic Hill. From here we caught our first glimpse of Loch Lomond. I leant on a stone wall at this point and took a picture.

A bubbling emotion rose in my throat. I had arrived, I was back in Scotland, and now the scenery could only get better, broader, more aesthetically pleasing on the eye. Soon we would be entering the area known as the Trossachs National Park.

We didn't actually walk through Drymen, instead the route stayed east of it and headed through Gateshead. Finally, we were picked up by our transport at a car park near the edge of Garadhban Forest at 5.30pm.

As a group we had done well. It had been a long day for some, travelling first then walking. Michael in particular must have been shattered, but he stayed very friendly.

Happy bunnies, we were bundled into the van and taken to Rowardennan Youth Hostel situated on the Banks of Loch Lomond. I had planned to have a swim if the weather was kind, but it had just started to drizzle. There was the usual commotion of sorting out rooms and holdalls but the guys had it pretty well sorted, and best of all Christ, whoops, Chris had already made a large pot of tea. He knew just what the punters needed.

We fell into two groups, those who wanted a shower first and those who just needed to collapse and relax for a few moments. Shauna and I were in the latter category. After the mug of tea we sorted out our backpacks and had our showers in turn.

Once we were all sorted almost everyone helped in some form or other in cooking the tea. I have to say Chris was so sorted and nothing was too much trouble. Supper was such a contrast from the Offa's Dyke experience. I knew now it hadn't been me on that trip. These people were so down to earth and the leaders so affable. We all shared the wine. The supper consisted of salmon, broccoli and potatoes, followed by melon and ginger biscuits. We shared the washing up, after which Richard gathered us together as he and Chris explained the format of making our own sandwiches in the morning and having bags ready for going back on the van for 9am.

They went over the route ahead because this was the first time they had really been able to chat to us formally. They mentioned if we needed any extra provisions, e.g. batteries or wine, we were to just ask them and the super duper van driver would get them. They were so approachable and professional and that was all that was required.

I went to bed and wrote my diary, very happy and physically tired. Wonderful, this walk was just what I needed.

Sunday August 13th 2006.
Drymen to Rowardennan - 13 miles.

I slept well, nearly always do, although I was awake early. I was first to get up and have a shower. I made a cup of tea at 7am; I am a creature of habit. I have always enjoyed that first quiet cup of tea before the hustle and bustle of the day. At work, in the quiet before my staff start arriving, I always make a tea.

Then I clear my desk, look at staff rotas, holidays and sickness absences, read and return correspondence, and check clinics are ready. That way I have always been cheery and accepting of what the day may bring.

Chris appeared and I helped lay out the breakfast things. This became the norm throughout the walk, so I will not repeat it again.

Breakfast comprised of cereals, toast, yoghurt and fruit, then we made our own sandwiches from a selection of options. In the back of the van there was a 'goodies' box consisting of fruit and different nutritious chocolate and snack bars, from which we selected our day's rations. I thought this was great because you decided how much your intake was, and for someone like me who didn't eat much going along, I could be selective.

We recommenced our walk at 10am. It was a fantastic day, the weather clear and glorious with just enough breeze to keep midges away. The forest soon opened out into open heathland. The ling and bell heather were splendid, adding vitality and colour. It was a great path that wound its way up to the summit of Conic Hill (358 metres), probably the best part of the day.

Here we sat on the hogsback ridge and admired the views. I savoured the moment. I was transported back in time, as in the distance the hills of the Isle of Arran could be seen, such was the clarity. Was that sharp point Goat Fell? I would like to think so. Luss Hills, The Cobbler and the western shores of Loch Lomond and some of its 30 or more islands were all clear.

Looking at the expanse of water, I was reminded of the

steam paddle ride I had experienced 37+ years ago and the photo we have of Dad stood on the jetty looking northwards up the loch.

Pivoting northwards there was Ben Lomond (974 metres), which is the most southerly Scottish Munro – mountains over 3,000 feet. I sighed, "God, it is good to be back." In the foreground the Endrick meandered into Loch Lomond. This fertile southerly point with its marshes has become part of Loch Lomond National Nature Reserve and is renowned for wildfowl and waders.

For your interest, Conic Hill lies on the Highland Boundary Fault. This is a massive geological fracture separating the Lowlands from the Highlands. The fault traverses Scotland from Arran and Helensburgh on the west coast to Stonehaven in the east. It separates two distinctly different 'physiographic' regions, mostly recognisable as a change in topography. A tectonic plate collision occurring 400-500 million years ago caused the major rift that now divides Old Red Sandstone from metamorphic rock. It can be visibly seen at the top of Conic Hill, as the fault runs through the southern end of Loch Lomond as is marked by the loch islands of Inchmurrin, Creinch, Torrinch and Inchcailloch.

Loch Lomond is the largest body of inland water in Britain, covering 27 square miles. It is also one of the longest Scottish lochs at 23 miles, its width up to five miles and at one point near Rowchoish bothy its depth is recorded as 623 feet. The loch provides up to 450 million litres of water for people in

Central Scotland. Creating a further impact on the loch is the leisure industry, bringing with it noise, sewage and destruction of wildlife habitat through the use of leisure craft and the activities of fishermen. Thousands of walkers, city dwellers and picnickers flock to its shores. (I was to witness this impact first hand; it was shocking – see later.)

To counteract this, Loch Lomond and the surrounding area of the Trossachs became Scotland's first National Park in 2002, offering it the best possible level of protection with funding and conservation management put in place.

The Loch also boasts huge diversity in its plant species. It claims to have a quarter of all known plants in Britain around its shores, 200 species of birds and 19 species of fish. It is said to be home of the lamprey, an eel–like parasite that can grow up to a metre in length, and the powan, a type of whitefish similar to herring.

Coming off the steep slopes of Conic Hill we took a steady descent via Fraser's Chair and Table. It was very warm. Then it was a rude awakening walking into Balmaha. I didn't remember people all those years ago. Now everywhere was thronging with hordes of people and cars. I called into a local shop for an ice cream, the temperature now reaching 25 degrees. The shopkeeper was not a very jovial chap. He 'hated the weekends', particularly in summer, and wished he could shut up shop. Everyone just bought beer and food, then dumped their rubbish outside. "No one cares any more and the noise goes on well into the night." He served me an ice and relaxed a little as I explained I was part of a group walking the

West Highland Way. "Oh," he said, "you aren't so bad, at least you are only passing through, although even some campers leave their rubbish on the beaches. We even have dedicated wardens now to clear up the rubbish after weekends." I felt sorry and horrified, and looking outside the shop window I could not disbelieve him.

I left him and pondered on this as I walked back to the toilet block in the car park and met the others. I wondered what on earth the shores would be like. Sadly, all his comments were true.

The second half of the day became slightly tedious as we negotiated parked cars on the shores, and tents put up in random places. I saw adults building bonfires, as well as vast quantities of overflowing litter bins with rubbish just left in bags (or not) around them. Beer cans were strewn everywhere. I felt ashamed to be human. This poem I wrote during the walk says it all.

The Loched Jewel

What do I give to you?

The glint of the sun.

Shimmering across the rippling waters of my body.

What do you give to me?

Cans of putrid tastes, smells, bags of diluted slime.

You are unfair in your treatment,

You scorn my shores in futile pursuit of something better?

You are lesser of those mortals, who know the jewel's moods,

Who respect, accept, its fragility and strength, its consistency.

Now

Ashamed am I feeling, scourged, sore from the belittling,

In the name of happiness?

Noises penetrate tranquillity, bouncing off the walls of towering peaks.

There to protect me.

What pleasure I could derive to live in harmony.

Infants, those fish like efforts have learned by me,

Their innocent achievements are mine, not yours.

Take your tents, your cold unimagined dreams and leave,

Leave just your memories.

Not your stench of rotting pestilence that scratches the pebbled shore

surfaces, of this jaded crown.

Evening laps.

Wraps the stillness,

Succumbing to darkness.

Winking in the shadowed depths I sigh.

Winter will return to these shores.

Crisp, spiked, ballerinas will dance on glistening rays.

Wind swept, howling blackened sheets will fall.

Natural beauty will echo off my walls,

My lungs will breath once more.

Rhythm restored.

Our leader found a beach which wasn't being used and we sat on the rocky shores munching our sarnies and taking in the sun. Loch Lomond was twinkling, the sun's glare bouncing off its still shores. I lay back relaxing, my feet feeling really good, and I could make out in the distance the shouting and laughter of people further along and the rhythmic lap of the water. I think all the group were very pleased to stop. Before moving off I dabbled my feet in the water. It was warm. I made a mental note that tonight I would be going swimming.

We carried on for another four miles, going up and over rocky ground, passing little coves and inlets, on through woodland and then finally after passing Rowardennan we walked the final stretch on the road to the youth hostel. It was with relief that we all piled in. Instead of partaking of tea, I ran and got my swimsuit. The water was cold but exquisite. Initially I thought it would be great to swim a little way out, but somewhere in the sensible side of this blonde brain the thought did strike me that I didn't know what was on the bottom. So I swam around in a big circle. Shauna doing her lifeguard bit sat and watched as I savoured it all. The last time I had waded into the loch was 38 years earlier!

I had a cup of tea and dried off on the grassy banks. Then I went inside for a shower as Richard was coming out for a swim. He couldn't believe I had just been in.

That evening my feet were fine but tired. Again we had a marvellous dinner. Starters: egg mayonnaise. Main: chicken casserole. Dessert: strawberry meringue. Yum.

We turned in by 9.30pm. I was fully relaxed except that I briefly lost my wallet and then found it in the bottom of my main bag. Panic over.

Monday August 14th 2006.
Rowardennan to Inverarnan - 14 miles.

After a cheery breakfast, we left the hostel at 9am. Our bags were loaded into the van as we were heading for new accommodation in the evening.

In my diary I wrote: '*The day was great. Fab company, fab weather, fab food, scenery around Loch Lomond very pretty. An easy day on legs as the path undulated around the loch.*'

To start the day, we didn't stay beside the loch. Instead we went into the forest near Ptarmigan Lodge and continued running parallel with the loch but amongst the trees, with an occasional glimpse of the water and views across to the Arrochar Hills. Ben Arthur (884 metres), affectionately known as The Cobbler with its three craggy peaks, was in the distance. The path boasts waterfalls but as the weather had been so good I cannot remember seeing really dramatic ones.

Walking on the higher level was a good choice, as traversing the roots of trees clinging to the loch's edge would have been tortuous and slow for a group. We finally descended to the shores again at Cailness. From here, we followed the trail through native woodland close to the shore as it undulated all the way to Inversnaid with its waterfall and rock pool. Here we sat and had our sandwiches on the lawn in front of a hotel.

It was a welcomed break as it was very warm. I think some people chose to have a beer.

After lunch, we continued following the shores through woods, up and down outlets and around small beaches. These were picturesque places and it was noticeable as we travelled north that there was less litter and better foliage and fauna. Across the loch, the hydroelectric downfall pipes that run to the power station at Inveruglas were easily visible. Water is pumped from Loch Sloy and its dam, which is hidden behind Ben Vorlich. The pipes are massive but from where we looked they weren't intrusive.

Shauna and I headed on. Richard gave us space to spread out as a group. There was only one path. I don't think Shauna and I realised how far we had walked ahead until we finally stopped where the path was clearly going to do something different. We were now at the part where we would be leaving the shoreline. The beach was delightful. It reminded me of a mango swamp. The shores were very shallow and lined by large rhododendron branches and silver birches. It was very pretty. In front of us was the tiniest of islands. We sat and waited for several minutes before Richard appeared. I think he was glad to see us and was pleased we had stopped, although we did get a kindly nudge to be careful next time. We understood. Anyway whilst waiting for the others he had a quick dip and no, we didn't look. I think I would have been tempted to have a swim myself if I had had my costume.

From here we made a steady climb above a farm and

crossed a burn where its sandstone had been sculpted into marvellous pools by the rushing water, creating a vortex of spinning eddies. We stopped here for a break, making the most of the last shelter before heading slowly upwards following the burn to our final view of Loch Lomond, now receding quickly behind us.

On the col near Dubh Lochan we stopped and took in the view, but for me the tantalising views in front were particularly important.

Finally, the day's walk finished at Beinglas Farm Campsite, just moments away from the Drovers Inn in Inverarnan. Here we were treated to a marvellous place of antiquity. Not to be missed. The jar of Guinness went down well. The pub is blackened with age and offers no luxury, but it makes up for it with its atmosphere. Plus you get the opportunity to stand next to a bear! Stuffed, I hasten to mention. What more could you ask for. As a group we delighted with this. Everyone was tired but still pleasant.

What cracked me up the most on this trip was our French lady companion Aurore who, despite us all being bedraggled, smelly and hot, still retained an air of composure and compactness. She remained elegant all the time. Her walk was graceful and minimal. She was a very strong walker but she never got dirty. I found that amazing. My hair was like a straw field and hers was tidy. Every day I got splattered, but she always looked like she had just come out of the laundry all pressed and pristine. We would look hot and she stayed cool. I laughed with her about it because she would say in her gentle way, "I don't know how I do it," and shrug.

We arrived by van at Crianlarich Youth Hostel at 6pm. There was much more room here. I had a shower and washed out my T-shirt. Dinner was pâté or humus, gammon and pineapple, followed by apple strudel.

Chris had brought in some wine and another throwaway camera for me. Everyone mucked in with the washing up. I wrote my diary and then crashed. A glass of wine certainly helps you sleep.

Tuesday August 15th 2006.
Inverarnan to Tyndrum - 13 miles.

We left at 9am and returned to the campsite at Beinglas Farm. The weather looked promising again. Most of our morning was taken up walking through Glen Falloch following the River Falloch, a string of pylons and the West Highland railway line. At one point there was an impressive girder bridge carrying the line over a valley. This sweeps around the contours of the mountains and is stunning. The mountains of Ben Glas and Stob Glas rose up to our right, these towers in the sky marking the beginning of the views to come.

Just after Derrydaroch the route took us under the A82 by way of a low cattle-creep. This tiny passage was difficult with our backpacks on. From here we followed the military road all the way into the outskirts of Crianlarich at the edge of a forest plantation. It was here we had a celebration for passing the approximate halfway point of our walk. Gosh, I thought, are we there already, but I suppose they meant from the start point in Glasgow. I wasn't sure but anyway Richard produced some whisky. I happily accepted two swigs. I must be getting a bit of an 'alky' – I hadn't drunk so much for ages.

From here northwards we went through a plantation. It was very dark in parts but interesting as we crossed bridges and the path went up and down, until finally we descended back to the valley floor and across the River Fillan using Kirkton Bridge. Remarkably the river was running dry but the shallow water that there was, was running rapidly.

The farm here was a scientific project. There were fantastic looking sheep in the fields. Cathy took some great photographs of their horns. Passing through the farm and the remnants of St Fillan's Priory, we sauntered along through a wigwam site. This seemed a bit bizarre but they did have a small shop and toilets. I can't remember whether or not we used them. My diary doesn't mention that.

Our day had been clear of rain up to now but dark clouds were above us. We weren't really that far from Tyndrum but we still got caught. So it was a wet trudge past Tyndrum, but we didn't really mind as it had been muggy up to then. Chris arrived with the van where the path joins the military road on the northern edge of the town at Clifton, near the cemetery. He took our rucksacks from us. We stopped there for a quick snack and then walked a further mile along the military road to where we picked up the van again off the A82. Here the impressive Beinn Chaorach (818 metres) was now towering behind Meall Buidhe, 653 metres above us. Personally, I think they wanted to us away from the Green Welly Stop! I will let you look that up on the internet. Since this trip I have also discovered a fantastic fish and chip shop in Tyndrum, an experience in itself and well recommended, and although a little expensive the choices are excellent.

Back at the hostel, cups of tea and lots of them. I was a bit dehydrated, or was it the whisky? This ritual at the end of the day was wonderful and highly entertaining. I had not laughed so much since the previous year. It was a marvellous tonic. Chris and Richard were so good at getting that pot of tea on. Again we would be moving hostel, so bags had to be packed. My feet were still excellent; I was very proud of them.

Dinner consisted of potato and herb soup, quiche and salad, and then trifle. All yum. And another dram of whisky! Plus another bottle of wine was shared.

That night I used one of my Horlicks sachets. A little treat. I was so happy. Physically tired but mentally chilled. I felt I could ring home now and check all was okay.

Wednesday August 16th 2006.
Tyndrum to Kings House Hotel - 19 miles.

I slept well but still woke at 6.15am. That time clock never changes despite any tiredness.

The weather was fantastic for walking. Ideal conditions: a slight chill to the breeze and clouds covering the high tops. This was a day of jokes, ice cream, Rannoch Moor, reflection, and my hips being slightly sore due to the military roads. It was a long day. We set off in good time at 9.30am and arrived at Glen Coe Youth Hostel at 6.30pm.

From Tyndrum we followed the railway line along the military road. The gradual ascent out of Tyndrum flattened off as we walked alongside the steep slopes of Beinn Odhar (901 metres), with Beinn Dorain (1,076m) rising in front and dominating this section of the walk. Occasionally we saw its top as the cloud cover changed. The A82, railway and military road were squeezed into the valley for a while. The feeling of grandeur all around us was palpable – or maybe it was the poet in me. I wondered what the mountain tops were like.

From here we descended to cross under the railway line by way of a sheep-creep. The views were spectacular as the railway swept easterly in a large horseshoe curve under the flanks of Beinn Odhar, Beinn a' Chaisteil and Beinn Dorain. The viaduct was almost dwarfed by the mountains' scale.

We continued along the Old Military Road, which was built by Caulfield's men (troops from Rich's regiment) between 1750 and 1752, into Bridge of Orchy. Here I became very excited as the memory of camping in the old railway sidings with my parents came so vividly to mind. I recall we had been looking for somewhere to stop for the night and the couple who owned the piece of ground offered a meagre piece of grass to put the Sun Medi tent on, with just enough purchase to get pegs intowhat? I am not sure. At the age of nine I didn't know the place name, but my mum confirmed it on my return home. I knew I had been right. The image is still clear in my head of that wonderful holiday with my parents.

At the Bridge of Orchy Hotel, we stopped and had a welcomed break of coffee and pee! Moving on and crossing the A82, we made our way up gentle slopes. The weather was still good, amazing. From here the views got even better as we looked across Loch Tulla to Black Mount, a Victorian lodge owned by the Fleming family. Very impressive. At Inveroran we had a delicious pot of ice cream, the day just lending itself to one. In the middle of nowhere. Even better.

The views of Rannoch Moor got better as we passed over Victoria Bridge and up the side of pine forests. We stopped for lunch before launching ourselves across the moor itself. All I can say is, we had the best weather for it. Everyone enjoyed this stretch as we were left to go at our own pace, even if it was hard on the hips. We met two ladies who didn't look totally equipped to be walking. Still, they had their billabong hats – important in the heat – but they were dressed as if they were going on a shopping spree! I smile as I type.

We also escaped the midges, as there was still a slight breeze. We were lucky; only one swarm. At Ba Bridge we stopped for another break to savour the bleak open moors to the east and behind us the peaks of Clach Leathad (1,099 metres) and Meall a'Bhuiridh (1,108m). Later, as we passed Ba Cottage, we saw how these monsters create the largest mountain amphitheatre in Scotland, known as Coire Ba. It takes your breath away and is humbling. I cannot describe the pleasure of this part of the walk. Here, there is a real sense of being miles from nowhere with all its grandeur. What a great place to camp. The scenery was fabulous.

During our break I restlessly climbed onto rocks with tumbling water from the River Ba. Jacques, our Frenchman, climbed down also. We bathed our feet. It was wonderful. There were some inviting pools, and if I had not been in company I would have skinny dipped.

We passed the ruins of Ba Cottage and climbed steadily to 450 metres. At this point to our left, although I didn't see it, was a small cairn, a simple memorial to Peter Fleming who died of a heart attack on 18th August 1971 while shooting in the Black Mount Forest. Peter Fleming was a correspondent for the Times newspaper. During World War Two he became a bit of an escape artist from occupied countries, including Norway, Greece and Burma. His brother was Ian Fleming, the novelist famed for his James Bond books.

As we came over the col, Kings House Hotel came into view, a substantial white painted building surrounded by wild scenery. It has been an inn or place of refuge for 200 years. Modernised and comfortable, it sits in remote and most inhabitable moorland but for a few pine trees, with the River Etive to keep it company and surrounded by the most impressive mountain ranges of Glen Coe. There was still a little way to go to reach it. The hard walking surface was beginning to make my feet warm and my hips a little sore, so it was good to see the end in sight.

As we slowly descended on the track, the Glen Coe ski lift became visible, ascending to 750 metres on the slopes of Meall a'Bhuiridh. It was built by Scotland's first commercial ski field company, White Corries Ltd. As we joined the valley, we passed the car park and the charming Blackrock Cottage. This well photographed cottage commands a unique position, and is used by walkers, climbers and skiers. It's owned by the Ladies Scottish Climbing Club. Even on this bright day it had its own atmospheric aura. It would be a great place to stay. It was all those tins of highland shortbread biscuits that came into mind as I stood in front of the cottage, which I had seen so many times on the lids.

Behind, the bastion and spearhead of Glen Coe Valley, rising and dominating the background, is Buachaille Etive Mor at 902 metres. This mountain is predominantly made of rhyolite rock, an extrusive igneous formation that is grey in colour. This, along with much of the surrounding area, is some of the oldest sedimentary and volcanic strata in the world. The mountain is photogenic and is found on many book covers and calendars. It practically represents the West Highland Way. Later on in my journey (see chapter seventeen), we were to pass it on our way up north when the early morning sun was just sitting on its top. A magical sight. I was glad my husband saw it then, as I had been ranting about it and the whole area on our trip back up to Scotland.

We finished this wonderful lengthy day with a well-earned drink in the Kings House Hotel. We went in the tradesman's entrance at the back. I enjoyed a cup of coffee. It was a pleasurable end as we waited for the van to take us to our new hostel at Glen Coe. It had started to drizzle; how quick the weather's moods change here. My feet were still in good shape. Thank you boots.

In my diary I wrote: *'Our room is very small tonight but what a laugh.'* The bunk beds were so tall and there was just one chair to share getting up and down. Every bunk squeaked and rattled, and felt as if they were only just staying together with a few pins. The intricacies of balancing, climbing whilst negotiating a swaying bunk, was so funny. The door had a dysfunctional Yale lock. It did not close quietly and was like a scorpion. You thought you had closed it and then it would make a final clatter as it fell into place, rattling the architrave as it went. There were six in this room and it was stuffy. This promised to be a good night's sleep then! Being on the top bunks, Nicola and I were crying with laughter. Everyone was very tolerant of our situation.

The room entertained me so much that I forgot to put in my diary what we ate for dinner that night. Sorry about that, or perhaps it was so bad that it wasn't worth putting in. Only joking.

Thursday August 17th 2006. Kings House Hotel (near Bridge of Orchy) to Kinlochleven - 9.5 miles.

This was our shortest day but with our only serious climb. Again, the weather was great for walking and I still had shorts on!

We started at 9.30am. Pictures were taken of the group

with Buachaille Etive Mor and the Bridge of Orchy (the distinctive metal bridge) in the background. We followed the Old Military Road, which rose in height as it climbed onto the slopes of Beinn a' Chrulaiste, before descending once more down to Altnafeadh, the head of Glen Coe. Here the views of the Pass of Glen Coe were dramatic, although the busy A82 was a little intrusive.

Before tackling the Devil's Staircase, we stopped briefly just to take in the views and prepare ourselves for a steep climb of 250 metres up to the highest point of our journey at 550 metres.

I thought the climb rather pleasant. The steps were easy to negotiate. Stretching the legs and getting the old heart pumping was good. The views just got more grandiose. There was a panoramic view of moorland, Meall a'Bhuiridh, Sron na Creise and Buachaille Etive, plus the tops of the 'Three Sisters' – Aonach Dubh (892 metres), Gearr Aonach (692m) and Beinn Fhada (811m) – which were outliers for the largest peak Bidean nam Bian at 1,150 metres. It was in and around this area that some of the scenes of a James Bond movie were filmed, and it was also the location of the Lost Valley. I relished the beauty.

Although sunny on the top, there was a gentle breeze keeping midges away and thankfully cooling us. Our lunch break was shortly after this. We sat beneath the flanks of Beinn Bheag (616 metres). I didn't fancy much for lunch, so Jacques and I decided to have a little climb onto the top. It was not far to the summit. We waved to the others, then we walked along its top until we could see our path to come, taking its steady descent towards Kinlochleven. To the north were the Mamores, a range of mountains in the Lochaber region of the Grampians, and way in the distance was the hump of Ben Nevis, our final destination. It was exhilarating and breathtaking, and we decided to have a race to see who could get back to the others the quickest. Foolish perhaps but good fun. I love running down mountains. In those few moments I realised Jacques was very much at home here; he was enjoying the walk in his quiet way. Richard said we could have stayed up there and walked off the other end, meeting the group along the path, but we didn't think that would have been right.

After lunch, it did not take long to get down to Kinlochleven, and we were in the town by 3pm. We had followed the track and the six huge water pipes from the Blackwater Reservoir all the way down. The track was a bit tiresome on the hips and even though it was the shortest day and probably the most spectacular day, I was more than pleased to reach the town.

Kinlochleven was created as a factory town for aluminium production but that is no longer in existence. Instead, the large smelter house has been transformed into the UK's highest indoor articulated climbing wall and the world's biggest ice climbing wall, drawing the outdoor fraternity to this otherwise quiet town. The river was also being utilised the day we were there, and as we crossed the Leven we enjoyed watching some kayakers being put through their paces.

Here, if we had wanted to, we could have posted some postcards or bought any items from the local shops. Instead, as it was warm we opted to enjoy a drink of coffee or beer outside the Tailrace Inn. This was when my day got slightly damaged, well my head more like it. I had bought a coffee and placed it on the table. Everyone was sitting at the wooden picnic tables outside. Talking (that was the problem) and not concentrating as I went to get both my feet under the table, someone sat down opposite and I miscalculated putting my left foot in. My foot lodged awkwardly and in trying to maintain my balance I fell backwards, my head hitting the pebble-dashed walls of the pub. Ouch! I felt the stone go in and come out again as I moved my head forward in reaction. But oh the stars. On reflection, I was lucky my leg came out from under the table and over the seat in one go. It could so easily have snapped. As it was, my head now started to bleed. Oh dear.

Actually, I knew I was fine. I sat for several moments aware of people being very supportive, but I knew that I had to assess the damage for myself and stay still for a moment. This meant my legs were still in the air, and now when I think about it, I had my baggiest of shorts on. Well, the view couldn't have been very pleasant down them. If you get my drift. How embarrassing but at the time, it was important for me to know that my neck was okay.

Richard and Chris were marvellous. All I kept thinking about was that my expensive new blue shirt now had blood on it. I was peeved at that. Chris, after a while, suggested I put my legs down and then I asked for my coffee to be passed down to me as I slowly came round from the incident. Nicola sprang into action and Jacques took some pictures of the moment. Later that year he sent me copies of this auspicious occasion. Shauna was horrified; visions of hospital ran in her head. But the head bleeds a lot and heals the fastest. I had taken loads of blows to my head as a child, as I vaulted the fence between our neighbours on a daily basis, sometimes misjudging or slipping only to end up against the brick wall in a crumpled heap.

I walked into the pub to check the damage. What a bloody mess my shirt was, bugger. There was a small band of instrumentalists creating some lovely folk music in the pub. I stopped and watched them and joined in for a moment.

Shauna came in to see what I was doing. Actually, it distracted me from the thumping headache that now started. Assuring everyone I was fine and 'please don't make any more fuss', the incident was noted in the accident book, and the guys took us on a lovely journey to the Corran Ferry where we boarded it for the small trip across across Loch Linnhe to Ardgour. This was brilliant.

Shauna was very quiet. I was so concerned that I had really upset her. We walked along the beach. I tried to apologise, that I hadn't wanted so much attention and I would be fine. I wasn't her responsibility. Perhaps she was just tired. I hoped that it wouldn't mar the walk for her.

On the way back to the youth hostel we took to singing. It was a very cheery drive back. I recall singing, 'The answer is blowin' in the wind.'

Back at the hostel, I washed out my shirt and had a shower. I was fine but aware that concussion could set in at any time. It didn't. I did take it steady though, my headache returning. I think this was tiredness.

Dinner was another gourmet delight: fruit cocktail, pasta and salad, rice pudding. I then wrote up my diary and turned in.

Friday August 18th 2006.
Kinlochleven to Fort William - 14.5 miles.

Our last day. As always I was quiet. I did not want to go home yet. My head was healed. The family was okay at home.

The weather was warm again as we walked out of the hostel. We headed along the B863 for a brief while, before our path climbed steadily out of the valley, zigzagging through lovely woodland. Although a bit of a wake-up call for the legs, it was a pleasant bimble up an ascent of 250 metres. Eventually the track widened and from here we had marvellous views of the ridge known as Aonach Eagach, as well as Loch Leven. The track (military road) slowly climbed to reach Lairigmor col, a point where the route headed in a north-westerly sweep towards Fort William. From here the path slowly descended, interspersed with forestry and the occasional sighting of Ben Nevis. We were exceptionally lucky to catch glimpses of the top when the cloud chose to move!

We did a 'wee detour' for lunch and came off the main pathway to stop and admire Lochan Lunn Da-Bhra. This was extremely pretty and the last place to savour our sarnies in the beauty of our surroundings.

The group were quiet, our journey almost over. It seemed a little tedious after lunch, going through gates and more forest plantation while descending all the time. Towards the end, we came down into a car park and then it was a short walk through the suburbs of Fort William, the Way and our walk finished.

Accompanied by photographs, hugs and congratulations, we stood in front of the official ending post. We were tired but overjoyed at finishing. Richard and Chris produced some bubbly and we toasted our success.

We had a delightful and eventful final evening. I thoroughly enjoyed it. After haggis for tea, the group were treated to a 'night out'. We were taken to a pub called the Clachaig Inn. What a treat. It was packed. We squeezed in and muscled our way to the bar. It was Friday night and the atmosphere was terrific. The long bar was something out of Spaghetti Westerns. One part dedicated to beers, one part wines and lagers and one featuring a fine selection of malt whiskies. Each section had a barman. A live band was playing great folk music and well known rugby songs, or versions thereof.

For me, having not been to a pub like it since the age of 18, I was transported back to my youth. Given half a chance I would have got up there and sung. As it was I sat in a Scotsman's seat. I didn't know it was his 'Friday seat' and I was advised to 'move' by his partner. On his return I could see he looked like he could get annoyed. I apologised and moved away, a bit embarrassed. Sadly, having just found a seat our group had to leave. There was a long day of travel ahead tomorrow. I did feel a bit tipsy.

The bikers who had turned up in the afternoon at the youth hostel were still at the pub when we left. They finally crawled in at midnight. Woken by this and because I kept needing a pee, I took all my bedding and slept on the sofa in the lounge. I managed to get a few hours' kip. In the morning I awoke to a few bikers crashed out in the lounge also. Snoring in a discorded fashion I pretended to conduct them. I hadn't heard them come in. I checked myself to make sure I was intact. What a sight they were to behold. Sleeping like lambs in their leathers.

Saturday August 19th 2006. Back to Glasgow.

An unremarkable journey back. Trundling along in the van, we retraced our steps along the A82 and savoured the last moments of driving through Glen Coe. I would be back and would be travelling even further north. I had loved every moment of this holiday. The group and leaders had restored my faith in human beings and the trauma of the previous holiday had been put down to 'just one of those things'. I vowed I would use C-N-Do again for A Cape Wrath Trail. When? I didn't know.

We arrived back at Stirling Station at 1pm and then Shauna and I caught a train back to Glasgow. By 2.30pm we had found the youth hostel and then wandered back into the centre and caught a bus tour around the city. This was a great way to see the sights and unwind. I was still very excitable; poor Shauna, she put up with a lot. Our tour finished, we wandered back through the streets and into Kelvingrove Park to the museum. Sadly, we didn't have enough time to truly appreciate it but it whetted my appetite. (See the previous chapter about the museum.)

We went back to the hostel and ordered a taxi for 11.30am the following day to take us back to the airport. Then we showered and sauntered off to find food for tea. A pleasant café not too far away provided our Mexican dinner.

Sunday August 20th 2006. Home.

Another new experience, riding in a taxi and a London style cab as well. What a treat, I felt like Lady Muck. This walk had given me so many opportunities. It may seem really odd to you how little I had done, but that is what becomes of someone who has lived 'in the sticks' all their life.

Our flight back was fantastic and we were home by 3.20pm. David came and picked us up. The walk and its experiences had all been brilliant. Now what was next?

CHAPTER SEVENTEEN:

FILLING IN THE GAPS

STRATHCARRON TO TORRIDON HOUSE; BRAESIDE, GLEN MORE TO

MORVICH VIA RATAGAN; AND FORT WILLIAM TO CORPACH.

DISTANCE: 50.7 MILES. DATELINE: SEPTEMBER 26TH-29TH 2010.

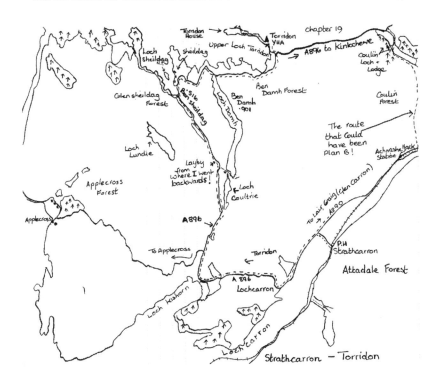

On reflection, this was by far the most unexpected, eventful, incredibly lucky, frightening and breathtaking part of my journey. Most of all, the accumulation of emotions as the end of my adventure drew to its close surpassed all before. (See also chapter eighteen.)

On this final stretch, David finally saw why I loved the Western Highlands of Scotland so much and how important the Cape Wrath Trail had been to me (chapter nineteen). All I can say is that the wagon got us there and back, a miracle by any stretch of the imagination. How my legs did this stretch in the time frame is also a wonder to me. I can only thank them for staying fit and to my boots for keeping me blister free.

Evening of Sunday September 26th 2010.
Northwards through the night.

Well, I was assured that the van would be okay. It had had everything replaced on it except the kitchen sink. David had toiled on our 'Pash Wagon' and it was time for me to put some faith in the old girl. My place of work had been extremely tolerant of this booking-and-cancelling lark. This time, it was achieve it now or wait until next year and devise another way of accomplishing the end. I was desperately trying to be philosophical about it but in truth I would have been like a petulant, spoilt teenager if we had failed again.

I had spent two invigorating days on Dartmoor, walking with my brother and his friends. David came at 6.30pm to pick me up from my brother's home near Romsey in the Pash

Wagon, and it was our intention to travel overnight, taking turns to drive.

We left my brother's at 7.30pm, having sorted out dirty clothes and a quick snack before embarking on our journey. It was misty getting back onto the A34 but it all went without a hitch. From here our journey was without incident and as we applauded passing Carlisle service station, it seemed the van was going to be okay. Soon after, I drove for a while until just after Glasgow, where we both power-napped and then had large espresso coffees. I am sure this didn't do David's head any good at all.

Monday September 27th 2010.
Strathcarron to above Loch Damh - 14.1 miles.

Dawn broke and we were travelling across Rannoch Moor. There was low cloud but clearer skies above. I kept jumping up and down in the seat. What a child, so excited as I pointed out where I had walked previously as the wagon crossed the white metal road bridge near Kingshouse. Even David lifted his eyebrows in amazement as the sun hit Buachaille Etive Mor, illuminating its grey stone peak in a glowing beacon of orange and purple hues thrusting above the low cloud surrounding it. In the watery sunlight it could not have been better.

I hoped the valley of Glen Coe would not be shrouded entirely by mist. We were not disappointed, although the very tops were hidden. We stopped at the viewing point near the Devil's Staircase where the cloud hung in the valley, suspended on an invisible string. We could see above and below. Even David drew breath at the sight. I was thrilled for him.

Although bright, the morning was very cold with a chilly breeze. We arrived at Ballachulish on the banks of Loch Leven at 8.30am. We found a petrol station two miles further north. Here we took on as much diesel as possible. Now our problems started. David checked under the bonnet. Oil was everywhere; my heart sank. The van was looking ill and we were so far away from home and our destination. We had pushed it too far.

Selfishly, I sat in the van with tears of anger and disappointment running down my face. On the forecourt of the petrol station, David looked under the bonnet and wiped away the oil to see where it was coming from. At this stage he couldn't find the source, but he did think it might be to do with the rocker box. In which case he felt we would be alright. Soon a large petrol tanker pulled in and the driver kindly gave David a hand, and then a local forestry guy came in and suggested we take the van to Chisholms MOT and repair garage in Ballachulish. His comment was, "They are the best, if they are open they will help you." He gave us instructions on where to find them, and thanking him for his kindness and the tanker driver too, we returned back to Ballachulish.

We crawled cautiously into the repair centre's forecourt. At first there didn't appear to be anyone there but then a bloke came out and David explained the situation. Well, I can only describe what accommodating people they were. Their shed was filled with a Land Rover they were working on and another car, and there were other cars and commercial vans lined up to be dealt with, yet they still helped us right away. Nothing was too much trouble, they were brilliant. They wheeled the

Land Rover off its pit stop and we drove in. With two gentlemen peering into the van's engine and taking a few bits off to get a better look, they and David came to the conclusion that it was a leaking rocker box gasket.

When David had changed the gasket previously, the proper standard rocker gasket for this van 'was not made any more'! He had had to make his own using round sectioned neoprene (1.5mm wet suit material). This clearly hadn't been suitable, but it wasn't going to be disastrous provided we kept a check on our oil levels. The chaps checked all the pumps, the radiator and the cooling systems, and cleaned the oil off the engine as best as possible. They were amazed we were on the road in our outdated transportation.

Once over the shock that we may not be going anywhere, I settled down in the garage and could see that the best was being done, and I had already prepared myself to be going back south. I love the smell of proper garages and felt at home there. We chatted about the Land Rovers, motocross, kids' cars, my journey, the business, the climate and last year's winter. Everyone was so friendly and we were so grateful. We were even offered a drink.

It was agreed we would be safe provided we took extra oil with us. David already had that on board, so even though I was nervous about going further, I accepted David's opinion that we should carry on.

We left at 10am. They did not accept any payment for their time or inconvenience. They only asked if we would put an offering in the tea money pot and if we had any problems to give them a ring. We put £20 in their coffers, which was plenty for them. "That will keep us going for a bit," was their reply.

How can I explain how grateful we were? I hope that anyone reading this will patronise that garage when the need occurs.

We drove on, a little nervously at first as you would expect, to Fort William and then out towards Strathcarron on the A87 and A890. I took to driving until David's head became so painful it was better for him to drive, to make him feel less sick. I don't know at this point what or who I was concerned about most.

The drive was stunning for David, his first time out here. I was pleased the day was bright and sunny and he could admire the scenery. Although his head and neck were aching, he couldn't have been more affected by the beauty. I was so happy to have him with me.

We arrived in Strathcarron and parked by the Henhouse Inn at 1pm and had a coffee. Here is where I would leave David to rest and chat whilst I started my walk towards Torridon. The plan was to walk until either I dropped or it got dark.

At 1.45pm, carrying just a day-sack with Gertrude tied on safely, I sauntered off. It was great to be back. It was a nostalgic moment walking past the little gate into the field where we had returned from our non-starter day on A Cape Wrath Trail (see chapter nineteen), absolutely drenched and the day had not even begun. I thought of Gill, and I wished she could have been here for this moment. I *knew* I would be back here.

I was quickly into my stride, walking at 3-4 miles an hour and I soon passed Lochcarron. I can honestly say it was good to be walking again and on my own. I really enjoy my own company, swallowing and wallowing in the surroundings.

By 5.45pm I was pooped, having walked 14.1 miles.

Darkness would soon be upon us. David caught up with me. He had stayed at the pub having another drink or two – chatting up the barmaid I expect. It was now time for us to park up. A small lay-by with a wonderful view looking down over towards Loch Damh and Kinloch Damph was our stop for the night. I was very hungry but mainly tired, having had only three hours' kip in the previous 24. I sorted out my kit for the next day, which unexpectedly would turn out to be a long one! I was in bed by 8.30pm.

Tuesday September 28th 2010.
Loch Damh to Torridon House - 14.6 plus 3.9 extra miles! Then Braeside, Glen More to near Morvich - 9.5 miles. A very, very long day. 28miles

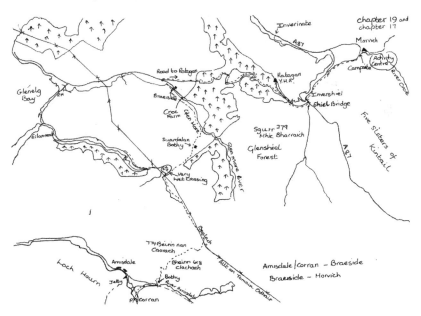

I slept soundly until 6.30am, when I made porridge and a cup of tea. Fantastic: I had not woken David. At 7am I crept out of the van, taking my clothes and snack bars off the side and leaving David happily asleep. I dressed outside, a bit chilly, then left at 7.30am in the first light of the day.

The plan was for David to get more rest and catch me up in Torridon. Easy, no problem, until…

I can honestly say I left my navigational head behind. How simple is it to walk down the road towards your destination? With, would you believe, the van pointing in the right direction.

Duh, clearly this blonde still had her sleepy head on, because she got out of the back of the van and continued to walk, dozy mare. The worst thing was, I followed the map. 'The map!' you cry. Yes the bloody map. I made it fit the location. I did question why no trees had come into sight. My answer for this was deforestation, but the lochans and the loch looked right? Oh dear, I didn't even recognise anything we had passed. I even noted the little shack at the side of the road as, oh that's like the one yesterday. How sad is that? I can laugh about it now but imagine my horror when I reached a right-hand road sign saying 'Applecross'. I broke out into a sweat, oh bugger, oh bloody hell. I pondered my situation: how could I have got it so wrong? Slowly into my one-celled brain came the realisation of what I had done. I cried out in absolute madness, "You stupid cow, now you have to walk back!"

At that moment a van, a knight in shining white armour, came from the road leading to Lochcarron. I had never been attracted to any man with a van before, especially a white one. It was a desperate woman that stepped into the road and waved him down. I would have not done such a thing four years earlier, and I hasten to add that this was totally out of character.

The van was an official vehicle driven by a young lad no more than Ben's age. He stopped; he didn't have much choice.

He said, "Are you lost?" "No," I replied, "just in the wrong place I think."

"Am I here?" I asked, pointing on the map. I don't know what I was hoping, that he was going to miraculously place me in Shieldaig, but instead he just affirmed my suspicions. I wasn't in Shieldaig.

"You need to walk up there towards Torridon," he said, pointing from where I had come. "Yes," I said, words failing me. I was so mortified, so in a disbelieving voice I found myself saying, "Well, how could I have possibly done that? I haven't done that before." Although blushing, I did recall Carlisle to Glasgow! I stood like some useless lemming and feeling totally despondent, grappling at the thought of walking back the four miles and worrying if David had already left, and wondering if he was worried why he hadn't found me along the wayside. It was at this moment that the young man kindly offered me a lift. He was going to Torridon and heading my way.

A new crisis entered my head. In all my life I had never, ever, ever accepted a lift in a stranger's car, van or lorry. I had never thumbed a lift and how many times had I instilled the same into my children? This was going against every grain of sensibility. I looked at the earnest, kindly eyes of the young man. He had an open face like Ben's. There was nothing pretentious about him, he wasn't pushy or demonstrative. He seemed genuine enough and wanted to help.

"Well," I said, "I haven't done this before. Are you sure? My husband is four miles up there with his van and will expect to see me today. If you wouldn't mind dropping me there, that would be good." Oh my God, I thought, what if he isn't there? What if I never see the wagon again?

"Look, it's okay, the van is an official one, and perhaps I shouldn't be doing this. Up here we are used to harsh weathers and helping people out. I can see you are in a pickle. I will drop you back to your van, don't worry."

I dithered at the side of his van for several moments. Looking in the window I could see it had electric windows and an interlocking door system. This did not allay my fears. I would have to keep the door ajar. My head was in a swirl: what else would this walk do to me? So many firsts. And with an 'okay' I got in.

In the van, I felt cold. I was trembling from head to foot as we headed back the four miles I had just walked on the lonely road to Torridon. His van had been the only traffic I had seen, so I didn't expect any more. My thoughts were, please let the wagon be there, I don't know if I can hold this door for that length of time and just keep him chatting.

With both arms holding the door semi-ajar and lights and beeper going off, we chatted about my walk and his job. He really was genuine but I still held on to that door with a gripped determination. He didn't think his mum would do anything like me and was quite impressed at what I had done so far. I commented on the fact that I didn't feel very clever at the moment. "Och," he said, "these hills can all look similar and the moors round here can look the same." He was very kind, his mother would have been proud of him.

Despite his kindness, I was so relieved when our wagon came into sight. I couldn't get out of the van quickly enough. He dropped me off and went on his cheery way, leaving this mentally deranged woman at the roadside.

I tapped on the window. The comical thing was David hadn't even missed me. He was just getting up having enjoyed his lie-in. He thought I had just got up myself and had been out for an early wander. It was 8.30am. "Yes," I said, "I am just off, I'll tell you later," and on that mysterious note I walked in the right direction. The whole episode had lasted 15 minutes from beginning to end, but the memory will last forever.

I would explain to David later in the day what had happened. When I did he just laughed. All he said was, "I wonder if you will own up to this incident in your book, bit of an embarrassment for you. Did you not think about your compass? And where did your map skills go to?" To this day I cannot explain my actions.

Our children laughed as well when I told them. "Aw Mum, you were living dangerously," they joked. Ben said, "I do that all the time, pick up old ladies or catch lifts." "You don't, do you?" I asked, my mouth and eyes wide open. "Nah, just winding you up Mum my dear," he giggled.

Somewhere in there I ignored Ben's take on 'old ladies', as I remember thinking he's a good lad not accepting lifts.

Somewhere along the way I had done a good job as mother. But I digress. On with the walk.

Now I had time to make up. I practically flew along until Shieldaig. I must return again to explore this most beautiful gem of a place. Shieldaig Island in the loch is owned by the National Trust and is covered in Scots pine. I noticed on the map there was a campsite in Shieldaig. This would be an ideal place to stop another time. Canoeing or kayaking would be even better in this sheltered part of Loch Shieldaig.

Alas, I had very little time but met up with David at a tiny point called Rubha na Feola. I had a bun and coffee here, and this was the last time I saw David until Torridon.

The weather was ideal for walking, still but cold. The views all along this route made up for the hardness on the hips and feet. They were not complaining too much. It was stunning scenery. At a viewing point with Beinn Damh (868 metres) towering behind me, I saw across the loch towards Inveralligin, and before that I could just make out my destination near Torridon itself.

People have to go there to understand the beauty of this outstanding area. It is almost indescribable. Everywhere is vast. As a walker you are dwarfed. It is easy to imagine being an ant here.

Moving quickly on, I made a steep descent past Torridon Hotel into Annat, at sea level. From here the bay swept around until I was in Torridon. I had walked extremely fast but had enjoyed every moment of it. I am aware though that to appreciate it further, I must go back and savour it more thoroughly. I can honestly say I did not do it justice.

Walking past the youth hostel, the local GP surgery, the small shop, the junior school, the inn and the café, this all took me back again to A Cape Wrath Trail (see chapter nineteen). I was again beneath the mountain known as Liathach (903 metres). This lump of a mountain dominates the road and to those looking up it appears almost vertical, with craggy terraces. Its main ridge has a peak on the western end called Mullach an Rathain (1,023m) and on its eastern end Spidean a' Choire Leith (1,055m). This range is part of Torridon Forest.

I met David briefly outside the café, and decided I would walk on until I had finished this bit, then have a well deserved break. I thoroughly enjoyed walking back up to where as a group the previous year we had taken a lift up to the waterfalls car park in the minibus during the Cape Wrath Trail I was not joking when I said to David, "I hope the van gets up there." It is a very steep climb as the road meanders upwards in hairpin bends to 100 metres above sea level.

I was so excited at being back here. David was very patient. We walked together for a bit and read the information board about the area. Ecstatic having finished, we returned to the café. I slumped in the chair, knackered. I had walked 14.6 miles plus the extra bit! And it was only 1.30pm.

There was still some walking to do. Rest was now important, plus a warm-down before doing the next bit. The weather had been so kind. Although cold, it was bright and sunny and at least we would be travelling in the warmest part of the day.

We had to get back to Glen More. Following a long winding road, it was going to take us a while. In fact, it took us well over an hour to get back to Braeside, Glen More, and by now it was pushing 3.50pm. I was stiffening up and was yet to walk anothernine and half miles.

Marathon comes to mind. Having devoured even more food and refilled my water bladder on the journey back, I braced myself as I left the van for the last time that day. This was to be the longest nine and half miles on my entire journey. Forget Carlisle to Glasgow, this was just a trial from beginning to end.

From the small bridge where the transit van had picked up the group at Braeside, the only way was up – a slow, lingering uphill struggle from 65 to 390 metres. Oh bloody hell, my legs were awful. It was agony as cramp set in. I was willing them to move and egged on by the fact that the light would soon be dimming. Thank God for a bright day.

I staggered in at 6.40pm in now failing light. David had followed as best he could on this terribly narrow and precarious road as I lurched along, but then practically ran onto the flat once more in Ratagan. It seemed an age to Glenshiel Lodge and down towards the road leading to Morvich. But I had arrived. Amen. Did I enjoy that? Not in the least. In total 28miles today. My hips felt sore but my feet were great.

We decided to travel back to Fort William, to Lochy Caravan Park near the town. The next day I would walk from the campsite to the end of the West Highland Way at Fort William then back to the campsite. After checking David, I would then walk to Corpach and back again to the campsite. This was a bit contrived as a way of covering the Fort William to Corpach leg, but I wanted David to be able to relax for the day whilst I messed about with the minor bits. He could then sleep or at least come round slowly. If we had stayed at Morvich it would have meant him or I driving first thing, which in turn would have meant getting up early. This way he could sleep in as long as he liked. It also meant my final two days would be spent walking to Mallaig.

I wanted to end my journey somewhere very special. We had also planned to take the train journey, as we had been told how scenic it was.

Our drive back to Fort William was uneventful. We arrived at the caravan park rather late, however the people were very friendly. After a shower and grub (a Vesta curry), sorting out the next day's walk, rubbing masses of deep heat gel on my legs, and putting porridge in a pan ready for the morning start, we crashed out. It was 11pm. I was exhausted. Wonderful.

Wednesday September 29th 2010. Lochy Caravan Park to Fort William and back - 4 miles. Then Lochy Caravan Park to Corpach and back - 4.6 miles.

I woke to a very grey sky at 8am, but oh boy didn't I sleep well. My legs had seized up, no surprise. But there was no great rush today. Trying to get dressed quietly in the confined space in the roof of the van was very difficult, with the maximum gap between me and the roof being two feet. I wobbled about a bit. David awoke. Apologising, I made a cup of tea and put my porridge on. If I could have sat and read I would have done, but in the confines of the roof space and with my joints feeling decidedly sore, I had to stretch. Having made tea and eaten my porridge, I headed off for another shower to get my limbs going!

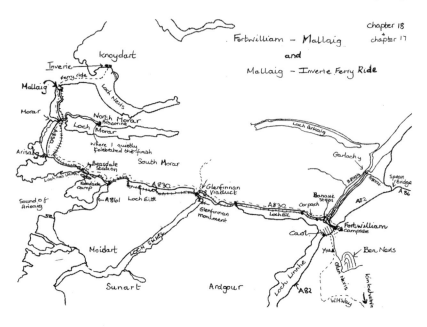

David stayed in bed, so gathering my belongings I headed off towards Fort William. It promised to be an overcast day, maybe rain.

There was nothing inspiring about this little saunter; noise was the only thing. Plenty of traffic, roadworks, that was about it. I had a flutter of excitement about walking to the end of the West Highland Way, and seeing the sign in front of which I had stood with the group in 2006 (see chapter sixteen). Was it that long ago? I didn't find it. There is now a statue in the town marking the end.

All those good memories flooded back. Well, look how far I had come. My time in Scotland almost done, the blonde got sentimental again. "Oh Gertrude, we are nearly finished my friend. What will I do after this last adventure? Will my confidence disappear once more?"

I didn't stop in Fort William; there would be time for this on our train excursion. I love the mornings, when I am at my best. Taking it slowly, I wandered back towards the caravan park.

Then it began to pelt with rain. It didn't matter, this was Scotland and the weather was part of its appeal. This may seem strange to you but Scotland had always been kind to me because of my acceptance and respect for what it offers. It may well be a long time before I return again.

Back at the van, it was still only 11am. David was just getting himself organised. I had a coffee and said I was off to Corpach. I could meet him in Corpach later; I'd text him, perhaps we could walk up the Banavie Steps together. I left him wondering what they were.

Still raining – it was bad – I made my way to Corpach. The A830 was very busy. But it was lovely just to stroll in drizzling rain and savour this brief walk. It didn't take long. I passed Neptune's Staircase at Banavie and wandered back to the van. It was still pouring with rain.

We had lunch and then we took the van back to Banavie so that David could understand what I meant by the 'steps'. By now the day had turned brighter and we were able to enjoy walking up the sloping pathway to the top of Neptune's Staircase.

This feature is part of the Caledonian Canal. The 'staircase' was designed by Thomas Telford, as was the canal. The staircase lock is the longest in the United Kingdom with a flight of eight locks, enabling boats to be lifted 64 feet (19.5 metres). It takes approximately one and a half hours for a boat to pass from one end of the staircase to the other.

The Caledonian Canal runs for 60 miles along the Great Glen from Corpach near Fort William to Inverness. For 38 miles of its length, the canal utilises three lochs: Loch Lochy, Loch Oich and Loch Ness. At Corpach the canal emerges into Loch Linnhe. Almost completed in 1822, it was built to bypass the hazardous journey for mariners having to navigate their sailing vessels around the north and west of Scotland. Sadly, by the time it was fully completed in 1845 according to Telford's original plan, many of the sailing vessels had been replaced by much larger ships, but until the railway came to Inverness the canal was still the most effective way to move from A to B.

The views of Ben Nevis on a clear day would have been exceptionally good, but it was a little cloudy to say the least, so sadly we didn't get that view. We bumbled back to the van.

Both of us were tired, so we relaxed. I wrote, David had another kip. After we had tea we went to bed. Don't we live dangerously? We know how to live. An early night would set me up for the next two days of hard walking.

It was with nervous anticipation and reflective sadness that I contemplated that my long journey would soon be over. In the quiet of the darkness, I lay on the slatted boards in the roof of the van, a flutter of butterflies in my stomach. How strange they should appear now, returning just like at the beginning. Was it fear of losing me again? Would my confidence just quietly drift away again and leave just the shell once more? Only time would tell.

I didn't take long to drop off. I was physically tired too.

CHAPTER EIGHTEEN:

A REFLECTIVE CELEBRATION ON THE ROAD TO THE ISLES

**CORPACH TO MALLAIG. DISTANCE: 38.5 MILES.
DATELINE: SEPTEMBER 30TH-OCTOBER 1ST 2010.**

Having filled in a few remaining gaps in the Scottish Highlands (previous chapter), this was the final missing piece of my long walk from the edge of Cornwall to the top of Scotland. I had longed to complete my journey somewhere very special – and I did, at beautiful Mallaig. The map for this walk is in Chapter 17.

Thursday September 30th 2010. Corpach to the tunnel near Beasdale Station - 27miles.

Sleeping overnight at Lochy Caravan Park near Fort William, I woke to torrential rain, well I call it low cloud cover. It looked as if it might be fine, eventually! To the west it looked more promising. Oh well. I had a bowl of porridge. David then drove me the short distance to Corpach, still in his pyjamas. He was going to go back for some more shut-eye, buy some provisions (I hoped not in his pyjamas) and get himself some magazines to read. It must be pretty boring being the back-up team. It's just a matter of sitting and waiting.

Anyway, I set off at 8.30am, at a walking pace of about four miles an hour. This was fast but the weather had some bearing on that. I just had my head down and ploughed on. My halfway point for the day was to be Glenfinnan. I can't really say much about the route. I was just pleased to be walking despite the rain.

Between Corpach and Kinlocheil (7.5 miles) the railway and Loch Eil were visible through the trees running parallel with the road. I remember seeing a large timber merchant but not much else. David caught up with me shortly after Kinlocheil. It was 11am and I was hoping to be in Glenfinnan for a late lunch.

As I progressed, so the scenery started to look more spectacular. I could only marvel at the water coming off the mountains. I passed some fantastic waterfalls on this walk. At one I recall, I had to go through it because the road was busy. It fell like a torrent on my head. I was drenched. It was like something out of a slapstick comedy.

I was becoming excited about reaching Glenfinnan. Was it food? Yes. Was it coldness seeping into my bones? Yes. My diary says very little. It really was a very wet day and I was a drowned, shivering rat when I finally reached Glenfinnan.

It's well worth a stop here. It is probably best to go by rail and enjoy the scenic ride on the Jacobite steam engine that runs in the summer on the West Highland Line, alongside the normal railway timetable. For those who wish to use the steam train, it is a must to book in advance as it was voted the world's best train journey in 2009 by enthusiasts. I could see why. As a visitor you can have a bite to eat in the Victorian carriages and savour another era. Then wander from the railway museum along the road to enjoy the views from the northern end of Loch Shiel.

It is here that the Glenfinnan Monument was erected in 1815 to mark the place where Prince Charles Edward Stuart ('Bonnie Prince Charlie') raised his standard and rallied his supporters at the beginning of the Jacobite Rising in 1745. A statue of an unknown kilted Highlander stands proudly on top, alone. Behind the monument, the views of River Finnan valley are dominated by a most spectacular railway viaduct. Over one hundred feet in height and made up of 21 arches, the viaduct was completed in 1901 by the engineer Sir Robert McAlpine and was the first structure to use 'mass concrete'. The viaduct in recent years has had much media exposure, as it was one of the locations for the filming of a Harry Potter film. Remember the flying Ford Anglia?

I was soaked, damp on the inside from sweat and very wet on the outside. We stopped at the National Trust coffee shop where, under the scrutiny of its inmates, I was glared at as I dripped across the floor and proceeded to take off my outer garments and hang them over the chair.

We had soup; I had become very cold. It took a good quarter of an hour to feel remotely human once more. The pink rinse brigade continued to glare as the soup barely touched my sides. As we left the small café I offered up my seat, but surprisingly no one took me up on it. Perhaps it had something to do with the puddles accumulating on the floor! And a rather damp seat!

The weather was no better. The rain, though finer, was cold as a bitter wind had sprung up. I did not stop to look at the Glenfinnan Monument. As a child of 11, I had been here with my parents and have old photos looking across Loch Shiel from it. I couldn't remember the viaduct, so I stopped and took pictures briefly before setting off on my soggy journey once more, leaving David in the comfort of the Pash Wagon!

The western sky in the distance was looking bluer. By that I mean it was grey really, with just a promise of blue in it. The light was different. I was still chilled and kept up a cracking pace to keep warm.

Slowly the rain fizzled to a stop and David followed me all the way. The walk alongside Loch Eilt became prettier and the surrounding mountains became more majestic in their protection of it. The railway was on the opposite side of the loch at this point, but we met it as we both made our way towards Lochailort. I became thoroughly tired but the reward as I slowly made my way towards Loch nan Uamh was stunning. The road slowly descended to a place where it passes under a viaduct and the walker can see through this into the loch beyond. My reward was seeing the slow burning red sun settling on the loch and reflecting through the arches. I cannot describe the intensity of pleasure derived from this one photographic vista. I stood in awe for several moments so it would be permanently captured in my memory. To me this made up for all the rain.

I met up with David at this point. By now it was 5.30pm and we didn't yet have anywhere to stop overnight. There was a small farmstead close by but the farmer waved us on, threatening us with his dogs – not verbally but with a few motions of his arms. We weren't going to argue. The evening was now bathed in this beautiful red hue. This empowered me to go further, so whilst David hunted about for a place to stop, I pushed forward on foot towards Beasdale Station. Here the road made a very long sweep to the left, with the valley below high above the loch.

It was a dangerous spot to finish at, but I came across the best lay-by that David and I had ever had the good fortune to stay in. It was cold but a beautiful evening. We had dinner immediately and to save my legs seizing up, I went for a little explore along Loch nan Uamh to the Prince's Cairn at this most eastern edge of the Sound of Arisaig. It is said to have been the spot where Bonnie Prince Charlie finally left Scotland's shores for France in 1746, after being on the run from government officials following the Battle of Culloden.

I sat amongst the rocks there for a while and gazed across the pretty loch, its numerous islands adding to the interest. It was a perfect evening. I didn't want it to end. I sat on the stones of the shore and hugged my knees. I thought of Dad, C-N-Do, Mallaig and my adventure, and felt nothing but inner peace.

The loch had become calm and then just as I was about to get up, I came face to face with two eyes only 15 feet away. In a blink of my eye the creature had gone. A seal! I don't know who had been more surprised. I scrambled back up from the shore so excited, straining my eyes across the loch to see more but I didn't. I thought I saw it again but I couldn't be sure it wasn't just rocks. I ran back to the van and David and I then scoured the loch with binoculars. Finally, David spotted movement towards the island. It could have been an otter or seal, we weren't sure, but what a treat in the most beautiful setting. Shortly after that we settled down for the night as the darkness soon crept in and the cold returned.

The only traffic along this road was that using the ferry crossing, so occasionally time was marked by a few mad moments of rushing vehicles travelling either to or away from Mallaig.

Friday October 1st 2010.
Beasdale Station to Mallaig (The Finish!) - 11.5 miles.

It was the early morning traffic heading towards Mallaig at 5.30am that woke me, still in darkness. Oh boy I was stiff. I dozed, tossed and turned until I finally got out of bed at 7.30pm to make tea and porridge.

After breakfast with David, I set off in the light at 8.30am.

The day was bright and it looked good for later. It was cold but the wind was light. I chatted to Gertrude about this being the last day of our adventure. I thanked her for being there with me, for enduring the tears and laughter, anguish and joy of this walk.

I was soon into my stride again, forgetting all the sentimental gibberish for a bit. I strode out like a demon possessed.

I wasn't alone for very long. After two miles of walking I was joined for half a mile by red deer. How amazing was that, a beautiful stag with two does wandering along the fence line on the roadside. They weren't startled by me, but just kept looking for a suitable place to jump back over the fence and into safety away from the road. I followed them in parallel on the opposite side of the road so as not to worry them. I managed to get a photograph and David, who came trundling by, stopped further along and took more photos of them. It was extraordinary, the deer were so focused on finding a way over the fence. Suddenly, they disappeared having reached a rise in the embankment. This was high enough for them to jump over easily, then they were gone. I have never been that close to red deer before and probably never will be again. It was only a matter of 5-10 minutes, no more, but what wonderful companions.

We stopped briefly in Arisaig for a coffee and wee break. It was quiet. The walk then became a little tedious as it opened up onto the exposed flat of the western shore. I can remember thinking I shall soon be at Morar. I was not disappointed; the wide mouth of the estuary of the River Morar with its beautiful white and golden sandy beaches is a fantastic sight as you walk across the bridge.

The sun was just catching the bay, but it was another two and a half miles before I finally stopped in Mallaig. The time was 11.30am. The views of Eigg, Rum and Skye were clear. I had truly been blessed with finishing on a warm sunny day. It was meant to be.

I grabbed the first person I could and asked them to take a picture of me standing in front of the quay where I had caught the ferry to Inverie (see chapter nineteen). A little bewildered at this messy woman who was grinning from ear to ear, the young lass who had a child in a buggy took the picture. I thanked her and then headed for the toilets, before tracking down David who was parked along the waterfront.

I was so glad David had come as he found Mallaig delightful. I treated us to a well deserved B&B for the night as a celebration. We stayed at a very comfortable place but not the one I had stayed in with the Cape Wrath crowd, as sadly that was full.

We wandered around the streets. I couldn't persuade David to come across by ferry to Inverie and Knoydart. It would have been a wonderful finish to the trip but he was so, so tired. It had been a very exhausting journey but I was still on a high. So instead, we compromised and drove back out to the banks of Loch Morar and followed the tiniest of roads as far as it would allow us and parked up.

I have to be honest here. I felt a little deflated. I would have liked to have shared this last chapter of the journey with a few more people. It all felt like an anti-climax, until I reminded myself **I had done it!** Then I couldn't stop grinning.

We had some lunch and in the warmth of the sunshine hitting the van David fell into a deep sleep. I took Gertrude, my book and coffee and found a suitable piece of beach by the loch and sat to enjoy the sun. It beamed merrily down whilst I dreamily looked across the twinkling water. I didn't need champagne bubbles, just this sparkle was enough to start me glowing with satisfaction. This was my celebration. A quiet euphoria swept over me engulfing my whole body. Tears of joy and poignancy trickled down my face as I quietly thanked everyone for this achievement, and as the text messages rolled in I held the phone to my chest and thanked God for keeping me safe.

I lay out and sunned myself for a while then read for half an hour, after which time I thought David would be awake. He wasn't though, so I looked about. I continued past the van and then walked towards the small hill of Creag Mhor Bhrinicoire (287 metres). I duly climbed it. From there the views across the loch were staggering. I felt I was on top of the world, and I stayed for a while. I sat hugging my knees and thought about David and his struggle to make it up here. I congratulated our little van for making the journey and it was right that David was in there, albeit asleep.

When I finally came off the hill it was 4.30pm. David had stirred but felt awful. It was a gentle drive back to the B&B, with showers and a decent meal helping him feel slightly better again.

Saturday October 2nd 2010. Train trip then home.

After a fabulous breakfast, we finished packing the van, leaving some clothes out for our journey home after doing what we had promised ourselves – to travel on the West Highland Line back to Fort William and then return to Mallaig. This was to be our special treat and afterwards we would head home. It was going to be another long day.

It was raining as we left Mallaig on the train, so the views weren't brilliant. However, the ride was excellent and a welcomed rest from all the walking. I found it interesting retracing my steps and following the road at certain parts.

On our arrival in Fort William, we had just enough time to drink a coffee, get some little pressies for the children and then catch the return journey back to Mallaig. We had a real giggle over a lady who, from the distance of the carriage we were sat in, looked just like my mum. Her mannerisms, hair, facial profile and shape all looked identical, even the colours she was wearing. Jokingly, as she came into the carriage, David and I both said together, "All she needs to do now is limp," and that is exactly what she did. We just went into fits of hysterical laughter. I was not wishing to be cruel, it's just that it wasn't until she finally turned around and faced us full on that we were convinced that Mum hadn't followed us up here. We were cracked up laughing. Mum definitely has a doppelganger.

Otherwise our journey was without event. We stopped at Glenfinnan next to the Jacobite steam engine, which was rather fun. Sadly, it had rained most of the journey so our pictures were obscure from the window, but it was still enjoyable.

We arrived back at the B&B in Mallaig at 4.30pm and then left for the long journey home. We finally arrived home on Sunday October 3rd at 11.30am, having stopped twice for breaks and power naps. I was tired but pleased that our next journey to Scotland would never be that rushed.

We crashed out and went to sleep. My journey was finished. My challenge fulfilled.

CHAPTER NINETEEN:

VISTAS ALL THE WAY

A CAPE WRATH TRAIL - MALLAIG TO CAPE WRATH.
DISTANCE: 162 MILES APPROX.
DATELINE: MAY 22ND-JUNE 6TH 2009.

On reflection this was to be the best decision I had made, choosing C-N-Do Scotland for my continuation up north. For me, it was about being off the roads and experiencing some of Scotland's and indeed Great Britain's remotest areas. Of course, I wasn't going to do this on my own. Although dim, this blonde knew it would be wild and bleak and to attempt such a task alone would have been foolhardy. I wanted to enjoy it, not frighten myself daft. (I am already that.)

All I can say is that C-N-Do did not let me down. I am a firm believer in 'you get out of things what you put in' and knowing how they operate was enough to assure me that this personality at her level of fitness would enjoy the challenge.

Words cannot really describe what a pleasurable trip this was. From the moment we commenced our first day of walking to our very last, I thanked God I was alive. I can wholeheartedly recommend that anyone who enjoys wild landscapes, lonely passes and glens, stunning coastline and the opportunity to spot some of our rarer creatures should undertake this trek. For me it surpassed all my hopes. My walking companions could not have been more interesting and enjoyable; every day was filled with effort, laughter and beauty, combined with the knowledge that I was edging towards completing my challenge.

I can honestly say that I did not wish to return from this trek. The inner peace I found daily was comforting. I felt protected from all cares and the walk gave me time to reflect and find myself once more. Amongst the majestic hills I succumbed, bowing to their creation far greater than mine, relishing the spiritual healing from these gods.

There was no infiltration of everyday clamour. No phones, no newspapers, no traffic, no computers, no benign chatter, no queues of impatient people, and no expectations, commercialism or exploitation. I found my senses once more open to Nature's cleansing properties and as I continued the trek through bogs and grasses, I was awestruck by the fact that no one person may have stood on this piece of ground before. It was so vast and barren in parts. I felt humbled and intrepid.

My journey started a few weeks beforehand in preparation, including taking on swimming, cycling and more walking in the Purbecks. It also meant a new pair of boots. Sadly, I felt that my faithful blue Scarpa boots, having walked almost the entire country and more, might not withstand this particular journey, and sentimentally I wanted to use them on the Durness to John O'Groats leg and the other missing parts of this journey.

Anyway, it was a good excuse to buy another pair. Once you have found a make that fits, it's almost worth buying two pairs – which is what I did. Blow the expense. Scarpa have never let me down! My feet have always been dry (although there was one incident, as I mentioned in chapter fourteen).

In January I had booked the flights and youth hostel accommodation. By then I had become blasé about such tasks.

Friday May 22nd 2009. Travel day.

My diary says: *'I am amazed I am sat here in Stirling Station. It is 12.30pm. I have one and a half hours to wait now and to unwind from all the worry of making sure I am on time. If anything had gone wrong with the flight or train journeys, I would have missed the C-N-Do pick-up time. Instead, here I am excited, really looking forward to the trip. (Anyone seeing me chat to Gertrude, who was in my rucksack, would have thought I'm mad. Those who know me know I am!)*

I have received some encouraging texts. Have grabbed a bite to eat and coffee and now waiting to meet my fellow walkers. I need these two weeks to recuperate and enjoy the next adventure. Why this terrible urge to walk and feel free, to breathe, and to feel alive? Forgive me, this space is so important. Thank you for letting me go.'

My flight from Southampton to Glasgow had gone without a hitch, although I had stood in the wrong queue for a while! Surprise, surprise, in the seat behind me was the father of one of Katy's friends. He was part of a group chartering a boat to sail along western Scotland. I sat next to an elderly lady who for safety reasons had had to wear a mask against air conditioning bugs. The previous year, she had picked up a virus having flown back from Spain.

The sun was out and the views from the plane of the New Forest and Solent were excellent, so was the remaining journey. I had good views of the Cumbrian Hills. We touched down at Glasgow Airport at 10.40am, I caught the bus to Queen Street Station in the city and then three minutes later I was on the train to Stirling. Everything went like clockwork. I counted myself lucky.

At 2pm we were picked up by the C-N-Do transit van. To my delight our leader was Chris, who had been the driver on the West Highland Way (chapter sixteen). I knew from that moment on that the walk was going to be great.

I soon settled into meeting my new walking companions and concentrating on not being sick as we made the slow twisty journey to Mallaig. Our driver was an interesting character called Pet. She seemed to know Scotland very well.

We arrived in Mallaig at 6.30pm and were placed in a B&B. I shared a room with Pet. That was interesting! Our twin room was comfortable with a lovely shower and bathroom. Breakfast was to be at 7.45pm. After so much sitting, I was pleased to walk out with the others, my bowels beginning to complain.

Mallaig was beautiful, the coast wonderful with the views of Rum, Eigg and Skye beautifully clear, and The Cuillins impressive against a setting sun. It was 10pm and still light!

The harbour water was like a millpond. Many fishing vessels were anchored in the bay, their colours reflecting in the water. I sat on my own in a restaurant, choosing not to go with the others because they were all eating fish and after such a journey I wanted to enjoy some pasta and a bit of space to savour my new surroundings. However after dinner, I went along to the restaurant where the others were and waited whilst they tucked in. I didn't want them to think I was being unfriendly.

Returning to the B&B, I retired to my room. No sign of Pet. However, during the course of my reading and writing she breezed in, and after a short conversation we went to sleep – only to be woken two hours later by some lads outside messing about. The room was warm and close and it took me ages to get back off to sleep. Excitement was bubbling away in my stomach.

Saturday May 23rd 2009.
Inverie (across Knoydart) to Barrisdale Bay - 9 miles.

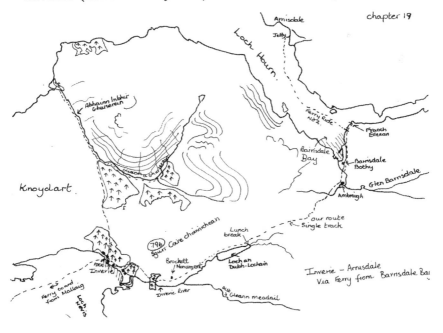

spirit. I was down first, Pet still lounging around in her pyjamas, Chris wondering where she was. Breakfast was very substantial and Chris gave us an overview of the day and asked us to have our bags ready for the van. This was it.

The group were all friendly. There were seven of us, two chaps and five ladies. From the start, I knew from the characters sat around the tables that this was going to be an interesting walk! Everyone was just a little on edge. It is always the same; people a little quiet before the start of a long journey. Me, I am always nervous because I don't know if my body will manage the challenge. Silly really; excluding our leader, I was the second to youngest! Looking at my companions who were in their latter years I don't know what the concern was. I smile as I type.

We caught the Knoydart Ferry to Inverie at 10am. The weather was quite fine when we left Mallaig, however the water was quite choppy and it was wet and drizzly as we neared Inverie. Welcome to Scotland.

As we crossed Loch Nevis, the surrounding mountains grew in stature as they rose out of the mist. As Mallaig disappeared into the distance, the sense of adventure rose up in me. I gurgled with delight.

I looked at the hunched shoulders of my new companions and took pictures. Chris was looking the most resigned to Scottish weather. I love ferry rides despite the weather; being on the sea is always good fun. The eldest walker looked to be enjoying it too.

We beached at Inverie, the bay dominated by the mountain

Sgurr Coire Choinnichean at 796 metres, although we couldn't see its top. I had never been in this area before. It is so pretty. It's a must-visit place.

Inverie village is dwarfed by its surroundings. It lines the shores of the bay with little homesteads dotted behind it. It is only accessible by ferry; there is no access by road from the rest of Scotland. There is a post office and a public house called The Old Forge, which boasts of being the most remote pub in mainland Britain.

The weather was inclement at this stage and we didn't have time to stop, even to take photographs. We soon found our path and headed easterly, before turning north-east towards Barrisdale. It was great to be in the hills once more. Our first point of interest was Brockett Monument, a structure built in vanity and self-importance by Alan Ronald Nall-Cain (Lord Brocket), once owner of Knoydart.

The path was brilliant and variable in width and the views just stunning. The copious rainwater running off the mountains had caused the rivers to swell, presenting us with some spectacular waterfalls. The rivers beneath the bridges hurtled with tremendous force. The day just got better, but the weather stayed misty and low cloud cover provided us with that damp drizzle that makes you chilly when you stop walking.

We stopped for lunch and sat on the fine sandy beach of the shores of Loch an Dubh-Lochain, meaning 'dark loch' which it was. The rain and drizzle had briefly stopped. For me, my eyes just absorbed everything. I was aware of three comrades pontificating over their lunches. I found this highly amusing as we had chosen our own. There was much chattering about what they were eating, which was to continue throughout the holiday. For my part, I enjoyed the peace and solitude as I devoured my sandwiches.

From here the low cloud and fine drizzle remained with us. It was chilly as we ascended over a long saddle. I took photos looking back towards our lunch break beach, and of the waterfalls that brought with them a cacophony of sound as they bludgeoned their rapid descent over rocks down the mountainsides.

We slowly made our descent towards Ambraigh and further still towards the bothy near Barrisdale. By now the rain had truly set in and as a group we were drenched rats. We stopped for a useful break. This bothy even had a toilet! I was grateful to get out of the rain. I don't mind the wet; it's the constant drumming noise in the ears as it hits the waterproofs that I dislike, and the fact you can't speak to anyone with any sense.

Unfortunately, the bothy was packed with people and with damp clothes! It was standing room only around the only heat source. A family of four (the children quite young) were enjoying the break, the weather outside quite atrocious. It didn't take me long to feel thoroughly chilled by this stopping.

Having had another swig of tea our group set off into the cold, dampening weather. It could not deter the spirits though and soon we were walking towards the flat marshy lands of Loch Hourn on our final stretch to the ferry landing near

Barrisdale Bay. Here the ferryman took us on the brief but interesting journey across Loch Hourn to Arnisdale.

Loch Hourn is Gaelic for Loch of Hell, so named because of the terrible spin drifts that have capsized many sailing boats. Happily we didn't experience this.

The ferry was an aluminium speedboat and all of us were only just able to squeeze in. Richard and Ann, who were at the bow, took the brunt of the bumpy, wet ride! I thoroughly enjoyed the trip; it was all part of the experience. The mountains dominated the shoreline. Although wet, I could imagine how pretty this coastline would be on a fine summer day. Everyone was very damp and some of our group were a little flat and quiet, but this was to be expected. None of us had had any real chance of getting to know one another yet.

Pet was waiting at Arnisdale with the van. She had enjoyed her day, and her cheerful smile and enthusiasm were fun. She was an extraordinary creature. She appeared so melodramatic, reminding me of a greyer version of Miss Piggy. A loveable character totally disorganised in an organised way, a warm heart and generous nature but also that 'don't cross me' attitude. She was fierce at times, quick to bite and you would receive the 'take that' moment if she didn't like your comment on anything.

Throughout the holiday I put all this down to her age. I smile as I type, for she certainly was the conversation maker most days. I suspect we all felt at times that she was frustratingly slow and disorganised, but for all that her love of Scotland, her knowledge, and her kindness towards one of the group not wishing to take part in the entire walk could not be faulted. What I liked about Pet was that she wasn't going to be sat on.

I think we were all pleased to see the van. What a great walk it had been. Stepping onto the jetty and sitting in the van, satisfied, my initial nerves over 'what ifs' had dissipated. I was really going to enjoy it all.

Arnisdale is a collective name for the area, which encompasses two villages: Corran and what was Camusbane. Arnisdale was once a major fishing port and had a population of over 200 people. Herring and other fish were processed and despatched to other parts of the country from here. Evidence of this can be seen at Corran, where the old herring sheds still stand. At one time Arnisdale had a school, blacksmiths, post office, three pubs, and a district nurse. Once a year, a coal boat would deliver fuel in the affordable amounts each villager could manage. The loss of the fishing industry due to trawler nets and restrictive catch sizes saw the decline of the village. Now it is a splendid tranquil setting and just the most beautiful and peaceful place to live.

We were going to be staying at Ratagan Youth Hostel for three nights. The journey there was delightful but I couldn't really enjoy it. Pet was chatting all the time and I was feeling very sick, my equilibrium only returning after tea! Pet and Chris made a very large pot of tea, which was wonderful and became the norm after each day's walking. There was always a packet of biscuits available. I really needed to keep up my liquids. I had not drunk enough because it was raining.

Our food for the night consisted of vegetable soup, quiche and salad followed by cheese and biscuits. All perfectly adequate. I did get the feeling that Pet was going to rely heavily on us to do the preparation, which turned out to be true throughout the holiday. Breakfast time was going to become a bit of a joke, which all added to the enrichment of the journey!

Oh it was good to be back in a youth hostel! The hollow mattresses, the squeaky doors, the dribbling showers and the knowledge that your bed was to be the only 'your space' of the holiday... I love every minute of it. The knowledge that there was nothing to worry about except sore feet or someone snoring can't be bad. I can't really describe how my mind empties on these walks. It just does.

Before bed I had my own Horlicks. This helped. It had brightened up outside, the dull day turning into a cold, bright evening. The views from the hostel over Loch Duich were wonderful. The Five Sisters of Kintail that dominate Glen Shiel and the easterly end of the loch were still shrouded in mist. There are actually six peaks: Sgurr na Moraich (876 metres), Sgurr nan Saighead (929m), Sgurr Fhuaran (1,067m), Sgurr na Carnach (1,002m), Sgurr na Ciste Duibhe (1,027m) and Sgurr nan Spainteach (990m).

I have been told that this is a wonderful ridge to walk, which I have made a mental note as a future challenge.

It was still light when I turned to my bed.

Sunday May 24th 2009.

Arnisdale to Glen More via Bealach Aoidhdailean -
10 miles (including 530 metres of ascent).

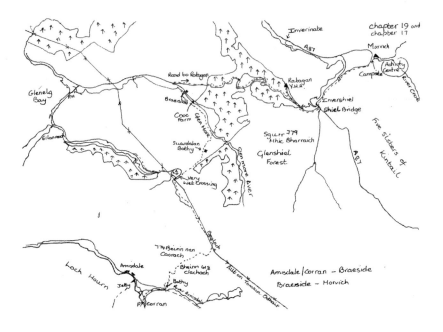

After a fantastic night's sleep (six and a half hours), I awoke refreshed and ready to go. It was 6.30am. I crept out in my PJs with my camera. The rising sun was poised between the hills. It was watery but ready to explode onto the loch. The colours were brilliant, the sun's glow creating a reflection on the black waters in the distance that dazzled the eye. I was so glad I had woken early, for the Five Sisters could easily be seen. I took several pictures and then a few of the youth hostel before going inside and having my first cup of tea in peace. Wonderful.

No one was about. I washed and got changed then laid

breakfast. By this point Chris was up. By the time the chaotic breakfast was over the skies had clouded over. It looked like we would have rain all day. Pet had not turned up yet, so we just helped ourselves from the foods available and made our own lunch packs.

This was always fun throughout our journey, as finding the bread and the fillings for sandwiches was a daily hunt. It was a surprise every day. Pet did well to cater for all the eating needs of the group as often as not, though we couldn't always find the supplies! I smile as a type.

Chris was really good at getting the group organised. I think quite early on he gave up hurrying anyone! We were packed and ready to leave by 9.10am and arrived at Corran car park, near the tea room, ready to start walking at 10.20am. I had sat in the front of the van, so I didn't feel queasy this morning. Chris had remembered I felt sick on long journeys.

The clouds looked ominous and the air was chilly. Still, we followed the river through Glen Arnisdale for a while. Here we saw a herd of deer, our first of this journey. We crossed the river to start the ascent out of the valley. Here at Achadh aGhlinne below the mountains was a bothy. This again was well stocked with comfortable chairs and old mattresses. After a coffee and a short break, we took our only serious climb of the day. Although drizzling we could still see the tops of the mountains. The path zigzagged approximately 500 metres up the col and was relatively easy, as it then flattened off into a saddle between the lower slopes of Beinn nan Caorach (774 metres) and Beinn Clachach (618m).

The path was quite ill defined from here. Chris kept us up as high as possible following the contours, so we dropped down onto Bealach Aoidhdailean with its power lines instead of climbing up to it. Needless to say, it was quite difficult terrain in the rain and cold wind. From here, we could see our way forward, the valley below stretching before us. The wind was cold so we sought refuge behind rocks as best we could and ate a small meal before moving on.

It became warmer as we descended and the path very defined as we followed the river to Srath a Chomair, a small boundary with a forest and high deer fences and deep rivers. At Ruighe na Corpaich we headed towards Glen More. It was very wet and the rivulets we crossed had become small rivers. We stopped at the beautiful Suardalan bothy for a breather. It just appeared; hidden from the path it suddenly stood beckoning. What a treat! I just thought it was brilliant, so wild. The weather was exhilarating but tiring, so we all welcomed the break.

With our brief visit over we walked the final mile and a half to Braeside, Glen More. We arrived at the van at 5.30pm. It had been a long day.

Back at Ratagan Youth Hostel, I had a shower and helped with dinner. This was tomatoes and olives for starters, then salmon, potatoes, peas and corn, with banana and custard for dessert.

I wrote my diary, noted that my feet were good, and turned in at 9pm.

Monday May 25th 2009.
Morvich to Killilan via Eas Ban, due to height of river
- 12 miles (540 metres of ascent).

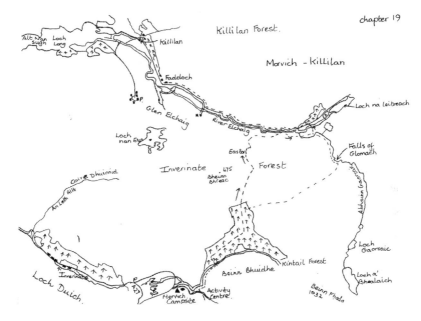

I slept well again. Breakfast over, we were ready to go at 9.10am. It was only a short drive around the bay to Morvich car park. It was going to be another wet day. Not yet torrential, just damp in the air when we started and very low cloud cover.

I think our walking companion Richard was already put off by the weather and was struggling, so he declined to walk and spent the day visiting a castle and doing domestics with Pet!! He later took our comments and teasing with good humour. I am not sure what his wife Ann thought of that, but she was cheery enough.

We left the car park and headed past the activities centre

and caravan area. From here we crossed a bridge with the water very high under us, as the first serious rain started to fall. For a time we were sheltered in the forest as we made a steady steep climb out of the trees up onto a high plateau. The waterfalls were marvellous.

Instead of heading towards the Falls of Glomach, we walked towards Eas Ban – a small cairn that was just a dot on the map – on an undefined path over rough moorland vaguely following a river. Chris did well to navigate through this, as so many of the tiny tributaries had become rivers themselves, and finding the correct one so as to pinpoint exactly where we were on the map in such poor weather had to be admired.

From here it was rain and low cloud cover drenching us all day. But I was thoroughly enjoying myself. The views could have been better but to me that was all part and parcel of the journey. We sat in the rain munching our soggy sandwiches. I have some great pictures of some very optimistic comrades smiling into the camera. It was either that or they were being very polite. Well actually, Rob looked like something out of the mafia in his dark glasses and all-black weather gear, delicately drinking his tea. I wonder what he was thinking.

It then became dangerous, the mist coming down quite thick. We never did quite see Eas Ban. Chris just pointed me in the right direction and everyone followed on behind as I picked a safe route off the mountain, skirting below Carnan Cruithneachd. Once below the cloud line, the views down to the valley of Glen Elchaig and its river were amazing. On a summer day this would have been stunning. Even so, it was by all accounts terrific.

We could see the path we would be using on the other side of the glen but getting down and across proved to be tricky, as the bridge we may have taken was under water. So we headed towards the Falls of Glomach path and its river crossing. Several smaller streams coming off the mountain were negotiated before we came to where the river of the falls met with the River Elchaig, and we crossed the bridge at Loch na Leitreach. This was very tiring; the group and our leader were much happier once on the valley's terra firma.

A good track saw us out of the valley and up towards Killilan. We sat near the edge of the loch and had a quick break. I took pictures of the Highland cattle there. Finally the sun decided to show up, allowing us the pleasure of some stunning scenery from whence we had come. The mist cleared to reveal the mountain tops. I sat against my rucksack, closed my eyes and enjoyed the sudden warmth. I was relaxed now and it was a shame to move on for the final five-mile stretch to Killilan.

It was a bit harsh on the hard tarmac surface when people's feet were soggy. Mine fortunately were still dry. Thank you boots.

We finally met up with the van at 5.30pm. Killilan is such a remote hamlet, just a few houses and a car park at the most eastern edge of Loch Long, with Ben Killilan (754 metres) as its backdrop.

The evening was spent packing for the next day's move with all our gear. Now I had a true sense of moving north. I had thoroughly enjoyed it up to now. My company was great fun. I found the Three Musketeers so entertaining (forgive me – you know who you are). I found myself laughing, which they may have found rude but I couldn't help smiling at their charm and conversations. It was Gill's raised eyebrows at times and the way she used to smile at the trio that made me giggle even more. Predominantly it was the conversations in the morning about food that cracked me up the most. That aside, I had great admiration for them. I hope I would still be walking with companions at their ages. They were so resilient, particularly the ladies with their dogged determination. I took my hat off to them every day and it is with respect for their intellectual and charming company that they are remembered with fondness.

Again we found ourselves helping out with the dinner. I am not sure what Pet did during the day. I appreciated she had a lot of travelling to do but sometimes I did wonder!

Dinner comprised of soup, chilli and cheese and biscuits. After washing up, most people abandoned social skills and sorted out their kit, as well as performing any doctoring required on their feet, along with other parts of the body!

Tuesday May 26th 2009. Killilan to Strathcarron - 12 miles (620 metres of ascent).

I slept well once again. Perhaps I was a little excited today, moving on to another area. We would be staying in Torridon

YHA for the next three nights. My legs were a little tired but my feet were really good. A change of mattress would help the legs.

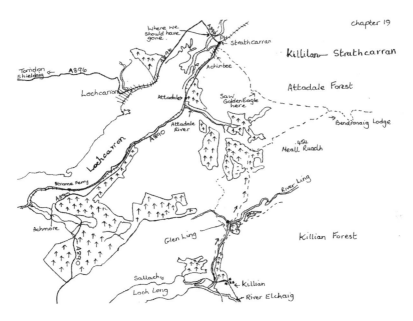

Breakfast was at 7.45pm after I helped lay it again. The weather was looking good; high cloud is always a good sign. Still, my wet weather clothes were at the top of my rucksack, plus the large emergency bivi for us all. Rob and I took turns carrying this extra piece of equipment for our leader.

Starting to walk at 10am, we followed the River Ling up through Glen Ling until we came to where the river divided. Here we stopped for our first break. The river was shallow but running fast, the scenery stunning. The weather was much kinder now. Blue sky, wow. I took pictures and rested against my rucksack. Ah, this was the life. A large tree root was jutting out of the riverbank shaped like a grizzly bear, and pebbles in the river sparkled wonderful colours of red, orange and brown. All was peaceful in my world.

Soon we left Glen Ling behind and headed north, slowly gaining height until we met the trees at Carn Allt na Bradh. Here civilisation had arrived in the form of telephone wires, which we followed into the forest. Walking on a lovely forest track albeit a bit dark, we had our first glimpse through the trees of the views to come. We saw a deer silhouetted against the mountains.

Views are so difficult to describe here. Everywhere you look is a changing vista, with no exception. For miles all you see are mountains. The air was clear, and the damp smells coming off the pine and heather just stimulated my brain. I found myself gasping with delight at this marvellous place.

Our path was a good track, taking us out among the hills. From here the day got better as we walked towards Attadale Forest (not a place with trees, just an area that may well once have had a forest). We stopped at a junction of paths and then followed a smaller track, Bealach Alltan Ruairidh, past Lochan Fuara as it went up and down and traversing around Carn Geuradainn.

Since Knoydart, this had been the most interesting path, so I bounced along quite happily. We had a hailstorm briefly, and had a giggle about this. Someone had said the day before that this was 'all we needed'. The day got warm again and in the afternoon it seemed we were permanently changing our outer garments.

Our most special part of the day came in the form of a

golden eagle. Well spotted by Ann, it followed the valley in front of us before disappearing behind us. What a spectacle. Some only briefly glimpsed it and I was one of those. We then came across three fishermen who had caught their supper.

Pet met up with us as we finally came down from the hills at Achintree and walked briefly along the road to Strathcarron. It was 6.15pm. Another long, brilliant day, very enjoyable. We saw the train pull into the station at Strathcarron. Our journey in the van to Torridon was a bit of a bone rattler again, but it was good to see the youth hostel.

We settled in but didn't eat until 9pm-ish. This was too late for me and my stomach was not good again. Again Gill and I did a lot of the meal preparation but we still ate – fruit salad, pasta and tuna salad, then ginger cake with cream. At least we didn't have to move our gear the next day, so I took the opportunity to do some washing and take a wander after dinner towards Torridon. I remember being in awe of the mountains behind the hostel. It had been the best Tuesday I had spent in a long time.

Wednesday May 27th 2009. Strathcarron to Torridon - 12 miles (450 metres of ascent) ...in theory.

Looking at the map, today was going to be a brilliant walk. I was well into my stride and accepting of anything coming my way. The day looked good – dull, overcast, a bit windy and chilly but okay by me. I had had a brilliant sleep.

How different the day turned out to be. It had rained

overnight. We arrived back in Strathcarron for 10am and were dropped off at the pub. From here we followed the river along its meadow bank through playing fields, and then after three quarters of a mile we hit our first problem. It had rained so much that what was once just a rivulet across the stream had become a hazard to cross. It took ages for people to get over this. I did not have a map at this time so I could not see the route, but it was soon after this that Chris, in his best judgement, decided to abort the day's walk. It was only raining slightly.

I was shocked we wouldn't be going on and was taken aback. Apparently the route would have been fraught with difficulties had we gone on, as there were many rivers to cross. It was with disbelief that Gill and I looked at each other. Chris did his best to explain, but at that point I wasn't listening. I was cross and needed my own time to cool off. I think what annoyed me the most was that there was no Plan B. To me, it just seemed an excuse to have a rest day.

Chris couldn't get hold of Pet, as she had already disappeared to do some shopping or something, so we sat in the pub and waited to be picked up and drank a complimentary hot chocolate. Big deal. I wish at this point I could have looked at the map, because I know Gill and I would have walked the road to Torridon if necessary. This abandoned part of the walk meant I would be coming back here and so would she.

I now became a spoilt child and spotting the piano in the corner, I sat down and played very loudly and awfully. Still, this vented my inner rage on an object, not another human being. I was disappointed and pissed off. Time was so precious to me that I couldn't think when I would fit in this bit of my journey again.

Pet finally came and picked us up and at 3pm we set off for a 'wee walk' beside Loch Coulin and Loch Clair. Admittedly it was beautiful, especially as the sun had come out, but looking at the map later I knew we could have done this earlier and walked across from Strathcarron to where we started this 'wee walk' – if a Plan B had been put in place. By 5.30pm we were back in the van to Torridon.

Resigned to the fact that a day had been wasted, I did not want it to spoil the holiday. Chris had made his decision based on previous experience and considering the members he had in his group. As a Venture Scout leader, I would have done the same, so as my annoyance dispersed logic and reasoning set in. Later in the evening, he came to apologise and again gave his reasons, which by then I had sort of accepted.

My protest was not to help with dinner preparation. I think I had done my fair whack of breakfast prep, dinner prep and washing up to earn a break. Dinner was haggis, then a mixture of Chinese chicken, sauté potatoes, celery, cucumber and mange tout. Dessert was cheese and fruit. My stomach felt bloody awful, having not done enough exercise to compensate for the dinners.

I rang home; it was Mum's birthday, all was good.

Thursday May 28th 2009. Torridon to Kinlochewe via Coire Mhic Nobuil and Coire Toll a'Ghiubhais route - 12 miles (680 metres of ascent).

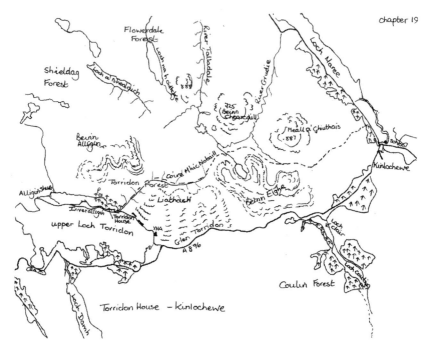

Slept well, up early again. We set off from Torridon in good time: 8.30am (a record).

At the start of the route, I had vivid memories of doing this bit following the river of Coire Mhic Nobuil. As a child I had not realised what a beautiful part of the country I was in. Jumping across the rocks in the river, oblivious to how lucky I was then, now I saw Torridon Forest as an extraordinarily magnificent place. The mountains were enormous lumps of rock rising from nowhere. The river took us eastwards behind the giants of the Liathach Ridge and towards the equally

391

magnificent range of Beinn Eighe massif. From the air it could be described as a large paw print with spurs as fingers. It forms a long ridge, with one spur classed as a Munro: Ruadh-stac Mor (Gaelic for 'The Big Red Stack') at 1,010 metres. Spidean Coire nan Clach ('Peak of the Corrie Stones') at 993 metres is the second Munro and is on the main ridge.

Whilst walking through Torridon Glen, we came across a lone German backpacker. He seemed organised and knew where he was heading. This would not be the last time we saw him.

It remained misty and murky but everyone was pleased to be walking again. Chris kept us as high on the contours as possible, as we skirted the edges of Coinneach Mhor (976m) and Sail Mhor (980m), part of Beinn Eighe. They towered above us. The highlight of the day was having lunch looking up at the Coire Mhie Fearchair, simply known as the Triple Buttress. Snow was still visible within one of the gullies.

The day brightened up again towards late afternoon. It was like walking on the moon as the topology of Beinn Eighe is composed of Cambrian basal quartzite, which gives it that distinctive light colour. We had a bit of a scrabble over the saddle as the path rose over loose boulders and scree while we made our way around Ruadh-stac Beag (896m) of Beinn Eighe, but we were rewarded with wonderful views of the northern edge as we left the massif behind us and slowly descended through the National Park and made our way to Kinlochewe. This was a wonderful path because we were let loose to go at our own speed. I really enjoyed my own company for a bit and absorbed the beauty.

We needed our sandals today to do two river crossings. It really was a great day. I didn't put much in my diary, but everybody was still in good spirits. The banter between Penny and Rob was very entertaining, with the odd whimsical remark from Lynn causing a stir. She was like the tonic added to a cocktail of laughs.

The sun was shining when Pet picked us up. It had been a tiring day but the weather now boded well. There wasn't a cloud in the sky and I hoped tomorrow would stay that way.

I think I was so busy packing up my luggage that I forgot to write down what we had for dinner. We turned in early as it was going to be a long day tomorrow and our bags needed to be in the van early – ready for the move to Ullapool Youth Hostel.

Friday May 29th 2009. Kinlochewe to Destitution Road - 16 miles (600 metres of ascent).

I slept well and was ready to leave at 8am. By 9am we were all set for another day's walking. What a difference the sun can make. Finally the shorts were on. It was 27-28 degrees in the glens. Not a cloud in sight.

Today it was so warm I drank four litres of water. What a relief not to have to carry warm hats and gloves, and I gambled on no waterproof trousers. Instead mosquito cream, sun hat, glasses and sun block were required.

We started at the back of a school on the outskirts of Kinlochewe called Incheril. The track was brilliant as we walked towards the Heights of Kinlochewe with Beinn Eighe behind us, the sun reflecting on its white quartzed top. Everyone had a chance to talk today and enjoy the warmth. We raced along; it must have been a break for Chris not to worry too much about us for a while. We followed the Abhainn Bruachaig river for two miles and a small bothy lay on our left with pine trees behind it. Very pretty. From here the track led into another valley, Gleann na Muice. Before we hit Lochan Fada we headed over open moorland for a while until the going got a bit tough.

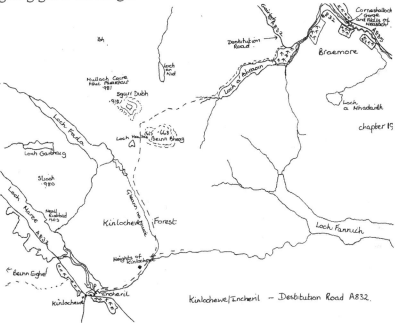

Kinlochewe/Incheril – Destitution Road A832.

We stopped at the lochan below Meall an Fhudair for our lunch break, surrounded by wonderful views of mountains. I went down to the shores of the lochan but it was very peaty and dark. Scouring the skyline and the mountain tops, I had hoped to see birds of prey or deer but couldn't. It was so peaceful.

We headed down the glen between Bealach na Croise (615 metres) and Sgurr Dubh (918m). It was then a bit of a mishmash trying to work our way over to the track that headed down to the shores of Loch a Bhraoin. Reaching the track around the loch couldn't have come any sooner. Everyone was very tired, the heat taking its toll. The track was very hard on the hips, having been churned up by four wheel drives, but it got easier as we headed towards the farther end of the loch. If I had been given half a chance, I would have had a swim but everyone else just wanted to get back to the van.

At the far end of the loch, there was a boat shed and a derelict house. Oh to stop and savour this place, but it was now 5.30pm and it had been a long, hot day.

Pet and Richard met us as we came up to Destitution Road (A832). The stretch of road between Dundonnell and Braemore Junction on the A832 is one of several in the region known as Destitution Road. It was built during the Highland Potato Famine of 1846-1857 to provide work for crofters in exchange for oatmeal rations. It was also a source of employment for those Irish who had had similar crises in the Great Irish Famine and had left their homeland for Scotland.

At this time, most crofters across Scotland were very dependent on potatoes as their staple diet, as these would generally grow in poorer soil. In the Highlands of 1846 potatoes suffered blight, the crops failed and the following winter was especially cold and snowy. With famine, severe malnutrition and crippling diseases, basic living conditions and financial hardship became inevitable. Many crofters left their lands and were reduced to living on the streets of the already overcrowded cities.

The authorities, having learned some lessons from the Irish Famine, did organise some distribution of oatmeal and other supplies, as did some landlords who worked to lessen the effects of the famine on their crofting tenants. However, crofters were not just given the rations – they had to earn them and were expected to work. Relief programmes resulted in the building of the destitution roads. A day's work consisted of eight hours of gruelling labour six days a week. Weekly oatmeal rations were set at 680g per man, 340g per woman and 230g per child. It is thought that 1.7 million people left Scotland during this period and it was part of a wider food crisis facing Northern Europe at this time.

I found this information humbling as we drove back to Ullapool, and a thoughtful reminder of how much we take for granted these days.

Ullapool is delightful town. It has the largest population in the West Highlands and is a popular tourist destination as a base for exploring the most stunning coastline in the British mainland (perhaps I am biased). It is also the main terminus for the ferry to Stornaway in the Outer Hebrides, and provides all types of accommodation from hotels to campsites.

Ullapool was, and still is, a fishing town. Prior to 1748 it was a small fishing village, however the British Fisheries Society employed Thomas Telford to design the harbour and quay to make it officially a herring port. When as a visitor you see it for the first time, Ullapool presents a uniformity of whitewashed buildings along its harbour walls, only separated by the road. The architectural lines of the harbour emphasise the money devoted to build it properly. Sadly, there was overfishing and by the 1830s it fell into decline. However, within 20 years Ullapool came to life again as European boats began to use the loch and the harbour as a safe anchorage. Since then the fishing industry has ebbed and flowed but there's still activity today, mostly involving local fishermen and touring yachtsmen.

The landscape that surrounds Ullapool is some of the prettiest and dramatic in Scotland, with Beinn Ghobhlach to the west, An Teallach to the south-west, Beinn Dearg to the south-east and Beinn Mhor na Coigich to the north. These giant blobs on the landscape dominate everything. As new travellers walking back and forth on the roads in this area, we were to see these massifs many times. It was wonderful, especially in the early morning and evening sun. I can honestly say we were blessed. I urge you to go and savour it for yourself.

We arrived at the youth hostel at 7pm. Gosh, this had turned out to be a long day. Our room was very small and hot but the view was exquisite. We overlooked the harbour. It was so pretty. It did not take me long to get changed and walk out into the street to take in this tranquil setting. The last rays of sun were creating the most beautiful colours right across Loch Broom. It was like a millpond and the reflections of the small sailing boats and trawlers were in perfect symmetry. The colours were as bright in the water as on the boats themselves. As my eyes swept round this panoramic view, I just absorbed it all.

The light on the hills across the loch gave them a purple hue and they were speckled with the white dots of whitewashed dwellings. I could not believe where I was, and I wished David could have been here. It will stay in my memory forever. I sound such an old romantic but this was a wow moment that brought tears to my eyes. What a cracking end to the day.

Walking across the street back to the hostel, I was aware that I needed to help with dinner preparation again. We did not eat until 9.30pm; way too late for me but who cares. We had melon for starters, then gammon, peaches, beans and potatoes with salad (what a mixture). Dessert was jelly and ice cream.

It was a very late night.

Saturday May 30th 2009. Inverlael to Duag Bridge - 15 miles (800 metres of ascent).

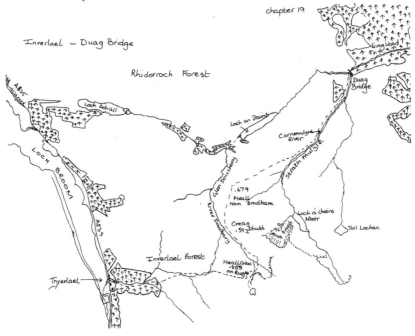

I had a disturbed, hot night. Revellers outside the bedroom windows at an unearthly hour of the morning laughed and crashed into things, only to be followed by the trawlers loading and unloading at high tide. The spotlight on the quay was bright and shone in our windows. I finally dropped off to sleep at 3.30am and woke at 5.30am, with light streaming in.

My towel had dropped off the window sill onto the ground below, so I quietly dressed and crept out into the cool freshness of the morning. I made a cup of tea, grateful that whoever had been sick over the front door had missed my towel! I then went over and sat on the wall. Although weary from lack of sleep, I was relaxed and my legs and feet felt good. All was still, and I said a quiet 'good morning' to a dog walker.

The sun already warming me, I hugged my knees and reflected. I hoped I would come here again. I would love to explore just this area. I thought of a friend who loved boats and had sailed much of this part of the coast. I could see why. I thought of the family; wouldn't it be great for them to see this. It would be great to bring canoes.

My thoughts were interrupted at 7-ish with Ann and Richard walking over for a chat. After a while, we went in and sorted out the breakfast things again. No sign of Pet yet, however we were all up, packed and ready to walk from Inverlael at 8.50am. The weather was glorious – it was going to be another hot one. I wetted my scarf and put it in a bag in my rucksack for later.

At Inverlael we climbed 500 metres out of a pine forest and took a north-easterly path. I think we went wrong here somewhere, but looking at the map now I can't be sure quite how. I am sure we came onto our main path from a slightly different angle. If we did, the group would not have been aware of it. Chris got us back on track easily enough.

It was wonderful with vistas everywhere as we made our way towards the River Douchary. We came over a wide saddle and dropped down to the river. It was extremely hot with no shade for miles. Still, we stopped and had our sandwiches with our feet dabbling in the river. We then picked up a main track circumnavigating Creag Dhubh (592 metres) and Meall nam Bradhan (679m), which took us into Strath Mulzie past Corriemulzie Lodge.

It had been another hot and glorious walking day. The views were tremendous. We had not met another soul. It was so wild and remote. We had stopped three times beside water, which was delicious on the feet.

We met up with Richard and Pet at Duag Bridge outside a rather smart bothy. Here we encountered our German friend again who had stayed there. He was definitely doing his own route to Cape Wrath. We were all relieved to see the van – it was becoming our friend. Some of the group were very tired now. I marvelled at how Lynn kept her spirits up. She was shorter than all of us and sometimes her legs must have been going like a terrier. I felt extremely fit.

On the way back to the youth hostel, we saw a herd of red deer. This was a consolation as we had seen none on our walk today. We had fish and chips for tea. I was expecting the fish to be extra special but it wasn't. Pet had managed to get another memory card for my camera, for which I was extremely grateful.

As we were staying for four nights in Ullapool we all clubbed together and did a large wash of clothes, which was great because everything dried nicely as it was so hot. After another fine evening I finally turned in at 11pm.

I wish I hadn't been so tired as I could have explored Ullapool a bit more. Our group dynamics had shifted slightly. It is interesting how the mind works when the body is tired. I could sense a few cracks, the odd snap, a sharp word, something missing, an annoyance or irritation. It happens. I think the youth hostel was cramped and this probably didn't help, coupled with the heat. The walk was taking its toll, but in the group as a whole our resolve was strong and the humour still there. I still can't help laughing at Penny as I am writing, going through her 'creaming rituals' and decisions on what she would take the next day. Bless her for being the source of my giggles this night as she packed and repacked.

The group was fantastic. They may never know how much I enjoyed their company, so removed from my normal life.

Sunday May 31st 2009. Duag Bridge to Loch Ailsh - 12 miles (210 metres of ascent).

When morning came I was very tired again, after a disturbed night. It was very hot and another person was sick outside our bedroom window. I had about three hours' sleep and felt a bit sluggish. So I found it difficult to be civil this morning, which is unlike me. I am not sure if anyone noticed. I hope not.

We set off in good time. By all accounts this was to be a much easier day, with fewer mountains and more rivers and forest tracks. We started at the bothy at Duag Bridge in glorious sunshine. The forest was quite young here and some of the puddles were fairly deep on the track. In the sunshine, I spotted a newt in one of them.

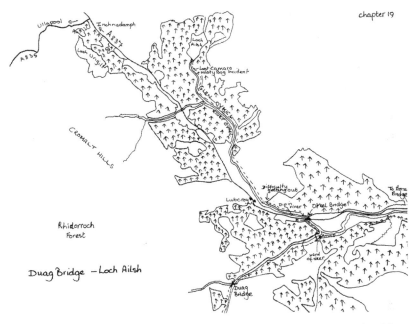

On reaching the end of the forest track, we had views looking across a small farmstead at Anat. We had the good fortune to spot a herd of red deer. There were many of them, so we watched for several minutes as they left the area quite swiftly in a long procession.

This was such an easier walk than our previous days. We went down towards Oykel Bridge and its hotel, this and its hunting lodge all part of the Corriemulzie Estate. I knew I had been here before with my parents. It was great to be back.

We stopped and had a cup of coffee and a decent toilet break. It was a treat not to be exposed for a change! We then passed over the bridge to pick up our trail once more, the large slabs of rock with water tumbling over them so inviting. On our lunch break, we dropped down to the water's edge and some shelves of rock. They were warmed by the sun. This was too much, so out came the swimming costume. My tiny towel covered nothing really but I found a fairly private spot to change. It didn't take me long to find a suitable plunge hole and a slab to lie on by the water. By 'eck it was cold but fantastic. I lay there adjusting to the temperature and then it was wonderful. The sun was right on me.

The others probably thought I was mad, except Lynn. Water is a magnet to me, I love it. It was refreshing and I can still feel that tingling sensation. Afterwards I ate my sandwiches and dried out in the sun. There was this wonderful sense of freedom from being the sensible mother or wife. I would strongly recommend anyone to try it.

From here we followed the river through the wood and then along its shores. The area was vast and wide. The estate had fishing huts along its banks. For a considerable price these favourable fishing spots can be bought for the week or day depending on your pocket. We bimbled along (for our first and last time) and stopped occasionally until we met the van at the southern end of Loch Ailsh.

Although a shorter day in terms of walking, it was still 5pm before we were picked up. We had had a slight hitch towards the end as we negotiated a bog. Frighteningly, Penny went in quite deep up to her knees. It was not funny; every time she moved she went deeper. Rob and I helped her. She had to throw her rucksack, and using sticks with Rob and I holding on to her arm we slowly brought her out. She was quite scared. In assisting I had not seen my camera catapult out of my pocket. It all happened very quickly.

Checking Penny was okay, we made our way to the van. Chris hadn't noticed anything and why should he, we were that close to the van. Having all piled in ready for the off I noticed my camera was missing. I was devastated. All those pictures. Rob kindly offered to retrace our steps back to the bog as there was just a possibility it could be there. If it was in the bog it would be lost anyway. I can remember trying to stay calm but was absolutely gutted and mortified.

We searched for a while before Rob found it clinging to reeds about a yard from the bog. I could have cried, but instead I gave Rob a big hug. I was so pleased, so relieved.

It was another long trek back to Ullapool but the views were stunning. We saw another herd of deer on the way. We were moving the next day to another youth hostel. I was informed it was a beautiful spot at Achmelvich and I would enjoy it. What other delights was I in for?

Dinner tonight was salad and bread, then couscous, sausages and stir fry, followed by raspberry and chocolate pudding with fromage frais.

I was hoping for a better night's sleep tonight. I rang home and learned that Ben had damaged his foot, Chris's 50th birthday went off okay and David was feeling slightly better. Relief. I felt guilty I had had such a good day.

Monday June 1st 2009. Loch Ailsh to Inchnadamph - 11 miles (400 metres of ascent).

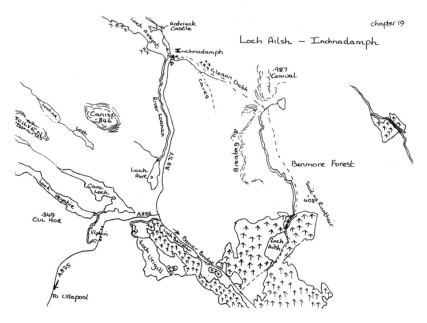

Yet another disturbed night, but only at 4.30am when the boats were loaded up again. I checked my phone and saw that Katy had left a message. Dad was okay and I wasn't to worry about Ben.

Breakfast was another chaotic affair, especially as we had to be ready with our luggage for the moving on. At least with the family okay I could enjoy the day.

We commenced walking at 10.30am. We were blessed with another beautiful clear morning, so everyone was in good spirits. Our first spot of the day: two ospreys feeding from the loch. What a wonderful sight. We also saw a couple sunbathing with very little on, their children playing near the water. They looked to be camping. What a brilliant location.

We passed Benmore Lodge, with its dog barking. We continued following the River Oykel into the area of Benmore Forest. We were now in a valley with wonderful mountains around us and as walked further into a quarry we had Breabag (718 metres) to our left, Carn nan Conbhairean (868m) on our right and in front of us Ben More Assynt (998m). It was breathtaking.

Chris kept us at 300 metres above the river so as to make our ascent easier over the saddle between Conival (987m) and Breabag Tarsainn (600m). There were no paths as such, so by climbing from the valley floor in this way we kept our height, and overall this was a lot better.

At one waterfall we came across some primroses in full bloom. Sheltered from the wind and on a southern slope there was moisture and warmth. We stopped and had lunch on the south-eastern end of Conival's slopes, looking over Dubh Loch Mor dominated by Ben More Assynt. It was here we saw a stag watching us on the horizon. Eventually it slowly moved off.

Continuing through the saddle we came across a mass of pink thrift and also an orchid. Now we had a noticeable path once more as we followed the steep descent of the Allt a Bhealaich river down past the caves by the River Traligill and continuing down Glen Dubh to Inchnadamph. It is only now, as I am writing up this diary properly, that I realise how much we missed travelling through this area. It would be great to explore it more. There is so much to see and the geology is fascinating.

Inchnadamph is a tiny hamlet yet it's a mecca for

geologists. The work of Ben Peach and John Horne from 1883 to 1897 played a major role in unravelling the structure of the North West Highlands, and in understanding the first thrust fault to be discovered anywhere in the world. A thrust fault is a series of several different layers of rock, often several kilometres in thickness or width and often with hard rock cap layers built on softer sedimentary rock layers visible at lower levels. Ben More Assynt is a good example of this, rising from a glen of limestone caves through sandstone terraces to a quartzite summit cap. A monument to the work of Peach and Horne stands at the most southern end of Loch Assynt. Since their day, much of rock dating has been done based on Highlands geology and this area is therefore still popular with geologists.

The Traligill Caves near Inchnadamph make up Scotland's largest cave system, but care must be taken. It is in fact advisable not to go in them. A little further along the road, the Bone Caves of Inchnadamph by Allt nan Uamh are easily accessible and can be explored. Once they contained relics of lynx, brown bears, arctic foxes, reindeer and a polar bear dating as long ago as 47,000 BP, as well as human skeletons dating from 300 BC. The skeleton of a bear thought to be 11,000 years old was removed from the caves in 2008. This is now kept at the National Museum of Scotland.

We arrived at Inchnadamph before Pet, at 6.30pm. Another long day. It was then a twisty journey to our next hostel at Achmelvich. We were all hot and tired.

Well, what can I say about Achmelvich. Forgive me, everyone should go there at least once in their life. This has to be one of the loveliest locations for a youth hostel. It is just yards from the most stunning bay. The sun in its western glory was resting on the still waters. Blow dinner, I just had to get stripped and run down to the shores and go in. Finding my bathing costume and dumping my clobber on the cramped bed, I told Gill where I was off to and then left.

There was one toilet and one shower, which were outside. At least by going in the sea I'd give the others a chance to shower and change. This dip would not take long knowing how cold the sea was in these parts, but undeterred I ran to the shores and went straight in. It took my breath away. The water was freezing. It numbed my body immediately but as I acclimatised I began to swim across the bay. This lasted for all of three minutes, when my arms started to get pins and needles. Well, I was certainly refreshed. I staggered back to the hostel, had a shower and then helped prepare the table for dinner. We had grapefruit, Spaghetti Bolognese and cheese and biscuits.

There were hundreds of midges around the hostel, so once indoors it was best to stay in. I wrote my diary and then crashed out very tired. The sleepless Ullapool nights had caught up with me.

Tuesday June 2nd 2009. Inchnadamph to Loch na Gainmhich - 10 miles (820 metres of ascent).

I woke early and crept out to have my usual morning cup of tea. It was very cramped in our bunk room. My thoughts turned to daughter Katy. She was 25 today, happy birthday my lovely.

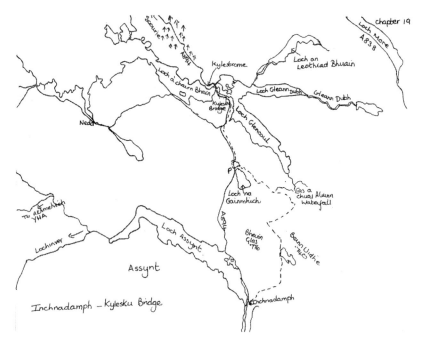

Inchnadamph – Kylesku Bridge

Another beautiful day had dawned but the wind had changed and there was a definite chill in air. Still bright with high clouds though. It was going to be one of those days when our coats went on and off.

In my diary I have written that today's discussion revolved around stockings and changing wheels. I can't for the life of me remember what it was all about, but I do remember the frivolity.

Our journey to and from Achmelvich was dominated by Suilven, a 731 metre high mountain rising out of a wilderness of moorland, bogs and lochans known as Inverpolly National Nature Reserve. Majestically and mysteriously the mountain stands alone, a wonderful sight. From one angle it resembles a giant death cap toadstool, and from other angles it looks like a pyramid. From Glencanisp Lodge it appears like a sleeping lion, its ridge forming the back of a giant rounded head. The area also features other bastions: Cul Mor at 849 metres, Quinag (808m) with its long ridge forming the backdrop to Loch Assynt, and Canisp (846m).

I found myself enjoying the journeys in the van as much as the walking, although I recall at the end of this day's walk that I had sat in something smelly at lunch and I was conscious of the odour as I sat in the front of the van between Chris and Pet. Oh dear! How embarrassing. But there was always tomorrow.

I digress. We headed off from Inchnadamph in good time. It was a wonderful route – an old stalker path that twisted and climbed over rocks and boulders in what can only be described as the remotest place I am ever likely to walk. I thoroughly enjoyed this interesting and challenging path. Everyone was concentrating on not twisting their ankle or tripping over. The views were amazing, as they were every day. Nothing as far as the eye could see but mountains and small lochans. I just bounced along, quietly enjoying the solitude of my own thoughts and absorbing the breathtaking beauty of this desolate barren wilderness.

The weather stayed dry but it was slightly chilly. We made a steady climb past Cnoc an Droighinn (477 metres) on our left, then dropped again past Loch Fleodach Coire before rising through the pass between Beinn Uidhe (740m) and Glas Bheinn (776m). The walking was terrific as we picked our way along the wiggly route over and around the 500 million year old basal quartzite and pipe rock formations. I felt I was paying homage to this marvellous creation, such was the lasting impression it left on my memory.

Finally stopping for lunch, finding a suitable rock that was out of the wind, we savoured our view. Miles and miles of grey and white rock peppered with lochs and small areas of vegetation. It was at this lunch break where I sat in some sheep poo. I had gone to find a suitable spot for a wee and with all of me exposed, I fell back and sat in poo. Oh great. I did my best to clear it up, but for the remainder of the day I had this sort of smell following me... You know what I mean. However, as my reward, I saw a ptarmigan. I had never seen one before. It still had some of its white plumage and flew like a giant, full stomached pigeon. I had to look twice to be sure it was what I thought it was. What a treat. I have never seen one since.

After lunch we followed the best path of the entire walk. Very slowly descending past Loch Bealach, we skirted the lower slopes of Cnoc na Creige (593 metres) to be rewarded with the most wonderful views of Loch a Chairn Bhain and the open sea, with all its inlets and coves. Much of the time it was hard to stop myself from crying with joy.

We had missed the Eas a Chual Aluinn waterfall, Britain's highest with a sheer drop of 200 metres. But we passed a small waterfall that plunged into a large hole in the earth, and we had to negotiate a tricky river crossing that had the remains of wooden boards sunk into its peaty edges, before we finally emerged onto the A894 in a car parking area south of Kylesku. This is where Pet came and picked us up at 5.30pm.

It had been a wonderful day. No swim this evening, although the sun once again was stunning. The chill and tiredness and the fact that we had to pack up again was enough to keep me out of the water. But that didn't stop me walking down to the water's edge again. I took photographs of the youth hostel bathed in evening sun; I wanted it to be imprinted on my brain forever. I also enjoyed looking in a very useful information hut explaining about the seashore and the area near the beach. It was so peaceful here. I vowed I would come back again.

My diary has not recorded what we had for dinner that night.

Wednesday June 3rd 2009. Kylesku to Loch Stack - 12 miles (600 metres of ascent, making the walk more like 13.5 miles).

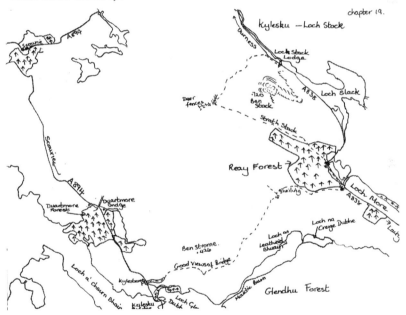

I must have been tired, as I had a great night's sleep and I didn't hear 'the commotion'. Apparently we had some late arrivals. I wouldn't have known.

Today we were moving on to Durness Youth Hostel, our last point of stay. Our Cape Wrath Trail was almost complete. I walked down to the shore for the last time, then had breakfast after which we were ready to leave this wonderful place by 8.30am. The weather was more chilly again, so a windproof was required. There was slight dampness in the air but it was clearer by the time we commenced our walk at 9.30am.

Our views of Kylesku Bridge that unites Kylestrome and Kylesku as it spans across the edges of Loch a' Chairn Bhain and Loch Glencoul were brilliant. Opened by the Queen, the bridge was constructed in 1984 to replace the ferry service, which had been in existence in various guises since the early 19th century. The bridge is 276 metres in length and spans a stretch of water 130 metres wide. It is a beautiful piece of architecture. Built by Morrison Construction Group, I feel the five-span continuous curve of pre-stressed concrete fits into its landscape. It certainly saves a driver a 100-mile detour if there wasn't a crossing here.

Our first incident of interest this day was watching a helicopter carrying enormous hoppers of ready-mixed cement up the valley to build a road or perhaps lay a foundation to a home. We weren't sure. It was fascinating as we watched the thick cables being winched down to a hopper and men attaching the hooks, before it went up and was suspended about 25 feet below the underbelly of the helicopter, swaying as it went. It looked very dangerous work and extremely noisy. We could feel the downdraft of the helicopter on our faces. Still, we didn't have all day and eventually we got going again.

To begin with, the track was easy. We bounced along, well I did. It was one of those paths you just wanted to fly along. We met a lady wearing a bright pink coat, matched only by equally bright pink walking boots, which I had to smile at.

We met up with our German friend again on a wide piece of mossy footpath towards mid-morning, and as we followed a very well heeled track we spotted a beautiful stag watching our small procession from above us. We then had a lunch break at some ruins. It was pretty chilly so it was a quick stop.

This was an easygoing day for me. I was well into my stride. The track got wider and prettier as we made the slow descent towards Loch More. There were marvellous views of Ben Stack (721 metres) to our left and in front of us Ben Screavie (332m), dominated in the background by Meallan Liath Coire Mhic Dhughaill (801m).

We went past Lochmore Lodge and then walked along the road until Achfary. This dear little village comprising of a few houses is part of the 120,000 acre Reay Forest Estate, owned by the Duke of Westminster's family. The hamlet was built to house the workers on the vast estate. It boasts a school, and a post office with an unusual telephone box painted black and white.

For the remainder of the afternoon, we walked below and around the wonderful mountain of Ben Stack, through what is known as Strath Stack and then out onto a very boggy piece of land, following the deer fences until finally turning easterly towards Loch Stack Lodge. The views of Arkle (787m) were wonderful.

It was becoming quite late but it was still dry. Even so, we all still had our coats and woolly hats on. We were picked up at 6pm, at a pull-in point along the A838 near Loch Stack Lodge at the northern end of Loch Stack. It had been a very long day and we were all delighted to see the van.

"But what is this?" came the cry. Pet had turned into a man named Frank. Our new driver was a very cheerful chap. I could see the smile of relief and gratitude on Chris's face. There was a lot of banter between them and so began our journey to Durness for the night.

Durness is the largest village in the north-western part of Scotland. It is located within Sutherland's North West Highlands Geopark. With a population of around 400, the village is part of the remote but large parish of Durness. Within this parish, there are other smaller villages and single homesteads. This area is noted for being sparsely populated and indeed is said to be the most sparse in Western Europe. Certainly for the visitor it is the absence of civilisation that strikes you most. Driving into Durness from Rhiconich, the telephone wires following the single track A838 road are the only hints that people live here.

Our drive to the youth hostel was exciting. It had been almost 40 years since I had travelled this far north and unbelievably the roads had not changed. The colour, the width, the views were as I remembered them. It was only the telephone wires I could not recall. I remember being overwhelmed by it all. This felt like a homecoming, such had been my experiences of Scotland as a child and how happy

415

they had been, and here I was again. Words can't describe the elation, the joy I felt on that van ride to the hostel.

Durness Youth Hostel was an experience in itself. The hostel was divided into two long, low wooden prefabricated WW2 Ministry of Defence huts. They were very rustic, their roofs made of corrugated asbestos. One hut housed all the dormitory space for men and women, separated only by showers and toilets. Between the huts there was open grass and a path connecting them both. The other hut provided all the living space, with a laundry and drying room (small but efficient), an open plan kitchen and a lounge area. At one end was a most marvellous coal burning stove with extremely old, faded but very comfortable lounge chairs. The crude but essential washing line that ran between the two huts proved to be useful.

It is believed that Winston Churchill visited these buildings during the war. It was very atmospheric here and a delight just to be staying in something from that era that had changed very little.

Although sunny, there was a constant cold wind. But it was very cosy and peaceful inside this building. The sleeping dormitories were a little chilly, the metal framed windows allowing in some fresh air! However, Gill and I managed to get single beds each. What a treat from being on a bunk bed. Oh joy!

The wardens of the youth hostel were a lovely couple. They had two dogs and this place was extremely friendly and welcoming. I would recommend anyone to stay here. Do remember though that it is self-catering, as are most of the Scottish youth hostels.

I was too tired to explore tonight, so instead I opted to sort out my suitcase for the final time, work out what washing could be done and relax for the evening. Frank, our new support person, was completely organised. On our arrival he made us all a cup of tea. We offered to help with the dinner and his reply was, "Only if it's needed." Well, what a change. Probably for the first time on this holiday, I was having a 'guilt trip' as I sat and watched while he did his chores in the kitchen. The fire was burning and I was sat in a deliciously comfortable chair with a hot cocoa, enjoying having a rest.

Frank had done the shopping and he prepared soup, steak pie, potatoes, carrots, peas and gravy, followed by fresh raspberries and strawberries with cream. It was extremely nourishing and all of the group devoured and savoured his fine cuisine. Nothing was too much trouble and he was such a happy cheery chap.

Tomorrow was going to be a shorter day, and this was rather welcomed by all. Much of the conversation was about us coming towards the close of our holiday. I was trying not to think about that. I did manage to get a mobile signal here so I rang home. David could hear in my voice how much I was enjoying it.

Thursday June 4th 2009. Loch Stack Lodge to Rhiconich - 7 miles (130 metres of ascent).

I had another wonderful sleep. I understand that the rain had let rip in the night. This morning it was chilly again and overcast. It looked like there could be more rain coming. I did not put much in my diary about the weather, but looking at my photographs I see we had our coats and hats on, mainly for the chill factor. But no rain on this day.

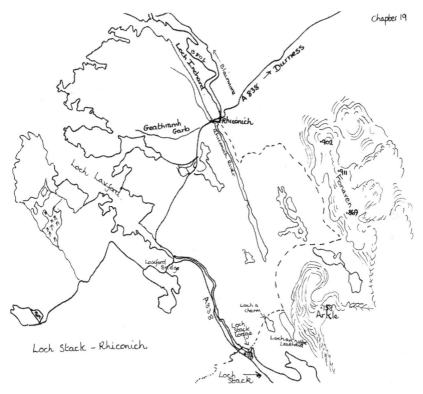

I got out early for my morning cuppa, only to find Frank was already up and about. Breakfast had been fully laid, tea was on the brew, and sandwich making facilities with choices available were ready for us to sort out. And breakfast was at 8am on the dot! So we were all ready to leave by 9.10am and were walking by 9.40am. Marvellous and all done with a smile. It had been a refreshing start to the day.

From Loch Stack Lodge we followed a wonderful track north-eastwards towards the imposing Arkle (787 metres) and we passed by some lovely lochans. In between Loch Airigh a

Bhaird and Loch an Nighe Leathaid under the shadow of Arkle, we briefly stopped for a small break. It had threatened to rain but this did not amount to anything.

As we skirted around the base of Arkle, we headed off in a north-north-westerly direction along two lochs towards Rhiconich. The path was barely visible and probably only used by fishermen. It turned out to be more difficult and tiresome than expected as we negotiated heather and rocky shorelines for quite some distance, before finally following the river into Rhiconich.

We stopped for lunch on a beach. It was strange. I have a picture almost identical to our first beach stop some 13 days before. However, at this stop it wasn't misty and there was a green rowing boat pulled up on the shore.

Everyone was tired now and looking forward to an early finish. Nothing however could take away the wonderful views of Arkle and Foinaven (911m) on this particular stretch. They dominate the area.

We arrived at Rhiconich and were picked up at Rhiconich Hotel at 3pm on the dot. Good old Frank. We then had our first taste of being mere sightseers. We were taken to Balnakeil Craft Village, this our first opportunity to buy souvenirs of our wonderful journey. This place is a community of its own. The homesteads, a collection of unusual buildings erected by the Ministry of Defence, were meant to be used by the military for radar as part of the early warning system for nuclear missiles during the Cold War. This never materialised, so they were decommissioned and sold off to the Scottish Council in the early 1960s. They were then advertised nationally for use as small business premises for a minimal rent, to attract new skills to come 'far north'. Many of the structures had no water or electricity and were basically concrete shells.

It was a quirky sort of place, and seemed barren on our arrival. As a visitor, it was up to you to ask for assistance. There was a café that also housed books and small paintings by local artists. There was also an opportunity to buy some postcards of the area. But yum, the chocolate factory here was a welcome treat and an opportunity to buy Chris a 'thank you' pressie from all of us. A sad reminder that our return to the real world was imminent.

We didn't stop long at Balnakeil but got back to the youth hostel. Gill and I shared the £3 cost of having our washing and drying done for us. It meant our suitcases would only have clean clothes for returning home, which made it is easier later as I would be returning to work the following Tuesday morning.

Gill was so easygoing and had walked so much of the country. I truly hoped she would finish the walk and would return to the part we had missed. I was going to miss her calm, whimsical nature.

After the washing was sorted, we went to explore Smoo Cave. The Three Musketeers had already left for a walk across the cliffs. The sun was out in a brisk northerly wind, nevertheless we made our way from the hostel down towards the bay. The tide was out, which gave us the chance to really look inside the caves.

These caves are unique in the UK as they were created dually by seawater and freshwater. The first chamber was formed by the action of the sea and the inner chambers were created by freshwater from rain and the Allt Smoo stream sinking through permeable dolostones. The mouth of Smoo Cave is the largest sea cave entrance in Britain, approximately 40 metres wide and 15 metres high, and the caves can be explored to a depth of 83 metres. This extends further via a sump at the rear of the inner chambers, but this has not been fully investigated due to silting. However, divers have apparently probed a further 40 metres from the sump.

Over time the caves have become made up of three main sections: the sea cave and entrance chamber, a waterfall chamber (the waterfall is often dry unless there is considerable rain) and a short passageway that leads to a further chamber. As visitors, we were allowed to wander into the main cave entrance. The cave is no longer eroded by the sea, as the tides do not reach the entrance except when there is a spring tide. This is because the cave is situated at the end of a 600-metre tidal gorge, which originally would have been part of the cave before its roof collapsed.

A coracle was moored to take visitors into the inner sanctum, but it wasn't in use when we were there. I think this is available by prior arrangement but don't quote me on this. Gill and I walked as far as we could in the outer chamber, peering upwards to the small glimmer of light where the waterfall would normally be.

At 6pm we wandered back to the hostel, having met up

with the others coming back from across the cliff. It was a treat not to have to worry about dinner. Frank was in charge!

He did us proud. Olives and garlic mushrooms on salad, followed by lamb chop, ragout and potatoes. Dessert was strawberries and cream. We were all stuffed; he was so well organised. Chris then spoke about our last route for the next day and how our belongings needed to be packed as there was an early start tomorrow. We would have breakfast at 7.30am to ensure we caught the nine o'clock ferry to Cape Wrath. We all mucked in with the washing up.

Frank being the professional turned in early. "I have porridge to make early," he said, and with that he was gone.

I went back to my bed. I could feel a sense of the holiday drawing to an end, closing another chapter. I felt bereft as I sat and wrote my diary. I fell asleep early.

Friday June 5th 2009. Cape Wrath to Blairmore - 12 miles (with the help of ferry and old minibus)

It had been a wonderful night's sleep, again. The day looked bright enough but with a very chilly wind. That was my observation from my bed; the day proved slightly different!

I got up to have some early tea but there was Frank with his pinafore on, already preparing the porridge. It did cross my mind: 'I hope everyone wants porridge today.' We were all very organised, making our sandwiches and standing beside the van by 8.15am – a record for this holiday!!

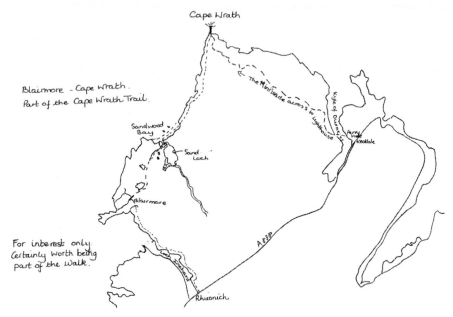

Blairmore - Cape Wrath.
Part of the Cape Wrath Trail.

For interest only.
Certainly worth being
part of the Walk.

Chris couldn't take any chances that the ferryman might leave
without us. Having checked with him the night before, it still
wasn't set in stone that the ferryman would remember that this
party needed to take the first ferry. And the time he would
actually sail seemed to vary! "Let's hope he is in a good mood,"
said Chris.

In the end, we had to wait a bit for the ferryman at
Keoldale. There was a queue of two waiting before us. Finally,
a tall larger-than-life fellow wearing a Breton cap and smoking
the largest cigar I had ever seen ambled over to the ferryboat
moored at the quay. He nodded and grunted his recognition
of our presence, and we watched helplessly as he slowly and
deliberately loaded four 10-gallon jerry cans of fuel onto the
boat. With his cigar slowly smouldering and the ash
occasionally dropping, he put all his belongings in the boat
before looking up, and in a brisk but jolly fashion he beckoned

us aboard, dismissing the unsuspecting couple until he returned again later. I remember muttering a small apology to them on his behalf. In my naivety I thought it won't be long before he was back. I had not reckoned on him being the van driver as well!!

We left the safety of our mooring and I remained concerned about the cigar, which by now was three quarters in length. Our ferryman didn't say very much as he negotiated the brisk voyage across the Kyle of Durness. I rather enjoyed this trip, which took approximately 15 minutes. It was a good chance to admire the dunes and the sandbars. I savoured the salt air and dragged my coat around me; it was going to be a cold day. Although bright at that moment, things were going to get a little wetter!

When we arrived on the other side there were two children awaiting the ferry to go across to the mainland – for school! We waited patiently as our ferryman went and fetched his minibus. Still he didn't speak as he transferred some of the fuel into the bus, collected the children and left us whilst he went back across for the two people we had left behind at Keoldale, returning with them and another ferryman.

Finally we were beckoned into the bus for the 11-mile jaunt across the Parph (207 square kilometres of moorland) to the Cape Wrath Lighthouse, where our last walk would begin and end as we walked away from our final destination point back to Blaimore. It was with a giggle that I watched the ferryman climb laboriously into the white mini bus, cigar now down to an inch in length, slump into the seat and with a big grin launch into this wonderful patter about the Cape. It was like a switch had gone on and he had finally woken up. I couldn't help but warm to this jolly, grumpy Scotsman.

Our mini bus now fully laden with bodies jumped into action, as we wound our way across the moorland to the most north-westerly point in Scotland. The only road across the Cape, known as the 'U70', was built in 1828 by the lighthouse commission. At times it is no more than a track but the views, although limited from inside the bus, were wild and bleak. The driver was clearly aware of every twist, turn, hole, camber and width as we trundled along for the 45-minute journey. As we swayed precariously in the passenger seats, I was feeling slightly nauseous as he carried on with his spiel.

The mini bus was from the 1960s but the upholstery was from a more modern era. Interestingly, such vehicles have to be taxed and MOT-ed despite never venturing far from Cape Wrath, but the last tax disc I noticed was dated 2001! I just hoped the mini bus was roadworthy and get us to our destination.

The ferryman was very funny as he explained the uses of Cape Wrath for NATO forces and that it was the only place where live ammunition is still used during bombing and target practice. The SAS trained there in the winter months and firing practice did not close the road, but he pointed out that, "today we are lucky, there is no firing but with US forces about, who knows?!"

Moving on, we had another giggle when we passed the lone MOD sentry box still occupied on days when the ground is used for military training. These are now manned by civilians. Our ferrymen reckoned the sentry boxes looked more like a target practice aids and many a time he had offered his wife to do a spot of duty!!

Slowly his cigar burned as more and more ash dropped in his lap. I couldn't help but smile. Apparently, even the mini bus got stopped occasionally by the military. At one time, the sentry box was next to an old school, where once there were enough children to be educated locally instead of going to schools further away. Now they just depict the beginning and the end of the firing ranges. The ferryman also spoke of the five dwellings now remaining on Cape Wrath plus the lighthouse. He told of the holiday flat, although he thought people ought to be paid to stay there, and he mentioned the two remaining shepherds who are allowed to keep sheep. He also said that three dwellings had been taken over by the military. The cigar was still smouldering.

He stopped briefly to show us the 'The Cathedral' (Kearvaig Stack) lying offshore some distance away. The sun was just hitting this unusual rock formation. The stacks marked the beginning of the Clo Mor Cliffs. These are the highest in mainland Britain, with a drop of 281 metres (921 feet). They are a major nesting site for our seabirds.

He briefly mentioned the tiny beach of Kearvaig to our north-east, as he shouted for us all to breathe in as he negotiated a small temporary bridge at breakneck speed with only inches to spare on either side. We all hung on at this point. Our ferryman was enjoying the ride, saying, "I got it right that time," and laughing as he continued forward. It was like being on a fairground ride.

This temporary bridge was built in 1981 to aid the mini bus taking its passengers to the lighthouse without stalling in the middle of the burn, causing everyone to get off and push. I did wonder that if this bridge was 'temporary', how long might it be before a permanent one was put in place. But that wouldn't be so much fun.

Finally we arrived at the Cape Wrath Lighthouse. Built by engineer Robert Stevenson in 1828, this was in response to cargo ships being destroyed in 1779, two surviving from a fleet of four vessels. It was manned until 1998 when it was converted to automatic operations. The ruins of the Lloyds signal station can be seen from the lighthouse. This station dates from the 1930s and monitored ships and their cargo. The only residents at the site have now converted one of the main lighthouse rooms into the remotest café in Britain. Called the Ozone Café, it was opened in 2009 by the Princess Royal. Sadly it was closed when we were there, although it claims to be open 24 hours.

I was tremendously excited to be here. We all were. We self indulged for a moment, congratulating each other on our achievement even though we still had 12 miles to walk. Nothing could take away this enjoyment as we took turns to take photographs. I took a photo of our ferryman. He was such a laugh and his cigar had lasted just long enough for him to re-ignite it and puff on the remaining stub as he rested against the swinging door of his mini bus

After a pee behind a wall – there were three of us so no privacy then – we set off with the sun barely showing through. It was extremely cold and a northerly wind straight off the sea caused enormous waves of spray rising up from the cliffs, creating a rainbow of colour across the rocks. It was stunning. I had on three base layers plus outer garments including gloves and hat and this was summer?!

The walk to Sandwood Bay was difficult. It was boggy, with no defined path across the cliffs, and we were constantly tripped up by bog myrtle and dogged by rivers of water. My emotions were very mixed. I wanted to really enjoy this last bit but my legs were giving up, yet I didn't want to go home either. I felt I had to withdraw from the group a little to ease the burden of saying goodbye to them. I was going to miss them by the bucketful.

The rain finally found us six miles into our walk. It was icy and just when we had to negotiate a large river crossing it became heavy sleet. Crossing rivers was a tedious job, everyone paying so much attention to their safety. Chris didn't want any accidents now. He was very patient.

Amazingly, again my feet were still dry. Chris allowed me to do my own thing with crossings. It was so cold waiting for everyone to cross that we huddled together for warmth. Proceedings took probably 20 minutes each time. I could feel I was getting colder.

We reached Sandwood Bay in the pouring, driving, sleeting rain. The waves were spectacular and crashed along the long sweeping sandy beach and against the stacks in the centre. The surf was clean, the sea clear. The beach had a pink tinge to it. We were all hungry so we found a small refuge behind rocks to munch our soggy sandwiches. In this huddled state with rain dripping down my neck and into my eyes, sleet on my back, I turned to face Lynn, who had that twinkle in her eye when she asked, "Are you going in for a swim today?" I just laughed and declined. "Oh," she said, "'I am disappointed in you Carol, I can't possibly think why you wouldn't today." We both giggled at her whimsical banter. I was going to miss her. She reminded me so much of David's mum.

It was easy to get cold very quickly so we were soon on our way again. As we left the bay so the wind dropped and a well-defined track took us the remaining way back to Blairmore and Balchrick car park.

Frank met us along this track and joined us for the final two miles. We were nearly done. At our final stop in the car park before we left for the youth hostel, Chris brought out a bottle of champagne and proceeded to spray it over everyone. It was a lovely surprise and a fitting finale to the best walk I have ever done. One I am so glad I have done with people who were genuine and kind. I felt the luckiest person ever.

We were all tired and then there was this mad rush to get back and get changed to go out for dinner. I wasn't too fussed about going out. To me it would have been much more cosy to have dinner in the hostel in familiar surroundings, with a glass of red wine in my hand. Instead we went to Smoo Cave Hotel. We gave Chris his present there and then returned late to the hostel to find that the lights were out.

There was no time for packing. Fortunately Gill and I had packed our bags before going out and only our clean washing had to be collected from the warden. These were our going home clothes.

Saturday June 6th 2009. Heading homewards.

Going home; what a thought. This part of my adventure was almost over. Breakfast was a rushed affair, everyone on auto pilot. I came back to my bed for the last time to find Gill had bought me a beautiful card showing where we had been. Her words on the back were so fitting. We had enjoyed the trip so much. I was going to miss my new chums terribly. We had had such a laugh and giggle.

Gill would also go on to walk right across the country. I felt I had been blessed to have met her and even now we stay in touch. I gave her a great big hug. I am a sentimental old fool and throughout breakfast and packing up the van it was difficult to hold back the tears.

We left Durness at 9.10am and had a long drive back to Stirling. I sat in the front between Chris and Frank all the way back. Between their jokes and conversation I could hide the emotion. I didn't want to go home, my brain screaming *please let me stay in these hills one more day!* Already I could feel the expectations lying across my shoulders; the responsibilities crawling into my brain.

We stopped at Ullapool for coffee and sadly we said

goodbye to Lynn, Penny and Rob at Inverness. They were hiring a car and staying longer. We then stopped for lunch at Aviemore until 3pm and then finally Gill, myself, Ann and Richard were dropped off at Stirling Station at 5.15pm.

It was more goodbyes to Ann and Richard, who were heading back to Edinburgh. Gill and I continued our journey to Glasgow. Here we parted. By now I was too tired from travelling to get too emotional, thank goodness.

I hailed a taxi to take me the short journey to the youth hostel. This place was becoming home from home for me, having been there with Shauna previously. I ordered a taxi for 7.30am the next day to take me to the airport. Then I made my bed, showered and changed and went to the local coffee shop.

It felt very strange to be in a noisy city once more. All those grotesque features of life that I detest were still there. Basically, I came to the conclusion that if I wasn't lonely I wouldn't notice these things. So I sat and ordered some food and drank my coffee and relived the walk. I had been part of a very demanding, physical walk. It had been a marvellous bonus to have enjoyed the daily company of others. The warmth of the memories will remain with me.

I went back to the hostel and had an interesting chat with a lady from Ottawa. She was asking lots of questions about where to go in Scotland. I found myself asking many questions about Canada. Then I turned in. It had been a very long day and tomorrow I was catching the plane back to Southampton.

Sunday June 7th 2009. Home again.

I was waiting for my taxi. I was not sure when I would be in Scotland again. I hoped that David would be well enough to share Scotland with me. He would so love this area. I hoped he fully understood my reasons for this walk. My heart and soul needed to breathe, and when I walk my frustration melts away and my confidence soars. To function on a daily basis, I selfishly need to look forward to these walks. I cannot explain the inner peace I gain from it. When I get home afterwards, I am energised to function for everyone else again; to be that strong pin who binds the family together; to go to work revitalised, ready to face the pressure again.

The taxi driver was a guitarist. We had an interesting discussion about bands. He thoroughly enjoyed being part of a small group who in their latter years did it for fun and for the social aspect. I chatted about Ben's band.

We soon arrived at the airport. My flight left without delay. This lady and Gertrude were on their way home.

CHAPTER TWENTY:

WALKING THE ROAD TO SNOW

**RHICONICH TO DURNESS, THEN DURNESS TO JOHN O'GROATS.
DISTANCE: 105 MILES. DATELINE: MARCH 26TH-31ST 2010.**

So reader, you are on the final leg of my journey. Actually, time-wise, I completed my entire journey back in chapter eighteen, in terms of finishing walking all the segments that stretch from the tip of Cornwall to the top of Scotland. But for me, this leg is all about when I returned to Scotland again with David, rediscovering places of my childhood and finally reaching the destination on the map that I had set out to do. Yes, I can hear you asking, "Wouldn't it have been better to make this your *final* walk?" I would respond, "But when did life ever go completely in the direction you wanted it to, or go in the correct order?" Remember, I am blonde!

Easter was early this year, Good Friday being April 2nd, so I booked the whole week off work to give me a full week without having to take the Friday as annual leave. My feelings about going this far north at the end of March didn't really register in the blonde brain. As far as I was concerned, it was nearly April and surely the weather would be better!! Did I think bank holidays are always doomed? No, that didn't cross my mind at all, such was the draw of doing a little bit more walking. Mad fool!

I did mention to Gertrude that she may get a bit chilly on this one. As for the Pash Wagon, my faith was still reserved. David had spent the winter months making some 'adjustments' and replacing bits and pieces. Don't ask me what. I am a woman.

In the middle of March I was busy, slowly gathering our food provisions for the journey. We needed to cover every meal, as we were expecting to sleep in lay-bys. No, let's rephrase that: park the van in lay-bys and sleep in the van. This meant we kept the cost down. The diesel alone was expensive enough. The other problem of course was finding petrol stations when there aren't that many far north, or indeed any shops open. The villages could not be relied on. Having provisions with us also meant I knew what I would be cooking once I finished walking for the day, which saved David from worrying about trying to find something we could eat.

We packed extra blankets and plenty of high energy bars. Water was going to be our main problem. If there were no campsites open we would have to rely on garages or public toilets. Fortunately the Pash Wagon had a 25 litre tank for water, and we took an extra 10 litre bottle for back up. This proved to be wise. It was amazing how much fluid we got through, and tea bags!!

Friday March 26th 2010. Travel day.

We finished packing the night before, and I had my clothes to change into ready in the van when David came to pick me up after work. I was extremely excited but nervous. It was a lot to expect the van to make it to Scotland and I was concerned even more so about David. He seemed so dreadfully tired of late and his headaches far more severe. Was I putting too much pressure on him? I questioned myself all the time, but I reasoned that if he wasn't doing this, he would be stuck within the same four walls all the time. At least he would see Scotland and I wanted him to enjoy its beauty. He hadn't been to the north of Scotland before. We were also planning to meet up with our friends Mandy and Alan at their holiday chalet in Aviemore on the way back.

After I was picked up from work at 12.40pm, we made good headway until Birmingham. From there it was all roadworks and speed restrictions until the start of the Lakes. Everything seemed to be okay with the van, but it was starting to get very hot as soon as we accelerated. It became so much of a worry at Southwaite Services near Carlisle that we stopped to refuel, only for the camper to die on us. The battery wasn't charging, so David's first reaction was that the alternator has gone. If we could get the battery charged, maybe we could limp into Carlisle and wait until morning.

There really was no one else about. It was 10pm, dark and damp. My heart sank. David couldn't see very well under the bonnet, so we eased the van under a better light and used our torches. He tested the power going to the alternator and as far as he could see, the alternator seemed okay. Finally, after much poking about, he saw that an electrical wire leading to the alternator had severed. It had been badly crimped, so much so that it had been arcing and that caused the wire to perish. A glimmer of hope entered David's voice as he said that if there was enough slack in the wire he could rejoin it, then wrap electrical tape around it to keep it together. "Right," I said, shivering and not that optimistic.

Like a surgeon aided by his trained assistant, David calmly proceeded to work his clinical magic as I passed him the correct tools required for the job. We didn't say much as he asked for more light, spanners, rag, spanner, rag, electrical pliers, more light needed underneath, hold this, hold that, electrical tape, more tape, more light… and finally a clean rag to wipe his brow. This all took a good half hour. I didn't know if I was shivering with the cold or with nerves as David started her up. He let her run for quite some time, re-charging her battery as I made a cup of tea and assessed our situation.

We pulled away at 11pm with our fingers crossed at our luck. Thanks to David's competence we were on our way. Now fortified with new energy and purpose, unbelievably David was happy to go on. He was very casual about it. "Should be alright," he said, "but if she conks out now there is no more room for slack on those wires." So we trundled on, picking up diesel wherever we could, as once past Perth we may not have found any.

Just prior to Perth in a lay-by close to the dual carriageway, we pulled in to get some sleep. It was 1.30am. Despite the constant noise of trucks hurtling by and causing the van to shake, we slept until 6am.

Saturday March 27th 2010.
Rhiconich to Durness - 14 miles.

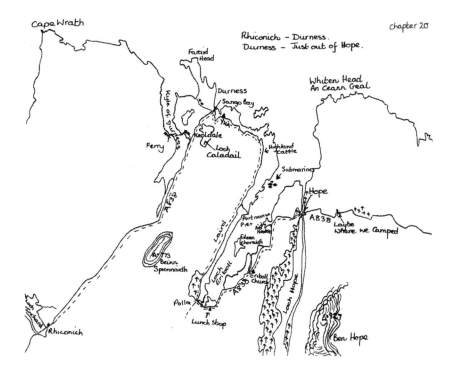

By 7.30am we were on the road again. We had a great run to Inverness and then on to Ullapool. We stopped in a café along the harbour front. David could see why I had loved the place. In the spring sunshine it was pretty. We then took the A835 to Ledmore Junction and the A837 past Inchnadamph.

For me it was terribly exciting to be passing places that I

had seen two years previously. David thought it very remote. To be honest, I just prayed the van didn't break down after we passed over the Kylestrome Bridge towards Scourie, because there was absolutely no one about. We collected diesel from the unmanned pump at Scourie, for which we were very grateful.

Finally we arrived at Durness. It was 2.30pm. I was back. The local shop was open and we asked if the campsite was operating. "No, it opens on the 1st of April, but the chap who runs it is about. If you ask him he might let you stay there. Or stay in the village car park, I don't think anyone will stop you." The shopkeeper pointed to the empty car park and grinned. We were grateful for his advice. So I asked the chap at the Sango Sands campsite if he would mind us stopping there. I explained what I was doing. He agreed and didn't even charge us – how kind was that.

The sun was still shining but the wind was intense as we parked the van a little way from the cliffs but still with views of Durness Bay. The rollers were clean and a beautiful turquoise colour. They were crashing against the rocks and this reminded me of Cornwall. Still, I couldn't linger, I had a walk to do.

David was going to follow me back towards Rhiconich, and I intended to go as far as I could before it got dark. Hopefully I would finish. I was tired but these 14 miles needed to be done and in record time.

Fortunately it was a bright windy day. This was ideal for speed walking and would give me more light. I needn't have worried. After all that sitting, my feet were glad to be doing something useful. Gertrude was in my pocket. I had no need for a rucksack as David was behind me. I didn't even have to carry water. It was the longest, lightest part of the entire walk.

I set off briskly, passing Keoldale where the ferry had taken me across to Cape Wrath. I took some pictures and it was rather nice to have the time to savour the view before setting off again on what seemed to be a downhill walk to Rhiconich. Some of that was psychological, I am sure. It was a cheerful, cold walk back. It didn't feel right doing this bit 'backwards', but as a walker I could appreciate the mountains of Beinn Spionnaidh (773 metres), Cranstackie (801m) and Foinaven (911m).

I rather enjoyed having time to read the map and see where the tracks from the few buildings led to. There was always the excitement of discovery. I soon ate up the miles and got in sight of the finish before the light faded.

I did finish at 6.30pm, with darkness upon us. We drove swiftly back to the campsite, parked up, ate our dinner, moved the clocks forward to British Summer Time, made our beds and crashed out for the night. What a day.

As we fell asleep, the wind was extremely strong. The temperature had plummeted; it was about five degrees and dropping fast.

Sunday March 28th 2010.
Durness to beyond Hope - 21 miles.

I woke at 6.30am, which would have been 5.30am before the clocks went forward. I was beautifully cosy in my sleeping bag but oh dear, it was pouring with rain and very windy outside.

Needing a pee persuaded me to leave the warmth. David was only just awake. I put the kettle on and got myself dressed. I gathered up my bedding so we had the roof space for David to sit up and have his tea before putting his own bedding away.

It was very draughty and cold this morning. We breakfasted and I was ready to set off at 9am, leaving David to sort out the port-a-loo and bring more water on board.

I had on three layers of garments plus waterproofs, two pairs of gloves and two hats. Does that tell you how cold it was?

After a sharp hill out of Durness past the youth hostel, then past Smoo Cave, I was on my way to Sangobeg when David caught up with me briefly. I munched on a snack bar and through the mouthfuls told him I was okay, and leaving him there I ploughed on.

David stopped at the ruined buildings of the erstwhile crofters in this area. There was a noticeboard here providing interesting details about what recent archaeologists have discovered. It is believed that there has been a diversity of inhabitants in this area for centuries. A pre-Christian burial site was discovered with skeletal remains of what was possibly an ancient Pictish inhabitant lying in the foetal position. Many other objects from medieval times and possible Viking remnants have also been found.

Sangobeg has a beautiful beach and the waves were just rolling in. My thoughts turned to the hardship of this remote place and how difficult it must have been to survive the harsh winters here.

I can only say the road was pretty. It dipped and rose and it was just a lovely amble along a very, very quiet stretch. The rain gave way to blowy conditions and heavy cloud. That rain was going to be coming round again. I could smell it in the air.

My next encounter with civilisation was with a herd of Highland cattle. I came over a brow of a hill and to my left these incredibly docile creatures greeted me. They were so pleased to see a person. Their long shaggy coats were being wisped across their faces and those big doleful eyes bore into mine. Behind the flimsy wired fence they each came up and said hello. Out of all the cows I have met walking, these are by far the loveliest, gentlest creatures I have come across. I fed them some meagre grass (they had plenty of buckets of grain and silage) and they happily licked my hands and enjoyed me rubbing their foreheads and giving them a scratch. They obliged whilst I took photographs of them and reluctantly I went on my way again.

Soon after this was my first eerie sighting of submarines. Like motionless grey whales half submerged, poised and lurking, they initially made my skin crawl. It was so unexpected that I had to get out the binoculars to make sure of what I was seeing. They were ghost-like on the water. Wrapped and racked together, the four submarines were sinister in their appearance. It sent shivers running down my spine. A few metres away from them, a grey frigate was there protecting them. They were covered in a netting camouflage. I kept on glancing over and felt I couldn't take a picture in case they weren't to be photographed. I was half expecting to be rounded up for spying. That's my imagination for you, going bananas. I was now intrigued about why they were actually there. Had I stumbled on some MOD secret? As I stealthily pulled my camera out and took a sneak photo, Mission Impossible came to mind. (I know, daft blonde.) Later I was to learn that often these decommissioned boats are kept there until sold for scrap when there is a good price for metal.

I have also since learned that Loch Eriboll has a history connected with the British Navy and its warships through the 20th century. This was the site of the surrender of the German U-boat fleet in May 1945 and during this time over 30 U-boats came into the loch. During the 20s and 30s, many warships used the loch as a safe anchorage and crew members would go ashore and leave the name of their ship written in large white stones. The most famous of these was HMS Hood. In 1937, what was the largest battleship in the world laid anchorage for nine days and during its stay the crew wrote the name 'Hood' in stones on the hillside to the west of the loch. Tragically, the Hood was sunk in 1941 by the German warship Bismarck, with the loss of 1,400 lives. The stones, some two metres high, stand in testimony to the tragic event and they have been restored twice since by local schoolchildren, in 1993 and 1999.

The village of Laid sprawls for two miles along Loch Eriboll's western shores, a township consisting of 18 crofts strung along the shoreline. Originally a thriving community with a school, the only evidence now appeared to be a post box and a telephone box with a noticeboard. Sadly, it felt that the whole area was in decline, but I saw smoke rising from some of the crofts, suggesting there were some inhabitants. The views of the loch from the road were stunning. I could only admire this beautiful place from the road. I could see the once Portnancon Pier that used to receive the ferry that came across from Ard Neakie, the only way to get across the loch until 1890 when the road was completed. At one time in Portnancon there was an inn.

In the centre of the loch I could see the island of Eilean Choraidh, otherwise known as 'Horse Island'. With white beaches, it covers about 49 acres. During the Second World War it was used for target practice by RAF Mosquito bombers, and prior to this the Reay Estate quarried lime there.

The wind was picking up. David had passed me in the van and I could see him at the end of the loch near a small place called Polla. This hamlet was basically made up of two cottages! I had decided to stop for a quick lunch break just past there, towards the hamlet of Eriboll itself. I thought I would be clever and cross the marshland using a small path, but it became extremely difficult following this tiny trail and my shortcut nearly ended in disaster when I fell into a large hole, slipping off a tuffet with the rucksack sending me sideways. After this struggle I got back out onto the road and made my way to the van for a well deserved cup of coffee, soup and a sandwich.

Fortified, I was heading along the eastern side of the loch when the rain came down. A fine Scottish drizzle crept into the open crevices of my coat as I slowly made the ascent above the loch once more towards Eriboll Church. It was at this point that the rain stopped.

Eriboll Church is a privately owned estate church. Built in 1804, it has essentially remained the same since then. In its earlier life, it was used as a missionary school, but in recent years it has been restored and still holds Christmas and thanksgiving services and wedding functions. The primitive whitewashed building was like a beacon standing above the loch, with large hills behind it and surrounded by dark grey clouds. I spent a few minutes admiring this little treasure before walking on.

From here the wind kept buffeting me forwards and the cold rain came in gusts. It was a long slow ascent above the loch, where I now had very good views of Ard Neakie. This interesting crescent promontory stretches out into the loch from the eastern shore. It creates two beautiful sandy beaches either side of its natural raised track. Ard Neakie was once the site of a limestone quarry and I could still see the kilns from the road. Prior to this, it had been part of the kelp collecting industry, and during the Second World War the kilns were used to store weapons and ammunition. It looked a very interesting place to explore and my thoughts were what a wonderful place to camp.

A car had parked further up the road and a lady was walking her dog on the promontory. If I had not had such a distance to go, I would have stopped and explored. The rain now ceased for a while as the road left the loch edge, and I headed inland along the same road to Hope.

This tiny village is the precursor to the most northerly Munro of Ben Hope (927 metres). Crossing the River Hope, a wide tidal river that feeds Loch Hope, it was with excitement and clarity that I saw the old C road that I had been on ages previously. As a child of just 11 years, my parents had driven our grey and maroon Ford Anglia alongside Loch Hope on the same road, not knowing really where we would be putting up our tent. The road went on for miles and finally we spent the night out with the sheep, next to the ruins of an old croft. It is a wonderful memory, so clear and vivid. I can still picture gathering water from a small stream and my mum cooking egg and chips in the main body of our erected Sun Medi tent, before the dark set in amidst the remotest of lands. It was the best meal ever.

I digress. Time was moving on and I was now very tired. Any warmth of the day had passed but it was a very pleasant late afternoon, the sun producing some weak blue sky and wonderful pink clouds. I hauled myself out of Hope village and climbed a steep 200 metres, and after another mile I stopped. It was 4.30pm and David had found a brilliant lay-by for us to park for the night. It boasted a large sign announcing 'North West Geopark, We hope you have enjoyed your visit'.

How the atmosphere can change. Dark rain clouds returned, then a brief but fine gentle drizzle changed the views across the moors, with Ben Hope rising eerily out of the mists, its top dusted in snow the only light in a lowering landscape. As dark began to descend it became very cold. Although the wind had dropped, it was still only three degrees outside as we munched through homemade Spaghetti Bolognese. Just outside the van we spotted a herd of deer. That was our final treat for the day.

I prepared my water bladder for the next day, made up a snack, put my clothes out ready for an early walk and then crashed to sleep.

I was disturbed in the night by a howling gale, snow and sleet buffeting against the roof. Shivering with cold, I put another jumper on. I eventually slept after worrying about getting snowed in.

Monday March 29th 2010.
Just outside Hope to just outside Bettyhill - 21.1 miles.

Layby Just outside Hope - Layby Just Outside Bettyhill

I awoke at 5am with it thankfully only hailing and raining. But snow gritters were rumbling through! This was our first indication of snow becoming an issue. I got up at 6.30pm, fumbling around in the dark. The storm of the night had passed. I made a cup of tea and my porridge. David was still in bed, all snug. It was freezing.

Gathering my belongings, I finally set off at 8.15am and what a fantastic sight. It was going to be a glorious day. The rising sun was just hitting the now snow-topped mountain of Ben Hope and other high hills. The red and purple sky created a heather-like hue of colour and in the distance the mountains appeared blue. The ground was covered with a sparkling frost and a sugar dusting of snow. This was my view as I took my first wee. The puddles in the lay-by were thinly frozen and the tussocks of moorland grass had captured snow, producing small deep pockets holding enough to make a snowball out of. My little bit of enjoyment was to lob a couple at the raised roof of the van, before taking pictures and then moving off. Even the van had snow on the top and on its bonnet.

Today the air was so clear and fresh. It felt warmer despite my breath coming out as icicles, so I was able to wear less – only one hat and one pair of gloves. There was no wind and nothing was moving. I can tell you, I was on a high as I headed towards the Kyle of Tongue. David would come along later. I savoured the loneliness and devoured the views. Only one car came along and that was the postie.

I was about an hour into my walk when the wind got up a bit, causing my cheeks to redden. This was one of those crisp, brisk, winter walking days; the sort that are made for families out walking after a wholesome Christmas lunch. It was brilliant.

I passed an old ruined house standing mournfully alone, its solitude only broken by geese flying across one of the lochans and on the other side of the road a herd of red deer quietly grazing, their muzzles pushing the snow away to get to the sweeter grasses. They did not stop grazing as I stood and watched them, embracing this chance meeting and glad of their brief company.

David came by soon after this, so I had a quick cup of coffee. He was warm as toast in the van and we both enjoyed the wonderful views. It was so bleak and barren yet picturesque amidst the feather dusting of snow. I was so glad he could come to Scotland.

I pressed on; it was 9.45am and I would soon be heading down to the Kyle of Tongue. This part was probably one of the highlights of the entire walk. The weather couldn't have been more perfect, and the views of the bridge, the wildlife and the four summits of Ben Loyal (764 metres) dominating the skyline, ever present and changing with every vista, were stimulating.

Heading towards the causeway over the Kyle of Tongue, the views of Ben Loyal became clearer and clearer, the four summit points accentuated against the blue skies as they reached above the low clouds. The air was so still and the surrounding colours reflected in puddles and small lochans. It made me catch my breath. The roadside was still peppered with snow, and like a black snake the road slithered downwards and across the Kyle. From the rise I could see my route stretching way into the eastern distance beyond Tongue. It was incredible.

I recalled the last time I had visited here in 1969, when it had been a ferry that brought the car and trailer across the Kyle, and now the causeway completed in 1971 enables the driver to continue along the A836 without stopping. For me, failing to stop would have been sacrilege.

David met me on the causeway where there is a pull in and viewing point. We stopped and had another drink. The water was like a millpond. The Rabbit Islands guarding the entrance of Tongue Bay were clearly visible in the distance. We could not take a single picture to capture the serenity and tranquillity of this moment, such were the panoramic views southwards across the Kyle towards Ben Loyal. There was no one to disturb our peace.

After David had driven on to get some fuel, water and provisions, I sat on the wall and watched redshanks and oystercatchers, and then in amazement as I walked further around the bay, I spotted a sea otter messing about on some rocks on the shallow shores, where the kelp left by the receding tide lay strewn. I was so surprised I moved too fast, and startled, it was gone.

It is these moments I feel honoured to have experienced. There is a tangible quiver of happiness that runs right through my body. This is why I was here, today.

Bolstered, I took a different path out of Tongue instead of the A836. I walked along to the pier and up to Wood End. Here, as I climbed above the Kyle, the views of its sandy shores and the islands were stunning in the sunlight. I savoured the shade, would you believe it! It became warm as I climbed up the steep road to meet the A836 once more and headed towards Bettyhill (a long way off). The road as it climbed skirted the lower levels of Ben Tongue before reaching Coldbackie, a tiny village overlooking a bay in the Kyle of Tongue. There was an artist at the roadside and a small café. I enjoyed chatting for a while and being in civilisation.

David and I had decided to meet for our lunch break at Borgie Forest, approximately three miles away. The road gently wound its course across some less hilly ground for a time. The views resembled a very large version of Dartmoor, with vast swathes of moorland bogs interspersed with tiny lochans. It is at these times I just settle myself down to do some serious walking, when I am not so distracted by my surroundings. I certainly felt alone here. I met just one elderly couple in a Morris Minor who stopped to check if I wanted a lift or not. They were so sweet and very difficult to understand!

David and the van were nowhere in sight. I suspected he may have been having a kip! The views heading down towards Borgie Bridge were stunning, the watery sun lighting the hilly backdrop as my road stretched before me. Blimey I was hungry, ready for some soup or a sausage roll. It was always a surprise what my chef dished up.

It was 2pm when I finally reached Borgie Bridge, which crosses the wide River Borgie. The weather was still being kind but the wind had a distinct chill factor. But I didn't have my waterproofs on, so that was a bonus.

Borgie Forest was the first managed forest in Scotland and is one of the most northerly. It is managed by Forest Enterprise, similar to our Forestry Commission programmes in England. It covers 7,746 acres of land and has some of the tallest Scots pine in Scotland. However it mainly has lodgepole pine and sitka spruce, with other conifers, larches and broad-leaved trees filling in. Borgie Forest is also surrounded by moorlands of 'Scientific Interest' due to the peatlands.

David came trundling along after a while. I was pleased to see him. It was a pleasant lunch; good to sit out of the wind and rest the legs for a bit. David had bought a paper at Tongue and some fuel, and used the garage to top up our water supplies. He had sat and then snoozed for a while.

I left David clearing up the dishes! He would overtake me later. Next stop Bettyhill. On the map there was a campsite and it was our plan to stay there, but given how quiet everywhere was, we had no expectations, just hopes. Six miles to go. Stepping out, it was delightful to be heading again towards Bettyhill.

It was the same place where I had stopped with my parents and brother for our two-second swim in the sea! I had never seen my father run so fast up the beach after just putting his toe in. Stephen and I ventured a little further. Even then with my young blood I cannot forget how numbingly cold it was. The beach was deserted and my mother had made sandwiches and in the wind-swept dunes we munched them. Now here I was again, marching along the estuary to the wide open mouth of the River Naver as it meets the sea. I was overcome with joy and sadness. I wondered what my father would have made of me being here. I think he would have been pleased for me. It was incredible I was here again.

I excitedly walked briskly across the bridge and up the slow ascent towards Bettyhill itself, with the most wonderful bright views of Torrisdale Bay, the dunes and opposite Bettyhill the small settlement of Torrisdale itself. The weather was brilliant, the sun catching the golden sands. Along the road a small white cottage was bejewelled with findings from the beach. It commanded the finest views. Then I saw a sign saying, 'The Store Bettyhill Turn left at crossroads open 8 days a week'. Someone had a sense of humour. It wasn't long before I was standing outside the store, which probably boasted all manner of items in it. The people there were very friendly, pointing us in the right direction for the campsite. "But it might not be open," were their parting words.

It was 5pm now and I was ready to stop. However, we couldn't find anyone at the campsite, so David drove on to find another suitable lay-by for the night, leaving me to continue walking.

Once the little sun that there was had gone, the temperature dropped dramatically. I carried on along the road past the houses, pub and museum, and finally having climbed a further steep bit of road, I chatted to a man with a black Labrador outside his cottage gate.

I found David in a lay-by about a mile out of Bettyhill. There were no signs telling us we couldn't stay for the night so that is where we stayed. Another beauty spot. The wind had stilled but the air was very cold and the sky grey.

Tea tonight was tinned mince beef, carrots and mashed potatoes, followed by fresh egg custard tarts and doughnuts. At least my clothes were dry. We had got into a good routine now, getting my next day's supplies ready, making sure I had dry socks, and putting my boot inner soles above the cooker to dry out the sweat. I cooked for David; he was very tired but doing extremely well in the cold conditions. Our toilet arrangements each evening were always different. Although we had a Porta Potty toilet for inside the van, the views using it outside were rather special! Let's just say the 'call of nature' is put into perspective.

Tuesday March 30th 2010. Fiscary (outside Bettyhill) to one mile from Bridge of Forss and Hotel - 24.3 miles.

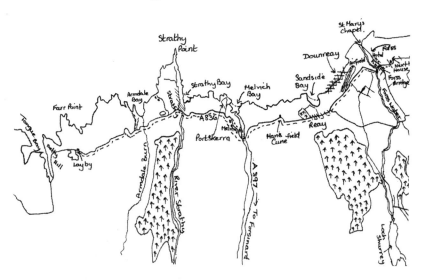

I was awake at 6.30am. For a brief moment at this time there was a flurry of traffic. It only lasted for half an hour. However, the most irritating thing was drivers beeping us in annoyance because we were parked in a lay-by.

I had slept really well. Still a bit dark, I made tea and porridge, leaving David in bed. I cleaned my teeth, had a quick flick of the flannel, got dressed and I was away at 8am. I was heading for Thurso, and the weather reports on the radio were giving the first indications that trouble could be coming our way in the form of snow. I felt the urgency to get a move on.

After his lie-in, David was going back to Bettyhill public toilets to empty the Porta Potty, buy a paper and magazines and some more homemade cakes, and then meet me en route somewhere. I was going to be on the road and as there was only one A road up here, he would find me.

It was freezing outside. Walking was extremely hard work and this was one of the toughest days physically. I battled all day against a north-easterly wind and snot running out of my nose, across my face and onto my arm. I felt truly buffeted. My nose became extremely sore. I had both pairs of gloves and hats on plus all my wet weather gear, just to keep the wind chill factor out of my bones. It was six degrees and the wind made it feel like minus six. At least it was dry.

I did not see a soul all day. It is rather pleasant walking through these remote parts by yourself, and when it gets tough you find you are a different person, digging deep into resources you didn't know you had. I usually think of something special, like the children's graduation, a romantic moment, a happy interlude, or someone's kind words. Today I felt Dad and Momma were there, and strangely a warm hand on my back pushing me forward. It was odd, maybe I was being oversensitive or it was just the wind, but there was this intensity in the centre of my back, a warm glow as the white line on the edge of the road became my focus.

It was a mainly uphill walk to Strathy, although the road did dip down a couple of times. Strathy is a dear little village and boasts a pub, but it wasn't open. There was a chapel and memorial with spectacular statues in the graveyards. There seemed to be a lot of graveyards placed outside the villages along this road, all strategically facing towards the sea.

The wind did not ease and I was tiring. I met David for lunch in the middle of nowhere at 1.30pm. It was so windy I could barely open the door without being blown sideways. Eventually I gave up and in the lee of the van I ate my sandwich and drank a warm cup of coffee. A plastic bag flew out of the van and I ended up chasing it down the road I had come from. I hate leaving mess. I was just going to give up catching it when it snagged on some barbed wire. After finally retrieving it, I slumped down exhausted on the step of the van. David commented it was the first time he had seen me not enjoying myself. Such was the struggle.

Getting cross now, it was sheer stubbornness and bloody-mindedness that got me through the day. At one point, I could hardly stand upright, but I had to keep moving to keep warm. I went through lots of chocolate on this day. David hadn't got his provisions at Bettyhill so he took himself off to Portskerra, half a mile away from Melvich where I was walking through.

Just prior to Melvich, there were signs declaring the border between Sutherland and Caithness. Melvich is a pretty village dominated by the sea. The waves were fantastic. I crossed the

River Halladale with its new bridge (the old one beside it) and then had another climb out into the wilderness again. Although the road dipped, it still seemed to go uphill all the way to Dounreay.

Before reaching the village of Reay, I passed an original bit of the road I would probably have come down in 1969, so I had to take a picture of course. There was a car park shortly after this, allowing the visitor to stop and look at an area designated the 'Marie Curie Cancer Care Field of Hope', where schoolchildren in November 2007 had planted 2,000 daffodil bulbs so that they would flower on the 60th anniversary of the charity being formed. It was rather thought provoking, as the disused nuclear plant at Dounreay could be seen in the background from this high point.

Was it me or had the wind dropped slightly? I spotted some interesting tracks at the side of a forest before going into Reay. In the soft mud at the verge of the road, I followed them until I lost them over the road and into a field, at which time they looked muddled. These were the tracks of a large deer, followed very quickly by large cat paw prints! I was not dreaming. I stopped for several minutes, following them back to where they became clear. I was intrigued as they appeared to be fresh. Had the deer got away? Maybe it was a large hound? I really wasn't sure.

On the map there was a campsite at Reay but that didn't exist any more, so I passed through this very ancient village with its Viking house and burial sites, stone circles, Bronze Age encampments and simple roundhouses. Its 16th, 17th, 18th and 19th century Scottish buildings sat alongside the more modern 1960s architecture that flourished with the construction and operation of the nuclear power plant at Dounreay.

The plant is still a large blob on the landscape, but it is slowly being dismantled since the start of decommissioning in 1994. The site of the first fast breed reactor, Dounreay's power was utilised by the National Grid from 1962 to 1994. In 1969 my family and I visited the plant with its futuristic dome. I can't recall very much about it, I just remember going up to the visitor centre with our trailer in tow along a very straight piece of road. I think naively I had no idea what an environmentally unfriendly place it was then.

I looked over the fence and across the runways and thought I still had a long way to go. Thurso was too far to reach, so I carried on walking until Bridge of Forss, with its water mills and hotel. It was like the M1 along this bit, as the mad flurry of cars with people returning from work pelted along with no regard for a walker coming towards them.

Throughout this walk, the person I most frequently saw was the postman in his red post van. I think the van spent its days going back and forth on the top road and I had heard I could have used it for a lift if I got stuck. This road was like Somerset, long and straight but with snow poles marking its edges... oh boy.

Bridge of Forss is very pretty. It is the site of two large water mills, one of which has been restored for comfortable homes. In the woodland behind sits the exclusive Forss House Hotel, its location very private and ideal for fishing and walking. I savoured a moment's peace – and a piece of chocolate – as I peered over the bridge waiting for David. I didn't linger very long as it was 4.30pm. I was extremely tired, battered and cold.

After David arrived, we drove on to Thurso but the campsite was shut there also, so we made our way back to Bridge of Forss and eventually found a small private lane that ran down the side of two cottages, half a mile from the bridge. I went in and asked if we could park there and thankfully they said yes, provided we left enough of a gap for the residents to pass behind us to reach their garages. Sheltering in the lee of the house was going to be a major bonus. The wind had freshened up again, the temperature was at one degree and the clouds were looking ominously like snow.

As I made a Vesta chicken chow mein supper, a text came in from our old friend Bob, saying the roads were closing in Scotland. The A9 was shut at Perth and others would follow shortly. Oh dear, could this be the end of my journey? No goddammit, I was not going to be beaten! If I got up early enough tomorrow, I could do the lot in one go. Up here we hadn't really been touched by what the eastern side of Scotland was experiencing. I said to David – nervously – that if all else failed, we should get to John O'Groats and then drive back to Durness and come down the western side, no problem.

It was a very early start tomorrow but first I wanted to do a little bit of walking/running. Dinner over, I ran back to Bridge of Forss and then back again to the van. I didn't want to miss an inch. Then I ate my yoghurt. This blonde was on a mission now!

We crashed out quickly at 8.30pm, just as the first hint of sleet spattered the side of the van.

Wednesday March 31st 2010.
Bridge of Forss to John O'Groats - 25 miles.

Bridge of Forss — John O'Groats

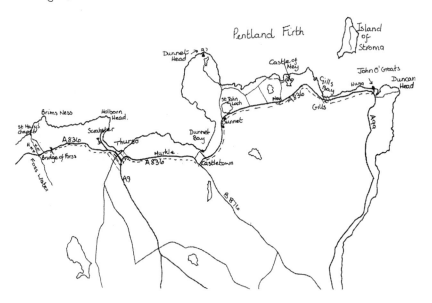

I was woken at 4.30am by snow hitting the side of the van. Large blobs were sliding down the roof window. It was cold. The wind was howling. Thank goodness the van was parked in the lee of the cottages, as up in the roof space I was being buffeted from side to side. I looked out, straining my eyes in the dim light to see the road. Snow was lying. Worried now, I tossed and turned for a while but succumbed to sleep until 7am, woken this time by driving rain. "Yes!" I shouted. The snow would melt and I could walk on. But there was now a north-westerly wind and it was freezing.

So this was my final day. I ate my porridge, left David in bed and stepped out into the semi-darkness at 8am. I had on every bit of clothing possible. The weather was abysmal but nothing could deter my inner excitement to finish. The forecast and travel bulletins were now painting a worrying picture. But I had to finish today.

The roads were slightly slushy and the rain had stopped, leaving running water at the edges of the road. I began my journey to Thurso, five miles away. David was going to meet me there after he had bought sausage rolls, filled up with diesel and got enough provisions to see us home. It was rush hour on the A386 as I headed off. At least four cars passed me one way and I think there was one going the other direction. The north-westerly wind buffeted my left buttock and arm and helped me along.

I met David in a car park near the river at Thurso. He was going to the bun shop and we arranged to meet for a cup of coffee at about 10.15am, towards Castletown. The weather had brightened slightly, although it was still very cold in the wind. I set off, leaving David to do the bit of shopping. He had done well to have lie-in and then get going to catch me up. Once out of Thurso I enjoyed my elevenses, before throwing myself into the elements once more. It was then a long straight road for about five miles to the outer edges of Castletown at Dunnet Bay, and it had started to sleet.

Walking extremely fast now, I just followed the white line at the road's edge, only looking up to ensure I didn't get run over. I was a bit sheltered from the northerly wind here but the sleet was freezing. Just occasionally a large blob of snow dropped out of the sky like it was pre-warning me of more to come. Remarkably, although walking in terrible conditions, I felt good. My feet felt fine, my body didn't ache. I was more surprised at how fast the traffic was hurtling along, considering the conditions. I guess that is what becomes of being a Southerner. To the Scots this was all pretty normal.

David stayed quite close by. I had given him a time of 1.30pm for lunch. He couldn't believe it when I waved him on, saying it wasn't time yet. I was being extremely strict with myself and him, as the weather was going to get worse by all accounts.

I soon passed Castletown and found David tucked in out of the wind overlooking Dunnet Bay. The waves were crashing in and the wind whipped up the fine mist. It was beautiful but great to be sat in the van for a while. I munched chocolate. It was with reluctance that I threw myself into the walk again. It wasn't quite lunchtime yet. David found this most bizarre but I still had 14 miles to do, and I wanted to break the back of it before I stopped properly for something to eat.

Walking past Dunnet Bay was a bit of a treat really, for although I couldn't see the sea it meant I was temporarily protected by dunes. I flew along this bit, but was soon battered once more as I edged towards stopping for lunch. For a time the sleet stopped. The road lay before me and I walked the white line again, trying to keep the chilling wind off my face.

At 1.30pm we stopped by a few dwellings near Whitebridge. I had nine miles to go. I hauled myself into the van, stripped off all my outer clothes and left them dripping in the back entrance, then sat in the front munching into peanut butter and marmite sandwiches, hot coffee and doughnuts. This was to be my last long stop before the end. When I say long, I mean half an hour!

Stepping out of the van, the wind hit me again. Now it had started to sleet once more. The sleet changed to snow but due to the wind it wasn't lying on the road. Instead it was coming horizontally through the bushes across the road, through the hedge again and not lying until it hit high ground. It was fascinating to see snow lying several field systems away to the south.

All down my left-hand side the icy rain splattered against me. My left ear and eye were thoroughly cold. I had two thermal hats on and my waterproof hood over that. The wind was blowing so I hard I walked diagonally against it to breathe. My head tucked into my chin, it was hard enough to raise it two inches. The roads were running with surface water. The consolation of all this was that it made me even more determined, and I walked faster. I was not to be beaten. I was just intent on reaching my destination.

I cannot really remember seeing anything on this last bit. I just saw the white line. I was extremely tired and the weather had infiltrated my inner sanctum of warmth. It was a very uncomfortable last five miles. I stopped briefly at Gills Bay to take a photo of the tiny harbour. I had waved David on to the last junction, for I knew mentally I just needed to see the van in sight for that final mile. I knew I was at my physical lowest of the entire walk. Never have I walked in such extreme conditions, or felt so continuously cold. My two pairs of gloves, one being waterproof and thermal, were now soaking after finally allowing water in. And I was cold, cold from the inside. My hands were not able to stay warm.

Despite all this, I stayed very buoyant throughout. This was what the walk was all about. I embraced the weather. My thoughts turned to my father, my childhood in the 60s and how I loved the snow. I thought of my children, of Momma and inwardly I was panicking about getting home.

Over the last mile and a half I became angry with myself. *Come on, get your ass in gear… where is the finish… this last bloody mile seems so long.* I was willing myself forward, slapping my legs. Then the van was there, a quarter of a mile ahead. David kept switching on the indicator lights just to keep me going. As I approached the van, he took some photos of me turning the final corner towards the last house half a mile away.

I had not been prepared for the northerly wind coming straight at me now. It completely took my breath away. The snow had stopped but the air was filled with a fine rain. My God it was freezing. I could not stop shaking. My face felt raw and my nose wouldn't stop dripping. It was raw like I had been having a bad cold for a week. My skin was being stripped of its layers. My eyes were half closed and very puffed.

We bought a few pieces of memorabilia in the shop here, which of course was deserted. It was exhausting having my photos taken outside against the John O'Groats signs. I was desperate now to get warm. I could barely stand up. Hyperthermia was setting in. David helped me to the van. I had to get out of those wet clothes.

David was extremely good. He turned the heaters on full blast in the van, and got a large dustbin liner for my wet clothes as I stripped off. Completely naked now, I put a towel on my head, got into a sleeping bag and wrapped loads of blankets around me. David made me a hot drink. I still could not stop shivering. I recognised at least that I was still doing that.

It was now 4.30pm. The sky was looking ominous. It took an hour for me to warm up enough to get on some proper clothes and concentrate on getting us home. The weather was beginning to set in and reports that the road conditions above Wick were worsening meant we had to get out.

The journey towards home was hazardous. It became dark quite quickly. We had no snow chains. We met the real snow just outside of Inverness; up to then it had just been a flurry in comparison. We counted our blessings it had happened no earlier.

It was our intention to reach Aviemore and our friends before the snow prevented us. We had already had a text stating that venison stew was on the menu! Well, fat chance of eating.

By the time we had reached Aviemore, turning off the A9 was out. We either continued our journey south or we would have been blocked in by snow. The snow was so heavy we missed the turning anyway. I was extremely disappointed, as the promise of seeing our friends and sharing the weekend with them was lost. However, we were actually extremely lucky because a snow plough had taken its last sweep of the A9 southwards for the night. It was about 9pm and we were the last vehicle to follow the plough's tracks as two police cars came up behind us after that and promptly shut the road.

Fortunately, there was a large truck in front of us keeping the road just passable. We followed it as closely as possible all the way back to Perth. Again, as luck would have it, we took the A9 towards Stirling and Glasgow. This was a fortuitous decision as on our arrival home, we learned that Edinburgh and the east had been experiencing horrendous conditions. I think we could have got stuck at the Forth Road Bridge.

We did not stop moving homewards. We collected diesel at Stirling. I was still exceptionally cold. David did very well as I dozed briefly once I knew we were away from the snow towards Glasgow. It was 2am when we crawled into a service area. We drew the curtains and I got changed into some normal clothes. My body was still cold. I wore two fleeces and we had the heaters on. We brewed up a coffee and had a tin of soup. I took my turn driving but after 25 miles I could feel myself dropping off, so as soon as we could we pulled in again, and then wrapping ourselves in blankets we both had an hour's power nap.

By 8.30am on Thursday April 1st we were in Birmingham. I was considerably warmer, having finally relieved myself of the blanket I had wrapped round me the entire journey thus far. David had continued driving through the night, stopping for five-minute dozes or drinking large black coffees. Remarkably, he seemed to be thriving on it. But at Chieveley service station just off the M4, he finally succumbed to tiredness and I drove the remaining distance home.

We arrived home at 11.30am after getting our weekly shop, just like you do after a gruelling 17-hour journey! My legs needed a stretch anyway. The van had made it. It had been a most remarkable, scary ride – one that without this brilliant walk I would not have experienced.

Two days later my eyes had returned to normal and my clothes, rucksack, and Gertrude were dry. I stood back and then enjoyed the achievement. It was then that I fully appreciated what we had done. For David it took a good week to get over as he nursed his head and slept. For me I was just grateful I hadn't killed him off and the Pash Wagon had got us home. Shortly after this trip the van broke down twice on the M5 and once on the A34! Bless its heart.

EPILOGUE:

POEMS FROM THE ROAD

BOOTS

If you walk towards number seven and stand at the door,

Tread carefully, for there, heaped on the floor,

Walking boots sort of, stored.

Not one pair or even four,

No a collective amount, of nine pairs or thereabouts at the last count.

The problem is most are for one person who happens to have, so the family say, an eccentric passion for walking over heath and dale, the odd wet mountain scramble, forest rambles, over peaks as well.

"These are my friends," I cry, as I stand and defend 'em, against insults, harassment for the uses, I need 'em.

So what if they take up most of the porch,

There doing no 'arm, carry your torch so you see 'em in the dark and don't go splat, over the laces that have splayed and strayed onto the mat,

That teenager's night out they didn't ask for you to be sick in 'em fumbling to place your key in the door,

They didn't ask to be peed in, or squashed as you slumped, to the floor.

"Let them be," I wail,

They look after my feet more than you,

When I cross certain pastures they protect me from cow turds and dogs do's.

Together we have scrunched over ice, over stones and rocks,

We've waded fast flowing streams, have climbed craggy outcrops,

Have slithered and slid through mud ridden tracks, through peat ridden bogs, been gripped by crevices and cracks.

My boots have changed more colours than the best bruises you have seen,

From shop new blue to slimy, blackened green,

Those ink, oiled puddles of rotting leaves 'ave clung to their sides leaving rancid smelling purple splodges to dampen their pride.

The gray yellow clay is still stuck to my friends 'cos the bristles on me cleaning brushes have come out of their ends.

"I haven't got too many boots," I plea, there is a reason for keeping so many pairs when there aren't so many seasons.

"They all do have a purpose," I urgently keep insistin' how could I possibly throw them out I stand defiant and keep resistin';

"I can't replace those ones there not made like that any more with leather as hard and thick as the varnish on our front door."

"I can't get rid of those ones because they are my winter boots, they take the strain of crampons to climb the snowy routes,

Although they are much heavier and harder on the feet they make my coming down much faster as I'm taken by gravity.

I can't chuck out those blue pairs they've a lot more yet to go, they have been more than seven hundred miles each and I'm nurturing that growth.

Although they're tatty on top, the soles are solid and sound,

Don't you even think of binning those?

I'd go to court, on sentimental grounds.

Last night I was a reflectin'

My friends, those boots;

We have kept going you and I,

My feet always comfortable, blister free and dry.

When laboured breathing has afflicted me on a climb, oh what a strain, as my lungs have gasped for air and my knees, red hot with pain.

When the bleak, rain swept moors, have battered me from all sides.

When my long hair wouldn't stay out, of my mouth or my eyes; And my nose has dripped in sequence with the continuous rain, and water had seeped into my rucksack, drowning me sarnies again.

But you,

I am amazed at your resilience; you have supported me in all I do,

You are as friends are, solid, reliable and true.

And in this quiet moment of pontification I was briefly interrupted.

Front door, opened, followed by commotion.

A resounding thud and blasphemous linguation the returning victim
had cried,

"Blinking heck Mum, (or worse), I'm claiming damages,

Keep your tenth pair outside."

The Loched Jewel

What do I give to you?

The glint of the sun.

Shimmering across the rippling waters of my body.

What do you give to me?

Cans of putrid tastes, smells, bags of diluted slime.

You are unfair in your treatment,

You scorn my shores in futile pursuit of something better?

You are lesser of those mortals, who know the jewel's moods,

Who respect, accept, its fragility and strength, its consistency.

Now

Ashamed am I feeling, scourged, sore from the belittling,

In the name of happiness?

Noises penetrate tranquillity, bouncing off the walls of towering peaks.

There to protect me.

What pleasure I could derive to live in harmony.

Infants, those fish like efforts have learned by me,

Their innocent achievements are mine, not yours.

Take your tents, your cold unimagined dreams and leave,

Leave just your memories.

Not your stench of rotting pestilence that scratches the pebbled shore surfaces, of this jaded crown.

Evening laps.

Wraps the stillness,

Succumbing to darkness.

Winking in the shadowed depths I sigh.

Winter will return to these shores.

Crisp, spiked, ballerinas will dance on glistening rays.

Wind swept, howling blackened sheets will fall.

Natural beauty will echo off my walls,

My lungs will breath once more.

Rhythm restored.

A Yearly Miracle

"Glad to be alive," she said.

Here it was.

The fresh air,

The crisp bite to the stillness as the sun stretched out its tentacles of warmth.

Mittens off, mittens on, decisions, not for long.

The frost had albeit disappeared,

Breath of those that walked could still be seen hanging on cool air.

Noses reddened, causing sniffles to annoy until the handkerchief could be found.

Eyes filled with glorious fusion of colours draped, strewn abound,
English woodland and hedgerows.
Mouths silenced,
Respectful to spring's murmured awakening.
"Glad to be alive," she said,
And,
There it was.

After The Walk

Returning to the beginning is painful,
Reminders drift back noisily,
Encroachment complete,
Senses dulled once again.
Verbal abuse bounces and television lights blaze,
Perspective becomes distorted,
Obstacles loom from the mist,
Sleep impossible,
Tranquillity destroyed.
Conscience clear,
Conscience harrowed,
Conscience forgiving,
Conscience furrowed.
Returning is painful in the beginning,
Slowly resolved as time passes and readjustment is complete.

AFTERWORD

In 1972 David, at the age of 17, was involved in a road traffic accident resulting in serious head injuries, accumulating in fractures of his skull, eye socket and mandible and jaws loss of the sight in one eye, loss of sense of smell and a broken collarbone. He also sustained tears in the dura mater from which cerebral spinal fluid (CSF) leaked. After six weeks in intensive care and then subsequently another six weeks of hospital care, he was discharged. At the time he appeared to make a full recovery and amazingly returned to work six weeks later as an apprentice Instrument Technician. He was a very young Scout leader and he returned to full activities of taking young Scouts for walking, canoeing, climbing and camping etc. He also regained the ability to become an excellent small bore rifle shot and clay pigeon shot. He went on to become runner-up for the Apprentice of the Year at the local refinery where he had started his apprenticeship.

At the time, the significance of the CSF leak did not become apparent until he contracted his first attack of bacterial meningitis in 1980. At this time, neither of us knew what this disease was. It had been the first case that even his GP (who had been practising for 28 years) had come across. Due to his diagnosis and immediate action, David was treated successfully. David's symptoms were that of a very bad headache and flu-like symptoms for 3-4 hours, followed by a progressively intense headache with flushed face, photophobia and increasing stiffness in the neck and back...

David was young and healthy and made a recovery within 10 days, and after three weeks returned to work with what seemed like no problems. However the leak remained.

During 1981-1982 David spent many weeks in hospital whilst they tried to locate and repair the leaks using advanced surgery. He also had two craniotomies. Each time he returned to work fit but tired.

In 1983 David contracted the disease again. Because he was aware of his symptoms we were able to get him to Casualty. (He had managed to drive himself home from work and then collapsed.) Speed has always been essential for a lumbar puncture to be taken, then diagnosis and the correct antibiotics. This time as the wife with knowledge, I was able to get him through Casualty reasonably quickly, despite them questioning my reasoning. David recovered in 10 days but this time he was exhausted and returned to work a little uneasy three weeks later, aware of the time he had already taken off and his place of employment constantly ringing asking when he was returning. Pressure basically drove him back to work too soon. At this point, David was a very optimistic person and was very rounded with a philosophical view on life and in no way had this disease, we felt, stopped him from enjoying life. We continued doing up an old house, taking holidays, water skiing, camping, swimming, sailing and canoeing, if anything just taking our hobbies slower but sadly giving up Venture Scout leading.

In 1984 I was pregnant with our first child. David contracted meningitis a third time. He had woken up feeling poorly. The previous day he came home from work very tired and grey and complaining of a headache, which was pretty normal for him because of the extra CSF in his head that created pressure. I rang the GP surgery in the morning and again he just got progressively worse, and before the GP could call I took him to hospital. The GP phoned the hospital to explain I was coming in and we were seen immediately. Early diagnosis of viral meningitis prevented David having a full-blown attack and he came home after 10 days.

It was clear by now that the neurosurgeons needed to locate all the tears and leaks. The CT scanners and early MRI scanners still were unable to completely find the problem areas, however with the help of ENT surgeons they were able to locate and plug another site of damage in 1985. We then had a period of calm. (Phew)

In 1987 David suffered his most severe attack of bacterial meningitis. It was winter. We had been to a dance at a wedding reception the Saturday night and had walked home from the event. It was very cold and frosty. On the Sunday we were both tired and David had his usual pressure headaches, but nothing different. On the Monday I had left our second child Ben in his cot, with David having the day off to lay some carpet in the hallway. He was still complaining his head was being a pain but was cheerful. I had taken our daughter over to a friend across the road and stopped to have a coffee when, within half an hour of going, David's father was frantically banging on my friend's window asking for me.

David had taken himself to bed in that time, rang his parents and said before passing out, "Carol is at a friend's house, she's the one with a Land Rover across the road. Can you ring an ambulance?" I rushed back to find David blue in the facehis tongue having gone to the back of his throat. The phone was hanging off the receiver, dropped as he had passed out. I rolled him into the unconscious position as best I could and shook him. He sort of came to and mumbled, but he was running a dreadful temperature and kept trying to put his hands over his head. I darkened the room, put wet flannels on his head and waited for the ambulance. He was totally incoherent but did say sorry.

In the ambulance he became still and started to speak again quite lucidly, telling them not to drive fast because his back was stiff and neck very swollen. I knew then we had another attack and by now he was looking very ill. He went very white and quiet and stopped talking again.

On arrival at Casualty I couldn't believe we became stuck in a cubicle waiting for a doctor to come and see him. By this time he was very agitated and was trying to get up and away from the pain. He kept apologising. After 20 minutes I went up to the doctors' desk, demanding to be heard and said, "You do realise this man has meningitis, he needs attention now. Get him to the infectious diseases unit now." It must have been my face; help came after another 2-3 minutes. By this time David was thrashing about in agony and then passed out.

We went in a lift with three medics and a crash trolley. Again David came to for a moment and we all held on to him to stop him hurting himself. Finally in the IDU, he went into a coma for six days. In the first two weeks, it left him unable to move his head or speak, and he had paralysis down his right side. He communicated with his eyes and small nods and he floated in and out of awareness. Soon after this, he had what could be only described as an epileptic fit, but it was almost like an electric switch had switched him on again. We realised he could not read or remember how to write small words and he had some paralysis, but he started to speak again even though it was pretty jumbled.

To me it was like a miracle. He was very weak but after another three weeks they had him on his feet, and with help from the physiotherapist he was beginning to walk again. David's own determination ensured he was able to communicate again, with the help of a speech therapist. Slowly his speech recovered. We started doing simple children's crosswords to get his brain thinking again, but knowing the word and trying to spell it were different things. However, even this slowly returned. His right arm remained weak for a time and he could not hold a pencil or any object for very long. Again, his arm has now regained full strength. The effort of concentration to remember anything was the worst thing, for he had lost all his memory of anything he had previously done or was doing, including places and people. He knew I and the family members were important because he had photographs. However, this was a short-term problem, although he still has no recollection of this time or much of the previous four years.

Slowly he was able to come home. The staff at the hospital released him for a weekend at a time for four weeks, to see how I would cope with two tiny children and David who still needed nursing care. Slowly he started to recall information, recovering from not being able to remember where the light switches were, or how to turn on the television on, or not having the strength to make a drink or remember to get dressed, or actually remember how to change a light bulb or fix a plug – all those DIY things he was so good at before. The frustration for him was terrible. The fatigue was unbearable to watch.

Over the years the first effects of the attack have diminished and partly vanished. Having taken at least two years to recover fully from those initial effects, he was left with no job, retiring from a water authority at 32 years of age on medical grounds. It was a very traumatic time. He did however receive a pension, which was generous considering he had been ill for many of those years spent with the employer.

In 1996 he had a fifth attack of meningitis but remained at home. Having been ill with bad headaches all week, he thought he had better ring the GP as his neck had felt stiff throughout this time. He stayed at home a GP called in and prescribed a large dose of covering antibiotics. The GP thought it was likely that he had had a mild attack but it was never confirmed, and if it had got worse they know I would have taken him in.

In 2000 still suffering with a CSF leak from his nostrils, more modern MRI and CT scanners were able to locate the leak in an inoperable place and a shunt was put in place permanently from his spine to his stomach to relieve the pressure headaches.

The after-effects now are that his body has aged 20 years, he has tinnitus, aching joints, fatigue, lack of confidence, poor sleep patterns due to constant headaches, a lack of concentration and he is only able to do one task at a time. He has poor memory, particularly short term (he uses lots of post-it notes). He has private physiotherapy for neck pain. He doesn't have a job, and he's unable to sustain activities for any length of time. No two days are the same in how he feels. He's mainly unable to pursue previous hobbies and he pays the consequences with bad headaches for days afterwards. Even walking jars the head. He has tried swimming but avoids public pools where possible, although he has recently tried canoeing again! He enjoys surfing for a limited time and now has a motorbike again. Sometimes frustration erupts but it is very rare.

On the positive side, David still remains himself and never complains. He has an even temperament and a wicked sense of humour. His enjoyment has been being home to see his children grow up into responsible adults and try and give them the time that so many children lack. He is a great house husband, a great cook, and has made beautiful harp dresses for our daughter. He has taught the children how to mend their cars, DIY, and patience.

The children have had to adapt to perhaps a different lifestyle from what may have been. Often money was short when they were young, and they had to learn to cycle early and walk miles (we couldn't afford bus fares). No friends could come home with them because of having to be quiet. Benjamin in particular didn't know his father well until he was five years old because of the illness. It took the two of them a long time to bond.

We swapped roles once the children reached 10 and 12, when I went into full-time work as we realised David was never going to work again. Previously I had worked at a school, pub, local shop, playschool, cleaning, cooking... anything that brought coppers into the house and fitted around the children and David at different stages. At one point I attempted to go to Teacher Training College but this had to be aborted. For Katy, our love of music meant we became involved in the local, Junior Operatic Societyand for Ben I became involved in managing and coaching a football team. I also went across the forest cycling, taught the children to swim and surf.

For me the saddest thing is that Ben never saw David at his best. Katy did briefly. However, the greatest thing we have as parents is we have gained two marvellous friends. On reflection, David's calm influence through the children's teen years was probably the very best of situations. Particularly for Ben. I was thrilled to see them share a love of motorbikes and I was very glad to hand over the reins when he left football behind.

We have always endeavoured to remain positive in rising to the challenge, and in return we have two children who are positive, highly motivated and fun. As a family, we have just got on with it all and support has come from very dear friends, relatives and fantastic medical teams.

To those people we are truly grateful.

Summary of mileage Lands Ends to John O'Groats

START	FINISH	MILEAGE	ROUTE
LANDS END	Gwithian	22.0	Road and SW Coastal Path
Gwithian	Mithian	17.0	Road and SW Coastal Path
Mithian	Treyarnon Youth Hostel	22.5	Road and SW Coastal Path
Treyarnon Youth Hostel	Tintagel Youth Hostel via Padstow Ferry	22.0	Road and Small path out to Youth Hostel
Tintagel	Stratton	18.0	Road
Stratton	Bideford	23.0	Road and Small path
Bideford	Barnstaple (Tarka Trail)	9.0	Road and Trail
Barnstaple	Wintershead Farm	16.0	Road, Track, Macmillan Way west and Two Moors Way
Wintershead Farm	Pooletown	15.0	Road, Two Moors Way (briefly) & Samaritans Way SW pth
Pooletown	Crowcombe	11.5	Samaritans Way SW path
Crowcombe	Bridgewater	13.0	Samaritans Way SW path
Bridgewater	Cheddar	17.0	Samaritans Way SW, small footpaths, road and track
Cheddar	Bristol	20.5	Sam.Way SW, Monarchs Way, Limestone Link, Community Forest Path and Road
Bristol	Severn Beach Railway Station	11.0	Road and Severn Way
Severn Beach Railway Station	Aust Services	8.0	Severn Way
Aust Services (River Severn Bridge)	Chepstow (Bridge Street)	5.5	Road
Sedbury Cliffs (River Severn)	Prestatyn (Offa's Dyke Trail)	182.0	As published in books
Nr. Worlds End OS Expl. 256 Grid Ref.235495	Wrexham Railway Station	8.0	Track, Clywedog Trail and Road
Wrexham Railway Station	Eccleston	10.5	Road
Eccleston	Chester Railway Station	3.2	Road
Chester Railway Station	Birkenhead Railway Station	18.0	Road and Shropshire Union Canal footpath
Birkenhead Ferry	Liverpool Dock	0	Ferry ride on the 'Royal Daffodil' across the Mersey
Liverpool Docks	Childwall	9.0	Transpenine Trail
Childwall	Ainsdale -on - Sea Beach	23.5	Transpenine Trail,(Liverpool loop Line) Cheshire Lines Trail and Sefton coastal Path
Ainsdale - on - Sea	Cocker Bar	21.0	Sefton Coastal Path, Road and track
Cocker Bar	Bilsborrow	15.0	Roads, Lancashire Canal tow path and footpaths
Bilsborrow	Lancaster	16.0	Road and Wyre Way
Lancaster	Sampool, Foulshaw Lane	18.0	Road, footpath, Lancashire Coastal Way and Cumbrian Coastal Way
Foulshaw Lane, Sampool	Ulverston	18.0	Road, footpath and Cumbrian Coastal Way
Ulverston	Carlisle Station (The Cumbrian Way)	70.0	As published in books
Carlisle	Kirkpatrick - Fleming	13.5	Road

START	FINISH	MILEAGE	ROUTE
Kirkpatrick Fleming	Lochmaben	14.5	Road
Lochmaben	Gubhill Farm	11.2	Road
Gubhill	Glenvalentine	18.0	Road, Track and footpath
Glenvalentine	Glentaggart Quarry area	16.8	Road and Track
Glentaggart	Strathaven	15.2	Road and footpath
Strathaven	Detchmont Hill Farm	10.4	Road
Detchmont Hill Farm	Glasgow Queen Station	13.0	Road and footpath
Glasgow	Fortwilliam (The West Highland Way)	105.0	As published in books
Fortwilliam	Mallaig	42.8	Road
Mallaig	Inverie	0	Ferry ride across Loch Nevis to Knoydart
Inverie	Barrisdale Bay	9	Path/Track
Barrisdale	Arnsdale	0	Ferry ride across Loch Hourn
Arnisdale	Braeside, Glenmore	10.0	Path/Track
Glenmore	Morvich	9.5	Road
Morvich	Killilan	12.0	Path/Track
Killilan	Strathcarran	12.0	Path/Track
Strathcarran	Torridon House car park	28.7	Road
Torridon	Kinlochewe	12.0	Path/Track
Kinlochewe	Destitution Road nr. Loch a' Bhraoin	12.0	Path/Track
Inverlael	Duag Bridge	15.0	Path/Track
Duag Bridge	Loch Ailsh	12.0	Path/Track
Loch Ailsh	Inchnadamph	11.0	Path/Track
Inchandamph	Loch na Gainmhich	10.0	Path/Track
Kylesku	Loch Stack	12.0	Path/Track
Lock Stack	Rhiconnich	7.0	Path/Track
Rhiconnich	Durness	14.0	Path/Track
Keoldale	Onto The Cape	0	Ferry ride across the Kyle of Durness
Ferry Ride	Cape Wrath Lighthouse	0	Mini-bus ride
Cape Wrath Lighthouse	Blairmore	12	Path/Track (this makes up for missing out Destination Rd to Inverlael WHOOPS!)
Durness	Just beyond Hope (how appropriate)	21	Road
Hope	Just beyond Bettyhill	21.1	Road
Just beyond Bettyhill	1 mile out of Bridge of Forss	24.3	Road
Bridge of Forss	**JOHN O'GROATS**	25	Road

1213.2

483